SE

LANDON CARTER'S UNEASY KINGDOM

Also by Rhys Isaac

The Transformation of Virginia, 1740–1790

Glynn Isaac and the Search for Human Origins in Africa

Worlds of Experience: Communities in Colonial Virginia

Killing the King

In 1776 the leaders of revolution in the Old Dominion made a Great Seal for their brave new republic. Their design is still the seal (and also appears on the flag) of the Commonwealth of Virginia. They were very explicit about the revolution they had just accomplished: Virtue, emblazoned with the insignia of Liberty, stands triumphantly with her foot on the chest of the overthrown tyrant. Quite evidently he is a king, for his crown has rolled away from his downcast head. *Colonial Williamsburg Foundation.*

Colonel Landon Carter of Sabine Hall (1710–1778), as portrayed by John Hesselius in the early 1750s. This master craved, but never received from humans, such fidelity and devoted admiration as he here received from his dog. *Colonial Williamsburg Foundation, reproduced by permission of Mr. Beverley Randolph Wellford and Mr. Robert Carter Wellford, both of Sabine Hall, Virginia.*

LANDON CARTER'S UNEASY KINGDOM

REVOLUTION AND REBELLION ON A VIRGINIA PLANTATION

Rhys Isaac

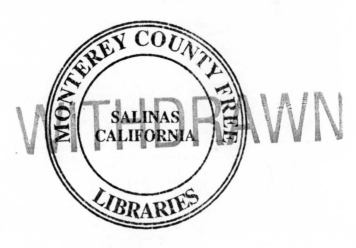

OXFORD
UNIVERSITY PRESS

2004

OXFORD
UNIVERSITY PRESS

Oxford   New York
Auckland   Bangkok   Buenos Aires   Cape Town   Chennai
Dar es Salaam   Delhi   Hong Kong   Istanbul   Karachi   Kolkata
Kuala Lumpur   Madrid   Melbourne   Mexico City   Mumbai   Nairobi
São Paulo   Shanghai   Taipei   Tokyo   Toronto

Published by Oxford University Press, Inc.
198 Madison Avenue, New York, New York 10016
www.oup.com

Oxford is a registered trademark of Oxford University Press

Library of Congress Cataloging-in-Publication Data
Isaac, Rhys.
Landon Carter's uneasy kingdom : revolution and rebellion on a
Virginia plantation / Rhys Isaac.
p. cm.
Includes bibliographical references (p.) and index.
ISBN 0-19-515926-8
1. Carter, Landon, 1710–1778.
2. Plantation owners—Virginia—Biography.
3. Carter, Landon, 1710–1778—Diaries.
4. Gentry—Virginia—Social life and customs—18th century.
5. Plantation life—Virginia—History—18th century.
6. Sabine Hall (Richmond County, Va.)
7. Virginia—Social life and customs—1775–1783.
8. Virginia—Social conditions—18th century.
9. Virginia—History—Revolution, 1775–1783—Social aspects.
10. United States—History—Revolution, 1775–1783—Social aspects.
I. Title.
F229.C32 I83   2004   975.5'2302'092—dc22
2003021863   Rev.

Book design and composition by Susan Day

1 3 5 7 9 8 6 4 2

Printed in the United States of America
on acid-free paper

For

Greg and Donna

and

Inga

companions in this journey—

friends and mentors—

always an inspiration in making history matter

Contents

The Argument

European Civilization took shape under the rule of patriarchal monarchies. Everywhere loomed the Father God. He reigned over the Holy Father Pope, the Imperial Father Emperor, and the Royal Father King. All those under this patriarchal rule were not equal "citizens" but hierarchically ranked "subjects"—defined by their subordination.

So, the declaration of the American republic in 1776 was one of the great events in all history. It accomplished the symbolic pulling down of patriarchal monarchy as the keystone of the cosmic arch of public and private authority. It gave the first comprehensive promise to mankind of freedom and equality in this world.

Drawing on a most remarkable diary, this book tells the story of the coming of the American Revolution as experienced by an apprehensive Virginia planter patriarch. He was unwavering in his commitment to his country's constitutional rights—even while he sensed that the overthrow of his whole world order would come from defying and then casting out the Father King. Uneasy in this awareness he began to write angry stories of rebellions in his own little kingdom.

The troubled narratives in the planter patriarch's diary are very revealing of his entire world. And so this book will be engaged in a search for the stories of the African Americans, the women, and the young persons in the patriarch's world. For them the Revolution seemed to bring promise rather than menace.

Are we not still haunted by that promise everywhere so unfulfilled?

First Words

From his birth in 1710 to his death in 1778, Landon Carter was ranked among the most wealthy and privileged of the planter elite of Virginia. In one thing, however, he outshone them all: the range of his diary writings have entitled him to a unique place of honor. In the book that follows I seek to do two things. First, I strive from a most remarkable diary to reveal the world as Landon knew it—and as he saw it coming unraveled. Second, I shall be presenting many of the little stories that Landon so strongly told in his diary. They are human stories to be relished as such, but my purpose is to show how they unfold a history far, far greater than themselves.

Here are two short examples of Landon's narrative style. They are simply two indications why he should have a place in early American literature as well as history.

The first is a story in which the antagonist is the younger son of the diarist, who bears the same name as his father.

Monday, October 24, 1757

This day near Sunset Landon Carter came home.

I, with great mildness, asked him if he did not think that, as he was to go up to Bull Hall tomorrow, he ought to have staid at home to have taken my directions with regard to my affairs. And if he did not think this Sauntering about from house to house, only to inflame himself the more by visiting a woman that he knew I would never Consent to his marrying, would not ruin him,—and was contrary to his duty?

He answered very calmly, No.

Then, Sir, be assured that—although you will shortly be of age—if you do not hence-forward leave her, you must leave me.

His answer, Then, Sir, I will leave you.

On which I bid him be gone out of my house.

He took up his hat, and sayd so he would, as soon as he could get his horse; and went off immediately without showing the least Concern, no not even to turn round.

This I write down the moment it passed that I might not through want of memory omit so Singular an act of great filial disobedience in a child that I have thought once my greatest happyness—but as a just Father kept it concealed.

We hear the strong narrative voice of the righteous patriarch. He makes a dire threat to disinherit this son if he makes a forbidden marriage, but there is a note of pathos in the lament of the rejected father, as he watched his son leave, *without showing the least Concern, no not even to turn round.*

The second little story—in a style all Landon Carter's own—is a lament for a dead bird.

Saturday, April 15, 1758.

Excessive hot day and no rain as yet—such are the Seasons I have had to crop in ever since 1751—always on violent extremes.

I can't but take notice of the death of my little Canary bird—an old housekeeper having had it here 11 years this month—and constantly fed it with bread & milk—and I wish the heat of this weather did not by Souring its food occasion its death—for it sung prodigeously all the forepart of the day.

At night it was taken with a barking noise and died the night following vizt, last night.

I know this is a thing to be a-laught at—but a bruit or a bird so long under my care & protection deserves a Small remembrance.

So much is there—note the careful attention to medical particulars and the self-idealization as lord and patriarch, one who gives *care & protection.*

Diaries are artifacts. The first thing in the great series is now a worn and battered old 8-by-10-inch quarto notebook, bound with brown leather.

That book was once a handsome new item purchased by Colonel Landon Carter in 1752, as he prepared to open a new chapter in his career. He meant to instruct himself by keeping a record of parliamentary procedures as he took his place in the colonial legislature. After a few years, Landon had thoroughly mastered the protocols and now devoted the book to his own estate. He literally turned the volume over, making what had been the back into the front. He dedicated it as henceforth his plantation procedure book, giving its new first page an appropriate heading: *Farming observations etc. continued.* Dated *September 21, 1756,* the back-to-front notebook became the repository of home concerns; but it was not yet an outlet for outraged feelings.

The long-kept diary, however, did not have enduring consistency of form any more than of contents—its physical embodiment went through notable changes. With the entry for October 24, 1758, that first surviving notebook was full; the plantation record, extending back now for three-fourths of the pages, had come to the place where the original parliamentary journal had left off. Landon Carter had to find a new repository for his habitual diarizing, but no immediate successor book has been found. There is a five-year gap; and then we see that Landon had begun to keep his diaries in the blank pages of the *Virginia Almanack* that was published year by year in Williamsburg. Three of those little $5^{1}/4$-by-$3^{3}/4$-inch volumes survive—for 1764, for 1766, and for 1767. There is none for 1765, the momentous year of passage of the Stamp Act. But we shall see that a profound shift in content began to occur in the volume for 1766. During this year, with the colonies in rebellion against the king, Landon, the planter patriarch, suddenly developed a compulsion to record rebellions in his own little kingdom.

Soon the diarist found that one little book did not provide enough space for a year's worth of scientific observation interspersed with angry narratives. He developed a new format that gave more scope for the indignant stories of disobedience that he needed to tell. So, each month he took a little stack of legal-size (foolscap) paper; he bent it in half; then he took the bent-over stack and bent it again in the same direction. He now had a $3^{1}/4$-by-8-inch oblong of folded paper ready to be made into a little book. He, or more likely a woman instructed by him, stitched up the center crease, while the outer creases were cut so as to open up the leaves. Six sheets gave 48 little pages at that rate. Thus were made the series of what Landon called variously: *these little books, my monthly books,* or—more usually—*my last year's June book,* or *my May book.**

---

* Only about half of these narrow homemade little volumes have survived—some 60 out of more than 100 that once were made and written in. They cover, though incompletely, the years from 1770 until just before the diarist's death in December 1778. It is mostly the contents of these little monthly books that have rendered this diary notorious—and they constitute at least three-quarters of the diary's total word count.

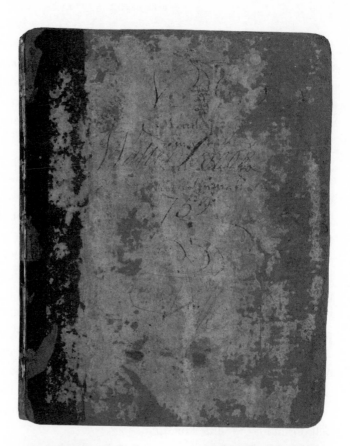

The three physical forms of the diary—top, the 8-by-10-inch leather-bound quarto notebook; right, the 5-by-4-inch 1764 almanac (a pocket calendar); and left, the 3-by-8-inch monthly book. *Special Collections, Alderman Library, University of Virginia.*

Into these steadily multiplying containers Landon poured not only his *Farming Observations*—which he vigorously continued—but also his torrent of stories about outrages against his patriarchal dominion. He came increasingly to feel that his fierce defense of American liberty was helping tear down the fabric of an old regime that he deeply valued. As he recorded this anguish, Landon accumulated a most revealing record of his momentous times.

The plantation that was so memorably recorded is situated in Richmond County, some 60 miles north of Williamsburg. (It is about 80 miles south and a little east of present-day Washington, D.C.) At the heart of the plantation stood Sabine Hall. This mansion that Landon built has been the keeper of Landon's stories. The papers were preserved in the Hall until recently, when, in the 1960s, they were at last deposited for safer keeping in the climate-controlled archives of the University of Virginia's Alderman Library. The house, however, is still proudly owned and occupied by the descendants of the man who built it.

Landon had been born into the American British colonial world in the third year of the reign of Queen Anne (August 1710); his death (December 1778) in the third year of the Republic of the United States of America, was an exit from a very different world.

The diarist's mother had been from a gentry family in the old country. His mother's family name of Landon was given at his christening to this particular son. His father was a wealthy Virginia-born merchant planter with extensive connections to London and all the maritime Atlantic world. Robert "King" Carter was (as his nickname implied) a grandee among the grandees. At the time of his death he had title to a third of a million acres and owned more than seven hundred enslaved Africans and African Americans. (Landon, who inherited only a fraction of this estate, was able to continue the accumulation of wealth. When he died his inventory showed that he was the owner of 401 slaves, setting him securely among the 10 or 12 wealthiest men in Virginia.)

In this immensely privileged family, however, Landon was one competing for his place with many. His own mother had four sons—among whom he was the third—and she had four daughters. His father already had one son and three daughters by his first wife. Surely the diarist's evident ambivalence toward women started there. He left many traces of bitter misogyny; yet he did marry three times, and his writings celebrated the married state as a happy one.

In 1719, at age nine, little Landon was sent with his two older brothers for schooling in England. Thus was he suddenly separated from his mother and his sisters, as well as from the big, vibrant plantation household that had nurtured him in his infancy. His mother's death is recorded as occurring in July of this year. (Perhaps that had preceded and precipitated the move; perhaps she was ill and the care of her sons was becoming too burdensome; or perhaps—as sentimentalists would want it—she died of pining for her fledglings.) Landon had been suddenly thrust forth into the wide world, but at his English school, run by the early linguist, Solomon Lowe, he proved an apt scholar. Despite the great expense, his studies were extended by four years beyond the three accorded his brothers. In 1727 he returned to Virginia to take on the care of his aging father and to learn plantation management.

Shortly after his father's death in 1732, Landon was wedded to Elizabeth, daughter of another Virginia grandee, John Wormeley, esquire. She lived only to 1740 but gave him three sons and a daughter. In 1742 Landon was remarried, to an almost child bride, the fifteen-year-old Maria Byrd, daughter of William Byrd II, one of the greatest grandees of them all. She died in 1744, giving birth to their only surviving child, a daughter named for her deceased mother. In 1746 Landon married yet again—this time to Elizabeth Beale, the daughter of a neighboring gentleman who had local rather than colony-wide eminence. She gave birth to three daughters before she died at some unrecorded time in the mid-1750s. At this point—which is also the time the domestic diary begins—Landon must have declared his intention to wed no more. In 1756 he arranged instead for his eldest son, Robert Wormeley Carter, to bring his bride, Winifred Beale, home to the family mansion that he would eventually inherit. (Winifred was the niece of Landon's third wife, and now she in turn became the lady of Sabine Hall; as we shall see, it was not a happy arrangement.)

Shortly after his first marriage, Landon settled on lands he had just inherited in Richmond County; there he began the typical career of a high-born Virginia gentleman. He rapidly became a justice of the peace in the county court, a colonel of the county militia, and a parish vestryman of the tax-supported Church of England, and he continued in these offices until revolution disrupted the whole system. In 1752 he was elected a burgess for his county and henceforth sat in the legislature until he was unseated in 1768. When the political crisis intensified, there came the last great step in Landon's career; from being a prominent bearer of the king's commission, he became, in 1774, as chair of the county's boycott committee, an active organizer against the king's ministry. He remained a militant patriot to the end of his life.

To be the historian who will present Landon Carter as a storyteller witness to the revolutions of his times is to be the scriptwriter and theater director of a major historical stage show. I shall introduce myself also.

Unlike the powerful diarist, I was not born to wealth and influence. I came into the world as one of identical twins, the first-born to kind and wise parents who never had much property but lived off their stock of learning as professional scientists. And yet we twins—born in 1937 at the Cape of Good Hope, in South Africa—were distinctly privileged since we were males. There was great privilege also in the fact that we (and our much-younger sister) were all children of the "white race." But there was alienation and exile lurking in that. We would come of age in a South Africa where severe penalties awaited any person who resisted the regime of racial segregation—apartheid, as it was called. We twins left the country at age twenty-one; and our parents and sister emigrated soon after.

Already at age nine, with our first viewing of Old World monumental antiquities, my brother and I had both been caught by the fascination of the past. Glynn became a famous archeologist, tracing the evolution of human behavior in East Africa. I, Rhys, became a historian of much more modern events. I was drawn to the study of the Age of the Democratic Revolution. An intended study of Thomas Jefferson brought me to Virginia, and there I became, as best I could, an anthropologist to that world in turmoil. As I was completing my first book, *The Transformation of Virginia, 1740–1790*, I became convinced that Landon Carter's diary, from which I had only snatched quotations and examples, should be systematically read for the riches it contained. Thus began a long journey that has led to this book.

I have analytically read, reread, and constantly pondered the great series of diaries, identifying the many genres of performance in which the diarist developed such virtuosity. I have also sought to understand the sources of those virtuoso performances. That quest took me first into the "natural philosophy" of eighteenth-century meteorology, agriculture, and medicine. It became clear that here was a whole fascinating cosmology—a very distinct way of understanding the universe, the beings in it and the forces sustaining it.

Soon I became aware of Landon's complex virtuosity as a teller of stories. I had to seek out the forms of cultural imagination, the blend of old and new narrative cycles that Landon used to craft the true stories in his diary. The inspiration from the emergent modern novel was apparent at many points. The old traditions of stories that masters have always told about their wayward laborers were more elusive. (I have called this genre "gentrylore," and after persistent inquiries I surmise that Landon's diary may be the biggest repository of such stories written from life in all the literatures of the world.)

But this account of myself goes too easily over the surface of events. Beneath the surface there are remembered voices, dreams, and nightmares. On one occasion I heard voices breaking silence. I was a beginner, on my first research trip to Virginia. Visiting scholars were just given a key to the old Colonial Williamsburg Foundation house where the microfilms were then kept; that way we could work round the clock if we chose. In those easy times the cleaners came in to do their work—sure—but first they would hang out downstairs and play cards a while. I could not hear the words they said to each other as they joked and dealt hands, but the sounds came up the stairs on the night air. Was it entirely fantasy that the timbre and cadences of their voices transported me vividly back to a house of my childhood in a little eastern Cape of Good Hope town on the edge of Xhosaland—with the sound of African voices talking and joking in the yard at night?

But memory carries grief and recollected wrong as well as enchantments. This came home to me sharply when one of my daughters, raised in egalitarian Australia, visited a South Africa that still replicates so much of my childhood. She witnessed scenes that reminded her of the master-and-slave draft chapter she had typed for me. She had watched the way African women, all along the street where she was, had been forced by poverty to sacrifice their own family's lives to the service of the white families with whom they must reside. Slavery was no longer the issue, but she wanted to be sure that my history would address the eons-old race, class, and gender exploitation that still continues everywhere.

History might seem a self-indulgence in the face of such moral urgency. But I know that it is not. We must know where our world comes from, if we are to plot for it a better future.

I wonder as I complete this work if it might not be considered as history's gift to literature. Landon's great diary has long been left to be pilfered for quotations by historians; but there are very good reasons why it deserves a prominent place in American literature. One reason is the vigor and expressiveness of its writing; the other is the memorable set of persons vividly brought to life in its presentation of day-by-day events.

The writing has great range. Dramatic weather narratives are the settings for reports on the labors of men, women, and beasts of burden upon the land. With the piercing eye of the scientific farmer, we even see through furrow and clod, turned by plow and hoe, to identify with the tender roots of the crop plants that seek to draw moisture from the earth. Then there are the human dramas: there are the *rogues* and *villains* who are the ringleaders among the slaves, and there is the defiant waiting-to-inherit eldest son. (The deep plot indeed centers on this *heir apparent*, together with his wife, a trouble-making daughter of *Eve*.) There are also the neighbors: there is old Captain Beale—a *fox* after other people's *chickens*, setting his children to ensnare Landon's offspring in stolen marriages. There is also the willful, card-playing parson; and there is the sinister old knight, the baronet, who smiled even as he plotted the destruction of others.

Inevitably, the most richly realized character in all the long series of these diaries—in the scientific observations, in the lyric pastoral writing, and above all in the flood of stories—is the diarist himself. If Landon Carter's diary had been the fictional creation, say, of John Barth or Thomas Pynchon, it would have been instantly hailed as a literary classic, and its central character would have been greeted as the invention of genius. So let this narrator, who depicted himself with such vitality, be now appreciated as a creative writer overdue for acclaim.

The diary has been transcribed and published in full for more than three decades. So, why has there been negligible literary acknowledgment? Many reasons can be proposed. There is the regional: if the diary had been kept in New England, we may be sure that a dozen or more dissertations would have come from it in both history and literature. There is also the matter of the sheer bulk of it: the gems of strongest writing are buried in a mass of more routine (though rarely dull) day-by-day recording. But most of all there is the problem of presentation. Landon wrote his best at white heat; the angry narratives came forth that way. His words spluttered off his pen; he kept getting ahead of himself with irate parentheses; his punctuation was erratic or nonexistent; and he never revised any of this vigorous writing. In short, he needed an editor.

Both boldly and cautiously, I have taken on myself the role of literary editor. I shall introduce the little and big histories that the diaries open up; at the same time I shall try to make more clear and intelligible the texts of Landon's own diary writings. I shall even be bold enough to intervene in his sentences. But I shall be careful to keep my interventions to a minimum: the diarist must not be supplanted as author by a historian writing out of turn. The many utterances from the diary that I quote or give as extracts will be thus *in a distinctive type face* (to separate Landon's writing voice from my own). The diary utterances will have supplied to them the rearrangements that I judge necessary to make them intelligible at first reading, rather than at the second or third attempt. I shall add no "inventions," but I shall supply or correct punctuation and insert missing words. All this will be done as unobtrusively as possible since my purpose would be obstructed by filling the lines with editorial marks. (Mostly I shall use the dash to mark the pauses I think readers need; and where, as often, the most lively narratives indicate dialog, I have given a new line for each speaker's utterance.) Where words are inserted for clarity, they will be in the same distinctive font, but in plain, not italic print.

Even when the diary text is rendered reader-friendly, there will be a challenge in accessing it. Landon was a virtuoso with the pen, but he did not usually write in a speaking style. His was rather an adaptation into English of complex constructions from the Latin writers he had studied so long and hard.

My already declared purposes in this book are twofold. First, to open for readers an understanding of Landon Carter's world as he knew it, and—as far as possible—as others around him knew it. And second, to show the Revolution as personal experience from the stories of rebellion that began to multiply. My strategy is to plunge the reader first into stories showing the turmoil of revolution, then to go back to the calm of scientific Enlightenment that preceded the turmoil. Only then will I trace the political developments that led to the crisis of authority and the sense of a betrayal on high. We see after that, the world running riot—as it appeared in the telling. Finally, we follow the diarist into the terrible rupture that the Revolution was for him. By then he was old and ailing; we accompany him through his last struggles.

THE CARTERS AND THE BEALES

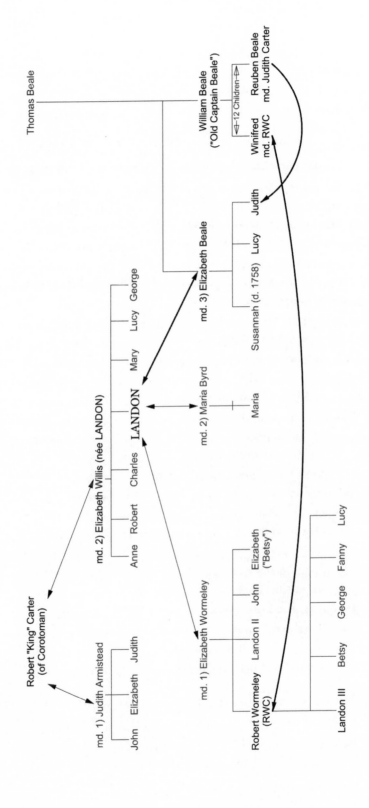

Sabine Hall—1770s Staff of the Dual Household

(The most prominent persons in the diary narratives are indicated by bold type.)

LANDON CARTER'S HOUSEHOLD

Stewards (managers): **Billy Beale**; Owen Griffith

Overseers (at various times): John Dolman (Doleman); William Lawson; John Selfe

Leading African American persons and families (as far as known):

Nassaw (valet/surgeon)
> father: Old Nassaw
>
> wife: **Mulatto Betty**
>
> grown son: **Nat** the coachman
>
> son-in-law: Phil
>
> children: **Talbot**; **Meredith**

Winney (nursemaid)
> husband: Joe
>
> daughters: Sarah; Winney
>
> sons: **Young Joe**; little Abraham

Talbot (various responsibilities): no family identified

Manuel (plowman)
> brother: **Will** (at down-river quarter)
>
> wife: Sukey
>
> daughters: **Sarah**; Peg
>
> sons: **Billy**; Harry

Johnny (garden supervisor)
> daughter: Nanny (with unnamed grandson)
>
> young sons: Johnny; Sam (?)
>
> son-in-law: **Postillion Tom**

THE PARALLEL HOUSEHOLD OF ROBERT WORMELEY CARTER (RWC)

Moses (valet to **RWC**): no family identified

Betty (Mrs. Winifred Carter's "favorite maid")
> husband: Sawney, brother to Simon the Ox Carter

PART I

REVOLUTION
IN HOUSE AND HOME

Landon Carter's diary is an extraordinary body of writing for its range and intensity, but it is most remarkable for the ways the personal and domestic resonate to the momentous events through which the diarist lived.

Part I assembles narratives of the challenges to authority that revolutionary times seemed to be calling forth. We feel the trauma experienced by an old-fashioned patriarch faced with rebellion in his great house and its surrounding estates.

The lower Rappahannock River—a portion of the map of Virginia prepared in 1755 by Colonels Joshua Fry and Peter Jefferson (father of Thomas Jefferson). Sabine Hall is located upper center; Gwynn's Island is in the lower right. (Present-day Washington, D.C., is some forty-five miles due north of the top left corner.) *Colonial Williamsburg Foundation.*

Chapter 1

Morning of Revolution

It is late June in the summer of 1776. Two months ahead lies Colonel Landon Carter's sixty-sixth birthday. One month behind lies the Virginia Convention's vote for independence and a republic. That decision had not come as a surprise for Landon—indeed he had long expected it—but it had been a shock nonetheless.

One morning in that late-June time, Landon woke to learn that what he had been dreading, what he and his peers had for so long been drawing down on themselves, had at last happened. The revolution had literally come home, through the door and into his house.

June 26, 1776:

Last night after going to bed, Moses, my son's man, Joe, Billy, Postillion Tom, Mulatto Peter; Tom Panticoe, Manuel, and Lancaster Sam ran away, to be sure, to Lord Dunmore,* for they got privately into my young steward Beale's room before dark and took out my son's gun and one I had there too, out of his drawer in my passage . . . They took my grandson Landon's bag of bullets and all the Powder, and went off in my Petty Auger canoe . . . and it is supposed that Mr Robinson's People are gone with them, for a skow they came down river in, is, it seems, still at my Landing.

---

* On November 7, 1775, Lord Dunmore, the royal governor, faced by rebel forces every day more numerous and daring, had raised the king's standard in declaration of war on the patriots. He had furthermore promised freedom to the slaves of rebels who would rally to that banner. Commanding the water, he had small craft manned by the Royal Navy and by Virginia Tories raiding the Chesapeake shoreline. His forces burned buildings, took off supplies, and encouraged slave defections. As hundreds of them came to him, he formed and armed a Royal Ethiopian Regiment.

These accursed villains have stolen young *Landon's silver buckles, my grandson George's shirts, Tom Parker's new waistcoat and breeches; and yet have not touched one thing of mine, though my door was open, my line filled with stockings—and my buckles in my shoes at the door.*

It seemed to be known at once that the leader was Moses, and that these named eight men (henceforth, the Eight) had run off to the hated and feared Lord Dunmore.

I shall interrupt the narrative a moment to picture for the reader the setting of that house where the diary was written, and where so much of the action of the diary occurred.

Sabine Hall stands about a quarter of a mile back from the tidewater shore. It is on the southern edge of a flat-topped ridge; a short way behind is a shallow ravine, now dense with trees. But the mansion was carefully sited at the point where the land falls off sharply to give a commanding view over the wide Rappahannock valley. Immediately in front and below is what Landon called *my Riverside field.*

Like most colonial Georgian mansions in Virginia, the hall is built of red brick, made from the clay on which it stands. The main houseblock was in three parts. The two single-story dependencies—originally a schoolhouse and a kitchen—are now joined to the main central house by solid brick hyphens, but in Landon's day the connectors were covered walkways made of wood, less elaborate but similar to those at George Washington's Mount Vernon. The central house had a hip roof with a cornice of white stucco all around. On either side of the classical porticos at the center of the long south and north façades, there are three great sash windows to each of the two stories. The more elaborate central features are of rusticated stonework; they extend the full height of the walls, and they frame grand portals that are approached by stone steps up to the raised first floor level. (In 1772, Landon's son added the amenity of a piazza, or stoop on the south side; it is still there, converted into a screen porch.)

Entrance to the house is through the great paneled central passage, a general-purpose living and entertainment space. It makes a wide hall, extending between the massive portals, giving access to two rooms of unequal size on each side, and to a grand staircase on the eastern side leading up to the great passage upstairs and the chambers off it. We know from the diary that the downstairs chamber on the eastern side of the great north portal was Landon's room, and that he most

Sabine Hall—now and as it first was. Above, a recent photograph of the south-facing river front, modified in the nineteenth century. The flanking extensions are recent additions. Below, a reconstruction of the main house in its original state. *Colonial Williamsburg Foundation; drawing by William Graham, Jr.*

probably also sat in the great passage to pen his diary entries, at least in summer when it was a breezeway.

Around the house there were some lawns, including a bowling green and possibly also a series of garden terraces, though Landon made scant reference to ornamental flowers, which he maintained but did not monitor in his diary. These features are still there, as is the Riverside field. Numerous outhouses and a walled garden complete the picture of a plantation that—as a number of travelers remarked about these Virginia great houses—looked more like a village than a gentleman's residence. There were tobacco houses, yards for the livestock, and stables for the many horses. Indeed, the Home Quarter for the household staff and the tillers of the adjacent fields also had to be close by. We need to imagine the sights and sounds of a little African American township. The other farming settlements that are featured in the diary—the Fork, Mangorike, Lansdowne, and Hickory Thicket Quarters—were all within a mile or so.

Unfortunately no archeology has been done that might enable us to determine the exact location, layout, and form of construction of the various surrounding buildings. The Home Quarter at Sabine Hall may well have had some formal architectural treatment, so as not to detract from the dignity of the mansion house. The outlying settlements perhaps matched the slave quarter carefully reconstructed at Carter's Grove by the Colonial Williamsburg Foundation. In this compact example, two long, low-eaved, shingle-roofed buildings are constructed to enclose a yard with a cooking-fire pit in the center. There are garden enclosures and fowl pens in the corners. The house floors are packed earth, and the walls are of what Landon called "wattled" construction—posts or stakes set in the ground, with flexible saplings (wattles) woven through them, and then sealed by daubing clay. This house arrangement (based on thorough archeology) captures a form that expresses a close communality derived from Africa. The yard between the houses was the common meeting ground for chatting, cooking, washing, child-minding, storytelling, music, and dance. The inhabitants shared or witnessed deep sorrow and joy, pain, anger and malice, loyalty and betrayal—in short, their own community life. This was the kind of setting in which the Eight had been raised. In such circumstances they had lived their lives until the moment of their exodus.

By the Rappahannock River, the shore is mostly high clay banks—small cliffs almost—to which scrub oak and other trees now cling, sometimes spreading their boughs in places over the tide-washed little beaches and the curling wavelets of the river itself. Where Bushy Creek comes down there is still the wide marsh to which Landon referred in his diary. To the side of the creek's little delta is the place where once stood the docks of a busy boat landing. Though we are some thirty miles upstream from Chesapeake Bay, and seventy-five miles from the Atlantic Ocean, the river here is a mile-wide estuary. It is indeed a murky mixture of the salty-blue seawater and the muddy streams out of clay-dirt foothills. The river's southern shore is from here only a low line of wooded terrain in the distance; but in Landon's time the scene was busy with large and small craft of many kinds. Sometimes tall-masted ocean-going ships plied up and down, sending off tenders to call at Landon's jetty. At all times small sailboats, rowboats, ferry punts, and paddle-driven periauger canoes would be moving people and cargoes up, down, or across the broad waters. Always, there above, commanding the landscape, presided the old plantation house.

"We hold these truths to be self-evident, that all men are created equal, that they are endowed by their Creator with unalienable rights, that among these are Life, Liberty and the pursuit of Happiness. . . ." These words from the pen of Virginia's great liberationist, Thomas Jefferson, had not yet been published when Moses and his seven companions made their bold bid for freedom; but those beliefs were already in the air, and Landon Carter knew that as well as did the Eight. (The master, after all, would interrogate his slave messengers returned from Williamsburg and find that they had taken in the latest talk of the town.) If the white Virginians were getting a heady draught of the rhetoric of liberty, then so were all the slave quarters in tidewater Virginia and beyond.

The master of Sabine Hall was certain these eight former slaves had run to Dunmore. He knew it from the very circumstances of their leaving. Slaves had run away all through this master's life, but they went singly when they needed to be with absent family or when their life circumstances became for the moment intolerable. Absenting themselves, they withdrew their labor and obedience—going on strike—either seeking refuge at nearby quarters or hiding out in the woods near home. (Much more rarely they would enter a fugitive existence as they made their way to a city such as Philadelphia, or a back-country region such as North Carolina, where they might pass for free.) Mostly they lurked locally where they could be fed and even sheltered by partners, allies, and kindred. After a time of defiance, everyone knew that such runaways would be back, often on negotiated terms. This June morning in 1776 it was different; and the master knew it.

To be sure, Landon had found some satisfaction in recording how, for all the audacious preparations for this running away, these men had not touched one thing of his. He carefully enumerated the circumstances that would have enabled them to do so, in order to console himself that some patriarchal divinity still hedged him and his possessions round. The master, indeed, went on to tell himself that his authority was placed so high above revolt because he had always kept these slaves in their places.

As his own rebellion seemed to turn against him, Landon Carter became deeply disturbed. He had the year before written angry reflections on the strategy initiated by Lord Dunmore's promise of freedom to slaves. Landon thought the *Scheme for the negro Command in the southern colonies. . . . a thing so inhuman.* But then—back in 1775—there were, he hoped, only *some thoughtless africans . . . sheltering themselves under the royal standard offered them.* Now on this late June morning of 1776, the revolution had called out people from his domestic staff. They had armed themselves in daylight, and they had gone forth to fight for their freedom.

By Saturday the 29th, three days after the departure of the Eight, Landon persuaded himself that this alarming episode might be over—or at any rate that armed white Virginia patriots had put a speedy end to this outrageous bid for freedom. He had heard that, at 7 A.M. on the morning after the Eight's dead-of-

An unknown artist's view of Yorktown, 1755. The Rappahannock River looked much like this at the time the Eight launched forth, though with many fewer buildings on its steep clay banks. *The Mariner's Museum, Newport News, Virginia.*

night departure, some minutemen at Mosquito Point, down the Rappahannock River, had seen the periauger canoe *with ten stout men in her.* (No doubt, then, these were his own eight and two of Mr. Robinson's.) They were *going very fast* over on the far side. The minutemen pursued and fired at them. Then, it was reported, *the negroes left the boat and took to the shore.* They were followed by the minutemen, who, by their firing, had alerted some hundred or so King and Queen County soldiers who were on guard along the southern shore. At that point the narrative tailed off into uncertainty; but, as Landon wrote, he expressed unequivocally his wish for swift retribution against these traitors to his patriarchal sovereignty: *It is supposed that Moses and many of the negroes were killed.*

Yet the exodus had been so painful and worrying that the diarist needed to know the outcome more certainly; he kept on inquiring about the Eight. By the middle of the following week—the July week of independence, in fact—Landon Carter could record that, on Monday at Richmond County courthouse, *we heard the King and Queen men killed a mulatto and two of the blacks out of the 8 of my people who ran away. . . . The remaining 5 surrendered.* But the changing stories filled Landon with doubt: *How true it is I don't know.* This had been the pattern ever since the fighting broke out about a year before; rumor, counter-rumor, reports sworn to and then disproved. This was how reports of war and revolution reached the countryside before the telegraph and daily newspapers.

Landon had to carry on as a planter, literally horse-trading, and viewing cornfields, calculating and comparing corn yields. . . . But those Eight defectors—whose departure symbolically threatened all his horses, all his corn, indeed all his way of life—could not be forgotten. By Friday, July 5, Landon still craved more certainty, *hearing so many contradictory stories about Moses and his gang.* On this morning Landon sent off his apprentice manager, Billy Beale, on a long circuit to get full information.* Billy was to inquire in all the lower counties on both sides of the Rappahannock. Landon had even given Beale ten shillings to bear his expenses.

---

* This William Beale was a gentleman apprentice plantation manager at Sabine Hall. He was the younger son of a younger son. His father was John Beale of Richmond County (d. 1766). He was thus a nephew of Landon's third wife; he was a cousin of the Beale siblings, Winifred and Reuben, whom we shall meet since both of them had marriages to Landon's offspring, Robert Wormeley and Judith Carter.

The gentleman made a demur about his breeches being dirty.
I told him dirty breeches are as certainly good to ride in as to stay at home in.

On July 6, the diary entry for the first time acknowledged explicitly that the institution upon which the diarist's way of life was founded was now undermined by the revolution in which all were involved. Landon's admission of the crisis was a notably self-serving rhetorical question:

Much is said of the slavery of negroes, but how will servants be provided in these times? Those few servants that we have don't do as much as the poorest slaves we have. If you free the slaves, you must send them out of the country or they must steal for their support.

Later, Landon would write words to legitimate the freedom struggle of the white Americans. Impelled by the climate of thought in which he lived, he used universalistic terms that—whether he acknowledged it or not—entirely delegitimized chattel slavery. The American patriots were in arms, he wrote, for *so Just a cause as the preservation of the rights of nature impressed on all mankind at their creation.* Though he would not, at that moment draw the conclusion, Landon was too devout a creationist in religion* to doubt that his enslaved people were children of Adam and Eve and so unquestionably included in that phrase—*all mankind.*

When, after three days, Billy Beale returned, he could bring no account of *Moses and his gang.* The young emissary in soiled breeches had been to the minutemen's camp on the point between the Rappahannock and the Pianketank River to the southward. He had *talked with the commander,* and had been told that *they had catched other people's negroes but not mine.*

Earlier, Billy had got a firsthand report from the detachment of minute men on the north side of the river. They were the ones who had first pursued the Eight out on the water. But they did not know what had become of the escapees. The frustrated diarist thought they could have overtaken the periauger canoe if they had tried. (Landon often found the younger generation cowardly or slack in the war effort.) Young Billy, following up this information,

---

* For Landon's "creationism," see chapter 7 below.

had gone *to ask for the Periaugur which the minute men had taken from my People*; but Captain Berryman of the Lancaster battalion had *with an oath refused to give it up.*

Meanwhile Guthrie, a tavern keeper in the neighborhood, had received a much more welcome report. *Some returning runaways told him that they saw some slaves who had run away from Dunmore.* These persons had reported *that they saw Moses on the Island* where the erstwhile governor Lord Dunmore, driven by patriot forces from Norfolk, was now encamped. (This inadequately fortified and short-lived encampment was on Gwynn's Island, just south of the Rappahannock River itself. The diarist remembered it as a desolate and unhealthy place that he had visited many years before.) A receptive Landon Carter was told by the tavern keeper that Moses swore to these double renegades, that *if he could get back he would return to his master; for Dunmore had deceived all the Poor Slaves.* And, Moses was said to have added for good measure, that *he never met so barbarous or so vile a fellow* as Lord Dunmore *in all his life.* Landon carefully recorded this fourth-hand report that he so much needed to believe. He was, however, aware that it had been tailored to his wishes, and so he discounted it. After all, it came from Guthrie, *who I have a long time known to be an egregious liar.*

The diarist was really no nearer to knowing the outcome of this unsettling episode. All that Billy Beale could add when pressed to say more was that the captain of that guard of minutemen who were laying siege to Dunmore on Gwynn's Island, had told him that *the slaves were returning daily, most miserably…, and did aver that the whole gang of runaway slaves must leave the Island as soon as they could get off.*

Experiments and speculations about the flowering and fertilization of cucumbers held the old planter diarist's attention for a little; but then on Saturday, July 13, Landon seemed to get more news about Lord Dunmore's camp and the betrayers of his patriarchal authority. The governor was said to have removed up the Chesapeake Bay in to the Potomac—or was it to the Maryland Eastern Shore? From talk at the courthouse, Landon heard once more that *our Gloster county battery and forces drove Dunmore and all his fleet from Gwin's Island, sunk 6 ships, took two, and disabled the men of war so much, they were obliged to go away . . . God send this may be true.*

Further rumor on July 13 seemed to confirm Dunmore's defeat and expulsion; but now the diarist heard, to his great satisfaction, that someone—who spoke with real certainty—had met someone else who had *bid* him *tell me that Dunmore last week sent off a load of negroes to one of the Islands.* (The West Indies were always a threat held over Virginia slaves, since an especially cruel form of slavery was known to prevail on the sugar plantations there.) Landon gleefully reported that this deportation measure had *so alarmed the rest of the runaways that the county of Gloster was disturbed with their howlings.* And the vengeful master went on to reveal the depth and nature of his concerns as he speculated that, *Possibly Captain Moses, the freeman, may be one of them,* sent there *to glut his genius for liberty—which he was not born to.*

Three days on, and Landon had a further stirring of his uneasy domestic patriarchy. There came a report that five of his runaways were across the river in Middlesex county jail. Then there was a lull while Landon's attention was drawn off to plantation doings. He also found occasion to wonder at the unaccountable *illumination* of the village of Tappahannock across the river. (This had probably been over news of the Congress's Declaration of Independence; Landon could get no explanation right away.)

More exciting by far for Landon was a report that meshed nicely with gossip about Lord Dunmore's sexual appetite, appealing to both Landon's outrage and his sense of humor. Someone *told me last night that, at Gwyn's Island, an 18-pound shot had come right at his Lordship. It passed between his thighs and cut a boatswain in two behind him. I don't doubt this shot cooled his latitudinous virility for that night at least.*

The depth of the psychic disturbance in Landon's subconscious was evidenced by the way he relived the trauma when it got to be a whole month since the Eight had gone forth to claim their freedom. The old man now had a dream about them: their armed exodus still obsessed him; he needed consoling.
A strange dream this day about these runaway people. One of them I dreamt awakened me, and appeared most wretchedly meagre and wan.

He told me of their great sorrow, that all of them had been wounded by the minutemen, had hid themselves in a cave they had dug; and had lived ever since on what roots they could grabble—and he had come to ask if I would endeavour to get them pardoned, should they come in, for they knew they should be hanged for what they had done.

I replied a good deal.

He acknowledged Moses persuaded them off—and Johnny, his wife's father, had helped them to the milk they had, to wit 4 bottles. Johnny was to have gone with them but somehow was not in the way; he declared I had not a greater villain belonging to me. I can't conceive how this dream came into my brain sleeping, and I don't remember to have collected so much of a dream as I have done of this these many years. It seems my daughter Judy dreamt much of them too last night. I am just weak enough to fancy we shall soon hear about them.

How, we might ask, could Landon forget that he had dreamt a similar dream only two-and-half years before? Like four of the six dreams recorded in the diary, that dream had also been about patriarchal authority overthrown. His daughter Judy had then appeared before him in widow's garb pleading to be forgiven and reinstated after she had eloped to marry against his express wishes. Perhaps Landon suppressed that memory, not caring to equate traitorous slaves with his own daughter.

The dream of *these runaway people* was so vivid in its detail that the individual who appeared can be recognized; it was Postillion Tom (see chapter 2). The idea that runaways might live secure in caves dug in the earth recurs in African American memories and legends (see chapter 10). Here—in this master's telling—it is associated with the rebels' loss of humanity as they live like wild beasts in the woods.

Despite the omen, Landon did not soon hear—or not before one of the long gaps in what survives of the diary. A surviving notebook does contain one flicker of rekindled excitement, showing that Landon remained keenly on the watch: he noted that there had appeared in a Philadelphia newspaper an advertisement concerning several slaves seized from on board captured enemy ships. Landon observed that *two of the slaves were named Moses and Jo,* and he resolved to write to a Virginia congressman about these, to find out *whether they are not from Sabine Hall, Virginia?**

There is a gap in the record until the early months of 1777. The diarist was calmer by then; yet the trauma of the Eight's leaving continued.

Thirteen months after the exodus of the Eight, Landon was once more confronted with running away. On July 9, 1777, a neighbor had brought to Sabine

---

* The American patriots were treating blacks on board captured loyalist vessels as slaves to be returned to their former masters.

Hall from down river *old Will, Ben and Molly—my runaways in Irons.* (These were a further wave of escapees; the British with their promises were still in the Chesapeake.) The diarist grimly recorded that he *had them separately secured & confined,* and that he was resolved they would remain thus *'till I can sell them.* Or indeed until, by one slave testifying against another, he could see to it that *one shall be hanged to terrify the rest.* A courthouse trial would be required for this, but Landon, as a senior magistrate, could certainly arrange that. And yet it seems that on this, as on other such occasions, the menacing master drew back from his threats.

Landon's renewed engagement with runaways on July 9 evidently opened the unhealed wound. He was impelled to justify the institution of slavery to himself by way of a defense of his own practices as a master. The whole of his next day's entry was given over to self-justification against those who had the year before left him for freedom. Indeed, he now mustered the Eight one-by-one on his page. Each of them owed him life itself—or so he endeavored to show. They were all styled "Mr."—a favorite irony in such narratives.

Thursday July 10, 1777

I am glad when I reflect on my own conduct to Moses & his gang of runaways—that I have no kind of Severity in the least to accuse myself of to one of them; but on the contrary a behaviour on my part that should have taught them gratitude if there ever was a virtue of the sort in such creatures.

1st, Mr. Moses—before I lent him to my son—was so very subject to worms as to be at times almost in the Jaws of Death. And yet by God's blessing my care constantly saved him.

2d Mr. Manuel—I really obliged by bringing Suky his wife to his quarter; he then took a fancy from a distant quarter. And at last I purchased the rascal's life though condemned by the law—and at the expence of £10—it being the smallpox time.

3d Mr. Pantico run a sharpened tobacco stick at his calf almost into his body & he— to the astonishment of Dr Jones—I saved by God's Permission.

4th Mr. Peter was so accustomed to bleed at the nose that—though often given over by the Doctors—I intirely cured, by the favour of heaven.

5th Mr. Joe to appearance struck dead with lightning, for some days, and yet by God's grace I alone saved & restored him.

6th Mr. Sam—a Sheep stealer under a process below which never reached him. I endeavoured to protect him.

7th Mr. Tom I ever used with the greatest respect. &

8 Mr. Billy—a fellow too honest, and mild in temper—who could not have gone away but to please his father Manuel who ever was a Villain, and . . . Manuel's brother

Will confirmed the same cursed breed. Will sent off two of his sons below & was contriving to get off more—but after 3 months trial I have catched him, and to Carolina he shall go—if I give him away.

Within a year and a half of that extraordinary entry, the old slave owner was dead. Only a few of the intervening monthly books survive, so we do not know if he did return to the subject of the Eight who so confronted him with revolution. Had they not armed and broken off their allegiance to him, as he had broken off his allegiance to King George III? By mustering the Eight one-by-one on his page he could present himself as a caring master, and so exorcise the haunting memory of their defection. In doing this, he was endeavoring to reaffirm the now-shaken system that had bound them to him—and him to them—all their joint lives up to that fateful night of their parting on June 25, 1776. He could endeavor, but we may doubt the actual efficacy of such an exorcism.

Although the fragmentary late record prevents us looking forward to see whether Landon could escape haunting by the Eight, we can look back into the relationships recorded in the extensive earlier diaries that do survive. We can check on the self-idealizing claims made in that entry of July 10, 1777. Moments in the lives of the Eight can be recovered, and so we can get both close-up glimpses of the individuals and a view of the system that they left behind when they went forth for freedom.

Chapter 2

The Egypt of This Exodus

The armed departure of the Eight had brought them into the Revolution; and it had brought the Revolution right onto Landon's plantation.

We know so well from famous documents such as the Declaration of Independence the terms in which Landon's fellow white American patriots proclaimed their rights and set about forging their destiny. We know from Landon's diary that the Eight who left Sabine Hall on the night of June 25, 1776, had responded to the call of liberty for themselves. We do not have a declaration in their words; yet we have their deeds.

Enslavement may perhaps be most deeply defined as being compelled to act out not one's own story but the story imposed on one by another, a master. With their exodus, the Eight had manifestly entered into startling new, hitherto unimaginable stories of themselves and their destiny. Landon's telling could not accept and could not evade this revelation. So he wavered in his reporting. On the one hand, he raged at the rebellion of the Eight, and angrily imagined punishments such as he had actually been able to impose on them all through the years they were in bondage. On the other hand, he denied to himself that they had really done what they had done. We have seen how he imagined their return to the kind of submissions that he had so long been able to coerce. But the new and different "story" of the former slaves' own making was there and could not be told away. *Captain Moses* had now gone forth as an armed leader. As a *free man* he was no longer to be constrained to act the slave part assigned to him. Now indeed he could *glut his genius for liberty*, giving the lie to his former master's sarcastic assertion that it was a condition he *was not born to*.

Who were these men?

They carefully planned to leave Sabine Hall. They equipped themselves to leave, and then they did so. They had last been seen on the river's farther shore, *going very fast.* Who were they as they left? Who were they seeking to become?

At first sight the question who were they is answerable—there is information about each one—but such a question is not adequately answered except with a person's own story, and the information that we have takes us back to Landon's telling. It is fragments of his stories that seem to hold the Eight for history. And these are, on the face of it, all that remain of the Eight. But these fragments, though fashioned by the master, are nevertheless so many monuments to the fact that Moses, Manuel, Tom Pantico, Mulatto Peter, Joe, Lancaster Sam, Postillion Tom, and Billy once were on the earth, living, breathing human beings, striving to survive. So, history owes them a review of the information that there is.

The master knew so very much—even as he was willfully blind to so much. His final listing of the Eight assuredly revealed his sense of the magnitude of their betrayals, with the greatest traitors first. Let us follow this order in searching the diary for clues that may give us at least intimations of these men's stories and may open up something of their world—at least as they shared it unwillingly with its diarist chronicler.

Moses

1st, Mr. Moses—before I lent him to my son—was so very subject to worms as to be at times almost in the Jaws of Death. And yet by God's blessing my care constantly saved him.

Moses was always first in mentions and listings, because he was perceived as the instigator, the archtraitor.

Through the record of his life up to the time of his exit ran the line of the greatest rift in the Sabine Hall household. Moses straddled the nagging, grumbling, unending quarrel between the old colonel and his son Robert Wormeley Carter—by 1776 the young colonel. Moses belonged to old Landon; he had never been formally given or settled on the eldest son, but had been lent, and then appropriated, in a way that continued to rankle. Thus, the appearance of Moses in the diarist's narratives was mostly upon occasions that aggravated father-son conflict.

The first time Moses appeared in the record was in 1764. The son Robert had refused his wife, Winifred, permission to have Moses ride as liveried *postil-*

lion when she went forth in Landon's chariot. (Nobles and gentry in Europe had for centuries put their servants in fine clothes that were a uniform, emblematic of their masters' status; the grandees of the American South had taken to doing the same with their enslaved attendants.) Landon Carter found his *graceless son* full of a determination to insult his father by meanness toward his own wife, Winifred. He should know that he ought to *treat her as a Gentlewoman as she lives in my house.* This conflict was between the generations of Sabine Hall Carters, and we hardly know its reverberations for Moses. Moses was a young man then, and probably the more inclined to riding forth in smart clothes. We get a momentary image of this, as the scornful father noted the inconsistency of his son. He begrudged his wife, but for himself he liked to take out the borrowed young man, riding liveried in charge of the luggage, *as a servant before his Grace's Portmantua.*

The record of Moses is small and uneventful for nearly ten years after that first appearance. Then, in September 1773, there was a near repeat of the first reported incident. Robert Wormeley had ordered his father's chariot to his service without seeking permission. So he was sharply reminded both of the disapproval he had long ago incurred about the livery and the ownership of *his man who* his father *only lent to him.*

Indeed, it is as a traveling servant and a messenger that Moses makes all his next appearances in the record—until the moment when he led the exodus. Probably it was both fine dress and the opportunities to travel and to cut a figure up and down the country that helped secure a transfer of Moses' allegiance from the old stay-and-mind-the-crops master to his son, the younger master, a gambling man, always on the road. Thus, Moses had been a defector of sorts long before he left both these masters for Lord Dunmore's army.

There was another flash of revelation of Moses as a young waiting man caught up in bitter conflict over a father's authority. Landon thought that he did well in keeping slaves *to their place*; but the young master, it seems, would portion off victuals from the old master's table to pass to Moses. And worse than that: when reproved, the son denounced his father's strictness, calling him *an inhuman creature* toward slaves. We may ask ourselves: what—behind the impassive mask he was compelled to wear—may have been Moses's feelings as he heard the old man angrily assert that he had *never used an angry word to Moses* or his fellow slaves?

By leading forth armed men, Moses had now acted to redefine himself. His name henceforth was sputtered into the record as the *Captain* of his band—the foremost in his *gang.* Suddenly he was endowed with speech, even if that speech was only fantasy utterances invented by others to please his former master. Thus he was believed to have expressed variously a longing to return home to submission and a detestation of Lord Dunmore and his false promises. Surely he had added his *howling* to that of all the others experiencing Dunmore's treachery. Or else, now that his feelings were central to the narrative, he was imagined repining slowly in bitter anguish under the cruelest of slaveries in the islands. Even the longed-for report *that Moses and his gang were all killed* temporarily relieved the outrage aroused by their exercise of revolutionary choice.

Manuel

2d Mr. Manuel—I really obliged by bringing Suky his wife to his quarter; he then took a fancy from a distant quarter. And at last I purchased the rascal's life though condemned by the law—and at the expence of £10—it being the smallpox time.

Manuel, next in the listing, was in every way an old hand. Throughout two decades of agricultural record keeping, the diary documented the work of Manuel as a skilled plowman. In addition, he can be found in the county court record some ten years earlier. Thus Manuel was the most fully documented of the Eight. This was partly because, being older, he had been around longer and was a family man. In Landon's patriarchal world view, children were always identified with their parents. When Manuel's offspring were mentioned, he too appeared. Furthermore, Manuel's special skills linked him closely to Landon. The old hand was a trainer and driver of teams of oxen, and so a cartage worker; but supremely he was a plowman. He had appeared in the first months of the surviving plantation diary, back in 1756. He was already *plowing my Fork land*. This skilled work made Manuel central to the plantation as Landon managed and recorded it.

To be sure, shared engagement with the land—the earth, its working, and its replenishment—could bond master and man. Just two years before Manuel left, the diarist wrote: *I went to Manuel Plowing my corn rows. . . . And to my astonishment I saw clods turning before his plow of near 40 or 50 lbs weight. He goes deep & really it is good work in a Prodigious hard soil.* Four years earlier, Manuel had been a seedsman, sowing where he had himself plowed: *I saw Manuel sowing the Rye at the fork. He is very sure that the 13 bushels of seed will sow full 13 acres. . . . He prudently left off sowing till what is upon the ground shall be chopped in—which I think is right as it is still raining.*

More often the closeness of this skilled worker to his master was perilous;

certainly, it was a kind of doom for Manuel. Since his master's patriarchal care extended strongly to his flocks and herds, Landon was ferocious toward those of his human underlings whom he considered neglectful or cruel in their treatment of livestock. And so there accumulated ample records of Manuel, for the plowman, as his master saw him, was a willful abuser of animals. That unforgivable misconduct was seen as surely linked to deeper moral delinquencies.

Some ten years on into the diary from Manuel's 1756 first appearance, there was a warning of the reproaches that were beginning to mount. In May of 1766, Landon wrote: *I find that it is not so much the obstinacy of my steers . . . as the Villany of Manuel. . . .*

By April 1770 Landon was expressing himself in his journal much more profusely, and with an ever more characteristic hyperbole:
Mr Manuel has at last compleated every scheme that he might have in hand to ruin me. Before this winter came in I was possessed of 8 oxen, 4 of them well used to the draft . . . In a little time he contrived that 3 of them should mire & die. . . . The other he contrived to lame.
Worse, the draft animals had large special provender allowances, and the master suspected that Manuel pilfered and sold this fodder.

The weakened creatures continued to perish. *But now as they*—the oxen— *were but 4 to work—two horses were allowed to go before them. . . . In a little time Manuel consigned two of those horses to death. . . .* The liquor that Manuel procured with stolen provender caused further destruction. While ostensibly training oxen to recruit the team, *he . . . came so late the morning after from his night revellings that they were turned out to graze.* It cost Landon two hands half the day seeking them, and still Manuel was unable to get them into action. Another three days were wasted, and then the plowman and his three helpers—as it seemed to the impatient master—only *pretended* to train oxen. The master came to an extreme resolution, which he confided to his diary—and probably he communicated it to Manuel—but he never acted upon it: *This is too much to bear—however I kept my temper & resolved to sell Mr. Manuel.*

At this point Landon entered a little biography of Manuel:
He was once a valuable fellow, the best plowman & mower I ever saw. But—like the breed of him—he took to drinking & whoring till at last he was obliged to steal, and robbed my storehouse of near half the shirts & shifts for my people—besides other things. For this I prosecuted him,* and then got him pardoned with a halter round his neck at

---

* This had been in 1744; the record of the case can be found in Richmond County's criminal trials book.

the gallows. For a while it—the narrow escape from hanging—*had some good ef-fect*—*but returning to his night walking*—*he turned thief as before, & killed beef*—*which was found upon him*—*but there was no proof of the* ownership of the stolen *property to be had for the prosecution. He again escaped execution.*

Here we look at an almost unbridgeable gulf between our sensibilities and Landon's. He and his peers took for granted hanging for criminality. All might have concurred with what was clearly Landon's view of his own conduct—that he had called down the terror of the law, while planning to combine mercy with a strong and salutary lesson. Certainly, the master expected the man to settle down to his duties in the aftermath of that contrived encounter with death. Manuel's feelings we can only imagine, but we may doubt that they in-cluded a grateful resolve to be more attentive to his duty. The diarist's narrative continued, bringing the story up to date:

Since then—*by means of the same practices*—*he has killed me 20 or 30 horses and as many draft oxen. He sleeps not at night and must do it in the day. And . . . by one bar-barity or another*—*he has as certainly killed these Creatures as ever he has been con-cerned with them. And now I will part with him.*

But Landon and Manuel did not part in 1770, nor indeed after many sub-sequent stormy scenes. Landon needed Manuel's skills, and perhaps had an emotional need for him as a scapegoat. The parting of man and master did not come until Manuel was ready to go. Meanwhile the ambivalence in their relationship was repeatedly recorded in the journal. Now they shared satis-faction in skilled work completed; now we see them locked in antagonism over neglect or rebellious misconduct. The system of enslavement is starkly revealed in the sword of Damocles that Landon kept suspended over Manuel's head.

On one July day in 1770—he having failed to complete a task as he had so often promised—Manuel was casually redestined for exile: *my long taken resolu-tion shall shortly be put in Execution.* By the following day, however, the relation-ship seemed to change to a playful teasing from both sides. Manuel was vaunting his skill and expertise, and the master wrote: *I thought I should catch Manuel.* The plowman had claimed that, with its fences moved, *the river field was as much work again as it was last year.* But his constantly calculating master tri-umphantly told Manuel that the land worked now *was bare 2 rows and ⅓ more than last year's.* And yet, from that teasing the master readily returned to angry scolding again. Once more it was this plowman's, among others', *unmercifull* treatment of the oxen, *by constant beating them*—*a villanous fault always in Manuel.* And so it went on for years, in alternations of laughter and cussing out.

Sometimes Landon ordered a less-than-extreme form of punishment—as when Manuel was whipped for breaking *the Oxtree of the cart . . . driving into the ditch*. It had been an accident no doubt, but Landon thought that slaves must suffer for their accidents.

Manuel's difficulties with his master were complicated by his having family to whom he was admirably loyal. They too got into conflict; he tried to protect them. This appears in the sequel to one of the most disturbing dramas in all the stories accumulated in Landon's plantation journals. Manuel's daughter had declared her pregnancy but was driven to work, whereupon she ran away. Then she was captured and imprisoned.

Wednesday, September 22, 1773 . . .

Manuel's Sarah . . . pretended to be sick a week ago, and because I found nothing ailed her—and would not let her lie up—she ran away above a week and was catched the night before last and locked up; but somebody broke open the door for her. It could be none but her father Manuel—and he I had whipped.

When there was still *No News* of Sarah by next day, Landon returned to his previous resolution. Sarah and another runaway who was marauding (with a *hue and cry and outlawyery* upon his head) *were two that I will sell—god willing*. Whether he did or not, we do not know. Probably he continued, with her as well as with Manuel, to make the heavy threat and then relent. But he left them always facing a terrible menace.

Manuel also had a wife in 1770 when the charge sheet against him began to blacken with the diarist's vituperative ink. Manuel's wife was then the (un-named) *cowkeeper* with whom the master believed Manuel should have arranged to keep penned those oxen he had picked out for training. Instead, he had left them to be turned out in the early morning with the rest while he was out *on his revells* till long after daybreak. But the name of this woman, whether she lived on, and whether she was indeed—as is likely—the mother of Sarah and Billy (last-named of the Eight), is uncertain. Perhaps she was that *cowkeeper, Sicely,* who was reported on April 22, 1772, as having *neglected her cattle yesterday and let a cow go into the mire below the Barn swamp where she perished*. Entering exclamations that he could not tell what to do with these *sordid creatures,* Landon *ordered the wench to be tyed up and severely slashed to keep her care if possible.*

Such are the broken chronicles of persons like Manuel and his family that whether Manuel left a wife or whether his daughter Sarah was still there when he departed for good cannot be surely known. We have only the near certainty that a self-perpetuating pattern of rebellion (including revells) by one side, and recurrent harsh repressions by the other (including the threat of being sold away forever) would have continued for Manuel all his days. But with the coming of revolution Manuel broke out of this and took one son with him. Two nephews also were encouraged to go for freedom.

Tom Pantico

3d Mr. Pantico run a sharpened tobacco stick at his calf almost into his body & he—to the astonishment of Dr. Jones—I saved by God's Permission.

Tom Pantico's second name referred to his coming originally from a slave quarter away from Sabine Hall, on the Richmond-Westmoreland county line. It was invoked to distinguish him from other Toms.

This Tom was a generation younger than Manuel. He was a fieldworker in one of the quarters quite close to the hall and was without special skills, it seems, beyond a steady hand and eye. He had once been entrusted with the task of measuring and *laying off the ground* that was to be hilled with hoes in the depth of winter (to better regulate the later planting of corn and tobacco). It was noted that in doing this he had sufficient vigor and judgment that *he keeps it well before the people*—that is, those following with their hoes.

The ghastly leg wound that the master chose to recall in his listing of the Eight was evidently caused by his stepping or falling down from the rafters of a tobacco house onto one of the sharpened stakes on which the thick-stemmed tobacco plants were speared in order to be hung—row after row—for curing under cover. That had been in the autumn of 1772, four years before Tom finally left.

Neither Tom's accident nor his wound had then been described in detail in the diary. Landon had no particular motive at that time to place Pantico in his debt, and so the matter was only entered as part of a quick review of cases then under treatment. It was also an instance of the diarist's ability to outdo a professional physician. Dr. Jones had *expressed great apprehensions about the leg*, evidently believing that the man would die of it—or at the least would have to endure amputation. But Landon knew better. He had recorded with satisfaction that Tom was put in his master's special care, and that only a few days of his treatment enabled the injured man to get up and go about.

Five months before the final listing in July of 1777, the diarist had named Tom in a discussion how *the great Pox* (one or another venereal disease) might be cured with a favorite Virginia herbal remedy, namely *rattlesnake root*. Tom's ailment probably related to the report on the troubled marriage that Landon also noted. The sexuality of both Tom and his wife alarmed and bemused his old master. Six years before Tom's departure, his wife was referred to in the standard terminology for slave owners, as *the wench Nelly*. She was to be *brought up to the house* since she was not at all well. Landon insisted on this, though the overseer had kept her *out at work*. But there was a moralizing as well as a medicalizing concern here. The diarist immediately wrote: *I wish that rascal Pantico and his new comrade may not somehow have injured her.* It seems there was another woman in the case. Landon had also heard that Tom *gave her a beating before she was sick.* Landon added: *I wish that may not be the worst.* Evidently he feared poisoning, perhaps associated with witchcraft.

We pass over brief mentions of her expected contribution to a fieldwork task to *be done by the Girls* and of the seasonal illnesses she shared with others. We come four years later to an even more dramatic entry.

Last night at bedtime Nelly came bellowing about her girl of about 6 years old, all swelled up to the eyes; I ordered the child to be brought up, but Mrs Impudence sent word she could not be brought up.

There follows a characteristically Latinate medical report:

I do suppose she—the child—has been stuffing Potatoes for some time—and is possibly full of worms as they are a fine pabulum for them. This morning I first gave her sweet oil, a spoonful, that if anything had stung her—the Poison might be enveloped & obtunded; And after that I ordered small doses Calomels with some apperients to dissolve her bowels—and then I shall direct a concoction of Marsh mallow tea and Saltpetre to promote her urinary discharges.

The obsessively medical diarist then noted with satisfaction that this treatment seemed effective. It was reported—from the quarter where Nelly, her mother, wanted the little girl to remain—that she *is grown brisk in the evening & is mending.* But tending to the child had not erased the memory of the woman who had so affronted her master, even demanding a house call for her child. He entered one of his characteristic *resolutions,* that he *will be particularly careful to have Nelly whipped when she is well.* (Either she had been sick also, or he was relying on the mother to nurse the youngster and believed a whipping then would make her incapable or unwilling.) Landon entered here a characteristic justification of his intended severity: he should make an allowance for a mother's fears for her child, but in this case, he set that down as *Pretence* and supported his view with an outburst that revealed more about his own views of womankind than it did of Tom Pantico's wife (or former wife) and the couple's marital conflicts:

She is a jade so firy in her temper & her lusts that the children are oft left by her whilst she is running about to satiate her desires. Perhaps she is the oddest creature in all my gang, a very fine woman but so Sallatious & ill-tempered withall that no husband will keep to her long.

How much did the Colonel know? Probably a fair amount of the gossip of the quarters reached him. Perhaps Tom and Nelly were still separated in 1776. Perhaps in the circumstances, Tom left no offspring acknowledged by himself and identified with him by the community in the way that Manuel's daughter Sarah and his son Billy who ran with him, were. We only know for certain that, in this case, Landon chose to treat as a flogging offense a mother's fierce insistence on the treatment of her dangerously sick child.

Mulatto Peter

4th Mr Peter was so accustomed to bleed at the nose that—though often given over by the Doctors—I intirely cured, by the favour of heaven.
Mulatto Peter had his recorded identification given to him by his skin color—to distinguish him from *Black Peter*. To prejudices concerning his skin color he probably also owed his recruitment to the skilled job that brought him some fifteen times into his master's plantation record.

Peter was also sometimes noted as *Peter the plowman*. His care and handling of horses gave additional opportunities for self-assertion—a kind of freedom through mobility. The master learned in the summer of 1771 that Peter the plowman was a *night Walker*. (Landon explained that term further by noting that *I have discovered he rides my plow horses in the night*.) Perhaps the sickness that was believed to have visited him in consequence of his excesses, and the associated exposure to the damp night air, was considered a sufficient punishment; more probably, though there is no record of it, he received lashes as well.

The anger of Peter's master did not change Peter's ways. (Peter was probably twenty or so at this time, he was not yet in charge of plows in 1766–1767, the previous block of surviving diary.) In the summer of 1775, only a year before Peter finally left, Landon reported that fastidious Mr. Beale, the plantation management apprentice already known to us for not wanting to go out in dirty breeches, was returning late; he had *Catched Mulatto Peter on the gray Colt*. Peter had been out with the young son of Gardener Johnny. (Johnny was the archvillain who loomed up in Landon's dream of these runaways as the chief instigator—though not participant—of their armed departure.)

Peter's nosebleeding weakness did get recorded once in the surviving journal. That was six years before the day on which Landon reckoned up the ways these defectors owed him their lives. On January 18, 1770, the diarist recorded that *Mulatto Peter has in one of his bleeding fits brought himself very low,* but he was not *dangerous ill.* Yet, there had then been real worry, as the disorder (and the low state of health) had lingered on. Within a week, the master had sent for Dr. Mortimer on Peter's account, though mainly at the insistence of his own son and his daughter-in-law. Landon justified his own reluctance (and demonstrated his care) by outlining the history of the case—which had hitherto always cured itself. He detailed his own diagnosis and attempted remedies. These were: *low and cooling diet;* having him *Cupped . . . between the scapula both with and without scarification;* the use of *warm baths to his feet for a delivation of the blood from his head;* and besides that *many styptics of the shops, as well as all the old women's methods of cold water to his head, to his privates, with Vinegar cloths and what not—and all to no purpose.*

The master, challenged by this case, had indeed called forth his claims to a deep knowledge of the body as he entered into contest with the doctors:
The evening before yesterday—imagining it to be a divided state in the blood—I administered 30 grains of the bark with 6 drops of Elixir Vitriol, and have continued the use of this ever since—with every now and then a cup of Comfrey decoction with saltpetre and gum Arabic, in order to . . . thicken the blood.
It seemed to pay off. The diarist noted two days later that Peter *has not bled to speak of since Monday 4 o'clock—Dr. Fauntleroy . . . seemed to think I gave too little bark.**

In vindication of his own skill and care, Landon declared that he was *sure . . . small doses administered frequently stand the best chance of entering the blood.* He doubted if the doctors—*such practitioners*—really knew *in such extraordinary cases.* Yet Landon had gone along with those who wanted these supposed experts called in: *It is the duty of a Master and I have sent for them to satisfye that.*

This medical drama apart, Peter's working role looms largest in the record for the same reason as Manuel's. A plowman's turning of soil was deeply meaningful to Landon, the agricultural improver. With his attention fixed on the earth, the diarist recorded the results of these labors quite frequently. In the first filled-out image of this kind of engagement, we see Peter caught up in his

---

* Quinine or "Jesuits' bark" is still sometimes used in the treatment of malaria. A sustained explication of the medical science of the mid-eighteenth century, as practiced by Landon, is given in chapter 6 below.

master's Enlightenment fascination with counting and with measured "grids" that could be laid out on the land: *Peter & two horses in his light plow has been ever since Monday plowing two furrows between each row of barley & Oats at 3 feet distance in 12 acres of tobacco ground.*

As fall was approaching, four months on, Landon penned another such idyll of practicalities. Wheat seed had been sown in what had been a cornfield, and *Manuel and Peter are now going with their plows from the Stiff clay through the light sandy land that it may be the easier to chop in.* By day's end, however, the seeming waywardness of his workers had shattered this pleasing prospect. *Neither Manuel nor Peter would plow up all my stiff land—pretending I did not order it.* The master justified his anger, reiterating to his diary that: *My orders were to plow my stiff land* since it was *to be sown with wheat.* And then—*Because there had been an old ditch that divided the rows, it seems they left off there & plowed no further.* Landon had, of course, set them right as soon as he knew. He *made them set in to it*; but he made also a characteristic resolution to have them whipped. *On Monday they shall pay for this. . . . Indeed I have not had any directions strictly pursued—so it is time to punish for it.* (Landon was much more likely to have followed through and acted on this quite routine order than on his other more final resolutions to sell Manuel away; but whether he did organize a flogging does not appear in Monday's record.)

Less than four years later, Peter moved decisively beyond this hitherto endless alternation between engagement in the master's work and facing his rage at real or imagined defiance of his purposes.

Joe

5th Mr Joe to appearance struck dead with lightning, for some days, and yet by God's grace I alone saved & restored him.
Joe, as one of the youngest of the Eight, had a record with very few entries. His mother, Winney, had long been *maid* to the Colonel's daughters. Joe's father, the elder Joe, also lived close to the house at the Home Quarter, but it was young Joe's illnesses rather than his father's work in the fields that came to be recorded.

The young Joe—who was being trained for housework—was first recorded in 1770 as a messenger. Thereafter his work as an attendant waiting in the house kept him close to the master day in, day out. Nevertheless, being young and low in the hierarchy, he was not that often noticed in the diary save when he or sometimes he and *little Abraham*, his brother (also in training), seemed to be the only ones there to give service. This would call forth the master's angry—or was it amused?—dismissal of the constant making of excuses. Only two months before the final departure of the young man, Landon wrote that: *This day has turned out so fine that I rode out from a quarter before 8, & got in a quarter after 10. But Mr. Jo had hardly cleaned out my hall, and called it*—the time I was away—*but a moment*. Once again the diarist, using his clock for this measurement, had caught out one of his people.

Not that young Joe always escaped the fierce retributions with which the Colonel sought to make felt his will and his displeasure. Years earlier, when he was even younger, a pair of handcuffs was missed. Joe had been *Ironed in them* while under punishment, or awaiting it. True, he seems to have gotten himself free. He then threw the cuffs into the well, where they were discovered some time later when it was drained. By then he had *sold the bolt*—*got his little brother Abraham to swear he saw black Peter take them, and carry them behind the Kitching.*

Young Joe was, however, at the center of one of the most dramatic narratives old Landon ever wrote—certainly one of those most pleasing to him. Joe's very day-and-night presence in the hall had seriously involved him when a lightning strike flashed through the house. Landon had written a very full account of that episode. In the extended narrative Landon dramatized himself as a God-fearing protector of his household. He also presented himself as a natural philosopher, engaged in the learned scientific controversies of his time. Those pages of literary prose were indeed a rehearsal for an account to be published in the *Virginia Gazette*. This is first and foremost a story about the master; yet it does also relate what was probably, for young Joe, the biggest event in his life up to the time of his running away.

The lightning had struck the eastern chimney of Sabine Hall and run down the hip of the roof on the northeast as far as the corner. There it divided; one flash went on a curved path down the north front of the house, shattering an upstairs window, but did not enter until it came to the downstairs window next to the door of the *great passage* or central hallway. (Landon considered it a great providence of God that he and his little granddaughter had both delayed their intended coming out into the passage, just the instant before the strike.) That branch of the flash had then *run along the middle of this great passage and out the riverside door . . . and in my Piazza struck young Tom Beale leaning over the rails of the Piazza, but did him little harm.*

The other branch was not so merciful; it went directly down the eastern end of the main house at the corner made by the *Communication building* for the eastern wing; and then it went through a small air vent, and into the *outer school room*, where it broke a chair leg, but left a seated man unhurt! From there it flashed out through the door, *and curved round into the little passage*, where it knocked down, *Mulatto Betty, Winny, and her son, Joe.*

The colonel's eldest son, going to assess the situation, had called out that three people were killed. Readers are then gravely told of the patriarch's response:

I laid aside my book, looked up to heaven for mercy & Protection, and humbly implored the utmost calmness; and went to them.

Winny I saw in a suppliant Posture, but stupid; Betty was recovering, but quite useless in her lower limbs, and Poor Joe dead to every Appearance.

So the master arranged for others to care for the two slave women and concentrated on Joe. When Joe was lifted, his head and limbs simply dropped, but the caring patriarch would not leave it at that.

As to Joe—finding no bone broken—I ordered the chamber bellows to be gently blown into his mouth, concluding it may have been only a suffocation; and, in doing of this— abundance of fetid air, like the smell of a foul Gun, was drove out from his lungs, and they began to play. I then ordered Nassaw to give him plenty of soft oily Volatiles, till— in about 10 minutes from his breathing—we got a Pulsation. Observing then a great difficulty in swallowing, I ordered first warm water to be given, concluding the sulphurious vapour that had rushed down his throat when the flash struck him, had excoriated his throat. . . . That made him vomit 4 yellow vomits. This brought him to know us all, but he was presently attended with such groans as were dreadful to hear; on which I durst not give him more warm water, but gave him a Paragoric chiefly of Pepermint water & Sydenham's liquid laudanum.*

Perhaps Joe began to regain consciousness. Surely he had some memory of this drama of his own return from the dead; but it is still not his memory but Landon's insistently medical narrative that preserves the story for posterity. The *paragoric* mixture made Joe vomit again.

*I then indulged him with cold water & Nitre—which by degrees cooled that violent burning complained of—and every now & then I gave more drops—so that in about 2 hours we got a Pulse tollerable regular—when I had him removed to his mother's room.†
He became tollerable sensible, though now & again he had a delirious rambling.*

---

* The laudanum was an opiate mixture devised by one of the great English physicians of the previous century.
† Joe's mother's room must have been in some part of the great house, because the master clearly meant to continue close observation and careful medication under his own eyes.

Now was time to begin to apply more of the armory of the standard medical practice of the day: suppositories.

Clyster on Clysters were administered to draw down that vapour, or whatever it was, from his head which began to be affected, and he became so sensible as to say the pain was now chiefly in his Stomach, but I durst not Vomit him till that Pain should abate; he grew by degrees easy in the night, and towards day began to mend; and as I am giving him a soft healing emulsion, I am in hopes that, by God's assistence, he may recover.

This draft for a published report continues in that vein, moving into a debate with the doctors about treatment for such cases, and with Benjamin Franklin about the nature of electricity. Indeed, the report was not in that month's diary book but in the Daybook where Landon wrote memoranda and sometimes extended notes on books he had read.

Thus, there had been a genuine return-from-the-dead scene in Joe's life, but Landon's July 1777 assertion that Joe had been *to appearance dead with lightning for some days*, was self-serving exaggeration. The same was true of the passage in the earlier narrative, in which we certainly find Landon writing his life as a sentimental novel:

Reader, whoever thou art, picture to yourself this dismal scene. Grandchildren—many, though unhurt—with every sorrowful countenance, though ignorant of the consequences, yet crying with Concern. A mother calling out for her babies—though they are in her company—and going from place to place to be safe, through some confused expectation; and Poor slaves crowding round and following their master, as if protection came only from him. . . .

After such a resurrectionary triumph, Joe's defection was perhaps for Landon the bitterest of all those eight blows in one.

Lancaster Sam

6th Mr Sam—a Sheep stealer under a process below which never reached him. I endeavoured to protect him.

Landon's assertive retrospect on how this sixth of the eight also owed him his life contains nearly all we know about Lancaster Sam, beyond the county designation that was perhaps given him only the morning on which the news of the exodus broke, in order to distinguish this man from the home-quarter Sam who was one of Gardener Johnny's sons. Lancaster Sam was probably just up at Sabine Hall on an errand from the quarter below where he lived and worked.

It is tempting to relate Sam to another striking report of revolutionary turmoil. In December 1775 an unnamed man was tried and convicted in Lancaster County Court for sheep stealing. This was just at the time of maximum shock at Governor Dunmore's newly-made proclamation of freedom to slaves who would come to fight with him. The *Virginia Gazette* tells how, when the convicted felon was being "allowed his clergy"* in place of hanging, the sheriff came to him in court with the hot branding iron. The man, instead of crying out "God Save the King" (as was customary), had, "with the greatest seeming sincerity," bellowed out "God Damn the King—and the Governor too." But perhaps Landon's uncharacteristically tentative statement in the reference to *a process* [prosecution] *. . . which never reached him,* and his assertion that *I endeavoured to protect him,* cannot refer to this dramatic moment of revolutionary awakening among enslaved African Americans in Tidewater Virginia.

Postillion Tom

7th Mr. Tom I ever used with the greatest respect.
Only according to some old Virginian standard could Landon's dealings with Postillion Tom be called respectful; to us, the recorded usage of Tom seems harsh. Landon had, indeed, once kept *Mr Tom in irons all night*—then whipped him. The master had resolved at that point *to turn him out to the hoe.* It is clear, however, that even on this angry occasion, the master saw this man as more weak and misled than wicked.

Postillion Tom was married to the daughter of that veteran schemer Gardener Johnny, a long-time subverter of plantation governance; and so Tom was seen as constantly led into the betrayal of serving his father-in-law more than his master. And Landon's patience was so frequently tried by Johnny's drinking, neglect, and pilfering to sell for liquor, that, back in the spring of 1770, he had demoted Johnny and promoted Tom. But only three months of that had been enough to persuade Landon that he might need to bring Johnny back in charge of the garden; Johnny *was a rogue that sold everything & this* Tom *is a villain that lets everything be ruined even by weeds, . . . and he does nothing.*

---

* As a felony, sheep stealing was in principle punishable with death by hanging; but, in the quaint Common Law formulation still applied for some generations more in Virginia, a first offender was given "benefit of clergy." In that case he would be "burned in the hand" with a red hot iron so as to mark him in any future trial as one who had already had his allowance of mercy.

After further months of frustration, Landon concluded that the problem really continued to be Johnny, and that young Tom was indeed *unwilling that his wive's father should be turned out.* After that overnight manacled incarceration of Tom, the master *put Johnny into his old place.* He entered a sweeping judgment against Tom, who was about to become again a postillion in charge of horses only: he was *too impudent & sawcy to follow orders; And the solemn fool* has *no command to make those* under him *do anything.*

In the bitterness of a revolution that had turned against him, Landon perhaps forgot the impudence of five years before. But what he had denounced as Tom's *solemn fool* characteristics evidently now seemed like welcome forms of docility. And so it had been Postillion Tom who had appeared in the master's dream, moving him almost to compassion with his *most wretchedly meagre and wan* appearance, and his tale of wounds and of hard *grabble* survival in a cave dug in the woods. Above all, Landon had been consoled by Dream Tom's plea to be taken back under his master's protection. The master was touched also by the phantom's acknowledgment of the harsh penalty the Eight were now liable to: *They knew they should be hanged for what they had done.* The imagined Tom further ingratiated himself by denouncing not only Moses but also—now, at last—*his wife's father,* Johnny. (This is how we can be sure that the unnamed apparition was Tom.) Thus, Dream Tom relieved in some measure the master's need to have an accessible target for his seething anger—for Johnny was at Sabine Hall, and still within reach.

Billy

8 Mr. Billy—a fellow too honest, and mild in temper—who could not have gone away but to please his father Manuel who ever was a Villain, and . . . Manuel's brother Will confirmed the same cursed breed. Will sent off two of his sons below & was contriving to get off more—but after 3 months trial I have catched him, and to Carolina he shall go— if I give him away.

The *honest* and *mild* character of Billy—as of Tom in the way he was now remembered—was as reassuring to Landon Carter as any remembrance of the Eight could be. There is no other record of Billy; perhaps he was too young. Remembered as an exemplary young slave, he now served to channel anger toward his villainous father, Manuel, who had led him astray. Since Manuel was at last where his master could no longer reach him, his brother Will was the available target for a tirade and a resolution to wreak the cruel vengeance of exile.

In that case, Will would be paying for both his and his departed brother's readiness to recruit the younger ones into the ranks of freedom seekers: *to Carolina he shall go if I give him away.*

The armed departure of the Eight truly showed revolution entering the plantation to threaten the world of the diarist of Sabine Hall with the second most fundamental overturn imaginable. Only a thoroughgoing gender revolution could have topped this one in confronting plantation patriarchy.

In the forceful way Landon wrote them, the records of the Eight and their families certainly reveal the slave-driving assumptions and practices of the master of Sabine Hall. They also reveal, in fragmentary glimpses, something of the lives and personalities of the Eight in their enslavement to this master. That record seems to reveal also the falseness of his anxiously self-comforting declaration, *that I have no kind of Severity in the least to accuse myself of to one of them; but on the contrary a behaviour on my part that should have taught them gratitude if there ever was a virtue of the sort in such creatures.* But Landon would not have seen the inconsistency that we see; he always persuaded himself that he had done his duty. The diary contains periodic declarations in defense of the floggings Landon ordered: *with conduct like this, to be sure correction cannot be called severity.*

These biographical fragments concerning the Eight give a close, almost experiential, view of the system of slavery as it was sustained at Landon's Sabine Hall. We see the individuals and their kin in vivid glimpses as their personalities and habits were described in very conventional terms by their master. Is that all we can know?

Can we in any way recover the Eight's own stories of themselves? Frustration is great in this regard, for there was assuredly a great deal of storytelling at the quarters. Manuel's return from the gallows, or Joe's return from the dead after the lightning strike, and all those stories of extraordinary recoveries from mortal sickness were surely subjects of powerful narrative performances; but we have only approximate ideas about how these stories would have been told among the enslaved.

Do the uncertainties leave the Eight without their own story? It need not be so. The suppressed stories are there for inclusion, even though they do not

come directly as individual utterances in diary, letter, and treatise form. Historians have begun to search out the stories of those who did not write for themselves. The traditions of their cultures are a collective set of the stories by which
African Americans knew themselves.

The Eight assuredly did not know themselves in a master's set of delinquent-
servant tales. The repertoire of stories with which they had grown up were the
trickster tales of Africa and the songs of a mystical world that "wise persons"
could manage. But their generation was changing and extending their culture.
The great eighteenth-century revolution worked most powerfully among the
African Americans in its Great Awakening form. It transformed their worlds
through the intensification of their appropriation of the great Judeo-Christian
story of creation, of a current state of bondage, and of a promised redemption.
The sacred history of deliverance—of Moses leading the enslaved children of
Israel out of Egypt—was becoming for them the central and most sustaining
narrative to live and to seek fulfillment by.

We may get a much deeper sense of the Eight's own story of their journey-
ing out by night and their crossing of the waters eastward into the dawn if we
understand their actions in light of that story of deliverance. Can it be an accident that the one whom everyone knew all along to be the leader of this exodus was named Moses? Manuel's name in that courthouse-trial book was
written "Imanuell." Can it be only his age and veteran status that gave the second leader his position in the ranking? Was he not also taken for a leader because he bore the name of the promised redeemer?

For cases clearly linking the Revolution to biblical promises of deliverance,
we turn further south. In South Carolina an enslaved man was tried for sedi-
tion in 1775. A report of the case carries the echo of the words of a Black
preacher—also named George—who, addressing "Great crowds of Negroes
in the Neighbourhood of the Chyhaw," had told them that "the old King
[George II] had rece[ive]d a Book from our Lord by which he was to Alter the
World (meaning to let the Negroes free) but for his not doing so, he was now
gone to Hell, and punishment." The slave George had gone on to proclaim:
"That the Young King, meaning our Present One [George III], came up with
the Book, and was about to alter the World, and set the Negroes Free." For
these words, George, the prophet or royal messenger of deliverance, had been
sent to the gallows.

In Georgia a black preacher named David (note this name) would have
been lynched had he not been hurried aboard a departing ship. He had
preached to blacks and whites together, prophesying that "God would send

Deliverance to the Negroes, from the power of their Masters, as he freed the Children of Israel from Egyptian Bondage."

There are only fragments from Virginia to match that; but we can yet take the step of acknowledging that the exodus of the Eight may have been a sacred epic story told in bold action. The traditional songs of their people certainly enshrine the story that made a pharoah of Landon Carter:

Go down, Moses, Way down in Egypt land,
  Tell ole Pharoh: Let my people go

And then:

We're travelling to Immanuel's Land
  Glory! Halle-lu-yah

Thus, we may get a sense of Moses and Manuel's joint story—and that entered into by their six fellows from Sabine Hall. We know that the prophetic narrative carried in their names was already becoming the triumphal faith of their people.

Chapter 3

"All for Love"

In Landon Carter's little kingdom an intense father-daughter struggle over patriarchal sovereign rights was fought out before the Americans' defiance of their King ever turned into war. In this personal struggle, Landon played a role not unlike that of King George III.

The struggle began with Landon imperiously attempting to exercise his father's prerogative. On Monday, May 11, 1772, he sent an ultimatum:
Nat the coachman *sets off with chariot & six to bring Miss Judy home from Pittsylvania. I wrote to her by Nat to bid her never see me, if she is ever to go into the way of her Amorato. For I desire never to see her upon such terms. He is a fellow I cannot be reconciled to on any account whatever.*

The *Amorato* was Judith's cousin Reuben Beale, younger son of a neighboring Richmond County family. His residence then, and his only means of support, was a small plantation in the comparatively newly settled county of Pittsylvania.

The May 11 ultimatum had a long history of family conflicts behind it. Landon ultimately was more in-law to the Beales than you or I, perhaps, would ever like to be to another family. His third wife—deceased since the mid-1750s—had been Elizabeth Beale. It had been a happy enough marriage that he sentimentalized in retrospect; but he was not delighted when, in 1756, soon after Elizabeth's decease, his eldest son married a Beale of the next generation. Robert Wormeley Carter not only married Elizabeth's niece, Winifred Beale, but brought her home to live and raise a family in the house of his widowed father. Antagonisms soon arose and intensified between the old man and his daughter-in-law. In 1766 Landon was already writing: *I see in her the cause of all*

The first Mrs. Landon Carter (née Elizabeth Wormeley), Robert Wormeley Carter's mother. The women of early Sabine Hall have left no words of their own inscription. This portrait was done by William Bridges for Landon Carter— one man commissioned by another. But we may hope that the lady felt that she had achieved some expression of herself. *Colonial Williamsburg Foundation, reproduced by permission of Beverley Randolph Wellford and Robert Carter Wellford, both of Sabine Hall, Virginia.*

the ill treatment my son gives and has given me ever since his marriage. By 1772 the relationship had gotten worse. And now Landon's youngest child, his little Judy, was taking up with Winifred's younger brother, Reuben.

That had been too much. A fierce quarrel between Landon and Reuben evidently left the old man angry and determined to prevent the match. There are, however, gaps in the diaries for late 1771 and early 1772 when this confrontation must have occurred; there is no record of the exact date and circumstances of the clash. From retrospective references, we may surmise that Landon warned Reuben away from Judith, and that Reuben angrily refused to leave off his courtship. And so words were spoken that Landon chose to hear as a direct threat that he *would have murdered me if his courage had not failed him.*

Ignoring many warning signs, Reuben and Judith went on courting, and continued even after the threatened decree of banishment. Judith was a determined young woman, for all she was only 21 years old. She came briefly back to Sabine Hall a few weeks after the May ultimatum; finding that she could not bring the old man round, she soon slipped away to be again with her beloved in the nearby house of his father. And so Landon began to enforce his stern decrees. Meanwhile Landon forbade his other young daughter, Lucy, to go to be entertained at the house of Captain Beale, Reuben's father, who was now harboring the exiled Judith. The diarist deplored Lucy's unwillingness to take his part in the quarrel. In August Landon was invited to a feast at the house of his brother-in-law, the same Captain Beale. He refused. He not only declared his breaking off of social relations with these in-law neighbors but gave as a justification that family's defiance of his sovereignty over his own offspring: — *only Claiming a right to dispose of my children as I please—and . . . not to be accountable to anyone for my reasons of objection.*

Some time in 1773, Judith went ahead and married Reuben, although it had to be from her father-in-law's house and not her father's. There was a long stand-off. Landon was continually angered by his own family's evident disloyalty. His eldest son, Robert Wormeley Carter, whom he sometimes nicknamed Robin, seemed to lead the way; he evidently preferred Captain Beale to his own father. Reuben, however, was the object of the diarist's most intense rage. Landon referred to him always as *the monster,* and eagerly collected evidence that his sickliness disqualified him as a fit husband for Judith.

Wednesday, February 16th, 1774. . . .

Yesterday—being Shrove Tuesday—my son Robin & his son went to eat Pancakes at old Beale's. Robin says the monster is not yet recovered—and my Poor girl is a mere slave to her affection. Now Reuben *has got the Piles. I have no concern for such a brute—but it is a favourable effort of nature to pass off that which—when settling on his lungs—would have produced a Consumption.**

Four days later, Landon felt further vindicated:

Those who never go from home—as they frequently say—all went abroad this day, and to My daddy's, as they call it; and . . . notwithstanding the badness of the roads . . . they got home well & bring account of the monster's being very bad.

Meanwhile, Landon's own health suffered from the deep distress he felt. By the fall of 1774 he was writing, melodramatically as ever, of *the wound* his heart had received from the elopement. Applying his medical expertise to himself, he elaborated with clinical detail. The metaphorically wounded heart was, he asserted, *the cause of my Present colic Complaint.*

The anguish of the father-daughter alienation could even bring the hated Reuben to appear in dreams.

---

* It was a standard part of medical theory in this time that an imbalance in the body if not expressed in one place would manifest itself in another.

September 11, 1773. . . .

It is comical. I dreamed—& told my dream—that coming from Francis Lee's I called in at the weaver's for water & went in and found there a Monster who had broke his leg, &c., and the next day it was reported he—Reuben—was in danger of an inflammation in his lung.

The father, alienated from his beloved youngest daughter, could not continue to find the affair comical. One day in February of 1774—a full year and a half after the banishment order of May 1772—Landon recorded a disturbing dream of Judith returning in abject submission:

I dreamed last night that somebody came to me in mourning—she acknowledged the folly she was guilty of, and all was made up. God only knows whether it will be so or not, I can easily forgive the deluded—if confessed and therefore corrected—and as there can be nothing to vibrate on my memory I think I can forget.

He could not name her. Did he know that by putting Judith in mourning he had willed Reuben dead? Had he not in a sense now killed the young man who, he had said, had threatened to murder him? His preoccupations anyway were with Judith and reconciliation: *God only knows whether it will be so or not.* When awake, he doubted whether there would actually be an act of contrition from Judith. But, if there were, he assured himself: *I can easily forgive the deluded. . . .* And then came the strange reference to there being *nothing to vibrate on my memory.* Here (as in some other places) he was using current medical-psychological theory: the mind, like a stringed instrument, resonates to certain notes. His wish was that there should be no more provocations; if none, *I think I can forget.*

But there were provocations. Abetted by her Beale kinfolk in Sabine Hall, Judith worked to secure a reconciliation without having to abase herself.

Not much of the diary survives for 1773 and 1774, so there may have been episodes we know nothing of. A drama in a churchyard that is recorded, shows how passion was mounting. The conspirators thought a church setting might call forth Christian forgiveness, but Landon's awareness of their designs only angered him the more.

Sunday, May 8th, 1774

A very fine day and I went to Church.

But there appeared the only disagreeable object to me in the whole world. For some time—as he kept from the place where I sat—I did not know him. But—taking him to be a stranger—I asked Mr. Williamson Ball who he was; on being told it was the only monster who ever injured me in my life—I took up my hat, bid everybody goodbuy and walkt away home—ordering my boy to fetch my great Coat & book out of the church and follow me with my horses.

The nonrecognition of Reuben was obviously a ploy. By asking aloud the identity of the young man, Landon could declare very publicly his reason for leaving the scene so abruptly.

Once home, the old man went straight to his diary to enter his narrative of that storming away from the churchyard. He followed it with a self-justifying resolution:

The way to forgive an injury is to forget it; and the only way for a much injured human Creature to forget the Person who injured him is never to see him—a resolution I have long taken and intend to keep.

Convinced of a conspiracy against him, Landon sarcastically defended himself against any charge of being unchristian. Reciting his grievances, he renewed his recollection of Reuben's threat of violence:

I do suppose this to be an intended thing. I am obliged to all who had a hand in it; If they had given me any notice I could have staid at home. For certain I am there can be no true religion where such objects are Perpetually bringing to remembrance the grossest of all injuries in the world. . . . A favourite child stolen from me—and by the man who would have murdered me if his courage had not failed him.

The diarist might resolve to forget, but he was not allowed to; Judith kept at him. With Reuben's sister living in Sabine Hall, Judith stayed well informed about his distress and his consequent ill health. A week after the public spectacle of Landon's enraged exit from the churchyard, Judith wrote and asked to see him. He had yearned for this; and so he recorded it in his diary: *I answered her . . . that—being satisfied of the pains taken to lead her against her duty. . . . if she came alone, my heart was ready to receive her as usual.*

So it was that, just over two years after the banishment order, Judith could come back, and reconciliation could begin. Perhaps its inevitable completion was already foreshadowed. Certainly it was a tender moment that Samuel Richardson or Oliver Goldsmith, among the eighteenth-century novelists, could have described. Any genre painter of the period could have painted the scene, though we should exclude the mocking brush of Hogarth. The diarist did not do badly in his short version.

Wednesday, May 25, 1774

Yesterday my poor offending Child Judy came for the 1st time since she was deluded away to be unhappily married against her duty, my will, and against her Solemn

Promise. . . . Tho' I resolved not to let nature discover its weakness on seeing her, I was only happy in that I could burst into tears—a poor miserable girl. I could not speak to her for some time.

In the middle of this affecting story, the diarist switched to a medical discourse, however. At the place where the elision points occur, the diarist broke off from the pathos of the reunion in order to assert once more his medical reasons for rejecting this marriage. Reuben was, he declared, *a man unsound by birth—as he descended from a man long before bedrid for months before his birth—which bad Stamen or Stock has once already made its appearance in a most Corrupted case, only relieved by an alarming fit of the Piles—which for a while has checked his Consumptive tendency; but such a stamen seems only to be for a while contended against by the Youthfulness of his solids, which must give way—Perhaps sooner than he thinks of.*

We know that Landon had read and was pleased to quote Laurence Sterne's self-mocking fictional memoir, *Tristam Shandy*; but we may doubt that he intended to subvert his own righteous indignation by introducing incongruities in the manner of that narrator. Soon the diarist switched into yet another discourse, one concerning that other kind of inheritance, namely family property. *How is such a creature as Reuben is, to maintain a woman who has always lived well and delicately, and he with only a poor Pittance of an estate—a bit of land & about 6 slaves? Indeed this fine girl has made a hard bed, such has been her deception.*

The patriarch used a story of an earlier Reuben Beale—an uncle probably—to reinforce himself in excluding Reuben from any property settlement:
I will contrive that she shall not want for Personal necessaries, but I will give nothing that either Reuben or his inheritors can claim.* I well remember the Case of his Namesake; the old Fox, Captain Beale, his father got all he had—whilst his widow got nothing, and Paid his debts to boot.

Sharing tender tears at last with his daughter had made it easier for Landon to maintain his rage against the young man who had stolen her away. He could use his sympathy for Judith's plight to confirm himself in his stand. He wrote once more with pathos:

---

* Under the very patriarchal regime that Landon sought to uphold, anything he gave directly to his married daughter was a gift to her husband.

A father reunited with his unhappy daughter. This is a detail from a 1745 engraving in a series showing scenes from Samuel Richardson's novel *Pamela*. (Prints from copperplate engravings were then an important part of education in sensibility.) *Colonial Williamsburg Foundation.*

Friday, October 7, 1774. . . .

Poor Judy and her new sister, Sally, came here. I could not help observing how easily that poor girl is made to believe in her distant happiness when I am certain she sees nothing but misery. She knows not whether she goes up to Pittsylvania county *this fall or next spring.*

I said it—staying here—might keep her the longer from being miserable—for she would be so as soon as she got there.

She answered: No, she should not be.

I am certain that the last time she was here, she told me there was no neighbors about the place within 20 miles of it. But possibly it was with her All for Love or the world well Lost.* She may be fond of that native nothingness from whence she sprung. I thought she

---

* "All for Love or the world well Lost" is actually the title of a verse tragedy by John Dryden. Landon was fascinated by this work; see below, chapter 10.

had from good sense been bred up in juster notions. But I see all the Beale brood are so now. . . . In short, the monster, like the uncouth Germans, has turned them all to such a mode of thinking. But possibly heaven may have something else in store.

So embittered had the diarist grown against the family that stole his children, that he was prepared to write a denunciation of *that native nothingness from whence she sprung.* Was this a reflection on the unsatisfactory Beales as a clan? Let us hope it was not a personal reflection on the memory of his late wife, Elizabeth Beale Carter, the mother of Judith. Soon after her death, Landon had expressed himself quite differently, when he had shared with this wife a pleasing poem, "The Wedding Day," and had noted on his copy of it: "read to the last Dear Woman & with consent she smiled."

Landon's anger at Reuben was now fueled by what he sensed as a renewed conspiracy of Beales. They had robbed him of a daughter; now they sought to get their hands on his property. So a new phase of this emotional contest began. Judith was determined to make Landon accept Reuben; and Judith knew how to manage the campaign she was commencing. On her next visit she let her father rage on about what he would and would not do. He assured her that he would try to secure her comfort; but he insisted that no property was to pass to her husband. When he recorded his tirade, he already knew that he had not beaten her down. *She made no reply—but only kissed me & took her leave of me.*

That had been in June of 1774; by October Landon was ready to show them all he was not going to be outwitted. He would now write his threat into legal form; and there would be a preamble to justify it. His words about this move are steeped in a bitter folklore of landowning families. The diarist raged against his former brother-in-law (now the father-in-law of two of his children), who had approved the marriage but was refusing to make a property settlement that would render Judith secure in the event of the ailing Reuben's death. He continued to designate Captain Beale by a folksy farmyard epithet. *Wednesday, October 5. . . .*

Yesterday I wrote my Codicil to my will and had it executed by witnesses this day. I had long ago suspected the Old fox in this neighbourhood—who had been ever tethering his Cubs out on other People—had only been instrumental in a late damnable trick—Judith's marriage—in hopes to get something by it. Therefore I tryed every way to fathom his intentions, and at last—I am privately told—he has not given anything toward his son's settlement and though he pretended to promise what he would do, has not done it, and only lends the possession; So in case of a death—with Reuben much to be suspected—an unfortunate creature—my daughter—is to be made much more miserable than she thought she should be.

Therefore it is that I have resolved only to furnish real Necessaries for the Poor unfortunate creature during her connexion—and to lend her a maid under the Cub's bond to return all again when demanded.

*As to Mr. Smart—*Reuben—*a beggar he was & a beggar he shall be found, to let Mother damnable* know that a good maintenance was much better than a barrell of Corn or two from a brother.*

Landon had checked into old Beale's plans; the two old foxes were now stalking each other. Judith was caught in the middle of their game. And it was part of the game at Sabine Hall that all of the patriarch's writings lay around to be read by his family. Thus, on the Thursday immediately following the change to Landon's testamentary arrangements, he could record the close attention given to the matter by his namesake grandson:

On Tuesday last I saw a certain Young Gentleman reading the fowl copy of my Codicil whilst it was lying on this table. Perhaps he may some day have the curiosity to read this book; therefore I choose to give him a few sentiments relative to himself.

There followed Landon's familiar advice about studying books and avoiding gaming tables. Suddenly we realize that the diary not only falls at intervals into the style of a sentimental novel, but that it might, at a stretch, be called an epistolary novel in the making. It was a kind of open letter to Landon's family that unfolded the household's life as the patriarch would tell it. Yes, if only they would all read its self-justifying narratives, they would understand not only Landon's feelings but the rightness of his conduct. Perhaps then they would alter their own conduct accordingly. At intervals the diarist even addressed these yearned-for readers. Just four weeks before he wrote the codicil, Landon had penned an address to his principal antagonist, his eldest son, Robert Wormeley. He wrote one thing that happened—*which I minute down believing the Gentleman who distinguished himself by it may one day read it.* . . . A year later Landon wrote them all an exhortation: *let those who may be curious in my life . . . peruse these little books to see how surprizingly they have treated a Parent ever fond of them & indeed kind to them.* Such apostrophes to Landon's family recurred; and we know he left his little books where they could be read, since he once had to cope with furor in the county when a visitor to Sabine Hall reported what he had seen written about the parson of the parish.

---

* Presumably *Mother damnable* was Reuben's sister, the detested Beale daughter-in-law, Winifred. The scornful reference to a barrel or two of corn is obscure, but it shows Landon imputing a mercenary nature to Winifred.

Landon was obsessed with the Beale plot. He saw everywhere at work the machinations of old Captain Beale, the predator of his children and his property.

A second letter came from the monster Reuben Beale to ask pardon & be forgiven his rashness to me. The patriarch of Sabine Hall stiffened his resolve by reminding himself that *the old fox,* Captain Beale . . . *has ever been tethering out his Children on others to cope* with them, and he has *hardly afforded them any education but that of stealing other Gentlemen's children—I do suppose intending to give his son nothing—he has put him upon asking to be forgiven—that is to have an estate given to him.*

Angry as Landon was, he could still relish a scornful play on words. And so he brushed off this approach:

I would not answer this letter and only wrote my daughter that I had read it but wanted no correspondence with the writer of it. . . . He says he was born to it. If so I am sure he was born to be a Villain. Some letter from Robert or Winifred . . . *has made this simpleton tell me my forgiveness will add greatly to the comfort of his life. But why should I consult his comfort who has robbed me of mine, and would have taken my life away if he could?*

Reflection on his grievances made Landon take up the idea that the *wound* he had received from Reuben's conduct had ruined his health. His sorrows, he asserted, were *the cause of my Present Complaint*—the colic. *Otherwise it is hard* to explain *that such a constant temperance* as I practiced—*with a sound constitution—could be thrown into such a weakness in solids as to become a Prey to every kind of flatulency.*

The shifting emotional claims and moral assumptions that tugged at both Landon and his daughter Judith were just one expression of altering personal identities and familial relationships that ultimately underlay the American Revolution.

From the late seventeenth century or earlier profound changes had been taking place that had many sources and manifestations; they were directly or indirectly connected to what has been called "the consumer revolution." From the later seventeenth century onward, a flood of new kinds of goods meant that, with money, a comparatively ordinary person could now buy the means to refinement and higher status in ways not formerly possible. Fashionable clothes and furnishings played their part, but other ways of transforming the imagination may have been even more important. There were mass-produced pictures in the form of copperplate engravings. (Hogarth's satires are the most enduringly famous of such market items.) And there were the papers and printed books of the new, fast-growing profession of journalism. Foremost among the new kind of books that were rearranging the consciousness of the age was the novel of sentiment. The novels told strong stories of self-realization and so contributed subtly but surely to the subversion of the ancient hierarchical order of ruling fathers. They were not set in a traditional hierarchical universe, where to live properly was to do your duty in the station to which God had called you. That was the patriarchal order for which Landon yearned; that was the old regime he felt slipping away as he and his peers combined to defy "Father George." By contrast, the psychological novel of the eighteenth century typically showed how the individual might discover and remake herself.

The feminine pronoun is not arbitrarily introduced; the protagonists of these first bourgeois novels were characteristically young women. This in itself was a revolution; neither Helen nor Penelope had stood a chance of giving their names to *The Iliad* or *The Odyssey*. But women now supremely embodied the new sensibilities that the novel was teaching. (*Pamela*, Richardson's first great blockbuster, was a story of a servant girl who became a lady by virtuously making the most of the literate refinement that she was cultivating as assiduously as she cultivated chaste virtue.)

Guided by love, the protagonist in this new story would choose her husband for herself, and that did not accord with the patriarch's *right to dispose of my children as I please*. That clash of moral claims is laid bare in the greatest and most sensational novel of the day. Richardson's tragedy *Clarissa*, was published in 1748. In this next book, a stern, unfeeling patriarch, James Harlowe, tries to impose an unwanted marriage on his daughter. She is driven into exile by this demand, but her death after the most severe trials secures her a kind of apotheosis. Her father is rendered contrite at last, and brings her body home for interment in the family vault.

Landon Carter, in a less sensational form, rewrote *Clarissa* from the point of view of old Mr. James Harlowe. It was a remarkable feat, and we are left uncertain as to what his models may have been. He had read Lawrence Sterne's *Tristam Shandy*, and he owned a complete set of the works of the novelist Henry Fielding, so it is very likely that the great books of the moralistic Samuel Richardson had been included in his library at Sabine Hall. In any case, the sentimental and subversive language of the new novels—the anti-authoritarian sensibility that they sustained—was in the air by the 1770s. Indeed, we have already seen Landon's writing in the idiom of these novels both in his narrative of the lightning strike at Sabine Hall and in his account of his reconciliation meeting with Judith.

In the forms of stories—now sentimental, now authoritarian—we can see Landon clearly as a divided individual facing two ways: he wanted to be a lordly patriarch like his father; and he wanted to be loved and understood like Pamela or Clarissa. His discourses were therefore also divided. I have emphasized the modernizing novelistic discourses in the Judith narratives, but we have already seen him enter into an ancient folkloric discourse with that farmyard image of *the old fox* after other people's *chickens*. In the stories that the diarist told with increasing passion as the Revolution came on, we shall see how much of the old-fashioned there was in Landon.

The next great step in the unfolding plot of Judith's struggle against Landon's decrees was disturbingly mixed up with Landon's determination to reform a recalcitrant slave. Nassaw we have already met in passing as the servant who helped attend the victims of the lightning strike. He was Landon's personal attendant and, in effect, his medical assistant; but, alas, Nassaw had an addiction. We would call him an alcoholic; Landon denounced him constantly as a willful drunkard.

It was a Monday morning in late summer when Landon wrote the most remarkable episode that we have in the cumulating record of his slow reconciliation with Judith. Landon was already churning with powerful emotions; he had just played God—or at least God's insistent deputy—to *drunken Nassaw*.

Nassaw was perhaps the person with whom Landon had the most sustained intimacy in these years of widowed isolation. They shared the healing work that was deeply part of the diarist's identity. But a drunken surgeon continually puts lives at risk; and so the reform of Nassaw had become a precious project to his master.* We may surmise that it was a terrible tyranny for Nassaw. With the drawn-out family crisis, issues of pardon and forgiveness were all churning in Landon's heart. To Nassaw he showed first the wrath and then the mercy of divine patriarchy. It proved to be also the time to turn from punitive rage to benign forgiveness in the treatment of Judith and Reuben.

---

* Surgeons were still classed as artisans; they did manual work, administering purges, letting blood, and sawing bones. They were still far from the white-coated professional status of today.

Nassaw's episode runs as follows. The slave surgeon had contrived to get rum after church on Sunday; so he was in a near stupor when he tended to a gravely ill overseer. After he had been found insensible in the fields, he was dragged back to Sabine Hall. His master made toward him *to give him a box on the ear,* but Nassaw, drunk enough to be incautious, *fairly forced himself against* his master. Physically a match for the staggering Nassaw, the old patriarch had tumbled him into the cellar. There he was *tied Neck & heels all night,* to await further punishment the next morning.

With the return of daylight, Nassaw was stripped and tied up to a tree limb. He was shown *a Number of switches Presented to his eyes* by *a fellow with an uplifted arm.* Now sober, he had pleaded for mercy, making before his master a display of complete contrition and abject submission. He had even sworn *that he never more would touch liquor.* Landon had accepted this—only expostulating to Nassaw about God, salvation and damnation, and the awful sanctity of solemn oaths. In the diary this is recorded with evident satisfaction: *After all I forgave this creature out of humanity, religion and every virtuous duty—with hopes—though I hardly dare mention it—that I shall by it save one soul more Alive.*

The Judith story at this point was intimately intertwined in the diarist's psyche with the Nassaw story. The deep source of inner conflict in both was an impending abandonment by Landon of his disciplinary stand against his beloved daughter and his hated son-in-law. On Sunday morning there had already been a decisive encounter leading to crucial exchanges with Judith. This had occurred in time before Nassaw's delinquency was known, and so before his close confinement, stretching, menacing, and release; but the Judith part of the weekend's dealings was only written down after the slave's ordeal and his pardoning had been piously narrated.

With a stark simplicity unusual for him, Landon told the painful story of how Judith at last broke down his intended stern resolution: *Yesterday I walked up to my daughter Judith in the church—though I at the door—to ask her how she did—and she hardly took notice of me.*

She did not come to him; she willed him come to her, and then she snubbed him. He needed affectionate reassurance; she knew he needed it. A long and painful Sunday afternoon followed. During this time Landon exerted himself to apprehend Nassaw—there, at least, was an offender who could be judged, punished, and forgiven. Meanwhile, Judith, no doubt sensing her advantage, made the next move: *At night, I received a letter from her, which—from one of less sense—might be overlooked, but from her it carried all the Airs of a Species of revenge, because I would not take her offending husband into favour.*

Judith's allies within Sabine Hall exploited the situation: *My son—who cannot yet help piping to his wife's affections, endeavoured much to get this unaccountable man restored, pretending more contrition in him than I dare say he will ever show upon the occasion—Robin would have had a mild tender answer written.*

Landon's own needs made him begin to buckle now, though he did so struggling with hostile emotions and a troubled conscience. He wrote to Judith: *But I put her in mind of her behaviour—and in answer said that—although it would be condescending to her undutifulness—and would set a bad example to disobedient Children— Yet she and her husband might come when they pleased & stay as long as they would at Sabine Hall—only declaring I would accommodate myself to such a trial if possible.*

Characteristically, the struggle with conscience took more words. Indeed, Landon was now in a bind; he had tried to reinforce himself in his stand by making it a cosmic imperative. Both in the codicil and in the diary he continually left open to be read, there were declarations that disobedience to patriarchs was not only an injury to the father in person—which should be forgiven in Christian spirit—but also an unpardonable offence against nature. Not to make an example of offenders, therefore, was to undermine the divinely appointed order of things.

Yet Landon now needed Judith's affection; and so he wrote—in the form of a prayer—a penitent justification of his capitulation: *Thus my God have I suffered myself to destroy thy divine order in governing this world; but thy religion is not only full of forgiveness but of the Social Virtues of forgetting injuries—though against the texture with which thou hast made man—and all for that grand and adorable end of a truely Social Virtue. We are thy imperfect beings in point of Right and wrong; but I beseech thee let not this be imputed to me as a crime. I have laboured and can only justify myself by the means of thy word—possibly imperfectly conceived by me. And if it is not too offensive to thy Justice in Mercy—save us all.*

This was in September of 1775. The American patriots had been by then for five months at war with the government of their king. The dispute was in some sense about whether it was the king or the patriots who had subverted *thy divine order in governing this world.* Landon deeply knew himself to be involved in that cosmic struggle over the terms of due obedience.

Almost inevitably, Landon continued to vacillate between forgiveness and recrimination. He returned to the diary after dinner on that Monday. He reverted from prayer to more of the dark folklore of family feud and intrigue. He spelled out again his doubts concerning Judith's allies; he described his answer as a kind of test to see whether affectionate reconciliation really was intended. Oh yes, he was watching to gauge responses. His twisted sentences reveal his anguish.

I could not but entertain a Suspicion that the letter received last night, was somehow in the artful schemes laid; Therefore I answered it—hinting at the situation of revenge the letter writer represented herself. I said only what my own suspicion suggested, being quite Satisfied—if there was anything of real sincerity—that what I consented to would be received—but, if not, the contriver must see the scheme defeated; and so it appears to be at dinner time.

There was therefore a note of triumph in his next-day's discovery of a Beale plot: *Tuesday, Sept. 12th. I thought there was an old fox in the grounds somewhere, and now I perceive where he is; but he may prowle about. I have no more fowls to be catched—& I am too old to be catched myself.*

But still the reconciliation proceeded. By Wednesday Landon could write: *Yesterday my daughter Judith & her Mr. Beale came here & are here still. I forced nature into a forgetfulness of Injuries—and gave a seeming easy reception as before.*

If only King George III could have brought himself to such accommodation of his rebel subjects.

It was time for a literal as well as a metaphorical healing. After the young couple had withdrawn again to the Beale's place, Reuben's continuing ill health provided an occasion for fuller reconciliation. Reuben had the need, and Judith, we suspect, had the wit, to ingratiate Reuben with Landon; they would flatter the old man's pride as a home practitioner of medicine. This certainly helped, as can be sensed in the complacent detail of the instructions and the dosages enjoined on Nassaw who was deputed to apply the treatment.

This evening Reuben Beale wrote to me for advice about his pain in his breast & costiveness without any Perceivable fever. I sent Nassaw to bleed him, if full in any manner in his Pulse. At the same time I sent opening boluses* of Senna, Jalap, Rubarb & cream of tartar with 6 grains of soap in each—to open his bowels & dissolve the hard faeces certainly in his bowels. . . .

By now Landon was keen to pursue this healing project; and so, he added: *And bid him come here that by enquiry I might find out his original disorder—which I take to be acidity.*

Perhaps because Nassaw was once again *really drunk*, or because this was the promising way forward to an inheritance, the newly acknowledged son-in-law actually took up the invitation to come back to Sabine Hall and be treated in

---

* A bolus was a medicine stirred as a paste and rolled as a little ball to be swallowed.

person by his father-in-law. *Reuben Beale came and I administered to him,* proudly noted the diarist.

Meanwhile, the record shows that Lucy, Judith's older sister, was preparing for her own marriage. It may be that this had been hastening reconciliation. Old Landon wrote only deadpan entries in his diary. Perhaps it was his way of marking the return of peace and of relieving the intensity of his record with some very masculine humor over Lucy's girlish foibles.

Saturday, 23 September, 1775. Lucy as usual is much in want of necessaries; first she was to go to Blane's Store; but on Catesby Jones saying there were more things at Hamilton's store she went there. I gave her 7 dollars to lay out. Note: her necessaries were first white & Coloured ribbons—and she was told they were in vast plenty at Blane's; but now they are at Hamilton's. . . .

And then: *My daughter Lucy got back by dinner—and has laid out £6 odd in necessaries—a fan, some ribbons, and several such prodigeous nothings. However I am trusted and that is her comfort.*

At some stage in all this preparation, Mr. William Colston, a neighboring gentleman, had done what Reuben Beale had been forbidden to do. Mr. Colston had approached Landon and told him how matters stood. He *discovered how . . . Lucy's affections lay,* was the way the diary recorded this. The two gentlemen then talked about the appropriate settlement of property. There must be a commitment both from the groom's side, and—by way of dowry—from the bride's father. Landon later recalled telling Mr. Colston that he *had only £800 sterling to give her as a portion.* We actually know this because misunderstandings and recriminations followed; it was when dispute arose that Landon wrote the surviving diary account of the original conversation.

There was a problem. Mr. Colston's estate was entailed in such a way that it would pass to others if he died without leaving a son to succeed him. (Thus was Mr. Bennett and his family situated in Jane Austen's *Pride and Prejudice.*) Mr. Colston indicated to Landon that he thought it sufficient that there would be a morally assured maintenance for his widow from his legal heirs, should he die before he had a male heir. But Landon wrote that he had insisted at the outset that the intending bridegroom must make *a settlement* on his daughter in such a way as to ensure her an adequate fixed maintenance; an unspecified allowance from those to whom her deceased husband's property would pass was not acceptable. Mr. Colston could only legally make such an arrangement with property not part of the entailed estate—that is, with the dowry supplied by Landon. But settling the dowry in that way would mean that the son-in-law's control and disposition of that property would be severely restricted. Readers must be wondering, as is the writer, why Landon had not proposed some such protected settlement in favor of Judith; perhaps, in that earlier case, it was because he had not wanted to do anything substantial for the rebel pair—or not yet.

Landon's diary carefully recorded his own tart response to Mr. Colston's proposal that the dowry be given without such restrictions. *The gift to you—only saying your widow shall be maintained out of the estate given to another, if you die without heirs—must leave my children in the power of others or of the law—and what would this differ from a Parent throwing his child into a river, that some kind hand might save her from drowning?* Mr. Colston had replied that Lucy *thought there would be no manner of occasion for such a settlement.* Landon then gave him the force of his views on the way young women in love prepare to ruin their own lives: *I answered she seemed to reason as she did on the present moment in the full shine of a honeymoon, but things of this* settlement *sort . . . could be only meant after his death, when perhaps the moons of others might never shine on his widow.*

So Mr. Colston was expected to provide an *instrument . . . any lawyer could easily draw*—for the dowry of £800 (mostly in slaves according to valuation) that was thus to be settled on Lucy personally.

Now we come to the almost-happy-reconciliation ending. The Sabine Hall disputes receded, and Landon found himself with two new sons-in-law and his youngest daughters more or less at peace with him.

Lucy and Mr. Colston lived in Richmond County; they visited every month or so. Lucy in time brought with her a new grandson. Certainly the diary showed how Landon longed for his daughter's company. He sent his chariot for her and the *little boy—for really I have been long without any company; and from a weakness in my eyes I cannot be occupied as I used to be.* He then used a Latin saying referring to the way a reader may be never less alone than when alone.

Alas, after four days only, it was: *My daughter Colston goes home—a short visit—but I must be content. Everybody is for themselves.*

Judith and Reuben lived a hundred miles away, however, in Pittsylvania County. Landon, therefore, had more often to be content with letters. There was one that he carefully noted in the diary. It vindicated him in that bitter struggle now past. He had rationalized his prohibition of the love match by reference to Reuben's sickliness. Now, word from Judith allowed her father both to have been right all along and to be active in his proud role as healer:

Wednesday April 3, 1776. . . .

I received this day a letter from my Daughter Judith. She complains much of Mr Beale's want of health. I could easily foresee the known family disorder of throwing Off his Vict-uals; but poor miserable girl she must now do the duty of a nurse for her folly, and I shall advise her to take the world as she finds it, now she has only relied on her own judge-ment. . . . She says much in praise of the pills I sent up. They only do him the least serv-ice; but she does not say he wants more.

In this diary entry, Judith was still *my daughter Judith;* she was not yet called by her husband's surname as her sisters were. When visits followed, the first re-ports revealed that the dosing of Reuben was the main satisfaction. But then at last, in August 1778, just months before his death, Landon could write that *Mr. Reuben Beale and his Lady my dear daughter got here yesterday—a comfort to me in-deed.* He even gave her at last the correct formal style of naming. But expecta-tion makes for disappointment; and so it was that this very last surviving Judith entry had its traces of bitterness; as he wrote that, *My daughter Beale who—when she came down was to stay till cooler Weather, & her husband go home—I understand today is to be in her way home.*

Landon had said once—when asked to persuade a niece to marry a gentle-man from Philadelphia—that *it was sending a child from her Parent out of the world.* Now he applied his saying to Judith: *But this child chose to go out of the world from her father. Farewell fondness. I will hope in God.* By the time of that little disgruntled note, Landon had already written a new codicil to his long and complicated will: "Item to Mr Reuben Beale, who has intermarried with my daughter Judith. . . ." There followed a bequest to Reuben of his equivalent to Mr. Colston's £800.

Landon had not suppressed or punished rebellion; he had not been able to sustain the patriarchal sovereignty he claimed. Instead he could only secure peace of mind by accepting Judith's declaration of autonomy. By his acquies-cence he restored the integrity of his extended family. How different was the outcome of that other struggle over sovereignty in which Landon was involved. Only under the duress of defeat in war did George III accept the Declaration of Independence of his former subjects; and the outcome was not a restoration of family unity but a permanent separation.

PART II

ENLIGHTENMENT CALM

The first domestic diary was a procedures book for methodizing the plantation. In that carefully kept 1750s record, we find an earlier Landon Carter. Before the diarist went into rebellion against his king's government, and began to write passionate narratives of rebellion in his own kingdom, the journal of his plantation reveals only a colonial gentleman practicing Enlightenment natural philosophy as modern science in both medicine and agriculture.

Pl. I.

Agriculture, Labourage.

Benard Fecit.

Plate I of Diderot's great *Encyclopédie.* Here is agriculture as imagined in the mid-eighteenth century. Technology is combined with subtle sentimentalization, including the evocation of the feudal past through the ruined castle. It was just such an old-world image of peasant labor in the fields that informed Landon's diaries. *Colonial Williamsburg Foundation.*

Chapter 4

Plantation Pastoral

*Rain yesterday rain last night and this morning—Thunder, Lightning & rain—rain all
the evening with more lightning and Thunder to the Southeast.*
Try reading these lines aloud, and feel in their cadences the lyricism that Landon, the agricultural diarist—and so weather narrator—was unconsciously striving for. The virtuosity he attained could be illustrated in hundreds of examples. The chapter that follows, attempts to condense one of the main streams of day-by-day information in the diary and to give a sense of Landon's artistry in his writing about sky and earth, field and flock.

Landon's first surviving plantation journal comes from a time when the term "literature" had a very comprehensive meaning. The word was not yet restricted to artistic belles-lettres but applied also to science, philosophy, and history. These day-by-day accounts of farmwork cumulated into a great pastorale in prose; they unselfconsciously extended an English-language tradition adapted from the ancients. Landon, of course, knew the Roman Virgil's pastoral *Eclogues* and his poetic celebration of country works and days in the four books of the *Georgics*, so the great poet's influence is pervasive. In the quality of his daily entries, and in his sustained recording over 22 years, Landon penned the most elaborated and revealing English-language farm journal coming down to us from the eighteenth-century age of agricultural improvement.*

---

* I have searched central and regional archives throughout England, Wales, and Scotland, and I have interrogated agricultural historians who are thoroughly familiar with the surviving

The Place and Its People

We have already seen how Sabine Hall was carefully sited on the brow of the line of low ridges just back from the northern shoreline of the mile-wide Rappahannock River. Looking out to the south over the tidewater, it was and is a box seat for the theater of the weather.

The name Sabine Hall given by Landon to his country seat took up the celebration by the ancient Roman poet Horace of his "Sabine farm" as a peaceful retreat from the vicious and strife-torn life of Rome. The "hall" component of the name is pure English. It harks back to an ancient mythology of Teutonic lordship—the Anglo-Saxon warrior lord holding court and feasting his followers in the heavy oak-beamed, smoke-filled building at the center of his fortified stockade. (A preliminary count of colonial Virginia estate houses that bore the designation "hall" suggests that most of them belonged to the great families of the north, the Carters and the Lees, who have been styled "the Barons of the Potomac.")

Having addressed the evocations in the name of the great house that was the centerpiece and command post of Landon's plantation complex, another important but elusive question arises. If this were not a diary but a landscape painting, it would be a first step in its appraisal to determine the genre that shaped and directed its manner of representing the rural scene. As soon as the question is asked, however, it is clear that the landscape with figures into which this diary transports readers is not the terrain of an America that was exotic to European archetypes. Landon, indeed, rather earnestly depicts a world imaginatively assimilated to the country estates of both the ancient Roman and the long English tradition. A famous declaration penned by William Byrd II, that: "Like one of the Patriarchs, I have my Flocks and my Herds, my Bond-men and Bond-women . . . ," made explicit an identification with the ancient world of the Bible that was surely there for Landon, at least in subconscious form. (These evident old-world evocations in Landon's diary may be proposed as a reason in addition to those already advanced in "First Words," as to why this diary has not yet been taken up by scholars of American literature, who tend to search for differences from the old world rather than continuities with it.)

---

records. I have found no leads to a day-by-day record of field planting, animal husbandry, and labor management that comes near to the close observation—not to mention the scientific reasoning—of Landon Carter's Sabine Hall diary. I have not been able to make so systematic a search of continental European records, but my inquiries there have also revealed nothing comparable.

Landon lived by the tillage of American soil and by the planting of Indian-derived crops of tobacco and corn. The Indians were long gone, and so the diarist's livelihood was the product of numerous enslaved African Americans, whose presence made this landscape seem exotically colonial to English travelers. We shall see, however, both in this chapter and in a later one on "The Master and the Slaves," that Landon narrated his world in a way that largely likened his workers to an ancient peasantry contending with their lord. Of course, this aspect is overstated the moment it is declared, for Landon can casually record extreme summary punishments of a kind that had long ceased to be available to English landlords, unless it were by order of a court, following a legal trial. Nevertheless, readers, as they proceed in this book, should at least bear in mind the question of what is most invoked, an ancient order of estate lordship or an exotic American colonial plantation world.

At and around Sabine Hall lived and worked Landon's large family in the old patriarchal sense. All the servants and slaves who were fed from his provisions were regarded as his family, because they were his dependents, living under his roof—although he utterly depended on them for his wealth, status, and identity. Landon referred to those who lived beyond the great portals of Sabine Hall but were around him under his command, care, and protection, sometimes as *my people* and comprehensively as *my out & in* doors *family*.

It was a numerous, restive, and rebellious family. Close around the estate house in 1756 were five habitations of enslaved workers—Mangorike, the Fork, Matheny's, Morgan's, and the Home Quarter. (Lansdowne and Hickory Thicket were also nearby—but they had been deeded to the eldest son, Robert Wormeley Carter, as part of his marriage settlement in 1756.) All these quarters were small African American settlements, usually (but not always) with a white overseer nearby. It was the men, women, and children of these little villages who worked the fields assigned to them. The number of mature men and women workers in the whole complex in the 1750s almost certainly grew over the decades of the plantation diary; during the 1750s it was probably somewhere between 40 and 50, indicating a total enslaved population of around 100.

Landon also owned more distant plantations; these lay in further parts of Richmond County, in Northumberland County down-river, in Fauquier, Stafford, and Prince William, and Loudoun Counties up-river, and in York, and King and Queen counties to the southward. These were operated by stewards and overseers who received either wages or shares of the crop or both as remuneration. The management of these scattered quarters only entered intermittently into the journal. At the time of Landon Carter's death, the officials of the court found that Landon owned 401 slaves in these eight counties. That number would have placed Landon in the top dozen property owners in the state according to a survey of wealth distribution in post-Revolution Virginia; by then the division of Landon's estate had left his son and heir, Robert Wormeley Carter, only in the top twenty. In all these places, near and far, the able-bodied workers were kept engaged in tilling the soil incessantly; they plowed it, hoed it, and dunged it, in order to keep it in production. On the 350 cleared acres of his home plantation, Landon would see to the tending of more than a quarter of a million tobacco plants; he also saw to a third of a million corn plants, so the slaves each year had to laboriously raise up some half-a-million knee-high hills, often in stiff clay soil. As well, Landon managed the sowing of more than 150 acres of wheat, oats, barley, peas, beans, turnips, timothy grass, and other soil-improving fodder crops. In all this, the estate's herds of cattle and horses were a vital resource, because of the haulage required for all the plowing, carting, and manuring. The well-being of the livestock was a matter of the master's most anxious concern.

The Seasons' Round of Toil

We have glimpsed the work of this plantation in tracing the recorded lives of the Eight; now we shall systematically follow the seasons' work of the Sabine Hall plantation complex from 1757, the nearest to a complete year's record in this *Farming Observations* notebook. But, for the later spring of 1757—when Landon went away to serve as a burgess for Richmond County—we shall follow the spring work of 1758.

SPRING

Did Landon look on March 1 as the beginning of the season of renewal? *'Tis now my usual time for observing on my Crops of Wheat on the ground,* he wrote on that day in 1757. What he saw did not delight him. February was *the most pernicious month in the whole Year to a farmer that cultivates low stiff lands.* But he must go forward: much heavy work was now on hand. *Began this evening to turn my dung at my house.* It must be forked up and be made ready to be loaded on carts to be trundled out and dug into the corn and tobacco hills that the gangs would be making or renewing in the fields.

Managing the dung was at the heart of Landon's self-conscious farming in the English manner; it was also heavy toilsome work. We see five days later the harshness of the system of work enforcement: *We are still turning dung at the house—they will not finish before Monday 12 o'Clock, which will make 5 days com-pleat with 5 hands, but three of them are my runaways—who I have been obliged to make work in Chains.*

It would be mid-April, after a month of hard toil before both dung heaps and the fields were ready, so that Landon could write: *Began this day to Cart out my dung.* Thus commenced another long stint for the teamsters and gangs. It would be slow at first—with *only one horse cart & an Ox Cart—by reason of Joe's illness,* but it would be relentless. Day after day the diarist entered the number of loads carried out, alternating daily achievements and cumulative totals—62, 121, 58. . . . By Friday, May 12, 1758, he could enter triumphantly that he had *finished carting out all my dung.* He not only drew up a complete tally but went on to estimate what total volume the *tumbrils,* each loaded with *40 bushels,* had hauled out. Allowing a bushel to provide for eight tobacco hills, he calculated that he had provided for exactly 264,960 hills.

The dung count provided the only triumphant entry the plantation would get during the whole spring of 1758. Cold, wet weather was followed by long drought and a plague of tobacco flies and ground worms; the crop prospect was bleak. Probably the insistent entering of dung delivery was compensatory; this was the one branch of the season's work that Landon could push ahead al-most regardless of adverse conditions. Meanwhile at the unloading end of the dung hauling, the tobacco hills had to be newly hoed up and the dung buried—a peck (or quarter-bushel) of it in each hill. It was only on May 20 that Landon could write: *Finished burying my dung & turning all my tobacco hills.* That brought a final note of triumph: that his tobacco ground was prepared *sooner . . . by 18 days than last year.* And so the gangs could begin *to weed Corn sooner than last year by 19 days.* But it was a hollow triumph. The master of Sabine Hall—like most of his neighbors, indeed most of Virginia in 1758— had almost no young tobacco plants to set in his quarter-million dunged hills.

Landon's workers had sown tobacco seeds in the *4 last . . . beds up at the house* on January 18. But now, as these first efforts were blighted by tobacco flies, there was a lot more clearing of further seedling *patches*; then there must be much raking, a desperate treating of the seed—with milk, with nitre, with any-thing that might bring success—and sowing, sowing, sowing. After all that came an anxious watching for transplantable tobacco seedlings. It all seemed for naught. Already at the start of April there was despair: *I can see no prospects of any plants at all.*

That gloomy prediction was the culmination of a sad meteorological story: *April 2, 1758.*

A white & black frost this day—Exceeding Cold—frequently snowing from Northwest—and the Clouds flying in squaley drifts.

That which used to be called April Showers in order to produce the flowers in May are now nothing but cold scudds of Snow—and I doubt not but many a poor cow goes to pot for it.

Wednesday, April 5.

This day a Frost—and so it has been this 12 or 14 days—a prospect of good weather— As a Farmer or Planter I must call it a bad season. The cold winds attending the Frosts have had their visible bad effects on everything. Cattle which not a fortnight ago were in fine order—are now much reduced. Oats lye just peeping the clod, poor & perish. Wheat again almost dead to the roots—and nearly blown out of the ground. The earth merely dust and flying as at midsummer.

In these circumstances Landon drove his workers harder than ever: *Thursday, April 20. . . . Sowed this day a small plant patch which I had well dunged & beaten fine and well watered immediately—and intend they shall be watered morn & eve. Saturday, April 22. . . . I find few or no plants anywhere—have therefore set about a large plant patch in a Nuke [nook] of my meadow, rich light & drye enough & convenient to water. . . .*

(He entered a design—a little "construction project"—for a watering apparatus: a box *with its bottom full of Gimblet holes!*)

By Thursday the 27th he was noting that the plant patches that *were pretty well off on Saturday last—have now scarcely a plant to be seen—such have the ravages of the Flye been this drye, Cold weather.*

Landon had his people try all sorts of expedients to beat the pest. The fine brush that had been layed on the beds as frost protection was now removed, so that, when the weather turned wet, he could *let the rains wash away if possible the Flye.* Another contrivance was *Frames,* like cucumber frames with glass sheets, to warm the plants and keep off the flies. He studied the creatures himself to try to see whence they came—out of the ground, he thought. But it was all to no avail.

By the last day of this grim April, Landon was resigned: *Very cold last night, excessively so this day. Prodigeous piercing hard wind at Northwest. This will in all probability . . . ruin the few plants remaining, and prevent the sprouting of those lately sown. Note: . . . I once heard an old Almanack maker say—if the world lasted long enough—midsummers day would change Seasons with Christmass day—it bids fair for it this year—for 'tis very probable the 1st May will be much colder than the 1st of January was.*

Finally, as June came along there could only be forlorn attempts at salvage. On the 6th, Landon was having his few viable tobacco plants put in *for seed.* And so by the 12th, his people *at the Fork* had planted out *about 10,000* into a small fraction of the 280,000 carefully dunged hills. This was ordinarily one of the great drudgeries on the old Virginia tobacco plantations; in most years it was performed in sweltering heat.

When rain did not come, Landon was driven to desperate measures. On June 15th, he noted that, *as it is a clouded dripping day, I have ordered many* surviving plants *(though no bigger than half Crowns . . .) to be drawn & planted in the hills.* The leaves should have been dollar size (1³/₄ inches across), but he had to move them to save them from the flies and the ground worms. (On the 11th, Landon had optimistically sent off his *Waggon & Six horses* to one of his down-river plantations for more plants; they never came, for they were nowhere to be had.*) As early as May 1st, the diarist had noted the talk at the courthouse: everybody was *planting corn in their tobacco grounds.*

Corn—the staff of life in Virginia—had already been planted in the fields originally intended for it. The planting of corn was another drudgery of late spring and early summer. It was like tobacco planting in the arduous hoeing of hills that preceded it, and in the bent posture of the workers through the long day as they inserted seeds, not seedlings, in each hill.

The Sabine Hall gangs had begun on April 11 *everywhere to plant Corn.* This was just before the carting out the dung had commenced. By April 22, corn planting was pronounced *finished* at the Mangorike Quarter. But these fields had their hazards too. Another diary tableau reviewing the plantation took the form of a list of disasters; one item read *Mole destroying Corn most prodigeously.* A week later Landon saw what damage birds could do; he resolved

---

* The price of tobacco rose so high that the Virginia Assembly passed an act (the Two-Penny Act) enabling all debts ordinarily payable in tobacco to be paid in money at two-pence per pound of tobacco. This currency fixing led to a clash with the imperial government.

that, *for the future I shall plant early & deep—& tread the earth that covers the grain well down.*

At that time the workers had been set onto the next of the spring-summer drudgeries. *I began also to weed Corn at the Fork yesterday.* Only the fact that they were still arduously *making the tobacco hills* at Mangorike postponed that imperative for the gang there.

Through the remainder of the spring and well into the summer, the heavy work of weeding alternated with the repeated work of replanting wherever the original planting in the hill failed or had been destroyed. This would be required for both corn and tobacco.

When Landon designated himself as a farmer, he linked his identity to the scientifically "improved" culture of wheat and other old world grain crops such as oats and barley, as well as fodder crops like clover, timothy, and turnips. (He reserved the term planter for his role as a grower of tobacco, the colonial crop.) Wheat and oats mattered economically and psychologically, but there was not much to be done about them during the spring. Early in the year, if they were being blighted by the weather, the diarist looked on helpless. He could only organize the cow-yarding to prepare next year's wheat lands, which would then become the following year's oat fields. (He wrote out the sequences of this rotation, *that it may not be forgotten what division follows the other in the order of farming.*) Landon had to wait for the moment when conditions allowed him to organize *cockling* (in effect, weeding) and *rolling.* In early April he could write with satisfaction: *My wheat now discovers the prodigeous service there is in rolling.* Later he would watch the crop anxiously: he would dread the effects of rain on its blooming, and he would see how it *ears* as the grain set. There was the possibility of rust, whose cause puzzled him (was it an insect?). The fly weevil might in the end consume everything; but those concerns lay ahead.

A bad spring like that of 1758 meant worry about livestock, also. Were the draft animals *overdone* with the plowing and carting—or was that an excuse of overseers and teamsters? *They did the same last year and did not eat the same* amount of *food—and were done before this.* Worse, the problem might be *owing to the want of care in my people that feed them.* Every year Landon would watch for the new growth in the pastures that would make unnecessary the further stalling and hay-feeding of livestock. There is pathos as well as science when, after the middle of April, he complained of the *very Cold keen Northwest wind . . . very bad for the Creatures who now stand in need of green herbage—even for a Natural Physical* medicinal *use to correct the gross & viscid bile made so by the long feeding on drye food—& the very cold weather.*

Feed would be a problem again if there were not continual foresight. So, on April 29, Landon *began to examin into the cause of the wetness of my meadow.* He found *near 20 strong dams made by the beavers in the Canals.* Those canals and the valve gates controlling them had been one of the scientific engineering construction projects that Landon had worked out the previous year. Now he discovered that nature's corps of engineers had worked even harder to *raise a great pond.* They had contrived also to *bore holes through the banks into the meadow.*

SUMMER

On June 8, 1757, Landon came back from a prolonged spell away. He was intent on pushing the plantation work ahead. *As to work, not a Cornfield touched but with the Ploughs—all the time since I went* has been *spent in planting the Corn and making the tobacco hills—& that in ground before plowed.* They had also been *spreading the dung,* he conceded; but he doubted if the heavy rains were indeed so great a hindrance as was said by way of excuse.

It was proving a wet summer, and weeds were the greatest problem in both the tobacco and the corn. Most of the work now was with hoes, chopping weeds whenever the weather permitted. By the middle of July the diarist could declare that at last the overseer *had begun to lay by his corn after it had been wed out* (further earthed up around the stem). At the same time, he had the tobacco *all cleaned out*—so he could *begin to have it topt a little.* The gangs would remove the central flowering shoot, and so force growth into a more limited number of leaves. At the same time, Landon had to see to it that the plants were wormed—scoured for the *abundance* of caterpillars that would devour those leaves.

The weeds and the waterlogged state of fields and plants prompted periodic exclamations of anguish at the way all these efforts were likely to come to naught. *Thus the Farmer is nothing without weather.* But Landon taught himself to be resigned: *The poor Farmer must always feel the weather and rejoyce when it is good and be patient when it is unseasonable.* Days later came a question bordering on complaint: *Am I always to be thus unlucky? I can truely say that from 1749 to this year I have not had one tollerable seasonable year.* Yet, there was relief at last: *The first easy rain . . . we have had this year—and I do expect we shall receive great benefit from it.* But upon its too-long persistence: *Rain all day . . . Farewell tobacco—by Timothy grass.*

Meanwhile, the ripening wheat gave the diarist worry, of course. With hired reapers—*but very few . . . so many Complaining of last year's reaping*—he got the harvest in. Although alarmed that it might be eaten by the fly weevil, he found it threshed out quite well and gave good white flour. (Landon carefully calculated what price he would have to get for flour—as opposed to wheat—if there was to be profit on that commodity after allowing for the cost of milling.)

AUTUMN

With the wheat and oats and meadow hay harvests behind them, the plantation workers had to cope with other harvests that demanded further prodigious labors. The tobacco had been sown just a little later than the wheat and had been much more laboriously tended through spring and the long summer. As fall approached, so did the time for crucial judgments as to when, with the shortening of the days, the tobacco plants would be ready for cutting.

The right weather would permit a final growth to give more size, substance, and ripeness to the leaves. Too much wet or dry, or early frost could spoil it all. The weather hazards, the stages of decision making, and the consequent work can all be followed through the intermittent reports in the diary pages for 1757.

It was with foreboding that the diarist wrote on Wednesday, August 24, of the *rain most of last night,* and then of more rain through the day. *Tobacco near ripe . . . will be bruised and I fear drowned.* By Monday Landon noted that *yesterday's Sun has shewn how much the last rains have Injured the forward tobacco.* Soon he must start the long and arduous work of cutting and processing rather than risk further such setbacks.

We find William Tatham, an English authority on tobacco growing, writing of the details that this Virginia diarist took for granted. He described the "cutting" as an "operation . . . assigned to the best and most judicious hands," who, "being provided each with a strong sharp knife, proceed along the . . . rows of the field to select such plants as appear to be ripe, leaving others to ripen." The chosen plants "are sliced off near to the ground, and such . . . as have thick stalks . . . are sliced down the middle of the stem," the better to release moisture." Then they are laid down "upon the hill where they grew, with the points of the leaves projecting all the same way. . . ." Some hours later, "when the sun has had sufficient effect to render them pliable," they may be taken up in "turns"—the word for an armful or shouldered load—by "the gatherers who follow the cutting." (When Thomas Jefferson wrote a similar description for a European correspondent, he was more erratic in his spelling and more imaginative in his expression: "It is . . . cut off below the leaves and turned on it's head upon the earth.

Before the evening the labourers go thro' the feild, gather up all the plants which have been cut that day and hang them on scaffolds.")

The hanging was heavy work. We get a clearer sight of it in a later year of Landon's diary keeping, when anecdote was entering the record: *September 8, 1770, . . . Observing Mangorike Will carrying in a turn of tobacco and raising it with some strain—I asked him if it was heavy—he told me it was by far the heavyest he ever carryed in his life. I had it counted—and it was only 18 plants.* Heavy work it was, indeed—and for long hours! The master was still celebrating ten days later; we doubt the enslaved workers were: *Yesterday's cutting upon the hill must have been a large one indeed; for all my people were hanging* tobacco *on the scaffolds till near 2 o'clock in the night.*

"These scaffolds," Jefferson explained, "are formed by strong poles running parallel with each other, 4. feet apart and supported by forks at the height of 3. f. from the ground." But before that first hanging, the plants had to be skewered at the base of the stem onto a stake sharpened at both ends. On these they would remain for the next month's successive arduous hangings and rehangings, until the curing was almost completed. (The maintenance of a stock of tens of thousands of these stakes was a demanding—though unrecorded—task of the days, or more probably nights, before the tobacco cutting began.)

The skewering and scaffolding stage could be postponed or even omitted by just laying the gathered plants on fences or stacking them on the grass until "killed" (fully wilted). But the next demanding step—the housing or hanging—could not be avoided. After a usual ten or so days on the outdoor scaffolds, the stakes, heavy with limp tobacco plants, had to be carried in and hoisted from hand to hand up into the rafters and hanging joists of the great tobacco houses.* This work was also dangerous, as we have seen in the biography of Tom Pantico, who sustained injury when a sharpened *tobacco stick* ran up the flesh of his leg so far that the doctor had despaired of his life.

Once hung—with so much heaving up to head height and clambering over joists—the tobacco plants had then to be closely watched and reported on. The great danger now was that rot would set in. ("Firing" or "house burning" were the names Landon used for what we would identify as a fungal blight.) With all the wet weather of the early fall in 1757, there were already signs of

---

* These tobacco houses were a distinctive feature of the tobacco-plantation landscapes. They were usually of notched-log construction, deliberately made with spacings in the walls to allow air to circulate. The always-exacting Landon, however, demanded more enduring and finished-looking buildings from his slave carpenters.

house burning by September 6. By the 11th, the diarist found that *the tobacco houses all stink*. By the 16th, he had his laborers up in that *putrid* atmosphere, taking down many of the stakes to *thin* the hanging and to admit more air. He was sure the problem had come *from their disobeying my orders—which was to thin every stick as it was handed in from the scaffold.*

The next step was also a standard procedure, especially when more rain and *very giving foggs* prevented natural drying. *September 17, Saturday . . . I this day—in order to save the tobacco in one house—made three or four Charcole fires—having thinned & opened the house everywhere.* By these means, Landon hoped that he had *brought the tobacco to a tollerable good state.* He noted that *it came to its Colour and had lost that earthy putrid Scent.* But then the return of *violent* rainy weather made him fearful of the long-term outcome.

While the early-cut, already-hanging tobacco needed rescue, the later-ripening portion of the crop had yet to be cut, wilted, and hung. The even-later portions still demanded the summer attentions of weeding, worming, and suckering. It would never ripen properly if the weeds choked, the caterpillars ate, or the secondary shoots debilitated it. Deciding when to cut it and finding the opportunity became ever more urgent, for the standing crop also was prone to the fungal blight. Thus, on September 10th Landon had lamented: *This is the 11th day that it has rained successively . . . but why complain? Has not every Crop this year been thus destroy'd? As to tobacco, whole fields have fired away* with the blight—*and not an hour that a planter would use to Cut in—however I have—against all the Common rules—cutt every warm day & have hitherto been lucky enough to get it either on fences or scaffolds and indeed some of it in the houses. But where it seemed wet or not well killed we hung it low and thin till it dryed.*

On Tuesday, September 27, he wrote: *Very fine weather—winds Northerly & Westerly. The tobacco house now dry & sweet.*

By early November, the next great weather hazard was overtaking this tobacco crop—*cold at night & white frosts in the morning . . . tobacco was like tinder.* But only the very last-ripening part of the crop was now still vulnerable as leaf on the stem. The greater part had already been hanging in the houses for weeks until, by the end September and early October, it was cured, or *in cure*, and had been lowered off the joists. ("Striking" was the naval-flag metaphor used for this operation.) And just when to strike was another crucial decision, calling for expert judgment. *I would this day have struck tobacco up here* at the Home Quarter, Landon wrote on October 9, 1770, *but neither the prize house nor the tobacco house are cured.* If the leaves were too moist, they would rot after packing; if too dry, they would be brittle and go to crumbs. Upon this subject—

whether the tobacco was "in case," was the term—it is William Tatham's description of "the method of trying" the leaf that is most vividly expressed. He tells how "it must be stretched over the ends of the fingers and knuckles, and if it is in good *case* . . . it will discover an elastic capacity, stretching like leather, glowing with a kind of moist gloss, pearled with a kind of gummy powder; yet neither dry enough to break nor sweaty enough to ferment."

Once struck, the tobacco plants were taken off the hanging sticks. Now they had to be bulked—that is, laid in heaps on the house floor. This promoted a fermentation and so generated some warmth that made the leaves sweat out excess moisture. From the "bulks" the plants were taken up and stripped—that is, the leaves were removed from the stems and bundled into "hands." Jefferson gives the most apt description of "every handful of leaves being bound round into bundles slightly at one end with another leaf." This task was usually enforced as night work. Furthermore, it was best done when wet or humid weather kept the leaves pliable. Each worker's output was weighed; no one could go to rest until they had done the minimum. (One early November, Landon recorded that he had selected an average-sized bundle; he found that it weighed 1 $^3/_4$ *pounds*, and he then set *30 bundles—52 lb & ½ each*—as a night's stint.) There was an additional operation that might be required for damaged or inferior leaves—namely "stemming." The principal veins had deftly to be pulled out of the leaf prior to bundling. That too was night work: *the people stemmed tobacco till the moon went down* was Landon's casual but revealing reference.

Silences. Even our clichéd images of the plantation tell us that the weariness of this night work was relieved as much as it could be by firelight song and storytelling; but of this there is no trace in the diary record. Landon resolutely turned a deaf ear to the ritual and celebratory life of his people. And the few old ex-slaves whose memoirs of plantation life we have (see chapter 9) did not choose to recall those night-work occasions as festive: it was drudgery.

Finally, the bundled tobacco would be deemed ready for stowage in the great casks weighing 1,000 pounds or more when filled. In these it would be shipped away across the Atlantic Ocean. Again, there was an anxious decision to be made concerning readiness. Jefferson explained that when a bundle was just dried to the point where, held by the end, it would not "bend with its own weight," it was ready for packing.

By late October, Landon might already have *2 hogsheads under prize*. The final packing of the cured tobacco crop was called "prizing"; the process involved compressing the crop into tightly packed containers. Thus, there had been demanding work for the enslaved carpenters and coopers over the months beforehand; they were required to make the giant hogsheads, or casks. This work might be rough, since these containers did not have to be watertight; but to withstand the pressure, the hogsheads had to be immensely strong. *October 12. . . . Toney says he shall be ready to set off to Rippon Hall tuesday next and shall leave 32 hogsheads behind.* At Landon's York River plantation hogsheads were also needed.

Thomas Jefferson is, once again, succinct in his description of the apparatus that he calls "a prize of very great power." It is, he writes, "nothing more than a leaver formed of the trunk of a tree of a foot diameter and about 20 f. length." One end would be "inserted in a loose mortice in a standing tree." (We must picture the beam seated in a generous cavity gouged through a great trunk still rooted in the ground.) "Close to the body of the tree the hogshead is placed under the lever which is then let down to press on the tobacco and the other end loaded with a thousand or two weight of stones." The pressing, or "prizing," was repeated as successive layers of bundles were packed into the great five-foot hogshead. The process continued until no more could be pressed in. By then the hogshead might weigh more than a thousand pounds.* Once the hogsheads were filled and "headed," they had to be sent by river on boats, or rafts of lashed periauger canoes for mandatory quality inspection at the nearest public warehouse. There—if they met the minimum standard, as Landon's consignments always seem to have done—they would await shipment across the Atlantic.

WINTER

It would be December or later before the packing of the latest tobacco crop was completed at the prize house. But Landon had long before that had his workers out preparing the fields for the coming spring and early summer's planting of the next tobacco crop.

Wednesday, November 23. This day finished breaking up my tobacco ground with the plows. It was exceeding hard—and besides being swardy—broke up in lumps from the drowth & the constant feeding over the ground with Creatures—and yet the two plows have—in 40 working days constantly imployed—broke up 80 and odd acres.

We must picture the plowmen, guiding their plows behind the straining teams. Behind them came the gangs, preparing the ground for the next May's

---

* Landon—never one to shorten processes—had an initial stage where the tobacco was "foot packt" in the hogsheads before prizing: *I see Simon, a heavy fellow treads it down well* (Oct. 20, 1770).

planting. *Monday, November 12. Rain yesterday & yet very cloudy. This day we were to begin hoing my tobacco hills.* On the 15th, it was still *too wet to begin to hill.* . . . When the ground had dried, the men and women were out in this wintry weather, working the near-frozen earth, drawing it up into the required hills. And: *The last day of the old year* brought a reviewing—*upon riding out*—of the conditions and of their labors: *The days indeed are at their shortest . . . & very short they have been, the mornings have been many days hard* frost *till about 10 o'clock—so that . . . they have been 4 days hilling only 26,000 tobacco hills & not done that as yet.*

Meanwhile, there had to be several million tobacco seedlings sown and tended during this wintry time. So around Christmas, the preparing and sowing the seedling beds was undertaken. *Thursday, December 29, 1757. Sowed the Mangorike plant patch this day with the sweet scented seed made on the plantation— and the Fork* Quarter *also.*

In order to accomplish this task, so bluntly told, plots of even ground had been heaped with specially gathered brushwood, which was then burned to scorch off weeds and vermin and enhance the earth with the ashes. The patches must be of the richest soil and near to a fresh-water creek or a well, because there would be watering if the spring season were dry.

There was continual resowing to meet the constant need for replacements: *Had all my tobacco beds hoed up again & laid off raked & ready for sowing. . . . Therefore gave possitive orders to keep the seed ready prepared for the plant patches—& sow as soon as the wind lyes.* . . . After sowing and germination, there followed an anxious period of watching, covering with brushwood to protect from frost and seedling-eating flies, and uncovering to admit light and air. This careful tending went on until the leaves of the plants were the size of a $1^3/4$-inch Spanish dollar coin. The tobacco patch preparation—like the intensive working of the winter ground for the oats—all foreshadowed the heroic labors that the spring would call forth. And so we come back again to the start of the cycle as traced from Landon's journals.

SLAVE DRIVING

The tasks of the plantation's great annually repeated round were numerous, endless, and mostly very laborious. What kept these workers to their arduous duties? What were the systems of incentive and control in this institution, the Virginia plantation?

Sabine Hall was sustained within a dominant worldview that imputed legitimacy to coercive systems, including the violence in them. That legitimacy was, of course, very much a master's construct. The belief systems of the enslaved workers largely elude us; we do not even know how far they had yet entered into the enduring forms of African American Christianity. (Perhaps that was already further developed than we have supposed—if parents or elders gave Emanuel and Moses their names, then an assurance of promised deliverance had been part of the belief system in some Richmond County quarters for half a century already.)

Landon, according to his worldview, knew that he had a patriarchal duty to all on his estate. *Care & protection* was what the feudal lord owed his dependent inferiors. In return, of course, they owed him service, deference, and obedience. This was very much how Landon saw his relationship to his enslaved workers. It was congruent with his own sacred obligation to his own sometimes-harsh, sometimes-benign master, God. This was most persistently manifest in his diary record of medical practice. Landon affirmed that *God is Mercyfull—& that he requires no more of us but our own proper humane Care—and that he will protect where it shall seem good to his infinite wisdom.* God, the protector, who gave the master the duty of *humane care*, gave him also the right of command and enforcement. God's commission empowered him to assign all that arduous toil; indeed, it was just such working of the earth that God in His wrath had assigned to Adam: "cursed is the ground for thy sake; in sorrow shalt thou eat of it all the days of thy life." So Landon knew that he had divine authority to keep idlers at their tasks. He knew he had a duty to punish as necessary the sinful children of Eve who were in his charge.

The master's commission was from God; but there had to be systematic delegations of his authority, a command structure. The continuities of daily life required that everyone—the enslaved, the overseers, and even the master—should live within a web of rules and conventions. But conflicting interests and the great cultural divide between English and African backgrounds ensured that violent resistance and brutal enforcement would be endemic to the system.

In 1756, at the time of the start of the surviving plantation diary, the work force around Sabine Hall was divided into two tobacco-growing task forces, each under an overseer. Each quarter not under direct supervision of an overseer was under a slave foreman. Landon allowed each of the overseers some ten strong hands (or equivalent) for the cultivation of tobacco. The overseer was given a stake in the productivity of his task force by being allowed a one-and-a-half share in the year's produce. A share was the total crop yield divided by the number of full hands who had produced it (the overseer was included in that number; women and children were counted as fractions of a full hand).

Landon expected each hand to tend 10,000 tobacco plants in their hills, plus 15,000 between them for the overseer's share. Thus, a gang of ten with an overseer should see to 115,000 tobacco hills; and Landon would arrange the assignment of fields to accommodate that. In addition, Landon kept a home farm more immediately under his control. As we have seen, he expected to tend, in all, more than a quarter of a million hills of tobacco, and so 70,000 hills, or seven hands' task, was the portion cultivated directly under the master's eye. That is how matters stood through most of 1757; but after experiencing considerable dissatisfaction with the work during that crop cycle, Landon changed the arrangement to reduce the number of overseers and bring in a manager, who would work for wages to supervise all the slave foremen and the remaining overseers.

On September 12—with a joking play of words—Landon noted that he had *agreed with John King to overlook my Plantations called Mangoright & Mangowrong. He is to follow my Directions in everything. He is to have 500 weight fresh Pork; milk of two cows, what corn his family can reasonably use—& £25 Current money the year; he is not to go abroad without my leave—& to use every kind of Diligence.* John King took up these duties on December 1, 1757. Landon kept the Home Quarter—*my farm*—very much under his own direct oversight.

The master's sense of authority derived from ancient writing and from living custom. Landon inherited a strong belief in the necessity of his own close personal attention to all the work. Varro, an ancient Roman authority on agriculture, had long ago declared, in a statement echoed by countless gentleman writers of advice books, that "the best manure for the estate was the master's footprint upon the soil." This belief Landon reiterated every time an absence or an illness had kept him from twice-daily or even more often tours of inspection. One pronouncement out of many says it all: *I see*, he lamented (or was it exulted?), that *go abroad what time of the year I will, the work that is then to go forward will stand.*

So, the delegation of authority was at best partial and grudging. Meanwhile, the master pushed his overseers hard, certain that only by keeping up their zeal and application would the work truly go forward. *Our fother not yet all in*, he wrote on Thursday, October 10, 1756; *such overseers I have never seen.* He had remonstrated with them: *They pretend it was stacked a good way off but that was not their labour. . . . I brought* it *in place after with my Carts.* (So, he did have reinforcements in reserve to hearten flagging work teams—another commander's prerogative.) Early the next summer he wrote revealingly: *Smart rain this day. We are overdone with it—and my overseer Watts as foul in his corn fields as can be. His hands*

& he are so dissatisfyed with each other that neither do anything. I was obliged to help him with two more plows this day.

His own intense involvement with the work of the plantation sustained Landon's belief that only his presence could ensure dutiful performance. This showed most clearly in the diarist's use of the pronouns "we" and "our" for the great collective efforts that he was continually calling forth from his overseers and laborers. *We began to sow wheat the 15th and have been sowing as we could get plowed ever since. We shall be a week longer here.* And: *Began to put our Cattle in our Cowyards yesterday . . . The Fork wheat is also sowing by means of one horse and a very pritty plow made for that purpose with one share—we plow better than 1 acre in every day. . . . I shall certainly try . . . these plows hereafter in all my light lands.* We see suddenly how that pronoun switch to "I" indicates the diarist's sense of his own particular role; special equipment and experimentation was Landon's to decide upon.

In keeping with the sense of collective endeavor that was indicated by Landon's frequent use of "we" and "our," there was, in this 1750s journal, a tolerance of failures that is in marked contrast to the vituperation so noticeable in Landon's later diaries. Thus, one tale of dissatisfaction with the ways of those in his service began philosophically: *It is necessary that man should be acquainted with affliction.* And, in the autumn of 1756, when the delay in gathering the corn was attributed casually to *the Lazyness of our People,* that explanation was produced to reinforce his sense of the necessity of his personal supervision, even though the prevailing sickness of his workers, which he also recorded, would have been a better explanation. When a similar delay was apparent the next year—with him present—he wrote that it was *not owing to any bad conduct but too warm weather.*

In some complaints there was, to be sure, a measure of scorn along both class and racial lines. The overseer at the Fork was *but a Chattering fellow—promises much but does little—for which I have given him a piece of my mind.* ("Fellow" in this context was a word for a social inferior.) And then Landon wrote that the exact way to plant tobacco seedlings in miry hills required *more care than negroes can be persuaded to.* Or, when the tobacco had been hung too thick, all sorts were denounced for *disobeying my orders . . . , because overseers & negroes think the work too tedious.* Disobedience seemed to be noted, like bad weather, as a regrettable part of the inevitable order of things. When penalties and punishments were imposed, the violence in them was matter-of-fact, and was recorded without disturbing the calm of the diary. Punishment as a topic comes only indirectly into this scientific plantation journal. Twice it is mentioned as malpractice by an overseer on a distant quarter. In this 1750s scientific journal, there are only three records of punishment at Sabine Hall. Significantly, all are related to time-and-motion observations. One (already quoted) is the disconcertingly casual mention of slow progress because the runaways have to work in chains.

The other two recorded punishments relate his monitoring the work in a kind of time-and-motion study:

My threshers of oats made a shift to thresh no more per day than they did when the days were twenty minutes shorter. . . . This was such evident lazyness that I ordered them Correction—which they took three days running—and then by setting them on different floors to discover the lazy fellow—they returned me 40 bushels per day. This I minute down to show that things are often judged impossible when obstinacy alone is the Cause of it.

And then the second telling—with even more explicit technicalities:

I am greatly surprized at the behaviour of my threshers. I had a Stack of oats without doors that must needs have been very tough—and though it was not half the dimension of my mow within . . . my barn . . . , yet out of the stack they got 918 bushels and out of the mow only 1,500 . . .—which is no proportion. . . .

They have been severely whipd day by day.

They have all encouragement given them—but they are such Villains* that they will not thresh them cleaner—so that I intend to thresh the straw that is left over again.

The casualness of that report—*They have been severely whipd day by day*—shows how routine a part of Sabine Hall life this punishment was. Unconcerned at that violence, Landon went straight into great detail on how much more easy to thresh the barn oats should have been. He also expressed the view that the problem arose because his slaves were told *that others don't thresh so much.* This subversive talk had come from an overseer of wheat production—*the farmer from Mr. Wormeley's*—who came to Sabine Hall after *a wench* at the Home Quarter. Landon resolved to send her to Bull Run, forty miles further off. But then—more constructively—he reviewed his actual work-system problem, and noted: *I observe negroes tyre with the Continuance of the same work—so that I will double their Number next year and work it quickly off hand—and then perhaps they will do better, for they certainly threshed cleaner and as much when they began as they do now.*

Although punishments went almost unrecorded in the scientific notebook,

---

* This is one of a very few uses of the word "villain" in the 1750s plantation diary; it became a much-used term in the 1770s diary series.

the cruel coercive system is fully apparent.* To the slaves, the cost of resistance was high. Of that there is a dark reminder in the little biographical fragment associated with the medical treatment of an old man: *George was for ten years a noted runaway—always in the woods & mostly naked—and now he has left that trade he is grown a sickly fellow.*

PLANTATION SCIENCE

Landon's lifetime vocation as a planter was coupled with high zeal as an improving "farmer" of wheat, oats, and other old-world cereals. That vocation and that zeal often brought him into a conflict with the traditional ways of his Sabine Hall work force as he drove them to do things his scientific way.

The heading *Farming Observations etc.* given to the turned-over, started-again notebook had a double meaning. The word "Observations" was central and stood both for the seeing of phenomena and for the written recording of scientific thoughts on those phenomena. The frequency and quality of Landon's musings on the reasons why things turned out as they did makes this, as already noted, one of the great diaries of the Enlightenment in the everyday life of the farm. In its practical yet eloquent way it opens to us a whole cosmology.

In his writing on weather, field, and livestock, Landon deployed a set of effective genres seemingly of his own devising. I have designated them for better review and appreciation by the following labels. There were "observation pieces" in which the writer noted some phenomenon (usually during a morning or evening round) and developed his thoughts upon it. There were "reflections" in which a train of reasoning was more general and less specifically developed out of a sight, sound, or smell. There were "plantation tableaus" in which the diarist let his pen follow his mind's eye, as it were, around the estate, rendering in concise prose its most striking aspects. Then, most important of all for the purpose of this journal, there were "planning reviews." These had aspects of the kinds of writing already noted but were directed toward the specification of future management. Most earnest of all were the "construction projects." Far from being merely prosaic engineering designs, these were often cherished flights of fancy that deeply expressed the desired persona of the di-

---

* To get a fair perspective on Landon's casual acceptance of all this violence, we must bear in mind that it was not then exclusively a plantation practice. White children of all classes, boys especially, were also whipped. The penitentiary was not yet born; white adults unable to pay the fines that were standard punishments for "misdemeanors," were publicly flogged; so, of course, were sailors and soldiers. George Washington was a flogging disciplinarian, and he had learned it from his British army experience, not from plantation custom.

arist. These "reveries," as I have called them, were very expressive of this age of the Enlightenment, when improvement was identified as the immediate goal of philosophy. In the 1750s journal, Landon's narratives were not stories about human clashes of the kind we have seen in the diaries of the 1770s; they were about sickness and attempted cures, or the weather and its consequences. Usually the drama in these narratives results from his reasoning about the interaction of the elements of sun, air, water, and earth.

A haunting story of emanations arising from the earth was strong in Landon's cosmological imagination; it recurred throughout his diaries. This idea surely incorporated a metaphor of an alembic or distilling apparatus in which rising vapors condense and descend as liquid. Thus, Landon wrote:

I have discovered fogs to be a sign of drye weather in Summer, and I suppose there is a Substantial reason, for . . . in Summer the natural moisture of the earth is so rarefyed that it ascends, and by the continued heat disperses away into air as the rarefaction continues, but in winter those vapours arise from a warmth . . . in such prodigious quantitys that they presently condense in the atmosphere naturally moist. . . , and then by their weight they fall again either in Snow or rain as the region of air is . . . hot or cold.

Applied science is the name we would give to all the earnest natural philosophy and medical case reports that Landon wrote into this notebook which was primarily kept for this purpose. The weather was where inquiry started, so the cosmological gaze went up to the heavens—reading clouds and wind direction as signs—and then down onto, sometimes into, the earth. Indeed, the weather had everything to do with the two related matters of deepest concern in Landon's science: sickness and crop production. Along with all the medical scientists of his age, Landon believed that the *Constitution of the air* had profound influence on the quality and balance of blood, bile, and phlegm. Balance or imbalance determined the well-being or sickness of human and animal bodies. (But that is a subject in itself; see chapter 6.) Like most of the philosophic gentlemen of that time, including Thomas Jefferson, Landon was a compulsive measurer; yet he did not measure the weather. Instead, he gratified himself with the descriptive narratives of which he became so great a virtuoso. There is no evidence anywhere of a rain gauge. At one time Landon did have a thermometer, but it appears in a single entry only (in 1766). Was the instrument literally dropped? Or was it just dropped from the diary?

At moments critical for the crops, Landon lowered his gaze from the elements above—the air and water of wind and cloud, and the fire of the sun—to scrutinizing the element of earth and how it fared under these influences. Was it *mud & mire* from too much water? Was it *baked* by a succeeding excess of sun? Had it become *mere mortar*? Had he succeeded in getting it as it should be—*well pulverized*—or was it *merely dust & flying as at midsummer, or grey as if divested of all richness*? The planter diarist often brought personal feeling as well as a scientific reasoning to these descriptions: *It began to rain at 9 at night and the earth has been most agreeably entertained with it all night.*

The same eye—with the same concern—looked not only on the surface of the earth but down into it as well to see or to imagine how fared the roots of the plants whose well-being the diarist monitored with such care. Looking at his winter wheat, Landon saw how, *if it proves wet . . . to an excessive degree, then the Land naturally spews by the rapidness of the Frosts—and thousands of roots are destroyed . . . as soon as the Sun grows warm.* Later he contemplated his experimental indigo plantings. *My stiff land baked much and must necessarily obstruct the rising of the tender sprout . . . although I frequently loosened the earth with great caution about them.* His oats looked poor—*I dread the crop. . . . It must then be owing to the very cold weather which withered the roots—and the rains being so late they had not time to put forth new roots before the heading season.*

This arduously acquired and lovingly displayed knowledge of earth and of botany (*vegetation*) was all brought together in Landon's declaration of himself as a *Farmer*. Here are his words as he compared his up-to-date English system to the soil-exhausting methods of the typical Virginia planter, who grew crops until the land would yield no more, and then returned it to the regrowth of trees for a long 30 or 40 years of fallow.

My method of introducing the English husbandry with the tobacco planting now seems to be exceeding good, and has only this inconveniency, that it frequently happens that the divisions of 50 acres manured each year cannot be land of equal nature—but everywhere it will be stiff and light so that in the tobacco crop it is evidently discovered that the same seasons . . . will not suit in the same field everywhere—but the tobacco will grow very unequal.

After discounting the particular problems of this wet year, he continued his celebration of his methods: *However this we assert—that either such land must not be tended at all in tobacco or—if it is—this is as likely a way to make it rich & profitable as any—although we don't always come up in Crop to the planter who culls his land—yet by our grain we more than equal him. . . . & 'tis evident that our lands run better into grass after such a method . . . and of course our creatures will improve and in time add to our profit.*

The coda here is most revealing of the struggles with his overseers and work-ers that lay behind Landon's need to affirm the superiority of his innovative methods. *Had I been at home I would have prevented a great deal of the raggidness of my Crop by planting after the season* of rain *was over and the land a little drye**—*but they followed the old way, & . . . sometimes the plant was plaistered in.*

Another topic that exercised Landon's mind not just as a farmer but also as a natural philosopher was the minute enquiry into the life cycles and condi-tions of survival of agricultural pests. Each of these was an *enimy* that threat-ened to nullify his and all his people's efforts. There were numbers of them, including *the hornworm, the Groundworm, the Webworm,* and the mole, who would eat corn *as well as a hog.* Two of these he thought he might defeat, using a mastery of the natural history of their ways in order to develop a system of counterattack.

The *flye Weavel* was a terrible pest that seemed to put a curse on the efforts of the plantation workers and on Landon's most cherished dream of being a successful farmer of wheat. These were little insects that ate the starch from the garnered wheat grains, leaving only husks that would yield no flour.

Landon closely studied the natural history of the insect, as he had done with the tobacco fly. Arguing against the folk remedies that his neighbors were practicing, he convinced himself that, by observation, experimentation, and sound reasoning, he had arrived at a practical method of eradication. The plan was to keep the mown wheat for a time unthreshed in a covered stack. He predicted that *the weavel would be destroyed in the embrio by the sweating in the mow,* that is, the heat-generating fermentation of damp straw. He clung to this remedy, even though there were clear signs that it was not working. Like many persons in the grip of an idea, he was sure that, if only he could perfect the method and eliminate human inadequacies in its implementation, it would be efficacious.

The project had a strong hold on Landon's imagination. His writing became very rhetorical.

I have frequently had in my thoughts the unhappy condition of the Country in the de-struction that attends most of the wheat by what they call the flye Weavel . . . and I have

---

* In time Landon would develop this idea into a controversial method of *dry planting* when weather conditions seemed to demand it.

reasoned on many methods to kill the enemy in its embrio—for no other way can their destruction be effected—because they lay their egg in the young Soft grain—and no steeping of grain before sowing . . . nor no affluvium . . . can affect them in the mow.

He hoped the sweating in close stacks would work; but his mind ran on into a plan that might make the outcome more certain. *I have therefore fallen upon the following kiln to give that heat should the mow stowed as above do no service.* He wondered if he had read of something of the kind; in any case, he affirmed that he had only *found an Hypothesis to be proved by practice.*

The plan that he came forward with was modeled on a poultry-egg incubator he had seen in a book that is still in his library. From this practical manual, Landon picked up the warnings that the bird eggs to be hatched might be killed by excess heat *where proper care is not taken.* Having the opposite purpose to the poultry breeder, Landon meant to take care that the insect eggs would be killed; he intended to apply enough heat to *open* and *destroy* these unwanted eggs while not attaining the temperature where *toasting* the wheat would result.

I propose then to erect the Kiln after the following manner. I shall build a house convenient to my Granary of the following dimensions—20 or 24 feet long and 12 or 14 feet wide. And so on and on he ran, elaborating measured specifications for a two-story structure with a brick-floored heat chamber, a communicating *arch which I shall call a Lanthern,* having many holes in the side *to let out the heat.* He would so contrive it as to allow of *going round to Judge* the temperature. In the upper story there was to be *a sheet of fine Sive work made of basket stuff.* It must be spread on *laths* set *to lye very thick* on *Sleepers*; these were to be extended across the building. On this *is my wheat to be laid and carefully stirred so as to drye it effectually.* When that was accomplished, and the weevil-fly embryos killed, the wheat was—*by a kind of hoppar spout*—to be thrown down *to my grainery floor to cool.*

Illustrated in figure 13 are a printed engraving of the Aegyptian oven (or incubator) from Réaumur's *Manner of Raising Fowls,* the book in Landon's library that was his inspiration. The elaborate specifications in the 1750s notebook conclude *See the drafts,* but, unlike some other sketches that were drawn onto the pages of the notebook, these *drafts* were rendered on separate sheets, and we cannot study the architectural drawings that would let us view just how Landon, as Enlightenment patriotic provincial inventor, envisioned his dream project. It seems that the elaborate plans were never acted upon; this was a reverie of scientific control—a "construction project"—that never materialized.

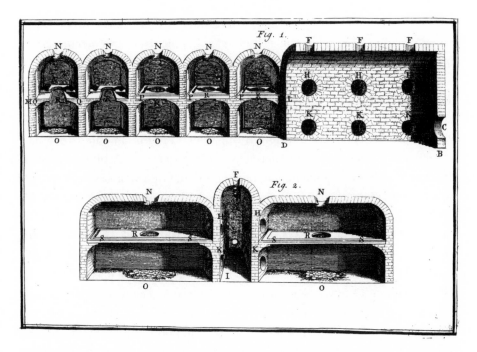

An "Aegyptian oven," or egg incubator, shown in vertical section. Landon had a cherished but unrealized project to adapt this design in a kiln that would both hatch and destroy the eggs of the pernicious "flye weevil" and so save the wheat crops of his region. (This plate is from an annotated book in Landon's surviving library: Réaumur's *Art of Hatching . . . Fowls. . . .*) *Special Collections, Alderman Library, University of Virginia.*

It is not clear with whom Landon was in conversation when he carefully wrote technical reports on the management of his plantation. Where did he get his ideas from? Whom did he share them with? Was he already writing to impress his challenging eldest son with the soundness of his management of the estate?

There are few clues. A botanical paper dated 1741 survives amongst an assortment of land surveys and mainly business letters that have remained at Sabine Hall, but it has no agricultural bearing, being a shocked (or prurient?) description of the flower of a wild plant Landon had just discovered. He found it remarkable because it carried close resemblances to human genitalia, male in one part, female in another.

Perhaps from a later gush of enthusiasm, we get a sense of Landon's long loneliness in his scientific avocation. In the late 1760s, Landon wrote a formal account of his fly-weevil observations for his cosmopolitan neighbor Francis

Lightfoot Lee. When in Philadelphia, the younger man, as was no doubt intended, communicated Landon's letter as a scientific paper to a meeting of the American Philosophical Society. The society published it as part of its "Transactions" in the *American Magazine,* 1769. A subsequent publication in the *Virginia Gazette* failed to win for Landon any acknowledgement let alone the commendations he was sure he deserved. The Philadelphia debut in the world of learned publications had a different outcome. Landon lamented (or was it boasted?) *that in me is verified the saying that A Prophet is not without honour save in his own Country.* In Virginia he had been ignored; but now a traveler returned from Europe was saying that the publication had made its author famous. He was flattered by the extravagant phrasing of his informant's account. *All Europe have agreed and have actually addressed me upon it (which I will soon see)—for they now have got a certain way of extirpating one of the most distructive insects that ever infested the world.* His admirers thought he should have been sent as a delegate to the Continental Congress—*my name would have given dignity to the very being of it, so great is the veneration that Europe has for me, as to pronounce me the greatest Natural Philosopher of this age.* He tried not to be vain about this report: *I shall only endeavour to deserve this good Opinion—that my old age may be happy in seeing its endeavors to serve mankind so generally acknowledged.* There is an amplification here of the 1750s journal at its most rhetorical; but nothing survives to suggest that he had sought to be a famous naturalist when he kept his remarkable records of observation and experiment.

The scientific control objectives of the 1750s plantation journal were evidently fulfilled in the recording of construction projects such as the kiln described above. They varied greatly in their degree of elaboration; some were indeed quite simple. There was, for instance, the hog pen—*a tall punchiond place,* whose carpentry and earth setting were specified so that the hogs could not dig their way out. Then there was a water-mill mechanism which Landon described in grandiose terms as *experiments in Natural Philosophy on the Axis in Peritrochio.* Indeed, dams and the channeling of water fascinated Landon. His most elaborately specified project of this kind is shown here only by way of one of the drawings that he carefully penned into his journal for March 7, 1757.

Although not accompanied by drawings, the design for a manufactory of manure was no less carefully specified. Dung (as we have seen) was essential to the "English husbandry" on which Landon so prided himself. His reverie on a kind of arrangement to enhance if not automate manure production was given in loving

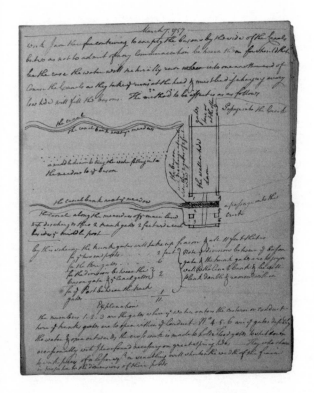

Landon as hydraulic engineer. The layout for valve-action tide gates to drain the meadow marsh on Sabine Hall's Rappahannock shore. *Special Collections, Alderman Library, University of Virginia.*

detail. Unlike other more elaborate designs, this one was actually built and found effective. There was to be *a line of Cowstalls double so as to hold 20 head of Cattle—& a Crib between that each may feed by itself.* From the outer posts of these stalls he would *raise a roof so that the food as well as the Creatures will be sheltered from the rains & snows and from the piercing winds*—which protection *I imagin will be equall to any food I can give them.* The reverie continued: *These stalls shall be raised with earth a foot above the level of the yard—and a causeway much like the hacks of a brickyard shall be carryd all round. These stalls shall be Constantly littered and cleaned out every Monday—and the litter thrown into the spaces between the stalls & the Raised hacks—which shall be also strewed with straw after every rain and every morning after the Cattle are turned out of their stalls. They shall be drove Gently about in these spaces and then turned out to browse about.* Then back went the enthused mind to the intended portability of the whole: *For the Conveniency of making these . . . moveable . . . to suit the grounds I am to manure, I propose to have the covering only thatched and the whole made so as they can be taken to pieces and carryd to the next year's ground.*

Four days more of the spring dung turning and Landon was ready to revise and expand his dream of a scientific manure manufactory: *As to dung making I now can possitively pronounce this rule to be observed—The Pens ought to be very large—at least 40 yards square for every 60 Cattle.*

In these notes, the evidence of *the difference of the goodness & quantity of the dung* was combined with scientific inference as to what was *rational*. There was also an eager engagement with the imagined dung-generating process: Where the space was too confined, the litter thrown down *will grow so thick & compact as not to rott or shorten the Straw.* But where it was more thin-spread, he noted, *it was all trod short,* and was *well trod—which is one good step to rotting it.*

Now the industrial chemistry of the imagined process could be confidently expounded: *And though we may be fond of the dung & Urin of Creatures—yet if we can get rotten vegetables we get the same—we get what makes those salts in their dung, their bodys being only the distillers—and effect the putrefaction the sooner—so that I say the salts of the same number of Cattle is—in the large pen—added to a greater quantity of rotten Vegetable—and in the lesser 'tis thrown on a smaller quantity not rotten.*

From dream to reality. . . . By the end of the year, Landon could look on the efficiencies he had achieved. Now his delight incorporated his loving observations of the ways of the beasts in his care.

I am much pleased with my new Cow stalls—they keep the cattle drye & warm enough—and their food drye—and by the Conveniency of the roof . . . a boy can fill the Cribs for 30 cattle in ten minutes because the flooring above the joist is open . . . and 'tis but turning over then what is left of the former feed—which I find . . . they eat . . . well—having no taint of their breath—and the fresh stuff is easyly pulled down.

We nowadays take scientific technology for granted; certainly the invention and design specification of new kinds of portable apparatus is quite unremarkable. In 1757 such innovation was an intrusion of philosophic gentlemen into customary vernacular farmyard arrangements. Its innovative aspect accounts for the visionary enthusiasm of Landon's construction projects as he wrote them into the 1750s notebook which was above all dedicated to such calculated dreaming of scientific control.

It was that reach for control—and the calm sense that it could be attained by reason and counting and calculation—that so distinguishes Landon's "Farming Observations" book. Agriculture could be narrated as the unfolding of the expected. The challenges faced by the farmer were the seasons and the weather, trials sent by God. The failings of human nature were part of that familiar order of things; they were not rebellions against it. And so we get the tone of a halcyon Age of Enlightenment; the study of improvement by learned gentlemen would assuredly contribute to enhancing the future of mankind. It is the air of rational calm that sets this notebook diary in such marked contrast to its 1770s successors.

Chapter 5

Landon's Library

It is Sabine Hall on a day or an evening, of uncertain date. Landon is bending over a book. Perhaps he already feels the eyestrain he later lamented. The book is one of his volumes of the mixture of facts and fables assembled by the early Greek historian Herodotus. This author is one of the great ancients; he is indeed a "classic," but that does not ensure respect. "Cicero must have joked," wrote Landon in the margin of his Herodotus, "when he call'd this man the Father of History—If anything it must be the Grandmother—for never were such inconsistent as well as bawdy stories in any history before or since." Again, at this moment the scornful reader dips his pen, and scratches into the margin of the page another protest: "Whip twang! A lie to be sure!" Was that established Virginia idiom that he wrote or a new-coined phrase?

But now, in the next of our visits to Sabine Hall, it is midwinter—February of the year 1779. Landon had died, late in the preceding December. He has at last left the great house he had built in the undisputed possession of his eldest son. A customary list of the personal property of the deceased is being prepared.

It is a minimalist art this inventory making. As he regarded the great central hallway of the house, the clerk wrote a meager list: "1 round Cherry tree Table, . . . 1 square Mahogany [and] 1 walnut writing table, 2 glass Lanthorns, [and] Spye Glass." But actually this wide entrance space is dominated by the library—although the clerk, challenged by this great collection of more than five hundred valuable volumes, promptly elevates the understatement of his kind to a maximum. He writes: "Passage 3 Mahogany Bookcases with Books."

For two hundred years more, until the early 1970s, Landon's library continued to stand in the crowded cases at Sabine Hall. There were additions and subtractions made by succeeding generations; but during all this time, the house remained in the proud care of the old colonel's descendants. The library and the building that housed it were together a fitting monument to one of the most learned readers and prolific writers among his generation of Virginians.

Over time, however, the extremes of cold and hot, of dry and wet that is the Virginia climate—and the ravages of moulds and insects—all took their toll. Many bookworms made visits. I was able to reconstruct the family story of just one pair. Displaying the taste of Landon's age, these insects headed for the great three-volume quarto set of Archbishop Tillotson's sermons.* The worms ate their way straight through the first volume; they tarried long and raised a considerable brood in volume two; then they all went straight through volume three, and out, perhaps to digest other, less-dated works. Volume one had a hole in the front and a narrow tunnel through the pages from front board to back (I observed the same with volume three); but when I opened volume two, I found myself looking into a great circular nesting cavity eaten out by these hungry homemakers. In the center of the cavity was a column of paper the size and shape of dollar coins; this is all that remains of the middle part of the printed pages. I could see that, if I lifted it up, it would be giant confetti in my hand. This was a concealed dilapidation. More evident to the anxious eyes of Landon's descendants living at Sabine Hall was the condition of the old leather bindings. They had very visibly become cracked; their gold lettering and handsome gilt rulings had grown dim or had chipped away. The same family pride that had kept this book collection in the house now required a further step to ensure its preservation for posterity. In 1979 the late Mr. T. Dabney Wellford organized a gift of the entire collection to the University of Virginia; the books are now safely in the climate-controlled Special Collections of the Alderman Library.

---

* Tillotson's sermons, first published as a collection in 1695, were for fifty years or more among the most widely read English-language religious works for educated persons. They were a vital contribution to the formation of a rational Christian outlook that was a part of the moderate Enlightenment, which prevailed not only in Britain but also from New Hampshire to Georgia.

∞

Those "3 Mahogany Bookcases with Books" that the clerk had recorded were packed with volumes, great and small. These had been read with much care and annotated at many points. They were filled with the wealth of the learning of the late squire's day—worlds within worlds. The inventory maker reduced it all to a single phrase: "with Books." How shall we open what that scribe had seemed to close with those two words?

Scholars have made many fine studies of old personal libraries. Nevertheless it still remains a puzzle for the historian, how to decipher meanings in something so complex and composite. One can analyze the assemblage according to its component parts. This can be done in a multiplicity of ways—by size, for instance. Thus reviewed, Landon's surviving library contains some 23 great folio volumes, 37 large quarto volumes, 98 octavo (still big by our standards); and 45 duodecimo and smaller (now impressive to us only for their leather bindings).

Then again, book collections are often analyzed by the subject matters treated in them. And so we may attempt to review Landon Carter's library under a plausible set of subject headings. In round figures, and in decreasing order of magnitude, the proportions can be summarized. The classics—ancient authors in the original or in translation—provide some forty titles (about 20 percent of the two-hundred books that make up the whole). Natural philosophy and natural history are not quite 20 percent—about 25 percent if the encyclopedias and manuals of trades are added. History and belles lettres are each at about the 15 percent mark, with religion coming in below 10 percent. Politics and law both fall below 5 percent. These last figures—and the important category of medicine, which simply is not there at all—are a clue for those who know Landon's diary. We know that we are not now looking at the library as it was left at Landon's death. In the practical country folk's world of Sabine Hall, those volumes that were serviceable for the pursuit of the liberal professions of the clergyman, the physician, and the lawyer or lawmaker must have been steadily culled from the collection. This probably happened over the generations at various times in the intervening two hundred years. (Perhaps the missing books were taken away to be used by aspiring young gentlemen among Landon's own descendants.)

There is another form of analysis that reveals a great deal. No private library worthy of the name is a sudden and instantaneous creation. It is always the slow accumulation of many years of collecting. It is informative to analyze the components by the time of their acquisition. In this case—since there are only occasional records of purchase—the accessioning process must be traced over time by the imprint dates shown on the title pages. (Whether or not a book was added to a library when it was new, the proportions of books that were published in one decade, say, as compared to another, is an important characteristic of the collection.) Analyzed thus, this surviving library reveals a very distinctive biographical and historical pattern.

In summary statement, the pattern of the imprints is as follows:

Before 1710:

The titles that date from before Landon's birth make up a mere 10 percent of the total. A few of these can be traced in an inventory of books owned by Landon's father at the time of his death. Furthermore, it may be noted that these works are almost entirely unannotated. Landon, it seems, did not interact intensely with books he had not procured for himself. But there is one notable exception—a seminal work from an earlier generation, which continued to be compulsory reading for the educated until long after Landon's death. It is John Locke's *Essay Concerning Human Understanding*, which Landon inherited as a big 1700 folio edition. It bears annotations in the hands of both Landon and his father.

1710–1730:

There is a larger portion of the surviving library that dates from the years of Landon's childhood and youth; it amounts to approximately 20 percent. Many of these are quite evidently schoolbooks; they are small-print, low-price editions of ancient Latin and Greek authors. They have scribbles and doodles in them, rather than annotations.

1730–1750:

In striking contrast to the school texts stand the books of the next twenty years. Although these are only a slightly higher proportion of the titles—a little under 25 percent—many are multivolume sets. Indeed, the books from these years seem by their character and their use marks to be accumulated aids for what we may think of as a prolonged period of higher self-education. There are French grammars and instruction books on conversation, and there are long compilations concerning the Greek and Roman worlds—a work entitled *An Universal History* amongst them. (Two well-used works of husbandry are surely a remnant of a once larger collection of manuals for Landon's self-training as a scientific farmer.)

1750–1760:

Perhaps there is no reason to divide off the remaining mature years arbitrarily by decades, but the 1750s were for Landon his years of ambition fulfilled. He at last entered the legislature; he then began the diary that has proved his most enduring life work. This decade saw the publication of 20 percent of the titles in the surviving library.

1760–1778:

These last years were both the lonely years when he settled to life without the companionship of a wife and the time of the coming of the Revolution. The remaining imprints—about 30 percent—date from these years. They show that Landon kept acquiring books until the end. If all the political works that he surely acquired and read had remained in place, there would be a higher tally yet.

Such forms of analysis treat a library as an assemblage of items; that is certainly useful and revealing. We get a sense of the person who made the collection, of the particular interests, and even of the stages through which reading interests may have passed. Nevertheless, such statistics stay on the outside of the books, treating them as objects merely. If the books themselves are to be opened and made to reveal more to us, a different approach must be attempted.

We shall begin with basics, asking: What is a library?

The practical answer: a collection of books assembled for use.

And next the seemingly needless question: What then are books?

Many answers could be given to that question. Books are objects, yes—artifacts of a certain kind—but books are artifacts of a very special kind. Perhaps their distinctive properties can best be understood if they are thought of as captured voices. They are indeed complex and enduring utterances in an even more complex exchange of discourses that is always moving on. That onward movement of the world to which books contribute, can be thought of as a conversation; and my questions, as I try to interpret the world of Landon Carter, are: what was the point in the conversation when the book was published and, more particularly, what was the point when Landon read it? (Of course, that means that I am now involving my readers and the books and the conversations in which Landon participated in a twenty-first-century historian's conversation.)

We know ourselves and the world about us largely through the stories we tell ourselves, the stories that we tell others, and the stories that we attend to. These stories come from and enter into our myths. And it is our own mythology that sustains us and our knowledge. It is our mythology that tells us what kind of world we inhabit; it tells us whence came our world, what kinds of beings are in it, and how they act and are acted upon. The term "myth" does not mean here, as I use it, what it is commonly taken to mean, namely, stories known to be untrue. Rather, as anthropologists understand myth, it is the very foundation of truth within any culture. The usual contemptuous usage is the way we designate the myths of others; it is in the nature of our own myths that they are only apparent to us through a great deal of close self-analysis. To suppose our culture is essentially free of myth because it is based on science is merely to identify the now primary myth of our own world. (Items from the mythology of our time understood in this way, and chosen more or less at random, might be "the atom," and "DNA," or "equal opportunity," to fasten on key words for foundation stories we now tell ourselves.) Appreciating historically the stories that Landon Carter's library told him, and the stories that he told himself as he read its books, requires us to try to enter his own mythology, the one he shared with literate persons of his day. Indeed, we need to find from him the more ordered and collected arrangement of myths that is best referred to as cosmology.

Taking cosmology as a fixing of myth, it is useful to start with a book that is not now in Landon's surviving library and that does not tell stories as such. The book in question was a cosmology that we know Landon was compelled to study closely at age thirteen, before he had even begun to assemble his own library.

In January 1724, Landon's father, Robert King Carter, carefully composed a letter concerning his son's schooling in England. John Dawes was the London merchant to whom the elder Carter had given the oversight of this matter; he now received instructions replete with very strong views. King Carter artfully attributed to his correspondent his own sentiments concerning education. He regretted that schoolmasters nowadays did not seem to keep "the old way;" if they did, they would still be using Lily's *Grammar*, that "we and our forefathers learned." King Carter was resigned to some departures and innovations, but he absolutely insisted on one point: his son must be put to study "the Janua Linguarum Trilingus in Latin, English and Greek, writ by John Comenius." It offered "the best stock of Latin words and in the best sense to suit the genius* of boys, even to their manhood, of any I ever met in my life."

Comenius's little book was thus thrust upon Landon when he was 13 years old; it was not, of course, his first introduction to stories. He must already have been told in song and story what the world was made of. School was for him—more than for his English fellow pupils—a reeducation. Many of his first narratives came from enslaved nurses and were radically different from the traditions of books; but to that first informal instruction we have no direct access.

The textbook prescribed for Landon gave him an early bookish encounter with a western outline of knowledge. It makes a convenient point of departure for this review of the knowledge into which Landon was entering through books.

The *Gate of Tongues Unlocked* was by a seventeenth-century Czech scholastic, Jan Kominsky, or Johannes Comenius, who used his text to undertake a simple, yet vast project—namely, to introduce a boy not only to "all Tongues" but also to "all . . . Sciences": in practice this meant Latin—plus the pupil's own language, and one other he was to learn. (Landon's father required Greek.) Three parallel columns, in the three languages, present all the essential terms in "Arts and Sciences," and thus a whole cosmology is unfolded in highly lingual form. In a thousand "sentences," grouped in one hundred "chapters," the student was to gain the essential relationships of all knowable phenomena.

Oral culture was still strong in schools, where reciting aloud was continually practiced; the first sentence is a spoken greeting. Sentence number two declares the project: "to know the differences of things, and to bee able to give its name unto everything." Preliminaries over, the work moves briskly into cosmic origins—"Of the beginning of the world." It declares that: "God created all out of nothing." Thus, Scripture has been recast into a simple language of metaphysics and poetic natural philosophy. Witness the chapter "Of the Firmament"; in it the pupil learns that, "Starres are lampes hanging up in the skie." The book proceeds through the four elements, from highest— "Of the Fire"— to the lowest "Of the Earth." It proceeds through the productions of the earth—trees and fruits. The living creatures come next, in their kinds according to their "elements"—first birds of the air, then water-living creatures, then

---

* Genius then meant spirit, or particular character or temperament—stage of development we would now say in this context.

beasts that labor on the earth. Then come "wild beasts"; and only then does it come to "man"—his body, outward and inward, his senses, his mind, his will and affections. Then the book traverses the works of humankind, from "things mechanicall in genereall," to particular arts—"Of the dressing and trimming of gardens" (mythically first, of course!)—through a rustic tableau of agriculture, the mill, baking, and on to "a house and its parts," including "baines, stewes, baths & and cleanlinesse." Next come the institutions of human society—"Of marriage," "Of childbirth," "Of kindred," until it comes at last to the "citie, or walled towne," "the Church," "the Court wherein law is pleaded," "the Princely estate" and so to "peace and warre." Then suddenly the account turns back on itself and reflexively addresses the learning that garners the knowledge of all these things. It summarily treats: "Of schoole," "Of Dialectick," "Of Rhetorick," "Of Historie," and "Of Physick," until it comes to such moral topics as: "Of prudence," and "Of Chastity." At last it reaches for finality in its concluding "chapters": "Of Death and Buriall," "Of Providence," and "Of Angells." And thus, it comes to "The Clause"—as the close is styled in this archaic diction.

Some basic underlying myths were deliberately brought to the surface in Comenius's little book. Returning to the review of the stories in the surviving library we shall see that these myths were recurrent all through Landon's life. The greatest, most encompassing, and abiding of these was the narrative of the Creation and the Fall. This story was present in Squire Landon's perception of his estate. We know that he saw the land and the sons and daughters of Adam and Eve who worked it laboring painfully for their subsistence. The signs of the pervasiveness of this origin myth are everywhere in the diary as well as in the library and its annotations.

The primal narrative of a single creation is alluded to in many ways in Landon's responses to what he read. There are little, but very significant, indicators of the assumed close-bounded unity of the cosmos. The universe as Landon knew it had great immediacy in created time, space, and range of forms. There was outrage when Landon met in Herodotus's *History* long retrospects in time. The chronology the ancient historian used was entirely incompatible with the current 6,000-year age of the earth as calculated by Bishop Ussher from the Bible. The pious Anglican squire was moved to exclaim: "a fellow of fine thought this—30,000 years he readily accounts for!" In another place, he scrawled: "17,000 years—bless us all!"*

Creationism in the eighteenth century carried an assumption that God would not be wasteful in producing multiple designs to achieve the same end. Landon thus was certain that the Creator had practiced economies in varieties of forms of species; he therefore confidently asserted an identity between an Asia-Minor tree frog and a tree frog that he knew in Virginia. So assured was he of this identity, spanning continents, that he corrected in his copy a traveler's account of a creature with sticky pads by which it clung to twigs and leaves. Landon wrote impatiently in the margin: "All this is a farce—we have the same frog in Virginia and it has toes, nails, and no glutinous matter." As an American with firsthand knowledge of native fauna, Landon proudly corrected an old legend. He denied that the rattlesnake "darts . . . poison from its head," but it might indeed "be the antient Basilisk w[hi]ch killed with his eyes, for I have seen their fascinating powers to draw their prey to them." The sage of Sabine Hall asserted the same correspondence of forms with regard to humans. In Herodotus he read how the mounted warriors of Thrace flayed the skin off the heads of those they killed and strung them on their horses' bridles; Landon wrote an exclamation: "Mere Indians."

After the Creation had come the Fall. It had come about through an original act of disobedience to the great Father Creator. Stories that both invoked and reinforced this primal myth struck a profound chord in Landon Carter. As a patriarch he knew only too well the subversion and defiance of subordinates who should be in the child relationship to himself.

There is real anguish in Landon's annotations on the willfulness and disobedience of children. Reading the works of Aaron Hill, he could ease a little the hurt he constantly felt by delighting in the poet's preference for plant "children" over human progeny. Gardening, the poet assured him, could offer "escape from that proportion of pain, which embitters our most tender reflections when they relate to our offspring of a less grateful and prunable kind." The poet therefore celebrated a retreat "into an enjoyment of serener satisfaction . . . under the increase of flourishing green families." Landon, the disappointed parent, who put more and more of himself into alternately combating his family and cultivating the earth, could seek relief as he inked the

---

*In 1658 Bishop James Ussher, an Anglican prelate in Ireland, had published a work (*The Annals of the World*) intended to relate secular history to the chronologies found in the Bible. By careful counting, he calculated the exact day of the creation—as it would be stated in the Julian calendar then used in Britain (October 23, 4004 BCE). His work enjoyed immense authority for generations, until geology, archaeology, and finally Darwin blew it away.

above quoted words into brackets; in the margin he wrote his own exclamation: "What a real truth is this! and how prittily is the thought dressd." Then, on another occasion he found himself contemplating Shakespeare's tragedy of King Lear; here Landon could find only the bitterest consolation as he shared his own pain. He apostrophized that tragic hero—that classic exemplar of indulgent and betrayed fatherhood: "Oh Lear, others have acted the same foolish part that you did, and have been as handsomely rewarded as thou wast by their Offspring."

Within the cosmology and mythology of traditional patriarchy, the terrible disobedience of children was related to the malevolent recalcitrance of slaves. In a notable exchange, Landon endorsed a denunciation of the base treachery of slaves. Pliny the Younger, an ancient Roman estate owner, had narrated the murder of a master by his slaves, with this comment: "You see to what dangers, to what affronts . . . we [masters] are exposed; nor will humanity or mildness be the least protection to us; for it is villainy not judgement that guides the [slave] murderers." Landon wrote in the margin: "Just observation this about Slaves—they can as little be humanized as bears; such a brutish ass does slavery beget—altho' they may be born Slaves." The afterthought deserves special note, precisely because it shows that Landon was hesitating whether to interpret the depraved nature he attributed to slaves as the product of environment or of heredity. Are they stupid, deceitful, and "brutish" because enslavement makes them so, or is it because of their inborn nature? But that was not the end of this library conversation; the text Landon was reading was a translation of Pliny with commentary by John Boyle, Earl of Orrery, an Anglo-Irish nobleman. His lordship protested at the old Roman's prejudice; in keeping with a newer humanitarianism, he urged upon all masters a "proper indulgence . . . to the meanest of our fellow creatures." Landon retorted: "Yes, my lord—and what will every indulgence produce? Nothing but a brute in human shape."

Adam's defiance of the Father's law had brought mortality, sin, and misery upon mankind; but behind the primal act of disobedience lay the scheming of an ambitious woman. During the later years of the master of Sabine Hall's diary, the story of women's subversive treachery is one that Landon told compulsively. Mostly focused on his daughter-in-law, it was for the old man a recurrent drama. The library annotations show how he made his books feed his deep fear. Landon's lurking misogyny was outraged at Buchanan's *History of Scotland*; it amply told the iniquity of Mary Queen of Scots, but its author felt compelled to reverence Mary as a sovereign lady. In the margin, Landon wrote:

A stricken Adam and a sorrowing Eve expelled from the Garden of Eden. Exquisite prints adorned many books in Landon's library. Here is the work of a pair of virtuoso artists—the painter Francis Hayman and the engraver Simon François Ravenet—from a 1761 edition of Milton's works. In the demeanor of the angel we see the story of harsh punishment sentimentalized. *Special Collections, Alderman Library, University of Virginia.*

"'Tis strange to read such a character [description] bound up with a book which makes her not only [a] Whore but a base adultress & Murtherer of her husband." Elsewhere, Landon encountered Clytymnestra, a far more famous husband slayer. He thought that if a modern playwright were to adapt her story, he would surely find that she had her equal in the latter-day world.

Yet, Landon did not always portray women as evil schemers. We know that he married three times; and, if the legend has truth in it, he had expressed such extravagant devotion to his first wife that he found it prudent, before bringing his second wife home, to expunge from her predecessor's tombstone his declaration that he would be celibate for the remainder of his days! We have already seen also how he recalled reading aloud to his last "dear woman," the poet Aaron Hill's "prettyest poem that ever was," in celebration of marriage.

In Landon's day there was already abroad a myth of human origins and destiny much more benign than the orthodox Christian doctrines of the Fall and the consequent vitiation of human nature through original sin. The alternative story of humankind keeps appearing in the library and in the annotations alongside the grimmer Judeo-Christian myth.

Since the Renaissance, a quickened spirit of inquiry in the west had encouraged a searching and speculation into the rise of human institutions; from that had emerged a more positive view if not of the human past, then of its future. In a nutshell, this was a story of a state of nature where instincts of "benevolence" prevailed: and these instincts, being "of nature" were still implanted in every human breast. Landon was evidently drawn to this newer account, this other myth of who we are and of where we come from. Ultimately, this second myth of origins was subversive of the old orthodox story; but during the eighteenth century and later, the two versions of origins coexisted, the newer account alongside the older.

The Genesis origin story explained not only where humanity came from but also its familiar life of sorrow, pain, violence, sickness, and death. The enduring benevolence origin myth had, of course, to have also an explanation for the evil and suffering so manifest in the world; and so it also told a story of a fall, but told it very differently. Not some primal act of disobedience but a slow corruption of morals (accompanying the creation of "unnatural" institutions among humankind) had made misery so general in the world. Since a benign and social humanity was known to persist, the malignant process could be reversed—indeed, it must be. A reform of morals and institutions would restore the primal prevalence of natural goodness.

The story of a happy state of nature was certainly one that Landon entertained himself with. We can see it very clearly in his engagement with a charming fantasy in the collected *Works* of Aaron Hill. The poem "The Happy Man" presents an idyll of Arcadian bliss. In this story, a man is discovered living in simple ease with his little family. All their wants are supplied from along the ocean shore, or from the hillsides, groves, and vales behind. But one day, Freeman (for that, significantly, is his name) is standing on a clifftop; he descries an approaching sail; he follows its progress toward the haven under the hill, only to see the vessel run upon a shoal; its mariners are drowned in the surf. At this:

> Freeman starts, sad revolves the changeful sight
> Where misry can, so soon, succeed delight,
> Then, shakes his head, in pity for their fate,
> And sweetly conscious, hugs his happier state.

It would be possible to discourse at length on the amount of cherished eighteenth-century masculinist mythology this little narrative encapsulates. It shows also both primitive simplicity and the advance of commerce, as portended by the sail. Landon was evidently charmed by it; but he therefore needed all the more to endow it with the traditional piety that was so strong in him. "What an instance for a religious thanks in pleasing adoration! Yet it has escaped the Poet's thoughts."

Origin stories must tell how the primal harmony was broken. Landon had a strong imaginative involvement in the story of the corruption of a blessed state of nature. Ambitious, scheming individuals were the agents of this downfall, as appears clearly in a series of interactions with writings of the early eighteenth-century English poet Alexander Pope. Landon read closely and made intermittent comments on Epistle III of Pope's poetic "Essay on Man," as edited and annotated by Bishop William Warburton. Both the poem and the commentary show the newer version of unhappy progress toward the unhappy world they all knew so well. Pope, in pregnant phrases, evoked an age when "Love was Liberty," and "Nature was Law." In that time: "States were form'd; the name of King unknown, / 'Till common int'rest plac'd the sway in one." Then came Warburton's note explicating Pope's lines: they described a situation where "men had no need to guard their native liberty from their governors by civil pactions [constitutional contracts]." He was sure that "the love which each master of a family had for those under his care" was "their best security." Warburton—a good English Whig—went on to attack the Tory doctrine of the divine right of kings as derived from the rights of the patriarch over his children. Landon the archpatriarch did not go along entirely with that: "Tho God might not confer the Regal title on Fathers, and as the Poet says 'common interest placed the sway in one'. Yet—as the obedience to parents was the effect of Nature in both Parents & children—it is not improbable that Man (represented as observant to both animal Creation, and obedient to the voice of nature) might copy from Nature in the Authority with which Kings began." An equation between monarchy and patriarchy was strong in Landon's mind; his later diary reflected a profound unsettling as, after 1765, he was impelled into rebellion against his Father King.

But Landon did endorse Pope's and Warburton's key proposition about the origin of evil in this once-happy world. He endorsed Pope's view (as extended by Warburton) that it was "The Policy of Priests" that first invented "Superstition" to accomplish "the corruption of civil Society." And Landon added another element that was very conventional for his time. The rise of commerce had been important in the process of advancing corruption. This is indicated by an almost gleeful note on an end flyleaf of Aaron Hill's *Works*. Landon raised a sharp rhetorical query as to whether one could find any instance of "a people long at once retaining Public Virtue and extended Commerce." (This comment is probably part of a growing inclination to doubt the prevalence of virtue in mercantile Great Britain while celebrating its continuance in agrarian Virginia.)

In a comment upon a passage in Warburton's *Principles of Natural and Revealed Religion* (London, 1754), the new positive account of underlying human nature was given broader application and made to resonate with the humanized theology of the age. The passage written by this staunch Anglican insistently distinguished the morality of the Gospel from that taught in the priest-ridden Church of Rome. The Gospel, Warburton boldly claimed, taught no complete system of morality; rather it directed mankind to discover within themselves, and then to practice, their own natural "human" and "social virtue." This passage the Virginia squire approvingly memorialized on the end flyleaf.* What is more, we know that Landon internalized this version of the history of humankind and its benign nature, for he used that phrase "social virtue" in his justification to God of his forgiving Judith and Reuben. Indeed, he made recurrent use of it in other powerful passages as well.

The implication of the state-of-nature myth concerning a human propensity for good was made altogether explicit in one book in the library. As Landon read in his 1753 edition of Milton's prose works, he entered a series of comments that were almost adulatory in their tone. But he did once break off revealingly to enter a disagreement. Milton had declared that "assuredly we bring not innocence into the world, we bring impurity rather," and then made a further assertion: "that which purifies us is trial, and trial is by what is contrary." Landon interjected a protest. He penned a very different schematic story of the course of human life. In tiny fine script, he wrote in the margin: "Here I differ in opinion . . . for if we are not innocent at our birth—Why is the Kingdom of heaven compared to a child? The trial which Purifies may be for the purpose of clearing away the evil gaind by life & not to purify a child [impure] when born." There it is—"we bring impurity" vs. "we are . . . innocent at birth"—original sin vs. abiding goodness in human nature.

---

* Landon greatly admired William Warburton, and wrote as much on the front flyleaf of the good bishop's treatise on the *Divine Legation of Moses.* Where Landon wanted to make extended comment on a book in his library, or to collect references for later consultation, he wrote his thoughts not in the margin but on the end papers, entering a page number to make a cross reference. Often there was simply an x inked onto the page at the place to be commented on.

Landon Carter, writing in his diary and the margins of his books was far from alone in telling a profoundly altered story of the Fall. An increasing number of others throughout Landon's lifetime were telling this story and were drawing more extreme consequences from it. Deists were explicitly setting aside—even mocking—the orthodox Christian version of origins and nature, in favor of a revival of ancient philosophy, or a new affirmation of human self-sufficiency.

The way of the deists, however, did not appeal to Landon Carter at any stage in his life. His library suggests that he refused to collect or to attend to their skeptical stories and commentaries. It seems he was only familiar with such writings through a few pious refutations of them. Thus, self-education in ancient and modern knowledge brought only one recorded direct confrontation with the kind of outright materialism to which God was irrelevant. The introduction to Landon's many-volume *Universal History* (published from 1747 onward) summed up the Epicurean philosophy of the Roman poet Lucretius. His cosmological poem, "Concerning the Things of Nature," had offered an atomistic theory of the origin of the world by the action of the sun on a "new-formed earth containing in it the seeds of all things." Landon wrote scornfully: "I suppose atomically & fortuitously form'd. A noble jumble indeed"!

Enlightenment anticipation of a moral regeneration that would reverse the corruptions introduced into human society by priestcraft, tyranny, and commerce was keenly linked to manifestations of technological progress. Closely associated with the idea of human perfectibility was the cult of "improvement." This was itself a rich set of stories that Landon Carter, and most of the literate persons of his generation, read and wrote with intense concern. This was a story that the Virginia squire was indeed enacting on his Sabine Hall estate in his search for improved ways of managing. At his reading desk, he accordingly found the story of rational progress in passage after passage in his library.

The fragments of the improvement myth that Landon thus inscribed served to locate him securely in an optimistic present time that was in strong contrast to earlier ages of ignorance and credulity. Herodotus's *History* provided ready instances. One of the few dated comments—noted as made in 1732—called this ancient sage "a dealer in sacerdotal lyes." And this view was scornfully summed up in one exclamation: "An instance of Philosophy in old times. . . ."

A momentous shift was occurring not just in origin stories but in social and economic values. Higher learning—"philosophy" for the slave owners of the ancient world—had been moral self-instruction for the leisured ruling class. Those fitted for book learning were assumed to be of a superior nature to those who did the material work that sustained the civilization; the elite and their valued knowledge should be as completely dissociated as possible from the servile preoccupations of those who worked with their hands. Greek mathematics had a kind of primacy just because of its abstracted immateriality. (Liberal arts were the ideal, and there was little notion of applied science!) This tradition was continued in the post-Roman Middle Ages and was embodied in the universities of that time; it only really began to be set aside with the fifteenth- and sixteenth-century rise of cities and of oceanic navigation. It was not until the later seventeenth and through the eighteenth century that the tradition was substantially—though not entirely—overthrown. (Even now it still influences attitudes.) By the eighteenth century, the most valued knowledge was coming to be a useful knowledge; the scorn of the "liberal" for the "mechanic" arts rapidly diminished, and educated men were garnering how-to-do-it information in every quarter. The famous French Enlightenment *Encyclopédie*, commencing publication in 1751, was a milestone along this new path. It was professedly the *Encyclopédie des arts et métiers*, that is, of productive trades. Learned gentlemen, intent on extending control, did not, however, merely study productive processes; they began to redesign them mathematically and "rationally," and to insist that the craftsmen surrender their age-old craft monopolies based on knowledge transmitted through apprenticeships. New procedures based on printed manuals were henceforth to have the greatest authority, and the industrial engineer was arising as a dominant figure in an emergent bourgeois capitalist society.

We have already seen Landon redesigning work practices on his plantation as he sought to extend his scientific management role. All this time, he was reading books in his library in pursuit of the same end. He was avid for practical ideas that he might experiment with; and he sought them in places we would think unlikely.

Travel literature was a readily available source. (Its authors pandered to this current taste; that was a reason why it was one of the most popular genres of the age.) Stories of productive practices observable around the world would bring home a multitude of improvements to those who studied to collect, adapt, and adopt them. It was thus with an improving eye that Landon read Charles Thompson's *Travels through Turkey, . . . the Holy Land, . . . and Other Parts. . . .* , 2 vols. (London: 1754). The book is presented in its preface as a kind of reverent, in-the-footsteps-of-our-Lord-and-his-apostles kind of work, but its author could not resist working into it an extended set of observations on customs, curious and useful—mainly useful. And Landon was certainly impelled to read it that way; his notes on the page margins and flyleaves pick out many practical prescriptions. There are notes on how to grow vines, on how to make fig trees fruitful, on a method to smelt iron ore, and so on. There is even a grand "construction project"—a description of the way the Ephesians contrived to build their great Temple of Diana on a marsh.

The Scriptures themselves were culled for practical lessons in technology. Landon would hardly write practically oriented annotatations in the sacred book itself; but he can be found culling what was useful from his *Dictionary of the Holy Bible*, 3 vols. (London, 1759). He developed a long note on "Zoheleth," the stone in the "fountain . . . just under the walls of Jerusalem" (I Kings 1.9); this he carefully cross-referenced to an entry on "Naemah"(Nehemiah) (the first that wove woolen cloth (Gen. 4.22). Noting the way workers in the Holy City would beat their cloth on the stone, his comment was: "this seems a good hint of our fulling mill invention; and I sh[oul]d think might be of service in families who cannot conveniently get fulling mills." With Aaron Hill's mainly poetic *Works* open in front of him, Landon was induced by the poet's correspondence about the cultivation of vines to take up his pen and enter some of his busiest notes.

Useful knowledge concerning agriculture had high priority. In 1750 Griffith Hughes had published in London a handsome folio volume titled *The Natural History of Barbados*. ("London Carter" [sic] is listed as one of the gentlemen from Virginia who had subscribed to support publication.) Included in this book was a description of an insect pest that attacked the sugar cane. Landon felt confident enough of the applicability of his own discoveries to retell a version of his fly-weevil observations; he used the generous, wide margins to reason out his own counterstory to the one offered by Hughes: "I am persuaded from what is to be seen on almost all plants[,] that such insects are not uncommon, but if we reflect on the nature of most insects, small ones in Particular, we shall then be convinced that instinct has only furnished the parents of them to deposit their eggs where there is a proper Pabulum [food] for them ready for their Subsistence. . . . Therefore it seems rational to conclude that the several plants on which we find these almost imperceptible insects are at first wounded . . . from which wounds the Juice of the Plant exudates[.] And the parent of the insect by instinct resorts to that exudation as a nidus abounding with a Pabulum sufficient to raise her brood."

The story of nature's care of her little creatures was one that Landon told repeatedly. Of course, he wanted humankind to learn these secrets to be able to take preventive measures. That marginal note may even have been an early rehearsal of the version Landon would tell in his learned paper on the fly-weevil that was communicated to the American Philosophical Society in 1769. The Latin words "nidus" (nest) and "pabulum" (food) were prominent in it, still carrying much of the explanatory force but coupled with a strong dramatization of the wonderful provision that "Nature" makes in guiding the "instinct" by which its creatures survive.

A passage from Stephen Switzer's *The Practical Husbandman* (published in parts, 1734 to 1735), reveals the probable source from which Landon adapted these very distinctive words with which versions of this insect-pest story was repeatedly told in various diary entries. Switzer narrates a cosmic drama involving the three terrestrial elements that support plant growth under the influence of the fourth, the power of celestial fire. The sun, activating air and water within the "Nidus, Couch-Bed, or Matrix" of the earth, produces the "Pabulum, or Food of Plants of all Kinds," and so calls forth the "great Work of Vegetation." *The Practical Husbandman* also includes a terminology of "juices" and "ascending vapour" that Landon echoed repeatedly; the book quotes a "great Naturalist" to show the cosmic system by which "the Air, being rarified by the Sun-Beams,... Vapour ascends visibly." This "is the certain Method which Nature takes to raise the Juices of the Earth to that Height she does in tall Trees."

There are continuities between the Comenius Renaissance cosmology in which Landon was first schooled and the vegetable dramatics of *The Practical Husbandman*. These continuities ran deep in the implied cosmology of Switzer's search for some active principle whose virtue animates life on earth. This was an ultimately archaic religious and not mechanical mode of understanding; an old animistic metaphysics persisted in covert forms. In this view, the principle so insistently sought was to the earth (or the plant) as the soul was to the body, and so ultimately, it stood as God did to the Creation. Therein we see the profound traditionalism that coexisted with the modernizing scientism of this transitional age.

While it is important to recognize the continuities and attachments to old traditions in the stories that the squire of Sabine Hall read and annotated in his library, it is even more important to observe the new and changed. If we go back to the cosmology that Comenius had laid out for that young schoolboy in those thousand "sentences," we can see how breath-takingly different was the imagined universe interactively constructed from the books that Landon was reading in the same space that he used to write his great diary.

Belief in the benevolent goodness of humankind and an avid study of Nature to discover the useful—the means of improvement—are not just curiosities of the worldview of Landon and his generation. This mythology, so apparent in the library and its annotations, was pregnant with history. It was this belief system that gave the leaders of the American rebellion the inspiration to embark on a revolution. It was from faith in the people and in the possibilities of endless improvability that they took a warrant for the daring of their great initiative. Landon shared all these beliefs; but in him the balance was different. He feared "the old Adam." He was a die-hard patriarchalist, who remained faithful to the old constitution in which a Father King was needed to balance the power of the people.

Chapter 6

Plantation Medical Science

The past, they say, is another country. There is no more startling way of experiencing the otherness of the eighteenth century than by paying attention to its prevailing medical beliefs and practices. The generation that saw the creation of the American republic gave us so much of our current political vocabulary and repertoire of concepts; but as to medicine, well, they inhabited another mental universe. And their ideas about health and sickness gave hidden meanings to their works of revolutionary statecraft, for their language of politics was largely carried by medical metaphors. In that time, as we shall see, the primary reference of the word "constitution" was to the make-up of the human body; and "corruption" referred to the inexorable falling of such bodies first into disease and then into dissolution after death.

Landon Carter's diary affords us a powerful experience of the very different universe he and his contemporaries inhabited. As a young scholar in England, he had interested himself in medical science; once back in Virginia, he kept ordering selections of the latest books on clinical theory and practice. His diary shows his pride in the expertise that he had gained from careful study; but while his knowledge was more technical than that of most of his literate contemporaries, it was not essentially different.

This chapter is not for the squeamish or fainthearted.

∽

Medical concerns provided the very first topic in the very first entry in Landon's 1750s scientific plantation journal; it was, in even greater detail, the subject of the second entry. Current beliefs made health and the weather joint concerns.

October 3, 1756

It has continued drye weather—Cold & hot to this day, & I believe the rain is now come. . . . Therefore to Conclude our Observation about the weather to this day: —from the 23d of July . . . we have had only two showers, one in August very slight & the other in September of no Continuance & quickly soaked up. My daughter—Susannah—still in her fever . . . but I think she has mended in her strength a little. God send that this moisture that we are now to expect may disperse & so remove the present prodigious unhealthy Constitution of the air. I have been sick myself ever since the 2d of September—& am far from being recovered yet. And now above 80 of us—the young & Old—have felt the effects of the Season—which has been attended with violent irregular fevers of a most bilious nature. Nay such quantities of bile have attended that some have many days (notwithstanding plentyfull evacuations of it by Vomits when they were first taken)—have voided it upwards & downwards till they were near Spent and I don't find above 2 or 3 cases that the quinine *bark has operated in at all favourably, for if the fever has been checked a day or two by it the Patient has been intirely Sallow— & all ages the same.*

Landon turned to measure his own scientific practice against that of professionals:

Neither do I know of any certain success attending any Physician. Do what they could the byle would flow again and the disorder return. . . . So that we must conclude that the Epidemic Constitution of the air was the Sole cause of it—which 'tis to be observed was all along drye, hot, & foggy at nights—excepting now & then a day when the smallest change—though but a Cold drye air—would revive the Sick.

In trying to come to terms with the strangeness of all this, we first of all are struck at once by the powerful connection that is asserted between *the Epidemic Constitution of the air* and an outbreak of the *violent irregular fevers of a most bilious nature.* The influence of the air was so pervasive that *the byle would flow again,* let the doctors *do what they could.*

Behind this report and its stress on the atmosphere and on the flow of bile stretched a long tradition of medical theory and practice. In our legendary history, the ancient Greek Hippocrates was its founder; but he must have derived much of it from now unknown predecessors. He lived and wrote his treatises about 400 BCE, and his system was taken up and elaborated by Galen, a Greek of the second century CE, whose treatises became the standard texts for more than a millennium. Put most simply: the human body according to Hippocrates and Galen was—like all material things—composed of the four elements—fire, air, water, and earth. The body's condition was accordingly governed by the influences of the four humors that sustained the opposed characteristics of the elements. Choler (yellow bile)—like fire—induced hotness and dryness; blood—like air—induced moist heat; phlegm—like water—induced cold wetness; while melancholy (black bile)—like earth—induced cold dryness. Health, in this paradigm, was the balance of these humors. External factors, such as the constitution of the air, might upset this balance, requiring intervention to restore it; but internal factors, notably the particular make-up or "constitution" of each individual were a very important part of the equation. The physician must be able to read in the patient both his or her innate individual characteristics and the current ways by which that unique balance had been upset. Only then might he seek a way to restore equilibrium. Evacuations as by vomits, and also, as we shall see, purging, bleeding, and blistering were the main balance-restoring therapies applied in this often-violent system of healing.

To us, this system of knowledge and the associated therapies seems more likely to kill than cure. To its practitioners for more than two thousand years, it was continually self-confirming; with their drugs they could make the body respond to treatment—vomiting, purging, sweating—as required. Often their patients did recover; and they, like we, had ways to explain failures and deaths without calling the system itself in question.

It was in this tradition that Landon conducted and recorded his plantation home practice. Usually the cases appear first in the notebook journal in the form of a resumé of the symptoms and the treatment so far. All this was already merged with his reasoning and prognoses. Thereafter, he would report at intervals on further developments. A close following of one such case can reveal in holistic impression the forms of practice and theorizing. Malaria, which we know as a mosquito-borne parasite invasion, was almost certainly the primary cause of the illness; but we must attend to the signs that Landon looked for.

On February 23, 1757, Landon sat down to a full set of reports on climate (and the causes at work in the weather) and on medical cases. Concerning one of the several cases whose care he was supervising closely, he wrote a narrative torrent of a medical report:

The boy Samson also very ill. His case was an ague & then a fever two days on the 12th of the month when I was abroad,—for which they gave him a vomit—which occasioned an intermission for two days,—when he went out after his cattle at night—but he relapsed again into a Cold fit & a fever, & as there were many twitching symptoms in his belly & his pulse very irregular—I gave him 24 grains Pulvis Bazilicus, believing there might be worms contributing to the disorder, & if there were not—the evacuation could not be hurtfull,—but this gave no indication of the disease—no worms were voided. *His head remained affected—and by watching his pulse narrowly every now & then yes-terday I imagined there must be a load of bile, for which I gave him a penny weight of Ipecacuana. This worked once upwards & brought off a quantity of green byle—&—tending downwards much—went off by stool,—and I think his pulse much mended, not so strong in the beats—soft & plyable to the touch.* The diarist then added as an afterthought to this resumé: *Note: I have two days before now endeavoured to loosen this bile by medecin—& Collect it for the purpose—& I hope it will answer.*

The improvement in Samson's condition was not sustained even to the next day. The fever continued, and was so bad that *at night his head was much disturbed and the fever high.* Landon decided that the man must be blooded. Judging the fever to be *of the inflammatory kind,* he had *near 4 ounces blood taken* from the arm. Closely examined, the blood was judged to have *a deep floridness inclining to a black colour—but with no Symptoms as if attended with a Cold.* (The scrutiny of the blood also, it seems, suggested that there was *but little serum,* and the consis-tency was indeed too thick—*viscid*—for health.) The need for this bloodletting was therefore confirmed, and the anxious planter noted: *I could wish my fears had permitted me to have drawn more off.* He reported that Samson's head now *grew quite easy—and his pulse more soft to the touch*; but his skin remained alarm-ingly *drye,* and his fever still continued. Landon introduced a new line of treat-ment: *I changed his drink to barley water, observing but little serum in his blood.* Then, *every two hours I gave him 60 drops of Spiritus Mindererius to act as a neutral salt to re-move obstructions that such a viscid blood must Occasion—& in order to promote a breathing moisture.* But no such salutary sweat had yet been produced—*although the boy acknowledges himself much better.* Indeed there seemed now some hope that *Nature perhaps by these little helps will be more at liberty to act.* The diarist added a coda next morning: *Note: he had a griping in the night & threw off 3 bil-ious stools.*

Dr. Nicholas Flood was the neighborhood professional whom Landon then regularly consulted.* He had been summoned to attend to Betty Oliver, a slave woman considered dangerously ill; but he had also seen Samson. Landon's next report, ten days later, on March 8, noted an exchange of letters with the doctor. The diarist wrote Flood that Samson had taken all his medicine, but

---

* By the time the later diary series resumed in 1763 after a hiatus, Landon had quarreled with *that devil—Old Nick* as he thenceforth called him. This became the most bitterly sustained personal vendetta recorded in the uninhibited later diary, as we shall see in chapter 10.

now there was a *Complaint he made about his throat;* furthermore, Samson's fevers had not left him. Dr. Flood replied that he believed Samson would *recover without any more medecin.* So Landon was reassured, and *left off going to see him— but sent him victuals punctually & . . . was always told he was clear of a fever & a great deal better.* But the master soon discovered that Samson was not doing well: *yesterday curiosity led me to see him—and I think him much worse—his fever still high— although without any complaint—but much weaker—& this morning the same—a moisture all over him—but it does not seem as if it came naturally from his pores—for the flesh is drye beneath & he had a great soarness all within him.* Landon found that *no Doctor can I get to him. . . . Therefore I must trye myself.* It was back to standard procedures: *I have ordered him a vomit.*

By the next morning Landon reported Samson to be better: *His vomit yesterday* having *brought off much viscid Phlegm and a powerfull sweat which I hope has opened the Pores.* The master was pleased at these promising signs, and recorded how he *endeavoured to keep this up by weak wine diluters,* and that he *twice threw in a Spoonful of rattlesnake* root *decoction.* That was his favorite remedy for thinning the blood, phlegm, and bile, and it seemed to work. *His sweat continued all night & till 9 this day. His flesh feels cooler & his pulse not so quick.* On the following day: *Samson easy but pulse quick yet & low, & He very weak but—I am in hopes—mending. He looks Cheerfull in the face—& his muscles not so flat as two days agoe. Neither is his flesh hot as before.* With that—apart from a passing mention three weeks later of Samson *but Just recovering*—he disappears from this record altogether. He did not die at that time since his name was not in the little June 1757 list of slaves recently deceased; but he probably did die soon after, for he gets no mention in the diary for 1763 and subsequent years.

In the detailed reporting of Samson's case we get a good sample of Landon's medical narratives and a striking instance of the comprehensive medical paradigms that directed his observations, that channeled his interpretations and lay practice. We are looking, indeed, at an application of that very stable, enduring repertoire of the Hippocratic therapies already enumerated. To be sure, the European colonization of the Americas, Africa, and Asia had greatly increased the range of drugs that were available for purchase and everyday use, but ideas about the effects of medicines had not fundamentally changed.

Yet, there had been momentous changes in science and cosmology between the time of Hippocrates and the 1750s when Landon's casebook diary begins. The universe had been profoundly redescribed in the course of the scientific revolution of the seventeenth century; medical science shared this transformation. William Harvey had proved that the heart was a pump that circulated the blood under pressure through a set of pipes and valves. Sir Isaac Newton, in the wake of Copernicus and Galileo, had demonstrated and reduced to precise mathematics the circulation of the planets in the solar system. In the new imagination, born of these transformative discoveries, modern mechanics had triumphed over the old Greek metaphysics. The machine now became the dominant model or metaphor for understanding the way things are—and how to act on them. The Hippocratic system with its concern for a balance of humors remained as an underlay, but in the new mechanical paradigm, the human body became less a cauldron of mixed humors and more a hydraulic system, its pipes and valves primed by the pumping heart. In this view, health would be promoted by managing the fluids and the vessels in the body in order to facilitate circulation. The thinness or thickness (viscidity) of the blood and the elasticity or rigidity of the solids (the conduits) were thus the crucial factors for the physician to assess and act upon.

From our vantage point on the ideas dominating medicine in Landon's day, we can see what blind alleys were the seeming great theoretical developments that had lately been incorporated into the old humoral system. The truly great paradigm shift—transforming both theory and practical therapies—would come nearly a century later with Pasteur's introduction of the germ explanation for infection and disease.

With some hundred or so of his own enslaved people in the environs of Sabine Hall—as well as neighbors who appealed for help—Landon's medical practice was extensive. As can be sensed in the sample cases described, the practice was also very intensive, bringing the master into intimate contact with ailing members of his large household. The diarist took care to write up cases that really challenged, interested, or troubled him; he sought then to reason his way to the bottom of them. Surveying over 160 of Landon's 1750s case reports, it becomes clear that the diagnoses and treatments were overwhelmingly concerned with fevers and agues—mostly malaria, we surmise. Coughs and respiratory disorders were usually looked on as conditions associated with a fever. Landon had very similar explanations also for violent pains in the head, belly, sides, or even limbs. For him, the pains were where the fevers settled and became localized.

Landon, in line with the prevailing philosophy, assumed that fevers and agues were caused by influences from the outside upon bodies that were resist-

ant or susceptible according to their constitutions. These outside influences included diet and exercise (or the lack of it), and other such habits that lay
within the control of each person; but weather and climate—seasonal, prevailing, or epidemic disorders—were known to be powerful contributors. The
air—its fogs, damps, or epidemic constitution—might disturb the bodies of
everyone who breathed it, always according to their particular susceptibilities.

Damp, unhealthy air was deemed to engender fevers and agues by inducing
an overload of bile from the liver, via the *Hepatic duct*, into the stomach. The
stomach where the disturbing excess accumulated was therefore the seat of
most diseases; it was the first and last concern in commencing treatment or
pronouncing a cure. Landon applied very consistent strategies. He wrote in
the spring of 1758 of fevers, *requiring long & gentle evacuations*. But in the hot
summer of the previous year, when *the Season* continued so long *sickly*, he had
been more forceful. He then prescribed *much evacuation by vomits, Purges & indeed constant sweatings*; he was trying to bring the fevers—however *irregular* at
first—to a *regular intermittant*. That way the recurrence of the fevers could be anticipated and timely remedies applied. These *regular* fevers Landon designated
as *tertian, quartan,* or *quotidian agues* accordingly, as they came at three-day, four-
day, or daily intervals. (This very distinctive, definable periodicity is what most
clearly reveals these fevers to have been malarial.)

Almost invariably Landon's first step was to administer a vomit. Indeed, when
it was near the *period* for the return of an *intermittant*, he was sure that it was
time—no matter what the doctor said—for the patient to be *given a vomit*. When
his daughter Lucy's symptoms told him that she had *a load* of bile *on the stomach*,
the need for a vomit was obvious. Ipecacuana root was Landon's favorite for
emetic purposes; it tops the list of his most used medicines—perhaps because
he also attributed to it a downward bowel-purging, and even a sweat-inducing effect. Sometimes he would just note his satisfaction that the patient had been *relieved by evacuants*. More often he scrutinized and recorded the product of this
vomiting. *The bile discharged seems now to be thicker & more rancid—I suppose owing
to the obstructions being longer continued by reason of the Cold evenings.*

Changing weather produced changing manifestations. In *the middle & last of
July* the bile was *thin*, whereas by mid-August it was *thicker*; and was notable for
its *Green & Yellow* color. In particular cases too, there were distinctive signs to
be read. Old lame George—whose fever had seemed to be removed by a previous vomiting—was found to be afflicted with a cough and *a prodigious difficulty
in breathing*. His new dose (10 grains of Ipecacuana plus a spoonful of Crocus
wine) brought up first *several Gulps of thick yellow Phlegm & one vomit of the same.*

Each case had its own features: thus, with daughter Judy, the manifestation was fever and *yellow bile & very thick*; while daughter Lucy, stricken at about the same time, was producing *green bile*. Examples of this careful recording of the bile, its color and consistency, could be extended and extended, though to little purpose. It is not clear just what the color, so often recorded, indicated to Landon; perhaps it was a persistence of diagnosis in the manner of Galen, where yellow bile was "choler," and so a mark of hotness and dryness. Certainly finding the matter *thick* or *viscid* was a sign—according to the newer would-be-Newtonian physical account of the body—that thinning, or *attenuating* of the *juices* was called for.

Feces (*stools*) were as closely monitored as the vomits, and for the same signs. Once in Lucy's case, the stools were *bilious & thin*; in Samson's case there had been *3 bilious stools*. Betty Oliver was searched for *green bile*, whether coming off *upwards or downwards*. Stools might be judged *purgative* or otherwise, presumably as they did or did not manifest a clearing of offending bile.

An alternative line of treatment after cleansing of the stomach by emetic was to *exhibit* (administer) a sweat-inducing medicine; this was to *attenuate* the blood, to *break* its *viscid* state. The thinning would help work noxious substances out through the pores. Landon never specified that bile would be eliminated this way, but he probably had such expectations. He certainly wrote of treatment that had *produced a breathing sweat & great discharges of urin—and insensibly as it were secreted the byle—and Carry'd it down its proper Channel.*

The preferred medication for blood-thinning and sweating purposes was the one for which Virginia was most famous—or notorious, since it was controversial. Rattlesnake root was only a few points behind ipecacuana at the top of the chart of Landon's most frequently used medicines. (It was named for an American plant, *Polygala senega*, that had a legendary association with the American snake.) Landon valued this medicine for its operation as an expectorant, thinning and bringing off phlegm that caused difficulty breathing. Landon knew rattlesnake root extract to be also a diuretic; but that seemed to be of small account with him since he recorded little concern with, or scrutiny of, urine (which is only twice mentioned and then in passing in the over 160 medical reports analyzed). Often the main intention in giving rattlesnake root was to combat a fever by moderate sweating. A *breathing moisture* or *breathing Sweat* was what Landon looked for as a favorable indication. If such a moderate sweat was not enough, then (as appeared in the case of Samson) there was the hope that *a powerfull sweat* would have *opened the pores*. The promise of effectively combating the fever seemed so great in Samson's case that Landon recorded with force how he *endeavoured to keep this* sweating *up by weak wine diluters—and twice threw in a Spoonful of rattlesnake decoction*. Samson's sweat evidently *continued all night* and till 9 o'clock next day; by that time the diarist found his *flesh* cooler and his pulse not so *quick*. By contrast, when Samson was found to have *a moisture over him* which did *not seem as if it came naturally from his pores*, it had not been a favorable sign.

Often—as Landon apprehended and we would predict—these violent vomits, purges, and sweat-inducing decoctions would produce pronounced exhaustion in the patients. This was then seen as a weakness in the stomach or as nervous disorder, or as both—an affliction of *the Nervous coat* of the stomach. Whole other ranges of treatments were then to be called upon. Here we see how eighteenth-century diagnosis and therapy had discovered the nerves and made them an object of concern second only to the stomach.

When Landon had a patient to revive, he was apt to prescribe *cordials* to stimulate the heart. In December 1757 Landon's beloved daughter Susannah, fondly called Sukey, was *dangerous ill . . . dead pale & blue. . . . He gave her a small cordial to strengthen her*. (It contained *salt tartar, Pulvis Cantian—each 5 grains—in balm tea*.) The next day Sukey's sister, Judy, seemed to have *lost her pulse for two hours*, and lay with *quite dead coldness—& hardly alive—with nervous Catchings in her hands & Jaws*, so that he *fancyed her death near*. He gave a more elaborate reviver—a *weak Julep of rum, water & mint*, with *Pulvis Cantian 5 grains, Salt tartar 5 grains* and *Pulvis Castor 2 grains*, mixed into it. After what must have been a very distraught *2½ hours* he could record his relief that *her pulse beat*; and then that—*after a good sleep—Nature seemed to recover*. Other patients, considered to be of much less delicate constitution, received similar treatment. The enslaved Windsor, driven *mad* by stomach pain, was given *Agua Mirabilis 3 drachms—with a large draft of Strong ginseng tea*.* When that gave substantial *ease*, the patient continued to be given this *cordial*. To remedy the *low state of Sukey's maid, Winney*, Landon prescribed some *warm wine & water—a little cordialed with Cinnamon Water*.

When the weakness—usually introduced by the heroic *cleansing* of the stomach—was clearly seen as *nervous*, a class of medicines that Landon called *proper Nervines* was called for. These were given quite frequently to his own frail-

---

* Readers who have any familiarity with Chinese medicine, now a widely used alternative to mainstream Western clinical medicine, will already have detected before the appearance of ginseng among Landon's medications that the millennia-old Western system practiced by laypersons and doctors alike had a lot in common with the Oriental.

seeming children as fevers (and harsh therapies?) laid them low. The most explicit application came when, on the morning after they both had a bad night, Landon, *being more composed to reason on* Judy's *case concluded that* what he had at first taken to be *the affect of the rhubarb* purge *on a stomach already vomited by the bile*, must, in fact, be signs of *a great relaxation or emptying*. So, *in order to give some degree of warmth to the Nervous coat of her stomach*, he *threw down—in some of her Julep—4 drops tincture Castor*. Landon gave these *nervine* medicines to his daughters upon need. Winney, however, was *with child*; and so, despite the way she grew *very nervously affected*, the diarist saw *danger in using warm nervines*. (Sal ammoniac seems to have been classed in this *nervin* category—as were castor, valerian, spirit of hartshorn, and perhaps oil of lavender.) The masculine character of medical practice became most overtly evident in the case of the enslaved woman Betty Oliver. Her nervous disorder was deemed to be *Hysterick Symptoms*. This patient, Landon thought, was *pretty full in Complaining, being of the kind of Moaning weak hearted Constitution*. For his female patients, this very patriarchal household physician turned most readily to nervins.

A related form of treatment was referred to as using *bitters to brace*, or just as *bracing*, or merely as administering *bitters*. There was a whole commonly accepted narrative behind this in the medical texts of Landon's time: it was a matter of strengthening the fibers. (Anatomy aided by the microscope had given new prominence to nerves and fibers.) An idea of a bracing effect was what gave such importance to the sovereign remedy of the day—Jesuits' or Peruvian bark; it was derived from the South American tree *Cortex cinchona* and is better known to us as quinine bark. Landon wrote a *Note*, in a retrospect on the late-summer fevers of 1757: *I was obliged to give the bark at last in very large doses, a drachm in a dose*. He went on, showing his pride in up-to-dateness: *This used to be the way formerly—but the modern practice has introduced much smaller doses as equally effectual—but this season the great relaxation of the stomach &c. made . . . the use of* larger doses *very necessary after the many large evacuations of the bile—so as to brace as soon as might be. . . .*

The two-year record in the "Farming Observations" notebook reveals clearly that Landon greatly prided himself on applying *modern practice*. He could certainly theorize and narrate cases using the language of physicians. And for his large household he had a whole dispensary. (A much later episode reveals that he referred to the locked room in which the stock of medicines was kept as *the*

shop; still later we learn that it was designated "the Physick shop" by the clerks who inventoried his estate after his death.) Analysis of the range of medicines Landon called upon shows some 64 medicinal substances, compounds, and named mixtures that were prescribed by him over the time of the 1750s plantation journal. An analysis of these brings out certain standard remedies continually employed, such as ipecacuana, quinine bark, and rattlesnake root, but he had many others in reserve for special conditions or rare disorders.

Landon also used surgical procedures. If a fever was identified as *inflammatory*, as in Samson's case, or if there was pronounced bodily pain, as he found amongst his Fork people, then an excess of blood was presumed to have unbalanced the body, and bleeding was indicated. But Landon evidently kept this to a minimum. There are only 14 references to its application in the 160 case reports, and it was never recorded as done to his children. (Bleeding—the drawing of 4 to 6 ounces from a vein in the arm—was not infrequently demanded by patients in the eighteenth century, partly, no doubt, because it was so strongly believed in, but also because it does produce relief, lowering pulse and fever, inducing brief euphoria.) Landon certainly used it to relieve symptoms, even when—since he was treating for worms—no cure could be expected from it. Blood drawn with a scalpel from the arm, was collected in a dish; it could then be inspected by the physician, or the head of the household acting in that role. Landon assessed the condition of the blood in various ways; most often the evaluation was by color and consistency. Thus, when the *near 4 ounces* that were taken from Samson's arm, had *a deep floridness inclining to a black colour*, it indicated that "thinning" was needed. The ensuing course of treatment was part dietary and part medicinal.

Bleeding was not the only surgical procedure designed to bring about a discharge of excessive or disordered fluids. "Blistering" like bleeding, reveals much about beliefs, though it formed a very small part of Landon's regular practice. (It was mentioned only six times—4 percent—compared to the 24 percent of physical procedures recorded for about this period in the Royal Infirmary in Edinburgh.) Intense and persistent local pain, usually deemed to be the settling of a fever in a particular part of the body, seems to have been the principal indication for blistering. (The procedure itself was the bandaging on of an extreme irritant compound which drew out serum by raising a large blister.) The diarist never specified what he used as his blistering compound, but probably it was Spanish fly as supplied by apothecaries—a preparation of the Mediterranean cantharides beetle that had been in use since Roman times. One example: Brickhouse Nanny's fever seemed to have cleared, but, by sitting out in the cold, she had given a *check* to the promising cure that should be *working off in breathing sweats.* The illness had returned as violent *pain in her neck, head & small of her back.* So, Landon *applyed a blister,* because, he explained, *there might be an obstruction in the upper vessels.*

Landon sometimes treated for what he knew to be invasive organisms rather than what he imagined as imbalances in the humors or obstructions in the flow of juices; his diagnoses and therapies then more nearly paralleled those of our own day. When the diarist came to suspect an infestation of worms in the stomach or intestines, he initiated therapies to poison and dislodge them. His description of the condition and its treatment could be most dramatic. It was mid-March 1758 when he *found worms to be the occasion of all the Coughs* that now afflicted his *people.* These coughs were *only such as the titillation of those animals in the stomach would occasion,* and, *although there was a Sort of expectorated Pus* (which was a favorable sign of the body expelling diseased matter)—*yet the pains were not relieved till the removal of the animals.* In order to effect the expulsion of the worms, the patriarch drew from a small arsenal of (mainly) mercurial medicines. In this case, after he had *bled to relieve the Symptoms,* he gave *Mercurius Dulcis in Purges . . . and a Course of* apothecary's *worm powders.* A close scrutiny of the *stool* would follow; he could then count the worms voided. Reasoning upon these observations, the scientific planter once concluded, from *all experience,* that what appeared like *slimy gourd seeds,* were actually what he could *pronounce to be parts of the Joint worm.*

A considerable part of Landon's household practice was inevitably on children; sometimes he reviewed their cases collectively, as with the *many Children* who *swelled after the fevers left them.* There were also *many negroe Children* who had been *ill with the ague & fever,* they had all received treatment with worm medicine. This latter batch of cases occasioned additional anxiety. Landon thought a strong remedy was probably needed for his own children, but fearing that they were too delicate, he did not give it to them. As a practitioner, this father knew the violence of his treatments, hence, the quite frequent *emolient* drugs, cordials, and tonics that he applied to *correct* for that.

The social and racial aspects of this part of the practice appear powerfully in one of the most skillfully shaped of the many medical narratives in this 1750s scientific observation book. Under the date December 13, 1757, Landon unfolded quite a story. There is a striking artfulness to the opening that this middle-aged widower gave to a narrative that would have as its main focus a daughter's stomach upset!

It is necessary that man should be acquainted with affliction & 'tis certainly nothing short of it to be confined a whole year in tending one's sick Children. Mine are now never well. Indeed I may believe there are many reasons for it besides the Constitution of the air— which has been very bad.

I have none but negroes to tend my children—nor can I get anyone else—and they use or accustom *their own children to such loads of Gross food that they are not Judges when a child not so used to be exposed to different weathers—& not so inured to exercise—comes to eat. They let them—*my children—*press their appetites as their own children did and thus they are constantly sick.*

Judy Carter . . . by being suffered after her dinner to sup some of her sister's barley broth—yesterday took in such a load as could not be contained in her stomach—& this day she was seized with a natural vomiting.

Landon went on to recount how, in spite of his intervention (with *Ipecacuana to help to clear the overburthened stomach*), and his initial success in *bringing off a good deal of filth & Bile*, the treatment had *too powerfull an effect on her weak stomach.*

Landon emphasized the difference between the bodies of young *negroes* and those of his own children. In this case and elsewhere he is postulating what we would call racial distinctions, although he remains within an ancient set of theories predating the evolutionary and genetic ideas that dominated later-nineteenth- and early-twentieth-century ideologies. It is clear from the records he kept, however, that Landon's diagnoses and treatments were almost never racially based. However, Landon must have been aware of a body of theory and practice that he was resolutely silent about in his diary: namely, the African American healing arts that would time and again have been the first and continuing resort of ailing persons at the Sabine Hall quarters. (As already noted in discussion of the worldview implied by Landon's style and range of reference in regard to the rural landscape, the diarist seems intent on maximizing an evocation of an old-world lordly estate, where control and meaning were supposed to derive from the culture of the master. The diarist must therefore deny the exotic, alien culture of the work force that his new-world colonial circumstances actually gave him.) The nearest we get to an acknowledgment of alternative healing practitioners was his free use of the term that then described them—"conjurors." Only Landon displaced his scorn, using the word as a way of dismissing the ill-founded theories (as he saw them) of his son and other antagonists in agricultural-science debates.

Landon's last developed medical narrative in this notebook unfolds not so much social, racial, and environmental themes, as cosmic, moral, and eternal-judgment ones. Judy, the subject of the preceding brief narrative, did survive her childhood ailments. Indeed, we have already followed how, by her elopement and forbidden marriage, she lived on to greatly vex her father. But Susannah, Landon's *dear Sukey*, did not live as long. She had received a high proportion of the diarist's recorded medical attentions; she was the subject of about a quarter of all his reports, nearly twice as many as any other individual patient. As her illness worsened, her frailty even made her father shrink from venturing to treat her himself. He kept in touch with the medical aspects of her case, yet his tenderness, and pious self-examination came to overshadow that. In reasonable health during early spring, little Sukey had gone to visit at a neighbor's house—Gilbert Hamilton's—where presumably she had a friend of her own age (although no mention of that is made). Within a few days her malaria, her intermittent fever, returned and never left her for a fortnight. The anxious father saw her then at that neighboring house. *Dr Flood could not be got to her* immediately; Landon wrote in anguish that, *My fears will not let me practice on her—as her case is of so Chronick a kind.* (Perhaps that was why he had let her remain at the Hamilton's house.) After one briefly successful medical intervention—predictably with *gentle evacuations*—the father withdrew and left matters to the doctor. In trepidation he awaited news. None is recorded for nine days—until April 16, when Landon wrote: *Received advice from Mr Hamilton's that my daughter Sukey was now grown very weak with her fevers. Dr Flood had sent her a purge. . . . which had brought off. . . nothing but thin Slime—& she could not move without help. . . . She was going into a hectic . . . so that I almost dispair of her.*

Six days later, matters were worse: *My dear Sukey is now most dangerous ill at Mr Hamilton's.* The doctor's continued purges had only brought off a further *abundance of Green Slime—but . . . no abatement of her hectic heat. She had by then also a tickling Cough and a Small pain in her chest.* Landon was brought now to a state of great fearfulness: *I dispair of her life.* He could only call on his religious faith: *God only knows—and I calmly submit. If she recovers I shall be greatly thankfull for the blessing—for she is the most Patient, most Sensible and most engaging infant that ever parent had.* The anxious father was schooling himself in pious acceptance: *If she dyes I shall remember the rod that chastises and learn to amend by it.* The next day's news was worse: *Poor Sukey near her last. Her disorder encreases and her strength decreases. Mr Hamilton thinks she must mend speedily or dye in a very little time.*

Two days later an early morning report heralded the end:
This morning Mr Gilbert Hamilton (at whose house my dear little daughter Susannah has been ever since her last illness) sent me an account of her death certainly approaching—And he says in his letter, although her face, feet and hands are all cold—& her pulse quite gone—& she reduced to the bones & skin that cover them—& dying very hard under the Severe agonys of her disorder—Yet does she preserve her Usual Patience to such a degree that he never saw such an Example before.

Seeking to control his emotions by accepting now what seemed already inevitable, the distraught father went on: *Severe stroke indeed to A Man bereft of a wife and in the decline of life—because at such periods 'tis natural to look out for such Connections that may be reasonably expected to be the support of Grey hairs—and such an one I had promised myself in this child in Particular.* The lament soon became the prologue to his epitaph for the beloved child he was losing even as he wrote. He used line breaks and capitalization as it might be for verse or a tombstone inscription:

For although she did not live beyond the very Dawn
Of humane life,
Such were the early discoverys of her growing Excellencys
It might be justly concluded That had the same Soul
Animated to a Mature Age A more healthy Frame
She would have been a Conspicuous Pattern if not inimitable
Even amongst the most Prudent, Good & Virtuous
Of her Sex
God Omnipotent.

Then came a grieving prayer in which the writer sought to find a redeemed sense of himself from the blessed character of this last of his progeny. He addressed himself to the God whose chastising *rod* he was teaching himself *to amend by*:
Could it have consisted with thy divine Purposes to have suffered this blessing to have continued to me—my happiness would have been uncommon—but as thou hast otherwise determined it—It is enough to lay the Obligation of a constant gratefull return to thy divine Goodness that thou was't pleased to Suffer me to be the instrument of so Promising a humane Creature—For in this shall I comfort myself that I was not myself altogether Corrupt—or thou wouldest not have so signally dignifyd such a Stock by a

Scion so universally applauded by All who knew her—and this before she could have received any of the Advantages of Education. In her therefore Pure Nature must have been pure Goodness.

Reverting to the scientific, "philosophic" purposes of his observation book, the sorrowing father, who had been comforting himself by finding vindication in his lost child, went on without a line or paragraph break to write a concluding midday medical summary of *poor Sukey's* end, as it had been reported to him. He thus added a little to his science of fevers and of the causes of death: *She dyed between 11 & 12—the constant period of intermission of her fever from the day of her attack and it never changed this from that day but once—when it was believed Dr Flood's medicin prolonged the time of intermission for more than 12 hours—but 'tis now certain her disorder lay in her breast—and I suppose the breaking of that impostumation finished her.*

Landon had set down a terse form of words in which he explained how *intermittent fever* had not been the killer in itself; it had been overtaken by a deadly *impostumation* or abscess. Yet this reasoning to a conclusion could not re-engage his interest in the science of healing. The diarist master had been closely following the development of the illness of Susannah's maid, Winney. He had brought her home and tended to her, even while he dared not do the same for his little daughter. With Sukey's death, Landon stopped analysing Winney's condition. Indeed, for two days he wrote no more than three words; and there were no more sustained medical narratives entered into this first of his plantation observation books.

Once again Landon's plantation diary—his thinking aloud about the scientific issues of his day—opens to us more than a specialized field of knowledge. Through his articulation of commonplace beliefs of his time, we see aspects of the cosmology, the imagined universe of those educated gentlemen who led in the creation of the American republic. Few if any of the laymen patriots who joined to declare independence and then to give "constitutions" to the new states of the new nation would have studied and practiced medicine as Landon did. But they all shared his understandings of health and sickness: they too saw the physical self as a microcosm of the vast system of the universe. The founding fathers in their search to endow America with sound "constitutions" drew on that cosmic understanding; they knew that balance was essential, whether the object of care was a biological or a political body.

PART III

POLITICS,
WAR, AND REBELLION

Landon's diaries crossed a great political divide. The first surviving volume covers sessions of the Virginia General Assembly for the years 1752 to 1755, and so it unfolds a record of colonial patriotic engagement by a loyal province of the British Empire, then at war with France. Toward the end of that struggle, the Americans as part of a "Greater Britain" could share in a general exaltation at the victories of their nation. But soon that exultation turned into the bitterness of rejection and betrayal.

The British Parliament's Stamp Act of 1765 levied taxes on the Americans without their consent; they seemed to be treated more as a conquered people than as equal participants in conquest. The 1766 volume of Landon's diary opens as all British North America is in outright revolt against the government of the protector king, who seemed suddenly to have turned tyrant.

The pair of chapters that follow show the two sides of the great divide: the first shows the diarist in devoted service to his "country" (always his word for Virginia), and so to his king and the empire; the second shows the trauma of embarking on rebellion—when no other path seemed possible.

Chapter 7

Landon, Legislator

It is time to reverse the turning over of that first diary, that leather-bound quarto notebook. It is time to go back from the Enlightenment philosophic observations of the plantation journal to the Assembly reporting for which the book was acquired.

That leather-bound volume in its first use is a little gem of a procedural handbook become political commentary and exposé. In it is strongly revealed the perspective of an independent country gentleman coming for the first time into his colonial legislature; he is shocked to find not free votes according to the merits of the arguments but everything fixed by the brokers of power. And then he experiences a face-to-face encounter with a manifestation of how cruel empire is to those who cherish illusions of their own liberty within it. Next, he is valiantly striving to provide for the defense of his country against the despotic French and their Indians allies. He certainly did not consider that the Indians might be striving to provide for the defense of their country.

Provincial Politics, 1752—An Independent Against the System

Landon Carter's burgess diary began when. . . . But no, like everything in everybody's lives, it really began long before he was born, when the ways of doing things and the systems of relationship that the diary both expresses and records were established and brought to Virginia. Those English ways were run up against the ways of the Native Americans and in time adjusted to live with and learn from the ways of the enslaved Africans. In the new land those ways evolved, but they remained self-consciously, even willfully, English. So this parliamentary diary project was already in gestation when little Landon was sent to school in London, the center of the empire, and it came another step nearer actualization when he returned home and became involved in local government. The diary did not, however, begin to take material form until 1752 when, at the age of 41, Landon was finally elected to sit in the legislature of his "Country."

Landon was already very well read in history, law, and politics—especially in the revered British Constitution and its law of parliament. He faced high expectations as he came into the Assembly; his family was part of the ruling circle in Virginia, and it is clear that he was already esteemed a capable man of business. Thus, Landon expected to move expertly through the intricate, custom-bound transactions of the legislature; his first notes were concerned with procedures. Before long, however, he went beyond that narrow objective; his journal became a rich record of provincial politicking. The proceduralist became more and more the wry commentator on his own independent gentleman's confrontations with the political *Byg man*—likened to a Pasha (*Bashaw*) of the despotic Ottoman Empire. The country squire presented himself as one who was governed by reason and the balance of the arguments; he depicted the Speaker of the House John Robinson as one who arbitrarily imposed his own will, making his fellow legislators into inconsistent and contemptible creatures. There is, however, a restraint in Landon's reports of the speaker's overbearing ways, a restraint not found in the angry narratives of the plantation-and-household diary of twenty years later. There is also a lightening of these narratives with flashes of the mirth enjoyed in this boyish debating club, where members attempted to practice wit at each others' expense.

Then in early April 1752, there had come the bombshell. Suddenly the burgesses and their legislative colleagues in the upper house, the King's Council, were compelled to face their true dependent and subordinate status in the great geopolitical hierarchy of pan-Atlantic empire. The governor informed them that the King's Privy Council had disallowed some seventeen of their statutes enacted at the end of the previous session of the Assembly in 1749. Thus were they abruptly confronted with the ultimate location of power in their colonial world.*

The subjects of the British monarchy on both sides of the ocean had long told themselves that—living only under laws that they gave themselves—they were the freest men on earth. But if some Britons wielded arbitrary power in the king's name, others would come under their heels. The requirement that the king rule through Parliament seemed to secure the liberties of Britons "at home;" but if those who wielded the king's and Parliament's power had no compunction about disallowing the laws made by the lesser parliaments of the colonies, the question arose: where then was the freedom of those colonial Britons? Landon's political life was led in the stress of this question. The problem became increasingly acute as the American colonies matured and articulated more and more of the rising tones of liberty-loving British patriotism. Certainly the diarist's career as a Virginia burgess was an education in the perplexity of these ultimately irreconcilable conflicts. But in 1752 no one yet questioned the system; they had to try to negotiate a way round the impasse by representations back home—as Landon and many others, like him Virginia-born, still called England.

First in his recording came the careful monitoring of procedures in this three-part General Assembly, modeled on the British Parliament. The elected House of Burgesses matched the British House of Commons; the King's Council was the upper house corresponding to the House of Lords, though its members, appointed by the king, could in no way be equivalent to the hereditary nobility of England; presiding was the lieutenant-governor, performing the king's part, though he too lacked the high majesty of a royal sovereign.

At the start the members had to ascend to the Council Chamber, where they found the councilors sitting and commissioned by governor to hear them

---

* There was another constant reminder of priorities in the empire: Robert Dinwiddie, Virginia's governor was actually only a lieutenant-governor. The Duke of Albemarle, who held the full governor's commission, considered his affairs in Britain too important to be left while he attended to the government of a mere colony. The duke paid a deputy, whom the king commissioned to act in his stead. (For brevity's sake—and because Landon made the same adjustment—Dinwiddie and his successor will be referred to as "the governor" throughout this book.) In 1768, when the next lieutenant-governor had to be replaced, the imperial authorities, anxious to do more to mollify their increasingly estranged colonies, insisted that the full governor must reside in the colony. Lord Botetourt accordingly came out in 1769. After his untimely death in 1770, his successor, the Earl of Dunmore, whom we have already met, was also a full governor—the last such royal appointee ever.

repeat a series of solemn oaths.* Once returned to their own chamber, they were summoned into the presence of the governor himself, and directed to *Return to the House and Choose a Speaker.* They duly reelected John Robinson, his fourth term in the office since his first elevation in 1738. The next piece of ceremony was thus to prepare and deliver a reply to that address—for which a committee must be appointed. Here Landon got his first assignment, in clear recognition that he was already an acknowledged penman.

Governor Dinwiddie's speech and the House's reply were both reported in the official *Journal of the House of Burgesses*; both are revealing of the prevailing ideology of colonial government. From the start, the governor had to present himself as the bearer of the king's commission; but, on his own behalf, he also gave assurances of his "Zeal for the Good of this Colony." His rhetoric was charged with the phraseology of the prevailing Enlightenment age of sensibility: it would be his "Inclination and Endeavour . . . to cultivate those Virtues of a social Nature;" and his "Affection" for them all would be "a Spring of Pleasure in [his] Breast."

The governor had also one great policy matter to lay before them; his most particular charge to the Assembly was an exhortation for "the cultivating a good Correspondence with the Neighbouring Nations of Indians." If the "Love and Amity" of these nations was secured, he went on, "our European Neighbours, who are settled to the Southward and Northward of us, would never be able to inflame the Indians against us. . . ." Then the governor's address returned to the ideology of the monarchy: if the Assembly did its duty in this and every other way to be expected from "good Christians and good Subjects," then it would not only "enjoy the Prayers and Blessings . . . of the whole Colony," but would "deserve the paternal Affection of his Majesty; and . . . be intitled to the Favour of Almighty God, who, that we might consider each other as Brethren, has not disdain'd to be called the Father of us all."

The reply that Landon drafted rang interesting changes on these words, through allusion, omission, and reordering: "We his Majesty's most dutiful, and loyal Subjects, the Burgesses of Virginia, . . . return your Honour our cordial Thanks for your affectionate speech. . . . Being truly sensible of his

---

* These oaths marked them all as truly sworn advisers of "His [Protestant] Britannic Majesty." The members and their clerk not only pledged their allegiance to the king but also had to enter a solemn recognition of their sovereign as "Supreme Head of the Established Church of England." Furthermore they had to prove themselves to be not even secret adherents of Roman Catholicism; they must declare their detestation of that church's dogma of the eucharistic transubstantiation of the bread and wine into the body and blood of Christ.

Majesty's Paternal Care, for this his most antient Colony, in appointing a Person of such approved Abilities. . . . When we reflect on those social Virtues, with which your Honour hath . . . distinguished yourself amongst us, we cannot but promise ourselves . . . an equitable and well ordered Government. And we . . . shall on our Parts endeavour . . . to . . . serve the common Interest of this Country. By such a Conduct we doubt not but we shall . . . obtain the Continuance of the Grace and Favour of that Omnipotent Being, who hath not disdained to be called the Father of us all."

Landon's draft was adopted. Then both it and the Council's reply were presented to the governor in a further little ceremony. Landon entered a proud note in that day's entry of his burgess diary: *All the best Judges say the Address of the House is by* far *Preferable to the Council's & so say I—by much*. In the exchange, Robert Dinwiddie had articulated explicitly the still prevailing patriarchal ideology of God as the supreme Father, with the king as the ruling earthly father under Him, in a cosmos still thus imagined as a great hierarchy of paternal authority; Landon, in drafting the reply of the burgesses, had affirmed this ideology from below. Landon was taking satisfaction in a little encapsulation of the assumptions sustaining the old regime of monarchy just two-and-a-half decades before its overthrow. Even when the crisis of the 1765 Stamp Act had introduced notes of discord, the Virginia Assembly was still making a claim for the patriarchal protection of their monarch; their "Remonstrance" of 1766 recalled how, as loyal subjects, "they had frequently applied to their King and common Father."

The English Parliament from its inception had been considered a high court in the realm—indeed *the* high court. Courts, after all, were still conceptualized as meeting places where subjects came to seek justice and redress of grievances from their sovereign rulers. The Virginia General Assembly was in this tradition, and there is a sense in which the House of Burgesses functioned like a county court writ large to serve the entire colony. It adjudicated cases (especially disputed elections relating to its own membership); it received petitions; and it assessed claims of many sorts. It differed from the lower courts (as did Parliament) in that it could pass statutes, by which it made new laws and revised old ones. Landon had already been doing this work in a county court for nearly twenty years; there the work was partly the administration of criminal justice and the resolution of small property disputes, but it also involved adjudication of claims and review of petitions for various forms of compensation. As a new burgess, Landon entered keenly into the more exalted version of this work; he maintained a pragmatic country squire's view that law must ultimately be reason and justice derived from common sense. He separated himself fiercely from the *Attorneys* in his reports on proceedings in the House; he would even disparage them as having only a kind of *Mechanical knowledge*— knowing merely from whom to copy the forms of words they were so pernickety about! On one occasion when he expressed himself strongly on a legal matter, he boasted that: *Mr. Attorney & the other Lawyers chewed the Expression over and endeavour'd to return it, but they could not. It was too true. Carry'd the motion by a large Majority.*

Most petitions to the House were received and reviewed by the Committee of Propositions and Grievances, on which Landon had a place. He brought in at least one of the petitions ("propositions") from Richmond and from Charles City Counties *for the restraining the Number of dogs kept by Slaves and Servants.* The committee voted the proposal to be reasonable; but two days later Landon had to record that, when the Committee's findings were reported to the whole House, instead of agreed action, there ensued *a great debate . . . in which Colonel Charles Carter, myself, Martin, and others Spoke fully but to no Purpose—It was rejected by two voices—the reason many members were absent.*

Landon persisted, perhaps because he counted on the support of those absent at that vote. This was his first legislative proposition, perhaps one he had promised his constituents to take up; he meant to see it through. That rejection had been on Friday, March 6; but on Monday, March 9, he noted: *I mov'd for leave to bring in a bill for restraining & Lessening the no of Doggs in Northumberland, Westmoreland, Richmond, Lancaster, & King George* Counties. He evidently secured that leave, although not seconded as promised by his colleague, John Woodford, the senior burgess for Richmond. (The counties named were all in Landon's own Northern Neck between the Potomac and Rappahannock rivers.)

On Saturday, March 14, Landon reported that he was going forward, and that the wits were preparing to ridicule him. *The bill for lessening the Number of Doggs in some particular Counties read the first time. Our Wise heads are full of Observations upon the distinction in the bill between Doggs and bitches, but nothing yet said* in debate. *No doubt they will get them ready to bring them forth.*

Then, on the Monday, *the Dogg bill had the 2d reading.* But there was trouble. Landon had reproached Benjamin Waller for supporting the speaker in another resolution of the House that seemed an insult to Charles Carter, the older brother Landon looked up to. *I told Waller it was ill natured to Oppose so reasonable a motion—upon which with great Warmth he vowed he'd throw out my Dogg bill—as he call'd it. Upon this I defyed him.*

This local bill to which Landon had devoted himself was in trouble from start to finish. Its author was proud of how he had steered it through the House, even past the third-reading stage and the mockery of the wits. *I got the blanks filled up—and then Made an Anticipating Speech—in which I raised all the Objections started without doors and answered them. Upon* which *the Buffoon Reddick—a* member for a southeastern Tidewater county—*got up and—because he was Ridiculous to make people laugh—Pleased many and Concluded with a Verse that now he hoped to send it to the Lethean Shoar where he hoped never to hear of it more.* Upon which I replyed that it was a humane failing not to know at what People laught or at* whom—*but if he delighted in being a laughing stock, I gave him joy of it,—and for his Verse I would agree to dubb him the Laureat of the house.* Also *that I could blush for him—but As I saw he was a stranger to Shame—I would pay him no such Compliments. . . .*
My bill Pass'd—and—by order of the House—*I waited on the Council to Present it.*

Alas, Landon's first legislative commission ended not on the statute books but in the graveyard for buried bills. He had taken it upstairs on Thursday, March 19. By the Saturday he knew the worst. *I hear'd this day the Council threw the dog bill out 4 to 3. No reason given for it—and indeed I must believe they had none—unless it was to save Doggs which some are fond of.*

Landon had some consolation in the applause he had been able to record for his engagement with other measures. He came off well against Mr. Martin, a keen debater and gentleman of consequence as a member of the mighty Fairfax family. Landon boasted that *if the Praise of Everybody and a Vote of the whole House but three—entitles me to value myself, I answered Mr. Martin as Close as the method he took Could bear. . . . Some Gentlemen told me—and not a few—so handsome a Speech and so Close an answer they never had met with.*

The *Dogg bill* was a side show and Mr. Reddick, the *Buffoon,* a cipher, when compared to the politics of Landon's clashes with the powerful House Speaker John Robinson. There had been some early tussles. There was disagreement about the authority over the Virginia burgesses of a *standing order of*

---

* In ancient mythology, the river Lethe had to be crossed to reach Hades, the domain of the dead.

"The byg man." A portrait of the House of Burgesses Speaker John Robinson by John Wollaston Jr. *Colonial Williamsburg Foundation.*

the British *House of Commons.* Landon doubted the speaker's ruling. *I never read any such* standing order—*and in my Speach I argued strongly against it. But, in a Private Conference with the Speaker,* Landon found that, although his reasoning was not disallowed, Mr. Robinson nevertheless insisted his own ruling should stand.

The extent of what seemed the speaker's improper use of influence suddenly confronted Landon when the House came to what was expected to be the most important work of legislation for the session. The legislators had to revise the Tobacco Act, which was a comprehensive set of inspection regulations to maintain export standards. This was no Dogg Bill; the official inspectors were men continually exercising real power over farmers' and gentlemen's livelihoods. On March 12, 1752, the House turned itself into a Committee of the Whole. Under this arrangement, its proceedings were secret, off the record, until, reverting to its normal form, it reported to itself the results of its committee deliberations. (This procedure, like so much else, followed the traditions of the British mother Parliament.) A change of chairman was involved. On the one hand, Landon's esteemed brother Charles had the very considerable honor of being chairman now in charge of the House; but, on the other hand, that enabled the *Byg man,* released from the restraints applied to a presiding officer, to present his own proposals and debate the proposals of others, undertaking political management in a very open way.

The House went into a Committee and debated sundry amendments in the tobacco Law. Every one of them proposed by a Certain Gentleman was agreed to <u>Natu Signisque loquuntur</u>.* If any dared to Oppose, some Severe Expression unbecoming the Speaker's dignity was immediately thundered out. For example, Carter Burwell spoke for amendment. . . . I seconded him.

Here that Gentleman rose, ridiculed the thing. . . .

I modestly answer'd that it was not inconsistent with this Assembly to do it. . . .

Upon which he told the Chairman I had no other method of Arguing but by making wrong Observations that I might hold forth upon. . . .

After this I opposed an Amendment for Certyfying the Sort of tobacco. . . .

But this Gentleman—according to his Usual Way—told the Committee I only argued against inspectors in General.

To this I answered in return of his Compliment that my words were plain enough—but the affectation of blindness I observed was Sometimes a proper method to furnish out a Speech with.

Here he said I was witty—and so the question was put—& carry'd against me.

He also overrul'd an Amendment of William Randolph's, I believe because I seconded it. . . . This was unanimously agreed to till that Gentleman spoke . . . —and then it ran against the Amendment.

Afterwards I proposed an Amendment that Inspectors should not be concerned In the Picking for their own profit *the tobacco Condemned by them. . . . Here he did not know what to say. . . . However, it was enough he show'd himself Against it—and so by a Great Majority the Amendment was lost—although many other Gentlemen said in the house they knew many* inspectors *to have gotten above 15 or 16,000 pounds of tobacco per annum that way. Of this Sort went it all day. Whatever he agreed to was Carryed—and whatever he Opposed dropt.*

To Landon, it appeared that the speaker had a consistent strategy whenever he wanted to manage every detail of the business under discussion: *he beckons . . . a Member whom he knows* will do his bidding. . . . *& having his lesson,* that member *moves for a Commitment to the* Committee of the *Whole House.*

The next day produced more demonstrations of the speaker's dominance. When the House resumed in Committee of the Whole, Landon tried to choose his moment:

---

* Approximate English: "They speak with the weight of high-born rank."

I waited till the 52d Section of the Act. . . . Here I moved for an Amendment That Inspectors might only Inspect the tobacco at the Warehouses. . . .

And as I told Colonel Thornton—so it happened.

The Byg man arose in Opposition after Mr. Woodbridge had seconded me—and—by throwing the most absurd arguments—endeavoured to Overset me. . . .

I told the Chairman that I expected Opposition and was so Unhappy as to know the very Spot from Whence it should Issue—but surely the Gentleman must be a better Judge of reasoning. . . . But I was in hopes the Committee would not always be bore down by weight without reason.

Mr. Ben. Waller, who had promised me to be silent in the debate—and who had before declared he knew nothing of tobacco,—Observing that the Speaker would now lose his Point—and taking a Nodd—and with the most ridiculous supposition . . . —expressed his dislike to the Amendment. And so—with this Union of Interest—only 25 on a division were for the Amendment.

Landon's own kin even seemed to play along: *I must Observe that Colonel Carter Burwell pusht me with his cain to make the motion—and then opposed it. . . .*

What then was the use of debate?

So fair well to Committees of the whole house. For there he sits—and what he can't do himself he prompts others to do by his nodds,—nay to hollow out aloud,—as the division must run to whatever side he sits . . . —and I'll suffer death if in these days he looses a motion.

It is not only my observation. Even his friends told me it would be so. And I did hear that Some Sessions agoe he lost a motion in the Committee of the Whole House—and he gave such proofs of his Resentment that no Stone was unturned to Please the Worthy Gentleman.

The consistency of these outcomes was Landon's proof for his diary record that power was overbearing reason.

I observed a Silent Joaker on his right hand never to leave him. Now I'll be hanged if—in such a Multitude of Motions etc.—it could be possible that two people—without any other influence than of bare reason—could always be so exactly of one Opinion. How unhappy must a Country be should such a man be byased with vitious Principles. I do absolutely declare that the use of any but this one Member is Needless—for 'tis but only to get all things into this Grand Committee and then he's all in All.

It is interesting that Landon stopped short of actually attributing *vitious Principles* to the speaker.

By the end of the next day (a Saturday) the speaker wanted to show the Carter brothers and their friends who was in charge. Charles, the Chairman of the Whole, needing to go away over the weekend, had moved for the next session of this committee to be on the Tuesday—*as he could not attend . . . soon enough on Monday. But Mr. Speaker nodded to Benjamin Waller—and by their joint interest it was put off only till Monday, and* it was said, *if the Chairman could not Attend, another might be appointed.* Landon could only comment sourly that, *This would be ill manners to any but a Carter, but to those it seems it is not.* He added a note: *A Gentleman told me that the Members all Agree that the Bashaw used me ill in the Committee of the whole House.*

A sudden turn of events soon ended Landon's frustrated isolation in the face of determined political management; the action of powers above and beyond Virginia came near to uniting the colonial elite at the end of the session.

There were still two tough political games being played in town, however. (Landon's reporting of both point up his sense of himself as an independent country gentleman suspicious of the machinations of courtiers.) One game was an attempt by some in the House to renew a failed earlier attempt to make a large gift of money to the governor. They had tried this once already; and he was sure that they had been so *Cunning as to design it because I was absent—for they knew I should oppose it.*

Now: *Ralph Wormeley . . . moved a 2d time for £500 to the Governour. Seconded by* Richard *Bland.*

I objected to the Regularity of it—reviving a matter already laid to rest.

And so did Edmund *Pendleton.*

But *the Speaker said the former motion not being entered* in the official Journal *it was as no motion—and therefore it might be moved again.*

I differed with the Chair. . . .

Bland then harangued in behalf of the Governour—as did *Power and Martin.*

I answered them all. Spoke long and modestly.

It was overruled again.

The other tough game was a push to get the seat of government moved away from Williamsburg; it was succeeding. Speaker Robinson was not exerting himself to oppose; probably he knew the King's Council would veto the scheme. So it proved. Four days later Landon exclaimed that not one council member supported the move, though some of them had been in favor of such a measure when they had been burgesses. *As Councillors they are against it.* Landon's sarcastic comment was: *'Tis a pity men should run like Bowls.* (Landon, like many Virginia gentlemen, had at his country house a green for lawn bowls; the

curved path of the biased balls made a striking metaphor to decry the devious-
ness of these politicians in the governor's ruling circle.)

By Tuesday, April 7, the Assembly felt itself to have done most of its business;
it was tidying up and winding down. Bills were being finished off; disagree-
ments between the houses were being adjusted; and the claims books were
finalized. Landon was doing part of what was expected of him by endeavoring
to look after his constituents; it seemed a time for small deeds in a very provincial legislature. And then, these games of local politics were interrupted by a
brusque assertion of imperial power. Landon's way of recording the sudden interruption is striking. His further commentary foreshadows the politics that
would later embroil him—and all the American supporters of the Revolution.

*In the God Sped of this Joye came News from England that ten of the Acts passed last
Session* had been *repealed by Proclamation. 57 passed the Royal Assent, and many lay
unobserved*—neither repealed nor assented to. *In the God Sped of this Joye. . . .*
What could he mean? Was it an ironic comment on the Council's vetoing of the
bill to move the seat of government to York and therefore closer to Sabine
Hall? Perhaps it reflects sarcastically on the joyless wheeling and dealing he was
weary of fighting. There is no doubt, however, that these lines mark a complete
change of mood and outlook. *This was a great damp—and will be the Cause of a
Sum* of money *to the Governor to get these things represented home—that they are in-
jurious to us—and also* it will be the cause *of a much longer Assembly.* With that,
Landon could only try to bring back to mind some of the juvenile humor that
had lightened work of the session. *Yesterday Reddick turned Rhyming buffoon
again—and had the happyness to be the Ass of the house.*

But the legislators were confronted with a necessity for action:
Wednesday 8.
*This day, after reading a few engrossed bills to send up to Council and receiving others
Just put in—the Governour sent us a Message . . . That he commanded the immediate
attendance of the House in the Council Chamber. Upon Which we waited upon him,
and in a kind Manner he communicated to us a List of the 57 Acts that had received the
Royal Assent and of the ten that had been repealed.*

It was serious. Among the repealed acts was the statute regulating, and so le-
galizing, the proceedings of the Colony's General Court since its passage in
1749. As he wrote the report in his diary record, Landon was impelled to go on
and review the meaning of what was happening to American colonists in the
empire of a nation supposedly dedicated to liberty but, in fact, governed by intrigues at its center. Acting by private influence on the Privy Council, British
opponents could get a Virginia law disallowed, or if these same manipulators

approved of a law, they could get it assented to, and then its amendment back in Virginia was obstructed.

By the by I must observe that an Act of Assembly is now a trifling thing—both from the possibility of getting them passed with *the Royal Assent or repealed in a Clandestine manner. . . . After the Royal Assent* is *obtained, it seems—although they may be amended or Repealed* in the colony, *yet it must always be with a Salvo to his Majesty untill his Royal Pleasure shall be known. By which means the force of the Act must be suspended for a long time. . . . And the Repealing of a Law not affecting the Mother Country but purely relating to the . . . Particular good of the Country where it is enacted, I say, passing such a repeal—without the application of that People—is to do them an injury.*

Suddenly Landon saw a whole system revealed, and in it the probabilities of abuse. Opponents of a law, whether British or Virginian, motivated by private interests, would not have to negotiate their objections before the representatives of the colonial people; they could arrange secret deals in faraway London. *Besides the suffering* inflicted on the colony, *such a Method of underhand practice must be introductory of All imaginable Bribery &c.*

The burgesses promptly made it their most urgent business to confer with the Council about ways to clean up the legislative mess created by the sudden annulment of laws actively in force. They already knew that they would have the arduous—and probably fruitless—task of preparing written statements in support of those laws they wished to have reinstated.

Landon's abilities and independence were esteemed; he was now enlisted as one of six leading men of business to meet with Council nominees to negotiate this all-important imperial matter. They speedily prepared and got adopted certain crucial recommendations: to reinstate the suddenly invalidated proceedings in the colony's General Court; to make representations *to his Majesty of our Unhappyness*, so as to have him reverse the rulings of his privy council; and to enlist the governor in those representations to the crown.

Meanwhile, the joint committee had to get on with the task of formulating the representation to be sent back *home* to England. *Many methods were proposed of Addressing his Majesty—but, as it is seeming to Prescribe to his Prerogative, the most humble is to be used.* That in itself probably did not sit well with the fiercely pro-liberty Landon. Besides he had a feeling that the address, however well drafted, might be futile:

This Representation is no ways disagreeable to me—and the Gentleman that drew it hit the Sense of the Committee, but whether it will meet the desired Effect is what I doubt of—because it all runs against a thing done by the Advice of the board of trade and of the

Privy Council at home—and it is not easy to imagine the King would consent to undo what they have advized him to do—or that those boards to whom this Representation and these reasons are to be referred . . . —would be easyly perswaded to contradict their own advice. However, <u>Audendum Si vis Esse Aliquid</u>. [One must dare, if one is to amount to anything.]

Then there was final business. On Saturday, the House learned that their *resolution for £500 to the Governor* as a fee *was refused by him*; so the words were changed to make it an unconditional gift. Landon felt now compelled to give support; he noted *that it would appear to us all that he would do the Services We required, vizt, the Soliciting our Representation to the King.*

At this late stage in his diary of this session, Landon reverted to his earlier project for this personal burgess diary notebook; he was again recording the details of procedures. On Monday, April 20, the House received the expected order from the governor to attend him and *to carry up Such bills and Resolves as were prepared for his* vice-regal *Consent.* Landon carefully noted the initial silence of the gathering, then the speaker's form of words, the positioning of the speaker's mace (on his left). There was a joint signing of the bills—by the governor first and, some distance below, by the speaker.

Then the Governor made us a proroguing Speech—and Prorogued* us to the last Thursday in October. And every Man with Joy Returned homewards. With Joy, I say for only they can tell the fatigue of such long attendance & attachment to one particular business. Thus ends . . . this Assembly—and, I think, from the Arguments Noted & the Several observations made, anyone may prepare himself for another.

In the lines below these words, the diarist entered the dates of beginning and end of the session and signed, with a flourished L and C, his name, *Landon Carter.*

The predicted fall session never occurred. The canny Scots governor, having gotten his £500 gift, instituted within a few days a fee, payable to himself, for land grants. Now he did not want to meet the outraged representatives of his province any sooner than he had to. The prorogation was extended; the next session was not called till a year and a half had elapsed.

---

* Proroguing was a procedure whereby the Crown both adjourned an elected legislature and set a (provisional) date for its reassembling. (Dissolving/dissolution was the form for ending the term of the elected house; in this case a general election would be required before a new body could meet.) The Constitution of the United States replaces by a fixed schedule this British sort of executive regulation of the legislature's meeting and continuance; that is one of the principal differences between these two versions of parliamentary democracy.

From the pen of this vain and acerbic, but very perceptive, commentator, we have this unmatched gem of narrative of the proceedings of an American colonial legislature, manifestly (though unconsciously as yet) moving into the kind of issues of disputed legislative sovereignty that two-and-half decades later would bring on revolution. At that time, as in this session, Landon would be both breathing defiance and longing for reconciliation through a restoration of the paternal care of his king.

The Clash of Great Nations

Landon did not participate further in the day-to-day work of the burgesses until August 1754. By then the relevance of the governor's 1752 exhortations about cultivating the friendship of the Indian Nations had become distressingly obvious. In 1754, Virginia began to take initiatives that would bring on the last great struggle between Britain and France for mastery of the North American continent.

On one side were the British peoples, their settlements across the Atlantic now extending down the coastline from Maine to Georgia and inland—but only as far as the Allegheny mountains. On the other side were their French opponents. They had much less in the way of settled territory, but from their control of the two greatest rivers, they had a pincer grip on the North American continent: French Louisiana was at the mouth of the Mississippi and French Canada lay athwart the St. Lawrence seaway that gave access to the Great Lakes and all the northern waterways into the interior. In a time when rivers were the readiest way to move cargoes, French trade networks went far into the territories of the inland Indian nations, while the fast-growing English population of the coastal plains found their access obstructed by the rugged Appalachians.

We shall be following a phase of the great struggle through Landon's legislative chronicles, but first a narrative overview will provide needed context.

The dragon seeds of a great conflict had already been sown when Landon became a burgess. In 1749 an armed party of Frenchmen had planted warning markers. From Lake Erie they came down the Allegheny River to what the English called the Forks of the Ohio (now Pittsburgh). From there they proceeded down the great river, and then up the Miami; at strategic points they buried lead plates bearing the name of their king, Louis XV of France.

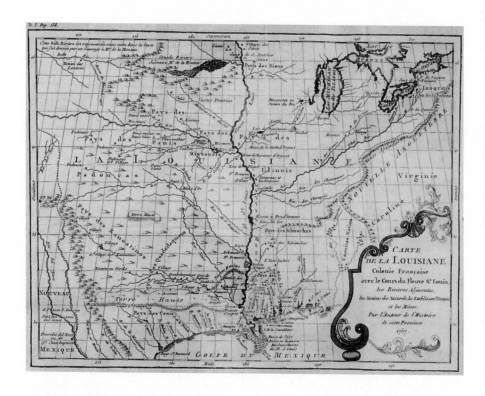

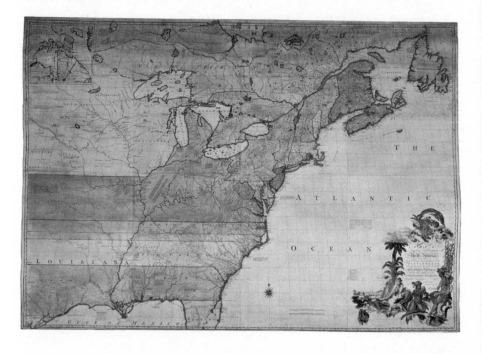

Britannia	Mars	Neptune	Genius of France	Mons.ʳ LePoliticiene	Jack Tar
Your Conquering Arms declare high Heaven is pleas'd, And sanctifies The Justice of your Cause: Maintain your Rights: Be Britains, and be Brave	*This for the Honour of The British Sword, Drawn by my Landfall and much-admired Son.*	*This for the Honour of The British Flag Conducted by the Nobly-Spirited Ansons.*	*Ave Maria; que ferons Nous: after our Massacres and Persecutions. Must Heretica possess this promis'd Land, which we so piously have call'd our Own!*	*jarni bleu! if our Fleet had not been lost in a Fog. We should have Trompe cut of 'tout L' Amerique Septentrional.*	*Hark ye Monsieur! now that your Map what a vast tract of North America; pity the Right Owner should take it from you.*

BRITAIN's RIGHTS maintain'd; or *FRENCH AMBITION* dismantled.
Addrest to the Laudable Societys of ANTI-GALICANS (The generous Promoters of British Arts & Manufactories By their most Sincere Well-wisher and truly devoted Humble Servant A Lover of his Country

Opposite top, from *Histoire de la Louisiane* (Paris, 1758), shows the French view—all the interior is theirs, and the English are tightly contained in the blank space on the eastern coast. *The John Carter Brown Library.* Opposite bottom, the English map (London, 1755) shows the boundless opposed claims of the British. Above, the allegorical caricature (also London, 1755) says the same in pictorial narrative: Britannia is supported by Mars and Neptune (plus the British Lion and a mocking Jack Tar). *The Colonial Williamsburg Foundation.*

The same territory was simultaneously being staked out from the other side. A land-speculating consortium named the Ohio Company was formed in Virginia in 1747. From London it received a very large land grant of western land on condition it moved promptly to survey, settle, and fortify its claim. The British authorities hoped to check the French largely at the expense of those who occupied the land. The authorities little realized at this stage that the English invaders' threat to their hunting grounds, far from winning over the Indians, would drive their well-organized confederations into alliance with the French, who came as traders not settlers. The same authorities soon made a similar huge grant farther south on the headwaters of the Tennessee River to another group of Virginians, the Loyal Company. (Speaker John Robinson was prominent in that consortium.)

In November 1751, the ambitious Scot, Robert Dinwiddie had arrived to take command as Virginia's new lieutenant governor. He understood the intentions of his imperial masters in London, but he also believed that zealous servants of the Crown were entitled to seek their own material rewards. He became a partner in the Ohio Company, and so stood to gain personally from moves to drive off the French. As we have seen, he also introduced the pistole fee—a Spanish coin (or equivalent) to be paid to the governor for every new land grant. This move ensured that most Virginians would see Dinwiddie more as a grasping Scot than as a stalwart advancer of the cause of the Greater British nation. Anti-Scottish prejudices were still running high after the Bonnie Prince Charlie rebellion of 1745. Undeterred, the new governor pursued an aggressive frontier policy; in October 1753, he sent the young George Washington on a mission across the mountains to scout out the French. In a report that Dinwiddie speedily published, Washington revealed that he had found the French at a fort on the Allegheny River, and that they would assuredly be coming further south in the spring.

Young Washington—who was both a surveyor for the Ohio Company and an adjutant with responsibility to smarten up the Virginia militia—was sent back in the spring with an armed company under orders to fortify the Forks and repel the expected advance. Unfortunately, Dinwiddie did not understand the difficulties of campaigning across the mountains. The militia had not been smartened up yet, and the governor could furnish neither the soldiery nor the supplies needed for success. What is more, when Dinwiddie had called a General Assembly in 1753 to help prepare for this counteroffensive, he had found the legislators more disposed to confront him head on about his detested pistole fee than to assist him financially with frontier defense.

George Washington had a small initial success; he overpowered a French-and-Indian advance guard. Soon, however, an avenging superior force overtook him, and with no time to complete fortifications, he was compelled on July 3, 1754, to surrender. Virginians found scapegoats for this defeat, and George Washington emerged as the colony's hero.

During 1754 a divided Virginia Assembly was unable to agree on money to be raised for defense. A sum of £10,000 was voted in the spring session, but we shall see how, in the fall, moves for a larger appropriation were blocked. The French, meanwhile, consolidated their victory at the Forks by converting the beginnings of a fortification raised by the Ohio Company into a stout structure they named Fort Duquesne. The British replied by sending out Major General Edward Braddock with two regiments of redcoats to capture this stronghold.

Ahead of them came a home-government promise of £20,000 and a supply of small arms to bolster colonial defense.

In February 1755, Braddock sailed up the Potomac to Alexandria and began preparations for his march on Fort Duquesne. It was a poorly managed expedition; there was jealousy between Virginia and Pennsylvania, the two colonies with an interest in the Ohio country; and the British regulars could not be well supported by a Virginia regiment that had been fragmented into ten independent companies in order to make captain the highest colonial rank and eliminate contests over the scope of command of colonial field officers. (Washington had resigned rather than accept demotion; but he served on the general's staff as a volunteer.) It seems that no one doubted that this army of regulars would overpower the French and plant the Union Jack at the Forks of Ohio. In the event, Braddock's men were surprised and surrounded; they were forced to retreat with heavy losses, and their general died of his wounds. The officer who succeeded him amazed and disgusted everyone by retreating all the way to Philadelphia; he left not even a rear-guard garrison against the triumphant enemy.

The Virginia troops were now depleted in numbers, ill supplied, and essentially unpaid; there was no viable plan to deal with the French threat. With funds very tight, Virginia could not overcome a chronic shortage of reliable troops, for its draft laws were proving ineffective. A series of British defeats to the north left the Old Dominion exposed. Virginia, meanwhile, adopted a policy of building forts along its frontier, which were costly but not viable as a defense against the raids of France's Indian allies, who were fighting fiercely to protect their hunting grounds from advancing settler encroachment.

In late 1756, a more resolute spirit began to prevail in Britain. William Pitt, "the great commoner," was ascending to dominance; he was an impassioned orator in the Parliament, and in his executive role he was a determined promoter of courageous and capable commanders. Canada was the main objective of this aggressive leader; but he would attack on several fronts. Brigadier John Forbes was specially chosen by Pitt to succeed where Braddock had failed.

Word of the new offensive reached Virginia in the spring of 1758. The Virginia Assembly was hastily reconvened at the end of March; it was told of Forbes's intended expedition, and of the British Parliament's provision for "the Levying, Cloathing, & Pay" of provincial troops. In the new comprehensive mobilization strategy there was a further a master stroke; to encourage colonial troops and the legislatures that sustained them, William Pitt announced that provincial (American) officers "as high as Colonels" would have command in the field over regular (British) officers of lower rank. By April 12, the Assembly had used the money made available from London to switch its whole recruiting policy. Two Virginia regiments were now provided for and rapidly brought up to strength, with Colonel Washington assuming command of the First Regiment.

General Forbes angered the Virginians by making his base at Lancaster in Pennsylvania, the starting point for his new road over the mountains. In the end, the vigor and success of his campaign compelled approval. On November 25, 1758, Forbes's army marched into the charred remains of Fort Duquesne. (The French had burned it days before, knowing they had not the strength to repel their attackers.) Virginia troops shared in the triumph; George Washington himself could make known to Williamsburg the capture of the burned-out remains of Fort Duquesne. On that charred ground arose Fort Pitt, later Pittsburgh. The power of the French to foster Indian attacks on the settlements of westward-moving Virginians was greatly reduced and would soon be eliminated. The Old Dominion now became a side show as the war went vigorously northward. In the fall of 1759 General Wolfe made his successful assault on Quebec. In the spring of 1760 Montreal was taken by the British, and all Canada was theirs. Early in 1763 the French had to sign a treaty that ceded the whole vast territory to Britain. It was a triumphant moment for English-speakers, but in it the seeds of great discord were planted.

Landon Carter missed two sessions of the Virginia General Assembly when the politics of the French and Indian War began to take shape. The first such session had been in November-December of 1753. He missed it because, as he explained, *I was . . . seized on my Way down with a Violent fever . . . of a dangerous continuance with as bad a relapse, so that I had no part in the same.* The second session, in February and March 1754—*he did not attend by reason of the Small pox's being in Town.*

For these reasons Landon had not been there in the fall of 1753 for the confrontation between the House of Burgesses and Governor Dinwiddie. The burgesses had denounced his pistole fee as a tax imposed without the people's consent. When they received no satisfaction from Dinwiddie, they sent the colony's attorney general, Peyton Randolph, as their agent to lodge their protest in London. From Sabine Hall, Landon took up the fight with a pamphlet spelling out the constitutional issues. (It was published in London, because Landon believed that the governor controlled the only printer in Virginia, thereby denying a free press to his opponents.) The strength of his views being known, Landon could record that he had been approached to go to England as the agent. *Some Compliments of this kind were paid to me, but my weak state of health and the Largeness of my Family made me decline having any motion made on my Account.*

The second session that Landon was forced to miss by health considerations was the one in the early spring of 1754. Alerted by Washington's report of the French advance toward the Forks of the Ohio, the Assembly moved *to raise a sum to maintain forces against the French, then taking possession of all the Lands West of the Allegany Mountains.* In order to levy £10,000, the burgesses had voted *a tax of 5 shillings for every Wheel on any Carriage contrived for ease or Luxury, and 15 pence . . . for every suit brought in County courts, and 2 shillings-and-six-pence* for law-suits *in the General Court.* But that effort had proved to be too little, too late, so the governor had reconvened the Assembly at the end of August 1754. He intended *to gain a Farther Supplye for the raising a greater Force against the French, who carryed on their encroachments with more Violence than ever, and had encountered our men twice on the lands on the River Ohio.*

The squire of Sabine Hall was already a man of science and letters; he was clearly now taking on the role of an informed patriot statesman, engaged for the salvation of his country. He began to write not day-by-day journals of proceedings but overview histories of the Assembly's sessions in this testing time. He prefaced his narrative of the August 1754 session with a brief account of Washington's initial success; but he noted that it was *only a Skirmish of a few.* The history of the subsequent defeat merited more attention.

I endeavoured to come at as true a Story as I could by enquiring privately of many of the Officers, vizt., Captain Pyrony, Captain Polston, and Afterwards Colonel Washington and Colonel Stevens, who were all in the engagements. The results of his inquiries Landon entered as a fairly detailed report of circumstances, including the human weakness and treachery he saw displayed. In another place, the diarist-turned-chronicler produced a very relevant paragraph on imperial geopolitics as he understood the subject. We get a clear sense of Landon's statesmanlike view of this opening phase of the war. Landon blamed Dinwiddie for not sending timely reinforcements to Washington's little expeditionary force, but he also grasped well the large-scale politics, and the need to foster Indian alliances to be protected against devastating surprise attacks.

The Facts appeared to be this: The Indians who pretended Friendship, however willing they might be to continue so, observing the Superiority of the French on those Lands, and the Slow motions of the Great part of our Army—dreaded their own fate should the French prove victorious. And they taking part against us, privately informed the French of our Weakness, which encouraged them to march out of their Fort they had taken from the Ohio Company. And though at a great distance off, Yet by coming down the Ohio to a place called Red Stone Creek, they had at that place well nigh Surprized our People there, who were not more than 300 in number, and had been—by Superior orders—instead of making a strong fort—*clearing a large road to that Creek in order for the marching of the whole Forces and embarking them in order for an attack upon the French. . . . Our Governour, it seems, was the Sole director of the Plan to be pursued, and he—too Sanguin on the Success of the first Skirmish—had ordered Washington to prepare these roads that there might be no obstruction to the marches of the whole body—which . . . were expected would amount in All to 600 men. Had this number Joyned Washington, in all probability the whole French Scheme would have been happyly rendered abortive for one Seven year at least. For the Certain bravery of those few of our men that were engaged, would, when aided by double their Number, have been vastly an overmatch for the French, who had evacuated most of their other Forts to make this Vigorous push. And the timorous Indians, instead of being compelled by Policy to take up arms against us, would . . . have . . . been, at least for some time, our Friends—and might have been imployed in driving the few remaining French from the Ohio.*

It was this understanding of the nature of the war and the crucial impor- tance of compelling Indian alliances, that Landon incorporated in his intro- ductory phrasing concerning the session of the summer of 1754—the second for that year: *Under these Circumstances were we when our Governor called us together in August, And upon our meeting told us the necessity there was for a Farther Supply.* He went on to report the conduct of the House of Burgesses and his role in it: *'Tis hard to point out the true disposition of the House at this time. They Suffered in General great declarations of their intentions to protect themselves against the Insults of the French; and they went farther in every design of . . . raising . . . money—for they de- sired and Obtained a view of all Copys relating to the orders that had been given by the Governour. . . . Yet—when they came in a Committee of the Whole House to consider of the thing—The Speaker, to whom it seems is a compliment due of moving first, Sat still and so did everyone Else. . . .*

Now was Landon's hour as patriot legislator:
Observing something like a Party that were not for Laying anything, I got up and moved that the Committee should resolve that the sum of £20,000 should be levy'd for the de- fence of the Country.

As soon as this was Seconded, the Speaker—very strongly Supported—moved that the question should be put upon £10,000, alledging that he did not imagin any sum we could raise would be sufficient, and therefore, as it would be but throwing money away, he was for throwing away the least Sum.

I soon perceived by the Speaches made by the others—of speaker Robinson's followers—*that they were also for nothing, and that every one had forged a most Specious reason. Waller alledged that we had told the king—when we gave £10,000—that we were very poor, and the levying £20,000—or any sum now—would be* implying we had been *telling a Lye—and much more of the like, which is but a low Popular argument, and could only Serve such a Purpose.*

And so I answered him: for, Although we were poor and had said so, yet that would not convey an Idea that we had nothing to loose, and our Levying now could only show that, poor as we were, we were so Much Alarumed with the visible danger that we were resolved to give up all in the Cause rather than be subjects to a Foreign Prince.

Having got them in this dilemma, that—though they wanted no levy—they had proposed a Sum, I moved for a question on the first motion—to which the Speaker— with Warmth—moved for the Previous question, whether the question on the first motion should be put or no.

I knew this would trye his Strength and argued against it, and he carried the Point, so that the question was put on the £10,000—and it went in the negative. And £20,000 was voted in Committee—and afterwards agreed to by the House. And so a bill was drawn accordingly. This Bill passed a Strict Scrutiny, and everything was calculated with a seeming Harmony. But the zealous would-be savior of his endangered country now had to watch his achievement put in jeopardy, and indeed brought to naught, by the actions of *the Party,* as he called Robinson's large following.

After this Bill was prepared and Considered by the Committee of the Whole House, The Party (against it or not, I know not) added a Clause for the Payment of the £2,500 to Peyton Randolph, Esqr . . . sent home in 1753 as an Agent. (When Randolph, the number two in Robinson's party, had been sent to London, his supporters had proposed to meet his expenses and compensate him with a payment of £2,500; but the King's Council, as the upper house, had rejected this—a right of veto which Landon and others held was not constitutionally theirs.)

The new maneuver now gave Landon double cause for alarm: his patriotic supply bill might be lost by a Council refusal on account of the inserted clause—"tacked" is the technical term. Even if the package were accepted, the burgesses, by submitting the payment for Council's approval, would have receded from their former assertion that appropriations of colony funds could be authorized by the House of Burgesses alone:

Against this Tack I argued Strongly that it was giving up the Point to the Council, who claimed a Negative or Concurrence in any . . . money Votes. . . . And such a point ought never to be rendered even doubtfull—and this Clause would confirm it against the rights of the House—A very dangerous thing perhaps in future.

And there was also Landon's other great concern: *Again, I argued, it was no proper time in the hour of imminent danger to hazard the passing of this bill, because— by it—it was proposed the Country should be defended—and it was more than Probable the Council would not agree to it—because . . . Persons discovering . . . pure Obstinacy were likely to Continue in it.*

Landon prided himself on his refusal to be beguiled on this crucial matter by the unfounded optimism of his cousin and other promoters of the subterfuge to get approval for the payment of Peyton Randolph:

But this obstinacy, I was privately assured, would not be the Case, and Colonel Carter Burwell was confident from some private Conversation with the Secretary of the colony—a Council member—that it would be the only way to get the money paid.

I believed . . . that he was told so—but I could not give Credit to the Intention—of the Council—because I think I know mankind, and very few deceive me—at least that Honorable Gentleman—Secretary Thomas Nelson—could not. I conjectured it to be all Artifice to draw the house into a Confession of the Council's right; and after the Bill should pass our House, their point would be gained; and yet no Bill should pass above. . . .

Accordingly, after the Bill passed with this Clause, it went up, and in one hour we heard that it was unanimously rejected. Then many were amazed, and in the Mouths of many nothing was heard but: "There's no believing mankind."

The most urgent matter, however, remained: the defense of the country.

Those who would not give up the patriotic Cause fell upon a very prudent stratagem to give the world a full view of the matter and justifye the behaviour of the House in not providing for the defence of the Country. The French and Indians had during the Session come in and drove off some of the Inhabitants, and they—the inhabitants—had sent an Express with a Petition to the House complaining of the Grievance; and they desired some Speedy relief.

The House immediately took this Petition into Consideration and Resolved that the Bill already passed had provided the relief required by the Petition; And also resolved that a Message be sent to inform the Council of the said Petition & . . . desire they would expedite the Passing that bill.

To this they sent a written message telling us they had rejected the Bill on Account of that tacked on Clause—with much specious reasoning for it.

And in a few days the house were called up and prorogued by the Governour— Nothing being done except a few private bills.

The malign ill-will of the grasping governor was seen in the whole disastrous outcome.

*This Prorogation Speech carryed all the Venom and all the Falsehood of an Angry Passionate man, and to mend the matter—it was spoke only to the House—as, if the Council had obeyed orders in what they did, So that many of the council were in doubt as to whether they should rise—*as they must if included in the address. *However, as this could not have been deemed a Prorogation, it being directed to only one part of the Assembly, the Printer was by the Governor's orders made to insert* afterward the words "*Gentlemen of the Council.*"

Every Burgess, I am sure retired full of Revenge, and in the month of September I wrote a Paper Published in Maryland, setting the Matter in a true and faithfull light, which has met with much Applause.

Thus ended Landon's history of his second Assembly, in which he saw himself as a leader above "party," rallying the patriotism of the worthy, but no doubt confused, majority. He had prevailed only to see his vital work undermined by a devious established leadership headed by the speaker. Just as culpable, in Landon's view, was an upper house that was obstinate in claiming rights they did not and should not have.

Yet, Landon did not have to wait long to see his efforts bear fruit. The governor could not leave the war effort suspended, especially since the deadlocked abeyance originated in the rancor aroused by his own self-interested imposition of the pistole fee. By the time the Assembly was reconvened in mid-October, His Majesty's Government *at home* moved to enforce a mediated settlement to the dispute that had paralyzed beleaguered Virginia. Landon took pleasure in writing another overview narrative of the politics that then unfolded. (For the moment, with the French still dominant just over the mountains, neither he nor his fellow Virginia politicians seemed disposed to express alarm at the power wielded by the politicians in Westminster; their right to impose a compromise involving fees that many deemed to be taxes was not questioned.)

October 17, 1754.

The Assembly met this day, And to give an Idea of what is to be expected I will venture to Call it the Harmonious Session. The Affair of the Pistole having been determin'd at home—and both Partys having got something—both seemed to hugg themselves with a Victory.

The Governor was pleased *in that he had got leave to Charge a fee on all Patents but only those granted after the date of this order of the* King's Privy Council . . . *and that are not under a hundred Acres—or that lye on this side the Allegany Mountains. . . . And also the King's Attorney*—Peyton Randolph—*was turned out for presuming to go home as an Agent.*

And The Country—the burgesses—*were pleased in that they had Stopped the fee on nearly all those pattents. . . . And farther they had an Assurance that if the Attorney ask'd for his Place, he was to have it again. And also that the Treasurer's Accounts should be pass'd with the Article of £2,500, the bone of contention, in it.*

I say these things were confidently asserted to the House, But his Honor could not forget his Rod at the last Prorogation—and, though he did not openly use it, Yet some twiggs of it were imployed in the Speech at the Opening of this Session.

Landon practiced a continued reserve toward the executive. *And so the business of Address drawing—in reply to the Governor—was laid on my Shoulders—which by the Private directions of many members I endeavoured to Sprinkle with a proper resentment—but all in implication work. It Passed <u>Nemine Contradicente</u>, and the Governor look'd upon it as Wormwood and Molasses. However, being tired with the heat and perceiving the House dispos'd to Levy money, he return'd only a mild answer.* Altogether banished were the 1752 sentiments of filial deference to the Father King's representative; Landon now delighted in the unanimity of the burgesses and the reminder to the governor that the sweetness of victory must be mixed with the bitterness of important concessions to his enemies.

In these circumstances, Landon saw his cherished defense expenditure bill gain passage at last. This time there was no tacked clause to pay Randolph, but the burgesses let it be known that, unless the Council approved that payment, the war-emergency levy would not get a final third-reading approval in the lower house.

As to our House we had no Contest about the money bill. It went for £20,000. . . . This was sent up to the Council—but not untill we saw the Treasurer's Accounts passed. . . . As it was the Olive Branch, we would not give the bill the 3d reading 'till that came in. At last it appeared—and, every member being satisfyed, the Bill passed and went up, where it was also Passed. But note: not Unanimously in Council—for the <u>Par Nobile Fratrum</u>—the noble pair of brothers (Nelson)—and Phillip Ludwell protested against it <u>More Magnatum</u>—in the manner of Grandees. How true then was my Prediction last Session that men Purely obstinate will continue to be so. Thus do they endeavour to make Lords of themselves.

The sense of patriotic engagement now prevailing among the burgesses was further enhanced by a message from the young leader of the military: *We received the Compliments this Session from Washington and his officers in return for our*

Thanks transmitted them last August. And we *desired the Governor to Recommend them for Preferment to his Majesty. All but George Muse, a Rank Scoundrel and Coward, and that Dutch Dogg Vanbraam, now in the service of the French. . . .*

The governor assured them that he would continue to recommend those officers. But Landon believed the governor could not be trusted and would rather continue to favor officers who were place-hunting fellow Scots, such as Colonel Innes from North Carolina. George Washington suspected the same; soon he resigned his commission, as advised by Landon and others, rather than submit to indignity.

Landon returned to the issues of war policies in his truncated account of the Assembly session of May and June 1755. The positions then taken by Speaker Robinson and his dominant following startled Landon, but the leaders' course of action reveals what had been going on all along.

For some five early entries—from May 1 to May 6—Landon reverted to daily diary keeping, but he left off after the first paragraph of a sixth entry for May 14. When he resumed at a later time, he switched again to memoir mode. He again wrote an overview of the session. Here is his narrative of the management of war finance:

I will now Comprehend the Votes and Arguments for the Supplye—which we brought by Resolution from the Committee of the whole House to £6,000.

I cannot but express my concern that men should be inconsistant in their Actions, a specimen of which this affair affords me. And to represent it truely I will go a little back to two former Sessions from whence the inconsistancy I mean will appear. When the £10,000 was granted—in 1753—it was so disagreeable a Subject that much Art was used to get one penny raised for the defence of the Country. And, although we had then certain intelligence that our Enemy had taken our lands, no steps were to be taken to endeavour to stop them. Our People—it was said—were too poor to defend themselves. But by a side Glance the money was raised.

And then, the initial levy being not enough, two Short sessions were employed last year—1754—to raise £20,000 more. . . . I joyned with and was indeed Active for the 20, that we might shew our Mother Country our own Sensibility of danger—and excite their Care.

We see Landon again emphasizing his own valiant patriotic efforts in the face of the indifference and hostility of the House leadership. But there followed a startling account of a reversal of the roles as reported in 1755. If we attend carefully to that, we may get an explanation of the strategy of the Robinson party truer than what is available in Landon's polemic. Indeed, we may get a sense of the unflattering account that Landon's opponents could have written of his role in the war-finance affair.

Landon, writing as engaged-participant historian, comes to the altered situation of 1755 by brief indirect reference to General Braddock. At the time of his writing, the army of British regulars (with American auxiliaries) was gathering for an attack on the French, and Landon was pleased to interpret the sending of this force as a response to the valiant efforts that he had helped call forth in Virginia. Now, however, he experienced a sudden turnaround of his opponents. They pushed for a further grant of money, and he was inclined to oppose it. He was quite evidently caught aback.

It may be said that those—like myself—who were for giving before are now against it. I own it in some sort—and have this reason: before we knew not exactly our Poverty, we had no kind of defence, no steps from home—and our indolence lulled them at home— of which our enemys were taking great advantage. Now we have found ourselves poor. Many steps have been taken—if not yet effectual—to rout, at least check, the enemy, and our Mother Country are strongly engaged.

But say they: shall we leave off and be inactive because our Friends are willing to help us?

I answer that what we have not, we cannot give, which must be a just excuse. Raise the money, that is shew where it is to be had, and I am ready. In short I own it is a difficult point to determin in—and it is possible there may be error. I have consented to this small sum—£6,000—in hopes that by way of lottery or some such means—it may be got. And—for this Purpose—A bill has been framed agreeable to the Resolution to raise the sum.

We can now gain a historical overview of the politics that Landon chronicled from so close up.

Marc Egnal is prominent among historians who have held that the original obstruction of patriotic response by the cohorts of Speaker Robinson was due to their alignment with the Loyal Land Company, whose interests lay south toward the Tennessee River. This faction—who have been termed "anti-expansionists"—would not, it is asserted, involve the colony in an expense that would advance the interests of their rival, the Ohio Company. The latter, it is held, naturally favored expense to reclaim their own territory, and they are referred to as "expansionists." In this view, Landon is taken to have been, if not an advocate, then a dupe of the Ohio Company. After all, that company was based in the Northern Neck where Sabine Hall stands; many of his neighbors were shareholders. But there are good reasons to question this interpretation. Careful reading of Landon's narrative supports a reassessment of what was going on.

First, Landon was not an Ohio Company shareholder, and second, his interests were not all concentrated in the Northern Neck—he both owned estates and had close kin by blood and marriage in the James River region. Landon was therefore well placed to make balanced judgments between the factions. There are also larger considerations above the personal. Is it seriously to be supposed that any Virginia leaders, wherever their own real-estate interests lay, could have contemplated with equanimity a French consolidation on the Ohio, blocking Virginia's line of expansion? Before long this inveterate enemy, if unchecked, would certainly extend a challenge to the Loyal Company's lands on the waters of the Tennessee, the next great river flowing into the Mississippi, whose entire basin the French claimed as their territory.

So—if an alignment for and against the interests of the Ohio Company was not the principal cause of division—what were the political options contested in the Assembly sessions that Landon reported? I think that Landon's line is clear enough; it is explicable without invoking personal financial interests. He knew that the enemy was on his country's borders, and he was saying that Virginia must arm against them. But how are we to understand the speaker's stalling? A clue to what was afoot—but could not be openly declared—appears, I think, in Landon's report of John Robinson's initial response to Landon's own bold 1754 initiative for £20,000. Landon reported that, *the Speaker . . . moved that the question should be put upon £10,000, alledging that he did not imagin any sum we could raise would be sufficient, and therefore, as it would be but throwing money away, he was for throwing away the least Sum.* The implication is surely not that nothing should be done, but that what had to be done was beyond the resources of the colony—be it ten or twenty thousand pounds. The strategy must be to do next to nothing until the Mother Country, sensing the extreme danger to her interests, would feel compelled to commit to the struggle. But Landon, the hotheaded patriot, could not get this hint! The political alignment is better understood thus: on Landon's side a David-and-Goliath patriotism that would pit Virginia alone against France, and on Robinson's side, a politics of realism that saw a direct interest in letting things get so bad that Great Britain would be compelled at last to engage her mighty self.

John Robinson and the Randolphs and the whole James River set associated with them had, over many years, effectively ensured their hold on power in the colony by brokering relations both with His Majesty's Government in Westminster and with the mercantile interests centered in the City of London. It was natural that they should look to solutions for the French menace from that quarter. Once Britain was squarely in the fight, why then: *shall we leave off and be inactive because our Friends are willing to help us?* Now, at last, good policy would be to show a willingness—as subsidiaries—to reinforce the imperial effort. How impatiently the Robinson realists must have regarded Landon, the well-meaning local zealot who did not know how to manipulate "home" policy!

If the imperial card was the one the Robinson leadership was intent on finessing, then they were right. The Braddock disaster and the following two-and-a-half years of futile efforts on the part of the demoralized Virginia troops proved as much. The war did not effectively turn in favor of the British Virginians until the impulse of the great William Pitt was felt in 1758. Money and arms were then sent, and the French were repulsed. Thus, and only thus, was established a British-American hold on the Ohio that would be unassailable.

Having recorded his valiant struggles to see his country properly defended, Landon kept no more burgess records, but he did continue an engaged and highly esteemed patriot.

In June 1758, Colonel Richard Bland, once his opponent in fierce debates, wrote him a touching poetic address in the classical manner. It was headed, "An Epistle to Landon Carter, Esq., upon hearing that he does not intend to stand a Candidate at the next Election of Burgesses." It begins by celebrating a pastoral idyll of retirement to a country estate. (Landon's great house was, after all, named for the retreat of the Roman poet Horace.)

"At Sabine Hall, retir'd from public praise,
You'll spend in learned ease your future days."

But—protested Bland—that must not be! Does Landon not recall the recent time of crisis?

"You then appear'd, your Country's surest Friend,
And did her Cause with manly sense defend."

The writer gives an assurance that it must continue so:

"The Country's Patriot once again appears
To vindicate our Laws, and calm our fears.

. . . .

Then stand once more, aloud your country cries,
(Nor do her prayers nor her commands despise),
Stand once again, and save a sinking Land. . . ."

Whether because of such encouragement or not, Landon did then seek and secure reelection. Two years later, in a letter to him from Governor Fauquier, his patriotic public character was again celebrated as "so illustrious an Example." This man who had replaced Dinwiddie worked far more harmoniously with the burgesses than his predecessor ever had.

Landon's public identity was greatly reinforced by his engagement as chauvinist politician of colonial expansion. The sentiments aroused in the defense of British America against the detested French influenced the future politics of Landon's entire generation. The magnitude of this influence can best be appreciated through a consideration of the real and symbolic role of the great man who came to lead the British-American nation to its triumphal success. Unexpected questions must at this point be asked. Of what nation was William Pitt the matchless hero? To what nation did Landon and his fellow Americans at this time feel that they belonged?

Mr. Pitt—Uniting a Nation Soon to be Divided

William Pitt was for Landon Carter perhaps the greatest man of the age. Before both their lives were over (they died in the same year, 1778), Pitt stood forth twice as the savior of the nation—first in the war with France to which Landon committed so strongly, and next in the nation-rending crisis of the Stamp Act. Many times after that, Pitt, by then Earl of Chatham, vainly strove to avert the final rupture as the king's ministers persisted in policies that destroyed a unity which he, like Landon, considered sacred. The nation to whose preservation Pitt's every effort seemed dedicated was Great Britain, but not the lesser Great Britain that we now know. It was the Great Britain of which Landon and countless Americans felt themselves to be loyal sons. It was a "Greater Britain" ex-

William Pitt's American apotheosis
(Philadelphia, 1768). An allegory engraved by Charles Willson Peale from a
painting he did for patriotic gentlemen of Westmoreland County, Virginia. The champion of Liberty points
to her statue, while busts of former
English champions support her altar
and flame. *The Colonial Williamsburg
Foundation.*

pected to share its destiny equally with "British America." Thomas Jefferson
pronounced the death of that nation in the Declaration of Independence: "We
could have been a great people together. . . ."

For Landon Carter's generation of Americans, no one had done more than
William Pitt to stir the conscious pride of Britons on both sides of the Atlantic.
That sentiment was part of the rising tide of what we now call nationalism, and
that rising tide would become a flood before the century's end, greatly aug-
mented by the American and French Revolutions. To call William Pitt the first
great nationalist demagogue of the Age of Revolutions, would be exaggerating,
but Pitt played his part in this regard. His chauvinist denunciation of the Peace
of 1763 was carried onto the streets by the "Wilkes and Liberty" rioters. As such,
William Pitt must be seen as one of the foremost—though least noticed—
contributors to the birth of the new American nation, as it emerged painfully
from the rupture of the short-lived pan-Atlantic Greater British nation.

On the back of Landon's almanac diary for 1766 appears a glowing tribute
to William Pitt. Landon penned in Latin an inscription suitable to be affixed
to a portrait of the great man and one of his associates. (I shall summarize this

eulogy in English; the full text and a discussion of it are given in the next chapter.) The Right Honourable W. Pitt had contributed mightily to save Great Britain by preserving the liberties of British America against their subversion plotted by George Grenville. Notice the close identification: to preserve the liberties of British America was to save Great Britain. This was a polemic accolade written in the time of the crisis occasioned by the first British attempt to directly tax America through the Stamp Act. But "Mr. Pitt," from his role in the Seven Years' War against France, was already the embodiment of British-American liberty-based nationalism.

William Pitt communicated a sense of vital, even furious, force. This strong statesman was a rare combination—great in oratory and tireless in commitment to the paperwork of government business, or at least to those martial and imperial branches that he was determined to master.

It is difficult now to reconstruct an accurate account of how William Pitt came to loom so large in the consciousness of Landon and his generation of Americans. The obvious historic parallel and comparison for William Pitt as orator and organizer rallying the nation is Winston Churchill. "Mr. Churchill" in 1940–41 was also an outsider to the ruling cliques that seemed to have brought the nation to the brink of disaster. Churchill, like Pitt, was brought suddenly into office by defeat and crisis. But Churchill had means to reach the people directly by radio. Everyone of a certain generation still knows the immortal phrases: "I can offer you nothing but blood, toil, tears, and sweat"; "We shall fight . . . in the fields and in the streets, . . . we shall never surrender!"; and "for a thousand years, men will still say: 'This was their finest hour.'" And since, in Britain, around the Empire, and even clandestinely in Nazi-occupied Europe, those phrases came to everyone over the wireless, the phrases were known and remembered in the distinctive Churchillian accent. William Pitt's oratory, on the other hand, could only reach the people in Britain and across the Atlantic indirectly—muffled, as it were.

Yet, every age has its own ways of knowing and experiencing the forms of power that direct its destiny. The newspaper was a rapidly rising presence and force in the middle of the eighteenth century, so William Pitt's career belonged to an early stage of press-sustained popular politics. Of necessity Pitt operated in the royal-court-dominated system of connection and patronage deals; but he also, both consciously and by unconscious instinct, cultivated a popular reputation that was sustained in the emergent national and pan-Atlantic political press—hence, the epithet "the great commoner."

Pitt's continual call in Parliament had been for British self-assertion as a maritime nation. Britain must be single-mindedly a naval power in relentless pursuit of the empire, colonies, and trade; these goals Pitt declared to be the nation's destiny. This advocacy, combined with long continuing opposition to successive ministries, won him great popularity amongst the tradesmen who dominated the boisterous politics of the City of London. And, since at this time the greater part of the news in colonial American newspapers were reprinted items from the London papers, press coverage throughout the pan-Atlantic kingdom was assured for any patriot leader adulated in London.

The creation of Pitt's charismatic persona was made possible by a political myth that haunted British politics in the eighteenth century. It was the myth of the independent representative of the people, who stood firm for the interests of his Country against the corruption sustained by the royal court. We have already encountered Landon Carter enacting this myth in his burgess chronicles. The pervasive set of political beliefs sustained by the myth were especially strong in late-colonial America, and have come to be known to historians indeed as the country ideology. Those who attempted to practice it—especially if they were seen by others in that light—were true patriots. This role had already been most effectively taken up by William Pitt in his years of vigorous opposition. Parliament was then dominated by Whig politicians—supporters of the House of Hanover, brought in to ensure that Britain had a Protestant monarch. Most of the Whig leaders, however, vied with each other to form ministries whose majorities would be secured by royal patronage. Pitt was one of a much smaller group of patriot Whigs who professed to despise such venal politics. In 1756 came the extraordinary coup by which the outspoken opposition parliamentarian became that almost inconceivable being, the patriot minister. This was a combination of incompatibles only made possible by the danger in which the nation stood.

These were dark days indeed, brought on by a series of engagements in which British and American forces, poorly led by British commanders, were crushed by the French and Indian forces they were sent against. Pitt put the political world on notice when Parliament opened on 13 November 1755. The ensuing debate on the ministry's outline of policies has since been identified as "one of the great occasions of the century." The session lasted until five in the morning, and its high point came after midnight. Pitt then brought together all the attacks on foreign and colonial policy in a great outpouring. "It was," wrote Horace Walpole, a great chronicler of his times, "like a torrent long obstructed." Pitt was superbly himself—"haughty, defiant, conscious of irony & supreme ability." This speech, "accompanied with variety of action, accents and irony, and set off with such happy images and allusions . . . lasted about an hour and a half, and was kept up with inimitable spirit, though it did not begin till past one in the morning, after an attention and fatigue of ten hours." Pitt came forth with denunciations of the way the war was being fought in Europe. He declared that at last a war must be undertaken "for the long-injured, long-neglected, long-forgotten people of America."

Two months later in a debate on supply for the armed forces, Pitt once more castigated both the ministry and their priorities: "This whole summer I have been looking for government—I saw none. . . . When his Majesty returned [from Hanover] his kingdom was delivered to him more like a wreck than as a vessel able to stem the storm." Were 140,000 soldiers ready to defend Hanover? "Who boasts of what numbers are prepared for England? For America? . . . Two miserable battalions of Irish . . . had been sent to America, had been sent to be sacrificed." Thus did he scornfully dismiss the ministry's vain effort with Braddock's army, whose destruction had left America's west indefensible and its patriots downcast.

In November 1756 the king was forced—at last and very reluctantly—to accept Pitt as principal secretary of state. He would lead in the Commons and have direction of foreign (i.e., war) policy. The bitter pill was sweetened by making the Duke of Devonshire the first lord of the treasury (as the prime minister was then officially styled). Thus, as author of the king's speech to the reassembled Parliament, Pitt could show his growing following on both sides of the Atlantic what he intended to do. A not unsympathetic bystander said of the speech: "It is an high style *ad populum* [directed to the people], and seems to promise great things." It undertook many popular patriotic initiatives. And most important for his reputation that was to grow across the Atlantic there was a ringing assurance of measures for the "succour and preservation of America."

The energizing of a complacent, patronage-dominated system was a difficult process; setbacks were inevitable. Pitt had immense popularity, but the Duke of Newcastle (the great manager of patronage) was now in opposition, and he had the numbers in Parliament. Furthermore, King George II was still hostile to this secretary of state, who in opposition had been scornful of the king's native Hanover as "a despicable Electorate." In April of 1757 Pitt was dismissed. The public outcry was immediate and immense. City after city—led by

London, of course—voted tributes to the ousted patriot ministers, William Pitt the foremost.

Nearly three months of political confusion followed. No other credible parliamentarian emerged able to cope with continual defeat in war. In the end, the king had to support the brokering of an alliance between Parliament's patronage man and the titanic patriot minister. In June 1757 the Pitt-Newcastle ministry was sworn in; it was an uneasy coalition that lasted a bare three years. But during those years Pitt was able to lead, and was seen to lead, to victory the great pan-Atlantic British-and-American nation that he, in this time of struggle, was helping to call into being.

Assuredly results soon came. America was thoroughly energized within half a year. Lord Loudoun, as British commander in America, had overseen a series of shaming defeats, and he had thoroughly riled all the colonial legislatures, and governors too, by his haughty way of demanding men and supplies for his army. In the autumn of 1757 Pitt began enforcing strong policies: Loudoun was recalled, and the American governors were empowered by notice of a new approach. Henceforth the charges that the colonial legislatures incurred in raising and supplying provincial forces would be reimbursed by Parliament; furthermore, it was ruled that "all Officers of the Provincial Forces, as high as Colonels inclusive are to have Rank, according to their respective Commissions"—they would be subordinate only to regular officers of the same or higher rank. The governors could see how much easier their work would become when they did not have to try to extract money and when the officers' commissions they issued were not despised by the imperial army. They lost no time in communicating these new orders to their legislatures—in the form of letters from Mr. Secretary Pitt.

In the narrative of the war in Virginia, we have seen how dramatic was the change. The Old Dominion suddenly had the will and the means to raise two well-manned, stout-hearted regiments. Such effects were general in America, and it was Pitt's drive that called them forth. Fred Anderson, in a recent major reassessment of the so-called French and Indian War, has summed it up in the following terms. "Pitt was, of course, scrapping some ten years of centralizing reforms by which preceding administrations had been trying to put the American colonies under more central control." (It was those previous centralizing policies that had so affronted the Virginia Assembly in 1752, during Landon's first session as a burgess.) But now suddenly Pitt, the new secretary of state, "only wanted to win the war, and no centralizing reform measure would help him do that." He was "a man to whom caution was no longer a constraint;" he was "a gambler either so desperate or so sure of his luck that he could stake everything on the next roll of the dice." The Americans sensed the new prospect of autonomy; it was headily combined by Pitt with a call to British Empire patriotism in an all-out war to expel the hated French. Anderson goes on to show how immediately the leader's presence was felt: "Pitt himself would direct policies, and insofar as possible, plan campaigns. The result would prove to be a series of victories unparalleled in British history. Pitt's policies would gain him not just the colonists' help but their adulation. Never before had the energies of so many colonists been engaged on behalf of the empire as they would be in the three remarkable years that began in 1758; never before had their affection for Great Britain been so heartfelt, or their passion for the empire burned with so bright a flame."

Results surely did vindicate Pitt's daring gambles. Between September 1757 and September 1760 there came, in rapid succession, news of successive triumphs of British and American arms. First came the fall of Louisburg, the gateguard fortress at the mouth of the St. Lawrence; then the capture of Fort Duquesne, the stronghold on the upper Ohio; then the taking of Fort Frontenac, a forward position on Lake Ontario; and crucially the fall of Quebec, the citadel of Canada.* The conquest was completed with the capture of Montreal, the center of the French and Indian fur trade.

Thus matters stood when suddenly, in October 1760, the old king, George II, died. This was ominous for Pitt. In the heady days of the height of his power, he had deeply offended both the king's grandson, who succeeded as George III, and his close adviser, Lord Bute. For the moment, the triumphant patriot was unassailable; but by October 1761, Pitt felt compelled to resign rather than accept responsibility for policies he no longer directed. There was immediately a hubbub that largely confirmed his reputation. Had not the great man been spurned after he had saved the nation in its dark hour? Had he not then led it

---

* This victory was gained as the dare-all-at-a-stroke British commander, General Wolfe, died on the field, in the very hour that he learned of the success of his bold assault. Some ten years later, Benjamin West, the expatriate American painter—who remained a fervent pan-Atlantic British nationalist—rendered the imagined scene yet more historic in a famous painting. Engraved for a mass market, that painting reached many viewers; it stirred once more the patriotic feelings of Americans, although they were by then in the midst of the conflicts that were tearing apart that greater British nation.

on to unparalleled triumphs and greatness? (Even the sardonic Horace Walpole was moved to declare that Pitt had created in three years an empire that far exceeded that of the Romans; Walpole would burn all his Greek and Roman books, "for they were little people.") Popularity, however, could not keep in office an out-of-favor minister, especially since the king had no longer any urgent need of him now that victory was secured.

From Pitt's heyday on, however, the reverence belonging to his name was unassailable in the estimation of Landon Carter and countless other British-American patriots. The *Annual Register,* published in London since 1768, presented an authoritative account of each just-completed year in politics; its summary of 1761, the year that ended with Pitt's downfall, expressed sentiments already very general in the political nation on either side of the Atlantic: "His power, as it was not acquired, so neither was it exercised in an ordinary manner. With very little parliamentary and with less court influence, he swayed both at court and in parliament with an authority unknown before to the best supported ministers. He was called to the ministry by the voice of the people; and what is more rare, he held it with that approbation; and under him for the first time, administration and popularity were seen united."

The editor, writing in 1762, did not need to state what was assumed—that "the people" he had referred to were the British political nation, and so included components on both sides of the Atlantic. Everyone already knew that no one had done more than William Pitt to raise the conscious pride of this entire dedicated-to-liberty empire nation.

The foregoing appreciation of the role of William Pitt in his times has been offered at some length for two reasons. The most immediate is to establish what Pitt meant to Landon Carter, whom we have already seen as a self-revealed, would-be patriot, independent legislator and rallier of his country in time of war. The second reason is to advance a much more general claim for William Pitt to be understood as the greatest stirrer of British-American nationalism. As such, he was a powerful originator of the primal American nationalism that was a transformation of that pan-Atlantic original. William Pitt is, indeed, to be understood as a mighty herald of the American Revolution, a revolution that flowed from the resentments of a British American nationalism when it found itself spurned and disallowed in Britain.

Before we can properly begin to appreciate the world-historic importance of

William Pitt, we have to set aside the anachronistic compartmentalization that sees him merely as English. In that view he belongs to British history; and so he is not eligible for a leading role in American history. We are not helped either by the practice whereby Mr. Pitt—the great commoner—is usually indexed, according to snobbish convention, as "Chatham, Earl of." A truer account must acknowledge Pitt as the first and last great popular leader of the pan-Atlantic British nation. The very popularity of his role helped to bring on the rupture of that unbalanced, overextended political community. It is only in this perspective that the great patriot's role in both Landon Carter's life and in American history can be properly appreciated.

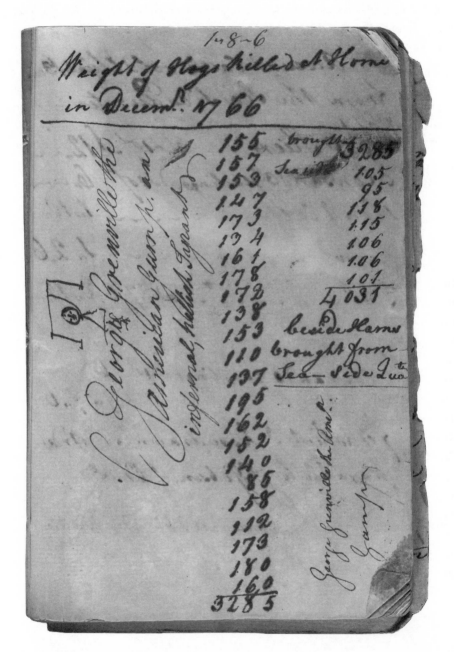

George Grenville imagined hanged—a seditious doodle (sideways, at the left of the page) from a Virginia gentleman's 1765 notebook. Notice it is the prime minister, not the king, who is the "hellish tyrant." ("Gump" was already a dialect pejorative—a fool or worse.) *The Colonial Williamsburg Foundation, reproduced by permission of Furlough Baldwin of Eyre Hall, Northampton County, Va.*

Chapter 8

Rebellions Begin

In the summer of 1766, Colonel Richard Henry Lee organized a procession to the courthouse of Westmoreland County just north of Sabine Hall. First came two slaves wearing the colors that their master also had donned, the blue and white colors of "Wilkes and Liberty." (Of Wilkes and this watchword of his supporters, more later.) Behind the banners came a crowd of planters and slaves together escorting others who bore two effigies of prominent but now notorious gentlemen. The effigies were hanged on the gallows at the courthouse. The next day the effigies were hanged again and burned, but only after Richard Henry Lee had read a mock "dying Speech." The effigies were of Colonel George Mercer, the Virginia gentleman appointed as collector of dues under the Stamp Act, and the Right Honorable Mr. George Grenville, prime minister of Great Britain, the notorious proponent of this hated tax. This pageant, showing a world turned upside down, was a symbolic rebellion in the face of what was declared an unconstitutional tax. At that moment the collector had not yet arrived in Virginia, but he was expected soon. He and his prominent family were left in no doubt about the reception awaiting him.

The passage of the Stamp Act in March 1765 provoked the conflict that eleven years later would lead to the revolutionary Declaration of Independence. The American colonies were to be taxed: all legal documents and newspapers had henceforth to bear a stamp purchased from tax collectors appointed by the king. Before the end of the year, all the mainland colonies of British North

America were in rebellion against this act. Thus did Americans find themselves in turbulent defiance of their Father King.

In this period Landon Carter's diary became a poignant witness to profound changes in politics. The Atlantic world was beginning to be wrenched off its monarchical foundations and reconstructed on democratic lines; the psychic disturbance of these deep changes in the forms of national, legal, and personal identity transformed Landon's plantation diary. As an ardent American patriot, the diarist participated in the rebellion, but as an old-fashioned patriarchal monarchist, he dreaded the consequences. His diary registered this deep angst; we shall see in this chapter how he now suddenly began to chronicle rebellions in his own little kingdom.

In order to understand the events with which American rebellion and revolution began, we must follow—mainly through the eyes of American onlookers—the course of politics onward from the end of the Seven Years' War. Those who watched felt themselves witnesses to the disruption of the Greater British nation that had been triumphantly led by William Pitt.

Euphoria never lasts; there had been internal dissension and dark forebodings arising even before the war with France was over. The swelling pride turned to fear and apprehension as the British-Americans observed developments in England. In October 1760 the 21-year-old Prince of Wales had come to the throne as King George III. Soon it appeared that the new king's new ministers were bent on extinguishing liberty and instituting tyranny.

On April 19, 1763, the close-of-session royal speech to Parliament celebrated the peace treaty. George III and his chosen counselor, Lord Bute, prided themselves on their achievement. William Pitt was outraged. Although the French by that treaty had ceded all Canada to Great Britain, the great commoner, already ousted from the ministry, denounced the treaty in a two-and-a-half-hour oration. Too much of what had been won with blood and treasure had been given away, he thundered: Britain's allies had been shamefully abandoned. Captured West African and West Indian territories had been given back to the French in order to achieve a quick settlement; it was a betrayal.

On April 23, John Wilkes published number 45 of his satiric newspaper, *The North Briton*. Wilkes was a member of Parliament; he was also a notorious rake, but through this publication he was soon to become the popular champion of constitutional liberties. The paper violently denounced the king's speech: the royal declaration that the peace was honorable and productive of "happy effects," was false; the ministers who authorized it were the "tools of despotism and corruption." Wilkes's article insisted that, since the king's address was known to be written by his ministers, the newspaper was only attacking the ministry not the monarch. But the young king was not placated; he believed he should punish everyone concerned with this newspaper polemic. And so it was that, on April 30, the secretary of state, Lord Halifax, issued a "general warrant" for the arrest of the "authors, printers, and publishers of the *North Briton*, No. 45." The charge was "seditious libel." Out of that hasty move, a year of riotous conflict ensued, the consequences of which reverberated through the Atlantic world and more especially through the already suspicious colonies of America. From these beginnings, it might be said, came the American and indeed the democratic revolution that was beginning to engulf the Atlantic world.

Patriots on both sides of the Atlantic saw a starkly divided nation: on one side, standing for the constitutional rights of freeborn Englishmen, were the friends of the British constitution with their popular slogan "Wilkes and Liberty"; on the other side was a corruptly conspiring, would-be-despotic ministry. The king should act as protector of the nation's liberties, but he seemed to have been persuaded instead to crush the opponents of his tyrannical ministers.

Watchers far off in the American colonies read reports of the persecution and of the silencing of John Wilkes with horrified fascination. The colonists were sure that the youthful king was in thrall to Lord Bute. That was extremely ominous; the Scottish nationality of Bute and his family name of Stuart made him synonymous with a covert revival of the dreaded papist tyranny for which King James II had been dethroned. English-speaking Protestants on both sides of the Atlantic still joyously celebrated that Glorious Revolution of 1688. They also remembered with a shudder the rebel Jacobite army of Bonnie Prince Charlie that as recently as 1745 had marched out of Scotland to threaten the return of the dynasty of Roman Catholic tyrants. The colonists already knew that it was the malign influence of the Scottish favorite that had driven out the great patriot William Pitt. Now the colonists must watch the use of illegal general warrants to stifle Wilkes and his denunciation of the shameful peace that followed Pitt's dismissal. The watchers from afar saw how the plot would have succeeded had not the ever-to-be-honored Mr. Chief Justice Pratt issued a writ of habeas corpus—that hallowed instrument for the protection of the liberties

George Grenville and the Scots Lord Bute (London, 1765). The Devil (with bagpipes) calls the tune as these two lead a dance beneath "The Oriflame," the French banner of the Stuart Jacobites. *Colonial Williamsburg Foundation.*

of Englishmen.* From the hearing that followed came the chief justice's order for Wilkes's release. It was greeted by the tumultuous acclaim of a people now roused in vigilance for their constitutional rights.

Alarmed Americans saw also how the ministry, thus thwarted, had successfully gagged Wilkes in Parliament. At the start of the new session, with the people still applauding him outside, Wilkes had stood ready to raise the issue of sacred privilege of members of the legislature. Such issues had customary precedence over all other business; but Prime Minister George Grenville produced a message from the king complaining about the *North Briton*, no. 45, and he prevailed on the House of Commons to hear that message first. In spite of William Pitt's powerful oratory, the paper and its author were then condemned without trial. Parliament, from being the vaunted bulwark of British liberties, had evidently become a corrupt, hireling assembly. Eventually, in January 1764, the appalled American patriots saw the Commons expel John

---

* "Thou hast the body"—under this ancient writ, associated with the sacred Magna Carta of 1205, jailers would be summoned to bring their prisoners into a high court. After a hearing in court, it would be determined whether detention was lawful.

Wilkes, canceling his rights as an elected member. The champion of the people was cast out. The hated ministry had organized this—and behind them was the king who continued them in office.

Prime Minister George Grenville had been in the forefront of these assaults on the constitution; then it was the same Grenville who promptly introduced a resolution foreshadowing stamp duties in America. How could this not be a conspiracy to raise more revenues to further subvert an already bought Parliament?

The leaders in Virginia's House of Burgesses had seen all these alarming signs of danger. They were not beguiled by Prime Minister Grenville's suggestion to Parliament that his proposed stamp duties in America were uncontroversial. Landon Carter, by now a senior burgess, took care that the Assembly did not miss the terrible import of the proposal. Such a tax imposed by the British Parliament on the American colonists would be unconstitutional, corrupt, and corrupting. Concerned colonists knew that when the Commons voted a grant of British money to the Crown, they themselves, as tax-paying property-owners in the kingdom, bore their share of that grant; now they were making free with the property of Americans so as to lighten their own burden. Furthermore, the revenue thus generated in America would be a source of patronage and so a means of political manipulation on both sides of the Atlantic. Everyone was clear that British constitutional liberty rested on free men not being taxed save with the consent of their own representatives. The only dispute was whether the Americans were or were not indirectly represented in Parliament through the members returned from such powerful cities as London and Bristol, with which the colonies had extensive commercial connections.

Those who managed the affairs of the Virginia Assembly had to determine a course of action; they set up a committee to prepare a response. We know from Governor Fauquier's report to the home government that there ensued conflict as to whether the language should be strong or moderate; the governor said that moderation had prevailed. Landon Carter later claimed that he was first in America to sound the alarm over the coming Stamp Act, so we may infer that he had been for the strongest wording. The committee was in any case tightly constrained. A colonial assembly could only transmit more or less deferential language through official channels. At best they could invoke an idealization of the constitutional regime under which they wished to dwell, and that is what they did in three documents—a "Petition" to the king, a

"Memorial" to the House of Lords, and a "Remonstrance" to the House of Commons.

To the House of Commons—sink of Bute's and Grenville's presumed corruption—the Virginia Assembly, perhaps spurred on by Landon, addressed the stiffest language. They emphasized the colonists' sacred rights, "which . . . must be infringed" by a Parliamentary stamp tax. They declared it "their indispensible Duty . . . to remonstrate against such a Measure" lest "their Silence, at so important a Crisis" be construed a "cession of those Rights." To the House of Lords, they appealed as "the fixed and hereditary Guardians of *British* Liberty," and so the proper authority to be alerted to "Measures . . . subversive . . . of that Freedom which all Men, especially those who derive their Constitution from *Britain,* have a Right to enjoy." To the king, their Petition was a reminder of their need for his care: they implored "Permission to approach the Throne . . . to intreat that your Majesty . . . protect your People of this Colony in . . . their ancient and inestimable Right of being governed by such Laws respecting their internal Polity and Taxation as are derived from their own Consent. . . ."

The burgesses sent off those carefully worded documents at their session's end in December 1764. But, we may ask: did they feel they sent them to the king, Lords, and Commons of their dreams or of their nightmares?

It was into their nightmares that the next news took them, for neither Commons, nor Lords, nor king even officially received their pleas. In February and March 1765, the already detested George Grenville swept the Stamp Act through Parliament. Parliament was heedless of the protests and warnings of the lone voice of greater-empire patriotism supplied by Colonel Isaac Barré. This veteran of the recent war in America said that he knew the colonists: they were true "Sons of Liberty." He warned that, while they were "as Loyal as any Subjects the King has," they were "a people Jealous of their Lyberties . . . who will vindicate them, if ever they should be violated."

Soon the phrase "Sons of Liberty" resounded everywhere in the colonies; it is a name that is now taken for granted by us. There lurks within it, however, a shadowy family drama in which all the subjects of King George were implicated by the struggles now ensuing. The mother of these Sons of Liberty is proclaimed in the name itself. The icon of the female figure of Liberty circulated widely in this time; her alternates were similar figures of Britannia and of Virtue. At first these brave sons must act in the world as fatherless men; but when they went on to cast out the king, had they not at once named and symbolically killed their father? Had they not done this, even as they cast off their old status as subjects, and established themselves as brothers and citizens who would rule themselves as equals?

Patrick Henry was a son of liberty, and he would now have his first immortal moment. He would have it because the authors of Virginia's strong but decorous appeals against the impending Stamp Act seemed paralyzed when the news of the brusque passage of the act reached them during their next session. They had been schooled to revere Parliament as the bastion of British liberty; they could not defy its statutes. How could they hope to get this one repealed when it had just passed against their strong protests? They chose to play ostrich. Then on May 29, 1765, at the tail end of the session, they faced a revolution from within, and—with all of British North America—they were overwhelmed by that revolution and swept along in its onrush.

Patrick Henry already had a reputation. In 1763 at Hanover Courthouse, in a speech that became part of his legend, he had urged a jury to set aside a decree of the King's Privy Council as tyrannical. Now, during the time when the established leaders were avoiding action over the Stamp Act, Henry and his associates were preparing for action. Williamsburg was too small a place for the secure concealment of conspirators. Rumors must have circulated that something was afoot. Many members preferred not to face hard choices; they preferred evasion over outright resistance to the king's sovereignty. They headed for home, leaving a rump House of Burgesses with barely a quorum.

One of Henry's group, a burgess for Fairfax County named George Johnson, took the first step. On May 29, 1765, he moved a motion, which Henry seconded, that the House go into committee to consider resolutions concerning the Stamp Act. Undoubtedly that was their intention, but it is not quite what the House journal declares. In the official record the motion calls for "a Committee of the whole House . . . , to consider the Steps necessary to be taken in Consequence of the Resolutions of the House of Commons of Great Britain relative to the charging of certain Stamp Duties . . . in America." Even when faced with the full force of a statute passed by both houses of Parliament and signed into law by the king, the traditional leaders who managed the journal still pretended that they were only discussing a bill still in process—some resolutions. (In this we see another sign of the paralysis of the old guard in the face

Patrick Henry romanticized in Thomas Sully's famous 1815 posthumous portrait. He seems to contemplate his country's destiny rather than to arouse passion with an inflammatory call to arms. *Colonial Williamsburg Foundation.*

of an authority that they dare not defy.) Patrick Henry was not so inhibited; he now produced a set of seven resolutions that he and his associates had drafted. For the next few hours the House was in closed session for its committee proceedings. There are no reports of the debates at this stage, but it seems a motion including the whole proposal was adopted as a procedural step.

In the event only the first four of Henry's resolutions appeared in the official Journal of the House; they were not very contentious, being but a terse version of the statements of rights that the Assembly had already sent off six months before. The fifth resolution put forward by Henry was adopted by a narrow margin, but it was rescinded and expunged from the record a day later. (This was a move with scarce any precedents; it has the hallmark of Speaker John Robinson's style of fixing, so detested by Landon when he first became a burgess.) The expunged resolution was certainly strong, for it had declared that the asserted power of the British Parliament to tax Virginians was "illegal, unconstitutional and unjust," and that, it would have "a manifest tendency to destroy British as well as American Liberty."

A vote on the sixth and seventh resolutions does not appear in the House's record, but a fierce debate on them is found in unofficial records. The sixth resolution sought to legitimate resistance by declaring that the inhabitants of Virginia—still called "his Majesty's liege People"—were not bound to "yield

Obedience" to any tax law that was not passed by their own Assembly. The seventh resolution put the resistance movement truly on the offensive. In effect, it incited attacks on all active officers of the Crown who might try to collect the stamp tax. It declared "that any Person, who shall . . . assert or maintain" the "Right or Power" of Parliament to "lay any Taxation on the People here, shall be deemed an Enemy to this his Majesty's Colony [of Virginia]."

This sudden move to have a colonial arm of the king's government defy the king in his imperial Parliament was traumatic. Those who remained in the House (39 out of 116 members) were about evenly divided between supporters of Henry's initiative and some very determined opponents. Governor Fauquier's report described supporters of the resolutions as mainly "young hot and giddy members." Fauquier gave voting figures showing that, however divided by age and temperament, the House had sufficient uncommitted members to produce variable outcomes in the crucial divisions: the attack on established authority was checked when only a bare majority of 20 to 19 could be obtained for the fifth resolution. The greatest majority for the least contentious resolution was 22 to 17, indicating the size of the initiative-blocking old guard led by Speaker John Robinson and Attorney General Peyton Randolph. Long afterward, Thomas Jefferson, who had then been a young law student listening from the lobby, characterized the debate as "most bloody." He remembered that "torrents of sublime eloquence from Henry, backed by the solid reasoning of Johnson, prevailed." Jefferson was "standing at the door" after that very close 20 to 19 vote; Peyton Randolph came out exclaiming, "By God, I would have given one hundred guineas for a single vote." On the next day, May 31, with Patrick Henry himself out of town, the old guard was able to organize the overturn of that fifth resolution and to get it expunged from the record. Despite this attempt to limit confrontation with Parliament, Governor Fauquier promptly dissolved the Assembly on June 1.

An unnamed eyewitness has left an account written within days of the events. (It is part of a journal usually identified as written by a "French Traveller"; but we may ask why, if he was French, did he write in English an intelligence report for the French government?) He was probably a disaffected Irish Catholic. The traveler came to Williamsburg on May 30, and learning of the excitement in the town, he managed to get into the lobby of the House, just as Patrick Henry ("henery," he wrote it) stood up to declare bloody war on tyranny. The spy was impressed by the regicidal wording this orator was prepared to use. Henry told the House that in former times both King Tarquin and Julius Caesar of Rome had each had their Brutus to stop them, and that King Charles of England had his Cromwell: "He did not doubt but some good American would stand up, in favour of his Country. . . ." The fiery orator was going on "in a more moderate manner"—no doubt to make a Wilkes-style identification of the ministry rather than the king himself as the present-day tyrants—when the speaker rose up, and said that Henry "had spoke traison . . .": the members should have been "loyal enough to stop him, before he had gone so far." With some of the ambivalence that would characterize the American resistance for the next eleven years, Henry now declared that "he would shew his loyalty to his majesty King G[eorge] the third, at the Expence of the last Drop of his blood, but that what he had said must be attributed to the Interest of his Country's Dying liberty which he had at heart, and . . . led him to have said more than he intended." It might be supposed that Henry had been humiliated by having to take a step back from the abyss into which none—not even he—were yet prepared to plunge; but Henry's response can be read as a tactical retreat that took nothing from the audacity of the speech. Furthermore, popular report outside of the Assembly made an instant hero of the fearless orator. All the talk of the ferrymen and in the taverns when this same traveler resumed his northward journey was boisterous endorsement of Henry's defiance.

Despite the halt called to his ferocious charge in the House, Henry's initiative succeeded. The effect throughout America was electrifying, because what the wider world learned was without hint of all the internal struggles just outlined. The seven resolutions that Patrick Henry and his young associates had boldly drafted, were assumed in the other colonies to have been passed by the Virginia burgesses. They had been posted northward and southward and were printed in newspapers in nearly all the colonies, starting with Rhode Island's *Newport Mercury* of June 24. (Virginia was the glaring exception; Governor Fauquier had a tight reign on the only newspaper there.) In time the resolutions were printed in the British press also.

With the publication of the resolutions the situation was suddenly transformed. Established leaders everywhere had assumed that an act of the British Parliament would have to be enforced until those who made it could be persuaded to repeal it. These assumptions were rapidly overthrown by the effect of Henry's resolutions and the violent outbreaks that soon made the act unenforceable.

The outcome was a triumph indeed for the young Patrick Henry. To Americans up and down the Atlantic seaboard, as they read the unexpurgated resolutions, the defiance was bold—and it was Virginia's. The reported response of the old Boston patriot Oxenbridge Thacher has entered into legend: on his deathbed he rallied to hear the resolutions read aloud; his dying words were a truly patriarchal endorsement of those brave sons of liberty in Virginia—"They are men!"

If we stand back to look at the nature of the drama that was being enacted in Williamsburg on those end-of-May days, and then throughout the colonies as the resolutions became a manifesto for action, we can see a great deal of psychological ambiguity and trauma. Once again the king had been both defied and not defied—because it was really the ministry. And yet the whole episode entered into a deep family drama. Henry's speech itself came right to the point of invoking Oliver Cromwell's regicidal action; the form of Henry's initiative extended the implication. In these proceedings there was contemplated the killing of fathers and father-impersonators—the king and ministers back in England, and a great many traditional colonial leaders in America.

The identification of a psychic family drama in the great struggles that were commencing in the time of the Stamp Act may meet with skepticism, even outrage, in some quarters. Many prefer to think that the whole of history is transacted at the level of rational consciousness. I maintain that deep shadow dramas always enter potently into the political realm as it is collectively imagined. This was especially so when, in its monarchical form, the state sustained a profound and explicit correspondence with the patriarchal organization of the household, and so of the social order into which every subject was born. But, it may be asked, had not the British constitutional monarchy, as established on a controlled and balanced basis by the settlement of 1688, already neutered the father aspect of the king? Not so, I respectfully insist. Attention to the daily forms of government reveals that the king was a real and enduring presence. He was there in nearly all exercises of power—even if those who theorized it (such as John Locke) had made their fame by teaching the limits of the kingly authority. A different and still pervasive body of teaching starkly asserted the patriarchal aspect of authority under the monarch. The Book of Common Prayer remained the official book of worship and instruction in England and in Virginia; its catechism taught every child that the fifth commandment— "Honour thy father"—demanded of all persons that they "honor and obey the king and his ministers," just as they must "submit" to all "governors, teachers, spiritual pastors, and masters," and indeed must act humbly "to all . . . betters." Thus was invoked a hierarchy of fathers stretching up to the king, and this was a hierarchy that extended back down from the king through the ranks of all those who bore his commission. This understanding of authority and connection was directly expressed by the Virginia General Assembly when, in an address of 1766, they recalled their anxious petitioning of "their King and Common Father."

The Revolution, of course, could not have happened if a great deal of change in outlook and attitudes had not already taken place; new conceptions had to have gained some hold. There was, indeed, a growing emphasis on government as based on a primal contract among the people to secure their own well-being, as seen in the writings of Locke and many others. However, to overlook the enduring psychic hold of the Father-King is to miss the trauma of the moment of the king's dethronement. How else shall we explain the long months of 1775–76 during which the united colonies were openly at war with the ministry but could only slowly and painfully bring themselves to declare an end to their allegiance to the king?

For the century and a half of the Old Dominion's colonial existence, the fathers and elders of Virginia had organized their own leadership roles as mediators keeping open channels of communication to London and Westminster. They had to combine two essential roles: they must protect the interests of the colony as they defined them, and they must maximize their own access to the patronage of the imperial monarchy whose loyal subjects they were. Patrick Henry showed how, in that role, they would now be pushed aside. (As it turned out these knowing politicians were soon leading and moderating the movement they had first tried to block; they both contained and co-opted the fiery patriot.)

Landon had been at Sabine Hall during this time. For the moment he had been spared taking sides; his own and his family's illnesses had kept him from attending the Assembly in the spring of 1765. On June 3, as soon as he heard of events in Williamsburg, Landon chose to respond not to Henry's resolutions but to the governor's June 1 action. With the Assembly dissolved, there must be new elections to replace the old House of Burgesses. In a letter that he sent to be published in the colony's only newspaper, Landon announced that he would not be a candidate in those elections. His decision was founded on opposite assumptions to those that inspired Henry's culminating resolve: Landon evidently still believed that the Stamp Act would inevitably be enforced. In such oppressive circumstance, he felt that "to be a proper Representative of a People divested of Liberty is to be a real Slave." On this account, "every prudent person, will rather choose to retire . . . than publickly be concerned where he must enroll his Country's Slavery." Evidently Landon was still unable to imagine the defiance called for by Henry. For the moment, in place of the rebellion in which he and most of British North America would soon be caught up, he saw withdrawal to a private station as his only honorable course. This resignation letter, however, was never published. William Royle, the only printer in the colony, thrived on government contracts, and Governor Fauquier forbade him to publish anything against the Stamp Act. Landon's own copy therefore had to be filed among his papers with an endorsement that it was "not permitted to be printed."

Proud of his early opposition to the impending stamp tax, Landon could never acknowledge the revolutionary difference between protesting against proposed legislation and inciting violent defiance of an enacted statute. Furthermore, Henry's course of action disturbed a sincere elder-patriarchal loyalty to the fatherhood symbol of the Crown; it offended a still-enduring emotional attachment to the person of the king, captive though he evidently was to ministerial intrigues. The older man neither accepted nor forgave the younger for seizing leadership in this struggle.

Virginia continued part paralyzed by the opposing forces that had checked Henry. The inward agony of a half-submissive political stance must have been considerable, especially as news of more outright forms of resistance came from the north. Tense months intervened before the days in October when Virginians could move into direct action against their newly arrived stamp-tax collector. As soon as George Mercer came to Williamsburg, he had to face an angry crowd, many of them leading planters who demanded that he should resign and promise not to bring the detested stamped paper into Virginia.

Meanwhile, there was the strange anti-Stamp-Act procession and hanging of effigies with which this chapter opened. Westmoreland courthouse, where the enactment took place, was only a dozen miles north of Sabine Hall, and Richard Henry Lee with all his family were neighbors and friends. In the effigy hanging-and-burning pageant of the world turned upside down, Lee had stage-managed a killing of false fathers. Indeed, it seemed as though Richard Henry Lee was intent on rivaling Patrick Henry in the role of the young man who would engage in violent assaults on old and hitherto sacrosanct forms of authority. And Lee was well positioned both socially and geographically to involve Landon. In June of 1765, Lee wrote Landon a letter crackling with the fierce rhetoric of "the cause of Liberty" against "tyrannic power." The young Lee exhorted his elderly neighbor not to withdraw from the polls but to stand as a patriotic candidate whenever the election should be called. Seven weeks later the young man sent another letter that escalated the violence of intended resistance. Already anticipating war, Lee expressed the hope "that America can find Arms as well as Arts to remove the demon Slavery from its borders." (Here, of course, he referred to political enslavement and not to the cruel bondage in which he, Landon, and the other Virginia patriots held Virginians of African descent.) This was strong language; such a call to arms amounted to treason,* and most Americans were hoping at this time that the rapid repeal of the Stamp Act might spare them the need even to contemplate such an extreme step. If Landon responded to these letters, his replies have not survived.

Soon Lee's own county of Westmoreland took the lead in announcing to the lieutenant governor that it would close its court rather than proceed using stamped papers. Lee then led in the formation of an "association" to refuse the use of stamped paper for any purposes. The signers of this agreement would enforce their stance on anyone who attempted to comply with the act. Shortly thereafter, Archibald Ritchie, a Scots merchant trading in Tappahannock across the river from Landon, threatened to break ranks. A crowd of four hundred or more prepared to march on him to force his recantation. Meanwhile, Landon's adjoining Richmond County did not form such an association, and Landon (unlike his son, Robert Wormeley Carter) did not sign to conform to the Westmoreland association. At this stage, the only record of the old squire's relationship to the threatened violence was that he arranged a meeting with Ritchie, designed to get concessions from him that might make the mobbing unnecessary. Much later, in 1776, when Landon was fully committed to armed rebellion against the forces of the King, he expressed notable hostility toward Richard Henry Lee's antimonarchical impulses; he even suspected Lee of having a hand in the writing of the anonymous, strongly antimonarchical pamphlet *Common Sense*, before it was known to be by Thomas Paine.

Landon knew Grenville and Bute to be traitors to the constitution. George III was implicated because he would not dismiss them. But for the moment, Landon looked to the king to save the situation. When the newspaper had resumed publication in Williamsburg, Landon was able to get printed a letter under a pseudonym that affirmed his identity as an American farmer. It was an

---

* Starkly stated, treason was "compassing or imagining the death of the king." The law would also brand as treasonous any collective action by subjects, without the king's commission, to act in such a way as to usurp his power and sovereignty.

Portion of an allegorical print show-ing George III with Britannia, Liberty, and America. Landon wished "that the Sovereign of the whole nation may be ever happy in the dutiful alle-giance of his people . . . , and that his faithful subjects may be equally blessed with his Royal protection." This portion of a 1768 print shows George III and Britannia with a dis-armed Liberty, grieving over North America (and Corsica—then being conquered by France). *Colonial Wil-liamsburg Foundation.*

answer to an English newspaper attack on American resistance to the Stamp Act, whose legitimacy the Englishman upheld. Landon's words were eloquent both as to his attachment to the king and to the British identity that the monar-chy still embodied for Americans: "An equality of constitutional rights enjoyed is the surest means of a steady connexion in the whole realm . . . ; where such blessings are interrupted in any part of the kingdom, a *Briton* can no more wish for life on one side of the *Atlantick* than he can on the other. That the Sover-eign of the whole nation may be ever happy in the dutiful allegiance of his peo-ple, even in the most distant part of his realm, and that his faithful subjects may be equally blessed with his Royal protection . . . , is the hearty prayer of A truly loyal and An HONEST BUCKSKIN."

The troubled aspect of oppression from above and incipient rebellion from below was marked both explicitly and implicitly in the 1766 almanac diary. Ex-plicitly, it was declared on the front and back; implicitly, it was threaded through the whole book by way of a new kind of narrative. This is the moment, already referred to, when the diary began to fill out with stories of rebellion at home.

The 1766 diary is significantly enclosed between two inscriptions relating to the Stamp Act and the resistance it provoked. On the front page there is a curious note: *This Almanack came enclosed under a cover with nothing hinting from whom. I examin'd it to see if it had been Stampt, but finding none I ventured to set my name in it.* The name is a signature with flourishes and a date—*March 8, 1766.*

Toward the back there is the previously noted undated Latin inscription for portraits of the two heroes who led the repeal of the hated Act. The words about William Pitt have been summarized in discussing Landon's admiration for that statesman; Lord Camden, we have encountered under a different name, when as Chief Justice Charles Pratt, we saw him order the release of John Wilkes.

A Proper inscription to be written under a picture of Lord Camden
and The Right Honourable W. Pitt.
C. Pratt et W. Pitt
Viri Honoratissimi
Qui Britanniam Magnam Conservabant
Fovendo LIBERTATES
Americae Britannicae
Contra Perditionem
designatam
Per
G. Grenville. Anno 1766.

(C. Pratt & W. Pitt, most estimable men, who in the year 1766 saved Great Britain by supporting the LIBERTIES of British America against the destruction plotted by G. Grenville.)

The first of the new kind of narrative eruptions to appear in the 1766 almanac diary came in the early weeks of regular chronicling. It was a labyrinthine set of reports of suspected slave robberies, cover-ups, runnings away, returns, further escapes, and cover-ups. It was all told in three diary entries from three days of revelation—April 24, 25, and 27; but the telling was full of retrospective narratives spanning a much more extensive period of time. The reporting of the episode is structured by the diarist's sense of a pervasive subversion that extended up into his own family, since Landon's detested daughter-in-law had protected the conspirators from discovery. That narrative begins a long series of stories of slave conspiracies and of the master's countermeasures. Landon as diarist suddenly began to reveal himself as the exasperated ruler of a rebellious kingdom. He was able to strike out in assertions of his authority, but he was not able to get the kind of control of the situation that he felt he ought to have. King George III, faced with cabinet intrigues of ministers and the Wilkes supporters taking over London, could also have written such stories.

The next dramatic episode in the 1766 volume of the diary is a more intimate family story. It is starts a long series of narratives of the primal rebellion of the son (urged on by the daughter-in-law) against the father.

It is a hot June morning. Landon has already been down to his boat landing where he made alternative arrangements for a shipment that a vessel in the river had not picked up as promised. Now the whole Sabine Hall Carter family—including Robert Wormeley, his wife, Winifred, and their eight-year-old son, little Landon—are waiting for breakfast to be ready. They are no doubt in the central-hall breezeway of the house. . . . But old Landon must be allowed to tell this story himself.

Friday, June 27. . . .

We had this day a domestic gust.

My daughters, Lucy & Judy, mentioned a piece of impudent behaviour of little Landon to his mother Winifred; *telling her—when she said she would whip him, that he did not care if she did.*

His father heard this unmoved.

The child denied it.

I bid him come & tell me what he did say—for I could not bear a child should be sawsy to his Mother.

He would not come and I got up and took him by the arm—he would not speak. I then shook him—but his outrageous father says I struck him.

At breakfast the Young Gentleman would not come in though twice called by his father—& once Sent for by him—and twice by me.

I then got up, and gave him one cut over the left arm with the lash of my whip and the other over the banister by him.

Madam then rose like a bedlamite that her child should be struck with a whip—and up came her Knight Errant to his father with some heavy God damnings, but he prudently did not touch me. Otherwise my whip handle should have settled him—if I could.

Madam pretended to rave like a Madwoman.

I showed the child's arm was but commonly red with the stroke; but all would not do. Go she would & she may. I see in her all the ill treatment my son gives & has given

"Madam then rose like a bedlamite. . . ." A masculine view of female anger as represented by the French artist Jean-Baptiste Greuze (1786). *The Metropolitan Museum of Art, New York.*

since his marriage. Indeed I always saw this in her as a girl—a Violent, Sulkey, Proud, imperious Dutchess—One fit to be Queen of a Prince—as the old _____ her father always complimented her.

As this child—my grandson—is thus encouraged to insult me, I have been at great expence in maintaining him but will be at no more. And so I shall give notice.

Family values in the eighteenth century still reflected a household-centered economic system that was thousands of years old. The family household as a command structure was very strong; it was still reinforced by the way the world then worked. In the mid-eighteenth century not only were there no factories or big stores but there were no corporations and office complexes. Nearly all the work that was done was still done in somebody's household, great or small. This might be a farm, a carpenter or blacksmith's workshop, a merchant's counting house, still situated in his dwelling, or, in Landon's case, on a large plantation. That meant there was no salaried employment as we know it—no opportunity to feel that you were your own person while working in an impersonal bureaucratic organization. You then lived and worked in a household; you were either the master in charge, or you were a servant, living under the master's patriarchal rule. Women, usually widows, might be female masters; as wives, they were in an intermediate situation—subordinate junior partners to the master; while as daughters, like sons, they were servants in their parents' or some other household. You could only be a master by acquiring, usually through inheritance, a farm, a workshop, a merchant store, or a plantation.

The extended-family situation at Sabine Hall was profoundly structured by this patrimonial inheritance system. *Go she would and go she may*—Winifred wanted out of that household where she could not be mistress since her husband could not be master. Robert Wormeley, however, felt he must wait to inherit. The girls—the young unmarried aunts who started the row by telling tales on little Landon—were similarly trapped. As the story of Judith's elopement and marriage has indicated, each must find an approved husband so that their portions would be given as dowries. Only that way would their new families have a plantation adequate to support them. Along with most of their counterparts in innumerable other households, all the younger persons involved in the *domestic gust* must await their inheritance—or a settlement of property in anticipation of inheritance. In this context we can see that, while the breakfast-time row was a clash of personalities, those personalities were historically conditioned. In this case, relationships were further strained by the situation of the married son living in the household of which his father remained the active head; that had been unusual for centuries in the western European family system of which Anglo-Virginian practices were an adaptation.

Old Landon, providing the point of view in this story, straddled two ways of negotiating family life. He operated with two ways of thinking about persons and their obligations, one ancient and one modern. Just behind him was an old regime of absolute patriarchy. His own father, a strong and very successful patriarch, had been known as King Carter; and in his own house he was indeed a king.

In the ancient regime of patriarchal monarchy just coming to an end in old Landon's lifetime, the Fifth Commandment, "Honor thy Father . . . ," was the *only* principle of government private or public. The arrangement can best be understood in a stark oversimplification as a cosmic descending sequence:

God was Father to the King

The King was Father to the Great Lords

The Great Lords were Fathers to the Knights and Squires

The Knights and Squires were Fathers to their Tenants

And the Tenants were Fathers to rule their households of wives, children, and servants.

(All save the king were aptly called subjects, defined by their subordinate status—for there were no citizens yet.)

Fatherhood was power; and power was a form of fatherhood.

Furthermore, the Christian churches—both Protestant and Catholic—taught that God was an angry God, and that human nature was deeply sinful. The more all those Fathers punished, the better it would be.

In old Landon's fifty-six-year lifetime, that way of imagining the world was being undermined. It had been severely jolted in the years leading up to the Stamp Act crisis; and in 1776 it would be symbolically overthrown in the Declaration of Independence.

As we have seen in the account of the world Landon culled from his library, a new positive view of human nature was working its way both up and down in Europe and America in the eighteenth century. This new view was expressed in (and advanced by) a revision of ideas about psychology and child-rearing that was coming from philosophers like John Locke and many of his successors. Innovation was also forwarded by such sentimental journalism as came in Joseph Addison and Richard Steele's immensely popular *Spectator*. Above all, the new view was disseminated by one of the boom products of the age, the sentimental novel. Have we not seen Landon unconsciously writing his own patriarchal point-of-view version of Samuel Richardson's *Clarissa?* During the eighteenth century the celebration of the stern absolute rule of punishing fathers was in rapid decline; among the fast-expanding, literate, cosmopolitan portion of society, a more problematic view of patriarchal sovereignty was coming to pervade both the political and the domestic spheres.

In the political sphere, expectations of government shifted away from kingly patriarchalism toward the more comprehensively participatory modes that would generate the ideology of democracy. The revolutionary alternative system came to be most boldly expressed in 1787 in the federal constitution of the United States; its opening words established the new sovereign—"We the People. . . ." That was a culmination still twenty years away; but in the 1760s, discussion of what would be best for everyone was already widely supposed to be the way government was directed—as was apparent when first Wilkes and then the American patriots used the press so effectively to protest the actions of the king's ministers. Government was no longer strongly imagined as a hierarchy of ruling fathers. As the idea of "the subject" faded, the idea of the "the citizen" grew stronger.

The values propagated in the narratives of the novel brought forward the feminine; the politics of republican rebellion foregrounded the masculine. Society as reimagined by the Wilkes-ites and the sons of Liberty, would be a confederation of males-only citizens who would rule themselves collectively in the public domain. As heads of households, they would rule their women and children and servants (or slaves) by natural manly authority in the now sharply distinct private sphere at home. We shall not understand the nature and the difficulty facing twenty-first-century democracy unless we understand how much its challenge was set in that first eighteenth-century disposition whereby equality was reserved for white men in the public sphere, while women, black slaves, and servants were assigned to continue as "subjects" in the excluded private sphere. This firmly assigned inequality has given promoters of gender and race-blind democracy the main continuing program for our times; and this work is not assisted by that other legacy of the eighteenth century, the reimagining of the family so as to sentimentalize women as the angels of the house.

There were, of course, other ways of thinking about the family very prevalent in this world—as there still are. The African Americans at the slave quarters would have told the story of that June morning "domestick gust" altogether differently from Landon. They had their own distinctive culture of family relations by which to judge and tell. The literate world also was not simply consensual. Benjamin Franklin's immensely popular *Poor Richard's Almanack* is redolent with a rough masculinism of the kind expressed in the old rhyme: A wife, a dog, and a hickory tree, / the more you beat them, the better they be."

The upper-class sentimentalization of family, however, is the key way to understand both the Sabine Hall "domestick gust" and its interconnectedness with the reimagining of politics in that time.

Old Landon had a "split personality": He wanted to be the unquestioned patriarch he had seen his father to be; but he also wanted to be a caring father and grandfather in keeping with the sensibility of the times. The diary narrative makes it clear how the grandfather had watched to see whether the father of the boy would exercise paternal discipline upon hearing the aunt's report of little Landon's *sawsiness* to his mother. Again, old Landon insisted that he did not strike the boy who would not come and answer when questioned. The patriarch was also at pains to show that he had not really inflicted hurt with the whip.

Old Landon's family thus were getting confusing, mixed messages. They were younger persons one or two generations further into changing times. They expected to be understood and persuaded, rather than just commanded. They were sorely tried by a father figure who demanded obedience but craved affection and companionship.

Every aging generation is caught between what it learned to expect from its parents and what it confronts in changed expectations from its offspring growing up in a changed world. At Sabine Hall in 1766, however, that generational conflict was very intense and historically very instructive, because it straddled a gulf that was opening into revolution.

There is a striking passage five years on in old Landon's record of his relationship with little Landon, now thirteen years old. It reveals most clearly the other side of this self-subverting patriarchy. This time the old man was not playing the stern, whip-in-hand patriarch, but his other (confusing) role of sensitive new-age grandfather.

I made it my business out of duty to talk to this Grandson & namesake—and set before him the unhappiness he must throw everybody into as well as himself. . . .

At first he endeavoured to avoid me, and went away.

I bid him come back;

he pretended to be affraid that I wanted to scold at him.

I told him no, it was my concern that made me earnest to advise him to imploy his good sence which god had blessed him with. . . .

At last he seemed to listen, and indeed shed tears at what I said.

I hope in God then he will learn to behave better.

Revolutions such as the one Patrick Henry had launched not only set person against person but they divide persons within themselves, and produce a mounting sense of impending chaos. It is to the diary revelations of a world felt to be profoundly disordered that this book will turn in its remaining chapters.

PART IV

A TROUBLED OLD REGIME

By contemptuously narrating disorder, old Landon would uphold right order. The stories of subversion of authority and neglect of duty that began to fill out the plantation diary from the time of the Stamp Act were at heart affirmations of an old regime.

Landon had been born under the British constitutional monarchy with all its hierarchical assumptions; now he felt the old order passing and his own rebellion contributing to the ensuing turmoil. The stories he began to write expressed a yearning for the restoration of the right relations of imagined better times. They are also an amazing revelation of that vanishing world as seen from within.

First we shall see how he tried to plot in cautionary tales the proper order of the master's rule of the slave plantation. Then we shall see how he tried to show whoever should read his diary that he upheld a tradition of service to the community in these troubled times, while others pursued their own selfish ends. In a third chapter we shall see his matching affirmation of a father's right to respect and obedience in face of the primal rebellion of his son and of his daughter-in-law.

Chapter 9

Master and Slaves

Lives in Bondage

It is Wednesday, June 12, 1771—a midsummer afternoon just after eighteenth-century dinner time, four o'clockish. The master of Sabine Hall turns to his current diary. Quill poised, he bends over his June book. He enters his initial review of the day so far. This is a confident day in a confident month. His eldest grandson's outrageousness has not yet toppled his mood. The diarist begins with the weather. Was it promising? Perhaps it was.

Landon had already been over to see the Mangorike tobacco field. The work there was pleasing enough; he plans how he will get done *the whole that I want*. Next he resolved to *clap a negative* on overspending by the manager of his down-river quarters, but he can note unusual accord with his Home Quarter overseer, Lawson. As Landon brings his diary up to that day's dinner just concluded, there is even the satisfaction of having detected (and no doubt corrected) female aberration: *My Cook wench cannot now dress a dish of beans or Peas but they come in quite raw.* That terse judgment had brought him to the bottom of the narrow page.

Now it is the end of the day. Using a candle, or the last of the summer twilight, Landon turns the completed page and resumes writing. He reviews the weather again, and his confidence is further boosted. Just as he had predicted earlier—*every chance of rain* has evaporated. Now he carefully inscribes an idyll. It is as though he had been preparing himself for this all the day, and even all the month so far. He writes clearly; he avoids the jumps and elisions that often make his narratives hard to follow at first reading:

I walkt out this evening to see how my very old and honest Slave Jack Lubbar did to support life in his Extreme age; and I found him prudently working amongst his melon vines, both to divert the hours and indeed to keep nature stirring—that indigestion might not hurry him off with great pain.

I took notice of his Pea vines a good store—and askt him why he had not got them hill'd;

His answer was—the Prudence of Experience Master—they have not got age enough and it will hurt too young things to coat them too closely with earth.

Inspired by the wisdom of the old man, Landon then turned away to inspect his own legumes planted on a larger scale in wide beds at Jack's quarter.

Aging and unappreciated at this time of his life—but confident for the moment—Landon carried away with him cherished wisdom from this exchange with an even-older man. So, he concluded his report on his evening round of crop reviewing with the consoling note: *Old Lubbar's observation about his pease being too young to be hilt comforts me about mine between the barley—which I cannot yet a while hoe and earth up.*

The encounter was ideal in both form and content. Certainly it is so as Landon recalled and savored it. He had sought out the old man, showing both a master's care for a dependent and a proper respect for old age. He had delighted in sharing a commitment to gardening in its productive and its health-giving aspects. The turn the exchange had happened to take had caused both old men to see themselves as fatherly protectors of *young things*. At least that is the part Landon was carefully collecting for the record.

The idyll of the aging master and the faithful old slave was resumed in time. Three years later, in 1774, turning to his current June book—already fat with reflections on politics and medicine—Landon composed some six pages of literary monument to Jack. It began: *I must not leave a very Particular case that has happened within this week to be only recorded in my memory.*

Once again Jack Lubbar was introduced as *my very old Slave*, but the contemplation of Jack's age now took the diarist's mind back to an earlier time. No one could be certain about Jack's age, but Landon recalled that *back in the year 1734 already I found him too old a man to keep as a foreman to my Mangorike Gang.* The humane young master—as he fondly told his diary—had avoided an abrupt humiliation, and had *privately bid* old Jack to relinquish the lead and *by degrees to fall astern of the rest.* Jack no doubt felt the pain of surrendering his masculine prowess and domination over the younger men and the working women—even though the change was imposed *by degrees.* Yet, Jack's pain was not part of the diarist's record; in the story that Landon unfolded, Jack was just thankful for the tactful consideration: *Ever since then he has been only as a Slave gratefully endeavouring to serve a very kind master.*

Jack was for ten years a follower in the gang that he once had led. Then, *At last about 20 years ago I removed him only to his ease as an overlooker at my Fork quarter with 5 hands and myself.* Jack would at last supervise from the side rather than follow or lead from out front; *in which Service he so gratefully discharged his duty as to make me by his care alone larger crops of Corn, tobacco and pease twice over than ever I have had made by anyone.*

But good times never last. Human frailty and human wickedness steal in. Under pressure, Jack *asked to be removed.* His age *almost deprived him of eyesight;* he found that *those under him—mostly his great grandchildren* continually took advantage of his infirmity and were encouraged *by the baseness of their parents.* Landon reported this, no doubt, from his personal experience of the ingratitude of children and grandchildren toward their progenitors. That alteration of circumstance was remembered as *about 12 years* before the penning of this elegiac narrative of the old slave and his master. The master had then brought Jack and *his wife,* herself a venerable authority figure described as *our old midwife,* to the *hen house* at home. For nearly ten years the poultry received the *good effects of his care* or their care. Then *about 3 years ago*—for reasons not given—Jack and *his old woman* had *at last* been removed again to the Fork. Their master intended that *there they were to live quite retired—only under my constant kindness.*

Jack found new vigor. With admiration, Landon reported that: *But active as his life has been—he there became a vast progger in catching fish, Beavers, otters, Musckrats, & Minxes with his traps.* ("Progger," says the *Oxford English Dictionary*, is an archaic word for an assiduous forager, living off the land; and the word was yet alive and well in the 1880s as a North American dialect word for clam diggers and oyster gatherers. It deserves to be resuscitated.) During all this time, Jack was a constant churchgoer. When the weather was *good,* he took himself to worship, *as erect and fast a Walker as almost any man in the Parish.* Meanwhile—in the manner celebrated in the diary idyll of 1771—Jack was also an amazing horticulturalist: he kept a garden well stored with *patches of pease & belly lumber, as it is called.*

Even a *sound constitution* must succumb eventually, however. When just recovered from a shin injury—aggravated perhaps by dropsy and Landon's idea of what was mild medication—the aged man had gone out unwisely, into the swamp. The fond master reported that Jack had heard of a minx that had *committed a great destruction* among the poultry. Still zealous to be of service, *he went into the run where the animal was suspected to reside.* There—*standing in the water so long* to set his traps, he had got a chill on his bladder that stopped his urine. When told of Jack's condition, Landon had applied all his practical and theoretical knowledge; but he found he could not reverse an inexorable decline toward death.

The master could not check the decline, but Jack momentarily could! Even after the despairing master had ordered his carpenters *to get some Planks ready to make him a Coffin*, Jack came out of his coma; he declared that, *if he could but make water he should do well*. He seemed still on the mend the next day: *The old fellow still insists that he is recovering*. Landon recorded his own redoubled efforts to secure *relief to my Poor honest Slave*; but at the same time there must be pious resignation: *Let God's will be done. I hope I do my duty, more I know I cannot do.*

Jack died within a day or so, having survived for ten days, a fact Landon later claims credit for.* More than a month later, Landon was still concerned as to whether he had done all he might have. Looking at recent medical publications relating to urinary disorders, and reviewing once more the course of Jack's illness, the diarist told himself that, with the treatment applied: *I should have cured him*, had not Jack been *so vastly old*. He had been, alas, already in the grip of mortal destiny: *I saw death on his cape*. The diarist had, however, already written valedictory epitaphs in anticipation; indeed, he performed this piety twice on June 25. First he had written:

Farewell to as honest a human creature as could live, Who to his last proved a faithful & a Profitable servant to his Master as every *remembered Conduct must testify*.

Then later that day, he noted that *Poor Jack is cold in his extremities*, and added: *Farewell I may say thou good & faithful Servant to me.*

The idealization and mythologizing is obvious. Writing these narratives, Landon could momentarily feel at peace; in time of revolutionary subversion, he needed to legitimate his now-problematic role as a master of slaves.

However, in earlier episodes and fragments, the surviving Sabine Hall diaries tell a very different story from the one Landon composed in retrospect. Jack's second retirement had been not twelve but six or seven years before the elegy; and there was absolutely no preretirement praise for Jack. What we read from the whole time of Jack's stewardship at the Fork is rather a string of complaints. Some six items figure in my reconstructed indictment:

---

* Landon's July book and the very end of his June book have gone missing, so we do not know how the devoted master recorded Jack's actual death; and we do not know whether in this altogether exceptional instance he recorded participation in a slave's funeral.

- He has imprudently pulled from the seedling patch the weeds that would blanket against frost —*though everything foretold a frost.*
- He has left a fence unmended—though particularly instructed on that point—so that the young corn under his oversight had been *all rooted up* by invading sheep and cattle.
- He has either stolen or carelessly allowed others to steal from the stock of corn *that would have kept the plantation a whole year.*
- He has neglected the all-important making of dung, he being *too easy with those* Fork *people.*
- He has failed to get on with the urgent task of working the earth for the planting of tobacco, and so: *no hills turned.*
- And then the culminating charge: he was a *drunkard.*

Landon was impelled to add angry generalizing reflections: *the more particular we are in our charges and the fonder we show ourselves of anything, the more careless will our slaves be.* Here was a sudden insight into the inevitable roles imposed by the whole system; suddenly we see the locked-in relationship of the master, incessantly slave driving, and the slaves, ceaselessly evading, while they sought their own gratification.

Slaves' offenses were a personal affront, especially if the offenders had been commissioned to bear authority under the master. So, the diarist characteristically generalized particular offenses into aphorisms about order and disorder in the plantation system. *Even the most aged whilst their lives are made most pleasant to them, are the most ungratefully neglectful.* And then, generalizing further: *This cannot but be a strong instance against the pretended honesty of a slave founded on Religious Principles.* That general reflection circuited back to the particular slave foreman, concluding with a Virginia proverb: *this old fellow Jack Lubbar is a favorite of that* religious *sort, but he has his inebrieties & whenever they interfere the devil may take his trash.* The problem lay in the nature of these workers; only a white man could offset that inherent problem. *Old Jack is . . . too deceitful and careless himself. A negroe can't be honest.*

The master told himself he should have known better—and known that deeper at the root of the disorder lay a human enslavement to appetite that slaves certainly could not overcome. *All is my own fault to think a drunkard could be reclaimed, or a negroe honest enough to carry on any business long enough for more than one year. I must get new overseers everywhere.*

The master had no choice, however, but to rely on his slaves. Another slave-foreman, George, did succeed Jack, but that only proved once again to Landon that even the ordaining of hierarchy could not sustain order long against nature. George's status and authority to command had, like Jack's, been marked by special rewards. Had not the diarist seen to it that he received *meat from my Smoak house*? For a time at the Fork, George had *carried on the plantation to a very fine prospect in corn*; then he had begun to fail in that command and in the competitive masculinity demanded of his role: *Having nobody but women to press him in his work,* he is *quite indolent with respect to any kind of care.*

Jack had pleaded failing eyesight and asked to be relieved of responsibilities around the year 1768; and then the intemperate outbursts of 1766 were repressed from memory. Jack's failings could be seen as relating to generational conflicts that the master himself contended with. This was the plight of a well-meaning man driven to drink by an ungrateful generation of children and children's children. Furthermore, plantation patriarchy as legitimating metaphor entailed both the right to drive the slaves and the duty to give them care and protection. So, when—in 1771 and 1774—Landon had needed to give himself an idealized self-image rather than to extract productive work from Jack, he had erased memories of a *lazy . . . stupid. . . . drunkard* and had penned a story of *my very old and honest Slave,* who was *gratefully endeavouring to serve a very kind master.*

Telling of Slavery

The Jack Lubbar of the 1771 idyllic evening visit and of the 1774 elegy upon a dying slave was clearly a figure from the realm of mythology. There had for eons been a rich set of old-world myths of faithful serfs or servants; now these were transposed into new-world myths of devoted slaves. But we must recognize that the careless, drunken Jack Lubbar of the 1766 diary was equally a figure from mythology. In both cases, the mythic quality of the story has the effect of stereotyping all the protagonists, most of all the narrator. There was profound truth in these narratives, since they arose from the bound together relationship of master and slave; nevertheless a striking variety of caricature was being produced by Landon's growing need to tell stories that would legitimate his patriarchal sovereignty at home.

SLAVERY REMEMBERED

While Landon was furiously narrating his dealings with his enslaved people, they were storing up their own memories. In the 1930s—just before it was too late—bearers of those memories that had accumulated over many generations

The most expressive portrait of a Virginia WPA ex-slave narrator. Mrs. Fanny Berry of Petersburg entered into very spirited interaction with her young African American interviewers. *The Museum of Hampton University, Hampton, Va.*

were sought out under the auspices of the New Deal's Federal Writers' Project. In Virginia nearly all these interviews were conducted by young African American men and women and were largely the result of the determined efforts of Roscoe E. Lewis of the Hampton Institute, now Hampton University. I am persuaded that these memoirs from the enslaved must be called upon to balance the one-sided, harsh account of the lives of their people that Landon left in his diary; but first I must say a few words about these recollections.

Former slaves were eager to pass on their stories to the young African Americans who, as college students, represented the promise of a brighter day ahead. In whom could these old timers more properly confide? Mrs. Jennie Patterson in Chesterfield County (just south of James River) said to her interviewer (Miss Susie R. C. Byrd): "I done told you I was feared to tell all I done seen in my lifetime, and I ain't telling white folks but so much even now in this new day and time."* Mrs. Fanny Berry said to the same young African American woman:

---

* In the 1930s it was felt appropriate even by African Americans to render the speech of black informants using the spelling conventions developed for the minstrel show. Out of respect, and for readability, I have silently replaced these with correct spellings—although I have preserved dialect forms of words. (If the speech of the white people whom the federal government set over all these projects were to be written as it was spoken, it would look just as quaint.)

"Now Miss Sue, take up [your pen]. I just like to talk to you, honey, about them days of slavery because you look like you want to hear all about them." Mrs. Minnie Folkes wished she "knowed how to write, and could put off a book on this here situation . . . these way back questions." The Reverend John Brown prayed for all those people "who has interested themselves to write this history about us slaves." He intoned "Dear Lord umm now let this . . . be the greatest book—next to your bible—um um um, for us colored people for Christ sake Amen thank you Jesus!"

The 1930s testimonies were the products of collective as well as individual memories, and the clustering of memories around certain themes shows the shaping power of a common culture. These stories, often heard from parents and grandparents, were stories to be told to children and grandchildren; in them were rendered that "way back time" of slavery as it needed to be remembered. Certain topics recur repeatedly: the cruelty in horrendous whippings; the distortions of morality as slaves were forced by hunger to steal; the class structures in the supposedly benign gentry and the mean overseers and patrollers; the heartbreaks when mothers, children, siblings, and cousins were sold; and the wish-fulfillment stories of successful running away. (Especially recurrent was a motif of runaways who raised families in snug hole-in-the-ground houses off in the woods.) There was also the surge of memories surrounding the triumph of the liberating armies. The Black Union companies had recruited escaping slaves; it was they who had raised the Union flag over the capitol in Richmond.

The voices of those 1930s Virginia veterans of the plantation are needed for any history encompassing slavery. Adding these individual expressions of the collective memory of their people to the history of the world of Landon Carter breaks a terrible silence and calls forth otherwise unspeakable truths.

Truth—let it be said—is not the same as fact. There is a profound truth in recording the facts of what stories an enduring people tell to preserve their own history. Virginia Hayes Sheperd told her two young African American interviewers that the Norfolk slave auction block had stood "between the Portsmouth Ferry and the Monument" (meaning the Robert E. Lee Monument); she went on to assure them that, "Lee's monument stands for all the devilment and cruelty that was done to the Negro during the days of slavery." The truth she communicated was not primarily factual about the location of an auction block; it was evaluative—it was about the different meanings of memory and memorials to one people and to another.

A FORMER SLAVE TELLS HIS LIFE STORY

The day was April 17, 1937—165 years and 309 days since Landon had sat down to write his fond report of his evening visit to Jack Lubbar's garden patch. The place was the clapboard dwelling of Horace Muse, an aged ex-slave. He was born not far from Sabine Hall back in the first half of the nineteenth century, and he may have been kin to the slaves in the Carter diary.

This is how old Horace Muse told his story to the two young African American students who sat there to write it down.

"I was born in Richmond County long before the Civil War broke out. . . . I was a young man when they was practicing for war. I remember when they was mustering before the war, but I ain't never seed any battles. . . . Master Riles was a mean man. He never knew when you had worked enough. . . . I had to do field work, plow, and keep the roads in shape. White folk was sure mean then. Better not look at them real hard. If you did, you was sassing them and they beat you to death. Yes sir!

". . . Sometimes you would hear the niggers way at midnight just a yelling, 'Oh master! Please master!' Yes sir! They beat them till they die. . . . Them was terrible times. . . .

"We worked from four o'clock in the morning till midnight. At night slaves would build bon fires to work by. Iffen you only work till eleven o'clock, you had to pick cotton after that. The little boys and everybody had to work. No rest for niggers until God he step in an put a stop to the white folks' meanness. In them days the only thing we got to eat was a ash cake and half a herring and water. . . . Only church we got to go to was the white folk's church. . . . No, ain't had a funeral. They dig a hole and dump you in it. After the war we had all the funerals we want. . . .

"When the war came, the news spread like whirlwind! We heard it whispered around that a war come for to set the niggers free. Master Riles tell us to pay no attention to it, that nothing like that ever gonna happen. . . .

"All white folks was getting little worried because the war was soon to start, but they keep saying, 'Niggers never be free as long as the world stands.'

"But praise be the Lord that the day did come!"

Unlike Jack Lubbar, the very old Horace Muse escaped having some "faithful slave" story imposed on him; he lived long enough through changed times to tell his story as an angry denunciation of the plantation, the masters, and the lives forced on the slaves.

MASTER'S TALES

All story is rooted in and crafted from myth. That proposition includes—some would say especially includes—true life stories. The mythology out of which Horace Muse developed his own true story of his young life as a slave was the great African American Christian story of themselves as a people held in bondage knowing that God will bring a day of deliverance. So, it told movingly of that bondage and exultantly of that day.

That leaves the question as to the mythology or mythologies out of which Landon Carter wrote his slave stories. The stories in Landon's diaries from 1766 onward were a mixture of modern sentiment and age-old folklore. The balance, however, was toward the traditional; the storyteller sought an antidote to subversion by evoking an ancient order of respectful obedience. In particular, Landon's stories of slave resistance are inscriptions of the folklore of the manor house that might best be called gentry lore. Such stories were the squires' counterpart to all those peasants' tales; these were the story versions of the master's endless dilemma: was his servant more knave or fool? was he more stupid drunkard or thieving villain? was she impudent wench or old shrew? These were story forms of the wisdom to manage and endure the endless variations of a traditional lord-and-peasant conflict—a kind of guerrilla war—that was as old as civilization.

From 1766 to 1778, the Sabine Hall diaries accumulated a considerable store of these masters' tales. Indeed, it may well be that Landon, the new world chronicler of a Virginia plantation, assembled the largest nonfiction collection of gentry-lore tales of forced laborer recalcitrance surviving in all the world's literature. This Virginia variant had readily incorporated the black slave in the role of the old-world peasants.

Though the seeds of later full-blown racism were already present, it would be anachronistic to label Landon's account of his enslaved workers as simply racist. The diarist's perceptions were conditioned by the traditional worldview with which readers of Shakespeare are very familiar: Landon did not see humanity so much divided into races, white and black, as ranked in their degrees. Society, in this view, was drawn out in an extended hierarchy. At the upper end was the noble and at the lower end the base, while in between were many gradations. But that ancient view had become undermined by the democratizing tendencies of Landon's own times; in telling these stories, Landon Carter, like King Canute, was trying to turn back an irresistible tide.

The passionately inscribed gentry lore of Landon's later diaries will repay careful reading. As the master of Sabine Hall poured forth intensely traditionalist stories, he illuminated a system and many individual lives otherwise lost to history.

Contested Mastery

My honest ones are now too old, and the young ones are all rogues, Landon was once impelled to exclaim. Against the story of the old and faithful Jack Lubbar stood a much longer series of stories of slave subversion and transgression. In these stories the words "rogue" and "villain" establish a clear link to the traditional cycle of master-and-servant narratives; and we can see that, while these stories presented actual slaves in actual clashes with the master, they stereotyped those slaves and those clashes according to formulas that the master's conceptions of plantation order demanded. Focusing on a small number of persons whose work or personalities (or both) brought them into recurrent confrontations with the master, I shall try to reveal both the personalities and the stereotyping themes.

MANUEL

As one of the Eight, Manuel has already had a version of his story presented in these pages; but it will be instructive to call up again the little biography of Manuel that Landon wrote into the diary as he worked toward a decision to sell the old slave away from home and family:

He was once a valuable fellow, the best plowman & mower I ever saw. But like the breed of him*—he took to drinking & whoring till at last he was obliged to steal, and robbed my storehouse of near half the shirts & shifts for my people besides other things. For this I prosecuted him and then got him pardoned with a halter round his neck at the gallows.

This is the easiest real-life story to match with a familiar item from the stock of gentry-lore tales. Manuel's career has been told as "the rake's progress"—with the twist of his being spared at the gallows, unlike the subject of Hogarth's famous print.

The angry biography traced developments from the time of that 1744 reprieve through the immediate present, to the intended future:

---

* The tracing of the source of Manuel's delinquency to "the breed of him" was probably compounded of a conventional idea as to what "negroes" were like, and of this master's knowledge of this man's own forebears, who had themselves been enslaved to the diarist's father.

For a while it had some effect—but returning to his night walking he turned thief as before & killed beef which was found upon him—but there was no proof of the ownership of the stolen property to be had for the prosecution. He again escaped execution. Since then—by means of the same practices—he has killed me 20 or 30 horses and as many draught oxen. He sleeps none at night and must do it in the day. And . . . by one barbarity or another—he has as certainly killed these Creatures as ever he has been concerned with them—And now I will part with him.

His master, raging at the loss of creatures in the plowman's care, repeatedly resolved to sell him away into exile. Yet Manuel escaped that fate also. He worked—and marauded—on at Sabine Hall for another six years and three months after the date of the first selling-away resolution. Then, on that fateful night of June 25, 1776, he armed himself and went off with Moses and the others to Lord Dunmore's camp. As far as we know, he was never in his former master's power again.

As we read Manuel's record of repeated condemnations and escapes, the gestalt can suddenly shift. Stories told at Sabine Hall assuredly came out of and fed into more than one cycle of folklore The reprobate rake of the Anglo-Virginian squire's angry story becomes the trickster of another laughing set of stories.

The Amaxhosa of Southern Africa tell an escape story that goes like this.

Lion, the Great Chief, made all the Animals dig a large waterhole. But Jackal would not join in the work. Yet when it was done Jackal was always the first to the hole, and muddied it for all the rest.

Lion set Baboon to guard the waterhole. But, with the promise of honey, Jackal tricked Baboon into letting himself be tied up while Jackal swam in the hole.

Lion denounced Baboon as a fool and had him severely punished.

But still no one knew how to keep the pool safe and the water clean.

Then Tortoise came forward with a cunning plan. He had the others cover him in a thick coating of beeswax resin; so that when Jackal came looking for Lion's guard he mistook him for a stone and stepped on him and became stuck. He soon found that, when he kicked at this "stone" and snapped at it, he became stuck fast by all four paws and his snout.

Then Lion came to pronounce judgement and arrange for a sentence of death.

Jackal begged at least to be allowed to die swiftly by some means of his own choosing; and Lion magnanimously agreed.

So Jackal cunningly proposed that Hyena should whirl him around by the tail and dash his brains instantaneously against a stone.

But that old Jackal had first shaved his tail and greased it.

Readers have already recognized the story of the Tar Baby and the not-so-dreaded exile into the briar patch. This was a story with as many variations in Africa and the new world as there were shapes and transformations for the Trickster himself. Surely it was with the framework of this lore that Manuel's two escapes from the gallows were told at the quarter.

JOHNNY THE GARDENER

Johnny's debut in the post-1765 story-laden diary was in a narrative about the telling of stories. The strongest dramas came from the unmasking of earlier stories by later ones. This series of reports is shaped by household gossip and its (late) revelation to the master.

The episode had begun in 1766 with Landon recording on April 24 that Simon the ox carter, who had run away on March 12, *came home*—meaning that he had returned voluntarily. The master thought he could congratulate himself on a successful pursuit; he had put a price on this runaway's head by having his outlawry proclaimed *in all the Churches.* Furthermore, Landon had laid an ambush for Simon (and for his fellow outlaw, Bart, also a teamster, "out" since January 1). Three of the leading enslaved staff of Sabine Hall, Talbot, Tony, and Tom, armed with *Guns loaded with small shot,* had lain concealed, watching for the runaways at the Home Quarter. (Simon's aunt and sister-in-law, who lived there, were believed to be harboring him.) The vigilantes had reported surprising the pair; they reported shooting Simon in the leg, but yet somehow they were not able to prevent his escape. That had been fourteen days ago.

Now, Landon supposed that the injured Simon, realizing the game was up, had turned himself in to be at his master's mercy. But, by the time of a later diary-writing session that day, it had come out that Talbot and Tom (and Nassaw) had concealed information in order to make the master believe *the fellow came in himself.* Landon also learned that the ambush of Simon and Bart had been in different circumstances than reported; the extent of Simon's injury had been greatly exaggerated; and—most outrageous of all—he had not come in voluntarily.

This was the true story that came to light: Will, the slave foreman of Mangorike Quarter, had seen the smoke of a fire in the woods; he had noted the place for investigation that night. He had found Simon and overpowered him, and then brought him captive to Sabine Hall. Since it was late at night, he had delivered Simon into the custody of Talbot, and Tom, and Nassaw—who next morning let it appear as a voluntary return. Landon had this story, complete with graphic detail—the hidden camp, the stealthy approach, and the fierce struggle that had ensued—directly from Mangorike Will, who had come back later in the day to claim his reward for the capture of the runaway. Will also said that Simon was not really lame, whatever act he put on.*

Simon would now pay for this: *I shall punish him accordingly.* And that was only the start of revelations that went on for three days. Next day Bart came back. He came genuinely of his own free will, it seems. He meant to appeal against his master's order four months before that he be whipped for indolence and lying. His appeal was disallowed—with a reminder of the general testimony against him back then; and now for staying out and plundering he was threatened with a trial in the king's court, where hanging was the penalty. He was meanwhile incarcerated. But Bart's network of persons who owed him a favor or who could not afford a court enquiry into his dealings proved stronger than Landon's determination to initiate such a process: *Bart broke open the house in which he was tyed & locked up.* It was somehow known that he had escaped *before 2 o'clock in the afternoon*; but it was not reported *till night.*

The frustrated master tried to identify the culprits. *Talbot is a rogue. He was put in charge of him.* Suspicion concerning the time the two had been out rested primarily on *the gardiner's boy Sam*, and Kit the Miller, whom he had already *given . . . a light whipping as having fed them by the hands of Gardiner Sam.* But Landon could find nothing conclusive.

The next day brought more disturbing revelations—this time from Lansdown Old Tom. (The report was the more galling because it reached Landon through his very critical eldest son, Robert Wormeley Carter.) Tom now revealed how the leading Sabine Hall staff had conspired all the time to conceal the outlaws; the details must have made everybody except Landon smile or laugh. It did not surprise the diarist that his daughter-in-law had obstructed his inquiries into the affair in order to protect her *wench Betty, wife to Sawney, brother of Simon.*

The runaways had been outlawed for suspected robberies; the militia had been summoned to hunt for them. (That is, the resentful dirt-farmer militiamen had been called away from their spring crop planting by their county

---

* The episode is analyzed—with closer attention to the loyalties and structural conflicts involved—in Isaac, *Transformation of Virginia*, 329–344.

commander-in-chief, Colonel Landon Carter, to search for his own slaves.) Now Lansdown Old Tom made Landon's ears burn with what he in turn had heard from little Adam, the grandson of Tom's present wife: *that Johnny my Gardiner had harboured Bart & Simon all the while they were out, sometimes in his inner room and sometimes in my Kitchen Vault. They were placed in the Vault in particular the day my Militia were hunting for them.* Gardener Johnny was revealed at the center of this slave conspiracy story; the master sent him to be locked in what he styled his *Gaol.* Johnny's son-in-law, Postillion Tom, who was later among the Eight of that revolutionary exodus, was also *locked up.*

After some further angry confrontations, Landon turned to reflect upon what it all meant. *These rogues,* he mused, *could not have been so entertained without some advantage to those who harbourd them.* Sensing a busy network in operation, he went on to link the protection of the thieving-and-conspiring runaways, Bart and Simon, to the *making away* of some of his wool and wheat. Since there must have been a lot of hard night riding to ply all this illicit trade, he now saw clearly into *the death* of so many horses. Gardener Johnny, as the ringleader, was evidently a scheming hypocrite: *I never rightly saw into the assertion that negroes are honest only from a religious Principle. Johnny is the most constant churchgoer I have, but he is a drunkard, a thief & a rogue.* Suddenly Johnny stood for all his people. *They are only* honest *thro' Sobriety, and but few of them.* Here in 1766, we see opened the long bill of indictment against Gardener Johnny in particular; we see also the start of the even-longer diary cycle of stories of rogue-and-villain slaves.

The scientific record of the 1750s Farming Observations book, with its measured tasks and performances, inputs and outputs, had assuredly been an instrument of control. But what of all this unpacking of stories?

It is hard to see a controlling effect achieved in Landon's recording of Johnny and the marauding Bart and Simon. In those stories a system of alternative concentrations of power became manifest. True, the diarist could write an angry moral to these stories: the master will always find out and punish. That is probably what Landon told himself was the purpose of his narratives, written for his doubting son and daughter-in-law. But it was long ago pointed out by William Godwin, an astute late-eighteenth-century commentator, that the explicit moral of a story may be more than offset by the disturbing tendency of its narration. If, for example, a story depicts a rebel as heroic throughout the story, despite the fact that in the end the rebel dies and thereby fulfills the need for a proper moral, the tendency of the story is nevertheless to celebrate the rebel. Out-of-control rather than under-control seems to be the tendency of this and all the other delinquent slave narratives that the master of Sabine Hall entered in his chronicles. Thus, Johnny and all his accomplices became a new kind of disturbing presence in the diarist's record of his increasingly rebellious world.

Johnny kept contriving subversions throughout the remainder of Landon's diary. The mutual but unequal bondage becomes clearer with every line: at the heart of the master's dependence on the slaves was the work he must get from them. Landon was certainly bound to Johnny by the work that Johnny was skilled in. The garden was a place of the greatest importance practically as well as symbolically. It was a zone of careful cultivation adjoining the house. (There was a space of flowers, although they only get mentioned a few times in the half a million words of the plantation diaries; and the formal terrace with graveled paths on the river side of the house gets no reporting at all.) As it appears in the diary, the garden was the place of cultivation of vegetables and salads for the dinner table at the great house. Supremely, it was the nursery for a great many crop seedlings. Also, in the domain of the garden—and so of the gardener—was the fold and shelter where the lambs, newborn in the depths of winter, were protected and nurtured.

After the 1766 volume containing the Simon and Bart episode, there was a gap with no diaries; then, with the new monthly books of the 1770s diaries, detailed stories appeared in profusion. We learn that it had gone all right for Johnny at the start of 1770. He is merely glimpsed on January 18, employing his gardening skills; but a month later there was trouble with the lambs in Johnny's care. This was a dangerous responsibility to neglect or cheat on; Landon, the good shepherd, was very engaged for his lambs and continually studied the conditions needed for them to thrive. A month after that, in mid-March, the trouble intensified: *One lamb fallen . . . one died last night through Johnny's carelessness. He wants his correction.*

Then on April 12 a bombshell burst over Johnny's head. Landon, as anxious manager of his conglomerate of plantations, was reviewing the situation at his Fork Quarter and comparing the serious livestock losses on the home farm. Suddenly he declared that he was *now convinced that this fellow Johnny is too damned a rogue to be trusted with any kind of care—and so are all his family.* So, Johnny was told he was demoted. The next day he came—presumably in a gesture of defiance—or was it reproach?—to dramatize his new reduced status as one of a field-weeding gang; the ensuing trial of strength was narrated with heavy irony:

Gardner Johnny was so pleased in being turned to the hoe that he came this morning at day break to tell me he was going—and the rascal took his row next to the hindmost man in my field. But—to show him I did not intend the hoe to be his field of diversion—I gave him the place of my fourth man—and have ordered my overseers to keep him to that. I observed it made him quicken the motion of his arm—which up here used to be one, two, in the time of a soldier's parade.

We see three things at once in the close-up of this story: Landon's intense surveillance of his workers, his attunement to the rhythm by which they kept their work going, and the system of delegated command on which he had to fall back for enforcement.

The master had now to rearrange the management of his garden. He felt he must put *postillion Tom*, another of the eight who would run to Dunmore, *into the garden but I have him to learn.* (Tom was Johnny's son-in-law, a relationship fateful for Landon's plans as it turned out!) Meanwhile, by working up his anger anew, the master bolstered his resolution to keep Johnny out and to teach Tom gardening. *I cannot be worse off than with Johnny—for with him I have not* for some years *got anything in my garden—and hardly ever a piece of work done like a workman who has been at least 20 years a gardner.* The diarist concluded with a judgment on Johnny's failings that was also a variation on the rake's-progress story of Manuel. Here was an overview of the whole process by which promising enslaved servants were ruined: *His perpetual pleasure is to be always stupidly drunk and right hand man to young Robin Smith.* (Landon names a neighboring small planter who had been suspected of trading liquor for stolen wool and wheat at Johnny's first diary appearance in that 1766 episode of the runaways.) The master's ire was truly up now; he was sure that Johnny had sold Smith *everything even to my plows for the sake of his throat.* The diarist raged on: *And in this stupid state has he for many years neglected to do me the least pennyworth of service.* In this temper, Landon readily justified his reprisal against Johnny and darkly threatened worse: *I have therefore thought it time to remove him to where he may be made to work or else I will sell him also—for a greater villain cannot live.*

The problems in the home-farm nursery department were not, however, at an end with Johnny's disgracing and replacement. In mid-July Landon found his modern improving efforts to raise fodder crops for his livestock nullified.

He had *last month at least 6,000 hanover turneps planted out*; they had grown well. Alas, Landon *being old & not going to see them often*, now discovered that the two ewes that suckled lambs—*by the carelessness of my new gardener—have been in and eaten them all down. That rascal told me it was my hogs* and probably someone else's responsibility, *but I at last found him out. I see by his carelessness I am not better off than I was with Johnny.* Tom, the postillion-turned-gardener, was already now incorporated into the same story lore of unfaithful servant as his father-in-law predecessor and with the same rogues-and-villains terminology.

By late the following winter, Landon, again reviewing losses, wrote wistfully: *I fancy drunken Gardener Johnny was a much better shepherd.* The master had never before lost *so many* lambs. By mid-March Landon had lost all patience: *Mr Tom says anybody that tells him he has not taken care of them lies, for which I keep him in irons all night, then whip him and turn him out to the hoe.* But, as he pronounced Johnny's sentence now on Tom, the diarist had a sudden awareness that he had been manipulated all this time. Tom had been reluctant to enter on the work in the first place: *I thought he might only be unwilling that his wive's father should be turned out.* Determined to show Johnny he was not indispensable, Landon had pressed on and had *now paid for it.* He was moved to recite the recent losses, and then he recorded an about-turn—justified with a piece of sentiment: *I have put Johnny into his old place—who promises to lay aside all his old tricks & mind his business that he may grow old in peace.*

Landon had not sold Johnny away; he had continued him in his service, to be continually stood over, scolded, punished, and forgiven. In this the master was undoubtedly acting out a deeply ingrained role of patriarchal lordship, with all its incessant demands for submission and its unreliable promises of ultimate protection.

But, we may ask whether Landon's gentry-lore tale of transgressions and patriarchal forgiveness is the only way this portion of Johnny's life story can be told.

The former slave Frederick Douglass, writing of his upbringing as a slave in Maryland, tells of the use by fellow slaves of magical elements to avert a master's anger or control his hostile intentions. A similar account appears in the Virginia ex-slave autobiographies. Robert Williams told a young Federal Writers' Project interviewer of the efficacy of charms. He had gone to a "hoodoo-doctor" when he needed help, fearing that his master's family was so angry that "they would kill me." He was given some powders and told "to sprinkle them" where his master would walk over them unknowingly. If possible he was "to put some in master's hat and he couldn't bother me." It had worked perfectly, the ex-slave believed. When he then put himself in the way of his master, the master had indeed begun to rage: "'God damn! Where in hell has you been . . . ?'" But the slave had stood his ground, resolved to seize a stick and fight back if the master attempted to beat him. The white man then had suddenly grown calm and merely ordered his resolute antagonist to saddle his horse for a ride to town. "From that day on he never did bother me."

For those who read portents, there were surely signs that Johnny had charms to protect him. In March 1770, just before Johnny's seeming downfall, *many little Children* among Landon's people had *died with tumified throats*. But in the case of *a Child of Johnny's taken in the same manner*, there was a favorable outcome. After three days, the gardener's now *stout boy* was *bright and runs about*. Was this a sign that Johnny had special powers to protect himself and his family?

Johnny assuredly was a survivor. His delinquencies resumed, but he retained his privileged position. Scarcely had six weeks passed from Johnny's March 12, 1771, promise to *lay aside all his old tricks & mind his business that he may grow old in peace*, when it was recorded (April 29) that *Gardiner Johnny is growing a Villain again*. In this case it was only neglect that was sarcastically charged: *he pretends to have been watering, but the earth is crackt where he waters*.

For a time after that, Johnny worked on without noteworthy transgression, until later in the year when the master became infuriated because a field had been laid waste where *the cattle under Johnny's care broke the fence down*; Landon's bitter comment was: *He did not care*. What there is of the diary for the following two and a half years only shows routine work by Johnny, until suddenly there was trouble again. The supply of tobacco seedlings gave out; the master knew why: *that fellow is always muddled with drink*.

Then the Sabine Hall water supply required maintenance, and Landon was faced with a whole archaeology of villainy dredged up from his great well. Amongst the *abundance of trash, mud & things*, the master's unsurprised eye fell *particularly* on *a Plow* that *Gardiner Johnny stole 3 years ago*. (That whole story seemed to be known—though no record of it survives before this one.) Johnny had intended *to sell that* plow *and another to Robin Smith*. But that known fencer of stolen goods had been cautious when offered the plow. Landon was no doubt being sarcastic when he recalled that his poor neighbor, *being a Penitent,* had *advised* Johnny to *go and put it*—the plow—*where it might be found* without suspicion presumably. As for Johnny—*being suspected*—he had *got whipped,* and in payback he *threw both* plows *into the Well.* Now that they had come to light again, the master resolved that, *a good whipping . . . Johnny shall have . . . tomorrow.*

There were a further two years without recorded outrage, and then Johnny was in the master's eye again. This story should be told entirely in Landon's narrative style, which here is almost as full of twists as Johnny's contrivances: *Thursday, July 25, 1776. . . .*
Gardener Johnny—catcht on Tuesday night riding a horse by my grandson returning from fishing, though locked up and tied neck and heels with his hands behind him, was broke out—and has not been seen or heard of since.

On the same day that old Landon wrote that record of Johnny's capture and instant escape, he had found himself in the grips of a dream *about these runaway people,* as told in chapter 1. Johnny now literally haunted Landon. The old slave's son-in-law and coconspirator, Postillion Tom, came to Landon in his sleep, where the phantom not only gratified the diarist by begging reinstatement but also at last unmasked his own father-in-law. Johnny had been a ringleader, he said, and *was to have gone with them, but somehow was not in the way.* The Tom of Landon's dreams denounced the slave patriarch who had ruled him so long: he *declared I had not a greater villain belonging to me.*

In the waking life of Sabine Hall, Landon kept contending with Johnny. On April 25, 1777—nine months after the dream—the state of the garden revealed *Mr. John as the worst servant a man ever had;* but that did not now provoke any change of arrangements. Two days later, a close review of lamb births and deaths revealed a systematic misreporting of twin births by *the Villain* Johnny, *that he may the more undiscoveredly sell one of them.* Worse was the realization that *it seems he had* done *this for many years.* There was the forlorn hope that it might be stopped by heightened security: *I have particularly had him observed.* Otherwise there was a resolve, probably not acted on: *I must seperate this fellow's Son from him—for he is his agent for marketing for drink.* (Son-in-law Tom had already separated himself by his exodus for freedom.)

It comes as no surprise to us, nor probably to the people at the quarters, that Johnny with his son beside him continued to supervise the garden and the nursery for lambs. Their last appearance in the diary record is in pastoral mode: *The two Johnnys this evening after tea pulling up the Jamestown & other high weeds in the Garden & Plant patch.*

∽

His master's diary narratives thus give several versions of Johnny to history. There is the capable garden supervisor, for whose competence there was no replacement; there is the churchgoer in the sentimental story, making resolutions for a new start, *that he may grow old in peace*; and, above all, there is the *rogue* out of gentry lore, stealing, dealing, drinking, and buying others with rum. That contriving Johnny was practicing *villany* to the end.

Behind these assigned roles the twenty-first-century historian wants to seek a persona more native to Johnny's African American culture at the quarters. Was he a Trickster? Was he both a man of God and a man of supernatural powers? The answer must always be surmise. The real Johnny is elusive. The strongest, most enduring attachment and commitment of which he gave evidence was to a position—and to the opportunities that the position afforded him to organize kin and connection around himself.

Technocratic Warfare

Landon's suspicious nature created extra distance from his people—a problem that was intensified by the scientific methods he introduced on the plantation. In Landon's diary we see an early stage of a process that in our own world has still not run its full course. Landon was carrying onto his estate that de-skilling, and sometimes re-skilling, of workers that has been part of the Industrial Revolution that continues to this day.

In the late seventeenth and through the eighteenth century a new figure rose to bestride the earth like a colossus. This figure has been mythologized as the inventor; but more prosaically he—emphatically he—was the engineer or works manager. Under this new taskmaster, the craft mysteries were being analyzed, measured, and rationalized, so that redesigned production methods could be imposed from above on the men and women who once had owned the ways of doing work. The factory was to be the most dramatically visible manifestation of this transformation; but the new control of work reached wherever cookbooks and other how-to manuals could take it. That is to say, it was going everywhere, including out to the colonial plantation.

With Landon's artisans, the conflict could be both very personal and very intense, as he strove to impose his engineering-style design concepts and they stood by their hard-learned skills in doing the work.

TONY THE CARPENTER

In March of 1770, there were repeated stand-offs between Landon and his carpenters; Tony (Toney) was only the most obdurate.

Mr. Toney shall as certainly receive ample correction for his behaviour to me as that he and I live. The day before yesterday he began to pale in the garden—and only fitted the rails to seven posts. When he began to put them up I was riding out and ordered him to leave the gateway into the garden as wide as the two piers next the gate on each side. Nay I measured the ground off to him and showed him where the two concluding post were to stand—and the rest at 8 feet asunder from post to post to answer to the tenons of his rails—and I asked him if he understood me. He said he did & would do it so.

Landon has been as technical in his diary as he was in directing Tony; he would show his mastery of these matters. Tony was not impressed: *I had been 2 hours out and when I came home nothing was done—and he was gone about another jobb. I asked him why he served me so. He told me because it would not answer his design.* That had been too much for the technocrat planter; an instant enraged action and a torrent of elaborate self-vindication followed:

The villain had so constantly interrupted my orders that I had given him about every jobb this year that I struck him upon the shoulders with my stick—which . . . made out of hickory so very dry & light—had been long split and tied with pack thread—therefore it shivered all to pieces—and this morning, for that stroke—which did not raise the least swelling nor prevent the idle dog from putting up the posts as I directed—in which I convinced him that everything answered. I say—this morning he has laid himself up with a pain in that shoulder—and will not even come out to take off a lock. . . . I might as well give up every Negroe if I submit to this impudence.

The complex of discourses here is awesome. Landon, the technologically literate gentleman, needed to declare that he was also a man of sensibility; he would not be inhumane to his workmen any more than he would allow them to be disobedient to him. But the diarist found that his sensibility rather provoked his workers than constrained them. Some two weeks later, on a Saturday, there was another confrontation:

I think my man Tony is determined to struggle whether he shall not do as he pleases. He has . . . been 2 days only paling in the dairy & henhouse yard. . . . I told him when I rode out this morning he would certainly get another whipping. He was . . . pretending the ground was uneven. I asked him if he could not pare the ground away. He stooped down like falling—but I imagine it was the Negroe's foolish way of hearing better. I rode out— when I came home the pales were all laid slanting.

I asked him why he did that

he still laid the fault on the ground and as his left shoulder was to me I gave him one small rap upon it. He went to breakfast afterwards & no complaint. This evening I walked there and then he pretended he could not drive a nail—his arm was so sore. I made Nassaw strip his Cloathes off & examine the whole arm—not the least swelling upon it. And every now & then he would tremble.

I asked him if I hit him upon the legs

he said his stroke was in his bone which made all his body ache.

Perhaps there was an African American medical lore in this; but the master instantly made his own diagnosis—the curse of his plantation visited on him again. *At last, looking full upon him, I discovered the Gentleman compleatly drunk. This I have suspected a great while. I then locked him up for Monday morning's Chastisement—for I cannot bear such a rascal.*

The Sabbath was to be respected; the retribution would come at the routine punishment parade, designed to control weekend transgressions.

The designation of Toney as a "villain" (and even the sarcasm of calling him "Mr.") safely returned this conflict to the genre of a gentry-lore contest of master and servant. But revolutionary disturbances of the whole Virginia customary system of authority had complicated the master's view of the situation; the next lines make reference to the religious rebellion then raging in Virginia. Increasing numbers of slaves and tenant farmers were breaking out of the established Church of England, where they found the traditional social hierarchy reinforced, and were attending illegal meetings held by itinerant "New Light" Baptist preachers. Landon knew that this latest form of subversion was extending onto his plantation: *I thought this a truly religious fellow—but have had occasion to think otherwise and that he is a hypocrite of the vilest kind. His first religion that broke out upon him was new light & I believe it is from some inculcated doctrine of those rascals that the slaves in this Colony are grown so much worse. It behooves every man therefore to take care of his own—at least I am determined to do what I can—Mine shall be brought to their piety—though with as little severity* as possible.

Tony was involved in no further recorded confrontations having the intimacy and intensity of those garden-paling episodes. But the subsequent diary does show Tony in a continuing aggravation over the on-and-off valuation and devaluation of enslaved craftsmen's skills. In June of the same year, 1770, he and his fellow carpenters were called from their adzes, saws, and chisels to work as a gang on the crop. There was another conflict over work methods, as Landon insisted that, with his careful measurement of performance, he alone knew how the hoes should be employed:

I visited my gangs three times this day—staying with them about a couple of hours each time. I had taken notice—when they worked up the hill—of the same strong heavy stroke which they had got into as they were *turning the stiff land before the rain. I put them out of it one day and they turned me then 40,000 hills—and this day by going from hand to hand every now and then I have got better than 30,000 hills turned. The earth was prodigeous weedy though otherwise light and clever.*

Close-observing managerial science was being pitted against workmen's custom. Once more in this entry, the same sharp attention to work practices had Tony under punitive surveillance: *Tony I see is the conductor of this idleness—he leads the gang & just as if every man had an equal number* of tobacco plants *missing—not one* of them *goes a hill before him—which is a certain proof of villanous lazyness—and all shall pay for it tomorrow.*

In August Tony was back in the carpentry workshop, but the record casts a casual slur on his craftsmanship. As a mere slave carpenter, he could only be expected to do makeshift work: *My Chariot carriage must now be thoroughly repaired—and as it is not worth employing a perfect artist/*artisan *about it—my Negroes, Tony & McGinis, are set to do it.*

Then, at the next tobacco harvest, Tony appears as the organizer of the making of the hogsheads and one whose reports and estimates are to be relied on. But by the next spring, he was in trouble again: *Toney had a great flogging for his yesterday's lazyness & impudence.* When he next attracted attention, in June 1774, the charge was malingering. Landon proposed a grim jest at the carpenter's expense: *Toney shall make his own Coffin to be laid up in and buryed; for he can now pretend to be sick when nothing ails him.*

Thus it would go on for Tony: now he was trusted, and now he was not. Furthermore, this was a pattern set to continue down the generations, for Tony had been given his own son to train as an apprentice. *Yesterday Toney's son, Toney, and Harry went to Indian Creek to John Beale to set up my tobacco hogsheads. I gave them directions to do it without using any nails. . . . And I wrote to J. Beale to make him understand it.* A deputy-master should first understand the specifications and then enforce them on the craftsmen.

At Tony's very last appearance, the task was renewal of the posts supporting the walkway from house to kitchen: *It takes much time & trouble. . . . But it must be done and with great care too.* The entry for Saturday, April 12, 1777, reads almost like an epitaph on this stressed relationship: *Poor Toney has a good Carpenter's genius but no contrivance. How Puzzled yesterday was he—and took all day to put up only 3 of his new posts in the passage to the Kitchin? I was obliged to turn out old as I am.*

MANUEL'S SARAH

The contending for and against mastery was more troubled, and the gentry-lore narratives were more filled with menace, when the conflict was with women.

The "villain" Manuel had a daughter named Sarah, who was as much inclined to go her own way as was her father. In late March, during a cold wet spring when the snows would not give over, she and other workers had been out in gangs with hoes, turning the stiff clay earth to heap the hills for tobacco and corn planting. There had already been a "punishment parade," where a voluntarily returned slave had received his whipping for having run away—*his correction . . . in sight of the people*; but this had not inculcated a submissive spirit in everyone. The master, needing to justify himself in his diary, gave a detailed report:

The 2 Sarahs came up yesterday pretending to be violent ill with pains in their sides— they look very well, had no fever and I ordered them down to their work upon pain of a whipping. They went—worked very well with no grunting about pain—but one of them —to wit Manuel's Sarah—taking the advantage of overseer Lawson's ride away to the Fork, swore she would not work any longer & ran away—and is still out.

The master and Manuel's Sarah had been at loggerheads for some time, and the diarist was impelled to write a kind of philosophic reflection upon her, and, indeed, upon slave womankind: *There is a curiosity in this Creature. She worked none last year pretending to be with Child—& this she was full 11 months before she was brought to bed. She has now the same pretence & thinks to pursue the same course—but as I have full warning of her deceit, if I live, I will break her of that trick.*

Landon worked to strengthen his resolve by recalling previous contests of this kind, in which he had prevailed by a ruthlessness that he narrated almost as though it concerned a scientific triumph over an obstacle in nature:

I had two before of this turn—Wilmot of the Fork whenever she was with Child always pretended to be too heavy to work—and it cost me 12 months before I broke her. Criss of Mangorike fell into the same scheme & really carried it to a great length—for at last she could not be dragged out. However by carrying a horse with traces—the Lady took to her feet—run away & when catched—by a severe whipping has been a good slave ever since—only a cursed thief in making her Children milk my Cows in the night.

Landon was striving to make his use of a horse and towlines to overpower a possibly pregnant woman compatible with his claimed humanity. His afterthought about milk stealing reveals that he knew there were no complete triumphs in such struggles for mastery. Women certainly would find a vengeful way of fighting back. We get a sudden glimpse of an enslaved mother's endless struggle to supplement her children's meager rations.

The story of the rebellion of Manuel's Sarah was recapitulated and continued some three weeks later:

Saturday, April 14. . . .

We have at last catched this infamous jade, Manuel's Sarah, who has been out now a full week yesterday. She at first pretended to be sick but having no discoverable complaint was sent out to her work—run away & not heard of till a robbery for meal—yesterday in the evening, overseer *Lawson observed her going to her Lodging and by a fair run catched her. She pretends to be big with Child—& perhaps may be so. I had her corrected & intended to lock her up till I could sell her. She begs hard—& is turned out to work.*

Was it humanity or the old duty of patriarchal protection that led Landon to spare Sarah the threatened banishment? Was it his need to continue to exploit her labor? The master allowed her to live on with her children and kin (presumably upon a promise to work in the fields without protest). How did Landon regard the whipping of a woman who might be pregnant? How shall we regard a patriarchalism that enforced itself thus?

Unsurprisingly, Sarah's defiance—like her father, Manuel's—did not end with that episode. Three-and-a-half years later, in the fall of 1773, the whole story came to be told again with variations: *Manuel's Sarah . . . pretended to be sick a week ago, and because I found nothing ailed her and would not let her lie up—she run away above a week and was catched the night before last and locked up; but somebody broke open the door for her. It could be none but her father Manuel—and he I had whipped.*

When there was *No News* by next day, Landon returned to his previous resolution; he now declared that Sarah and another runaway (who was marauding with a *hue & cry & outlawry* upon his head), were *two I will sell, God willing*. But whether he did sell this defiant woman out of his and her family's life, we do not know. Probably he continued with her as well as with her father, Manuel, to make the heavy threat and then to relent. The sword of Damocles was always over their heads.

The vividly recorded stories of Manuel, Gardener Johnny, Tony the carpenter, and Manuel's Sarah all show that, powerful as he was in law and fact, Landon could not conclusively win in his incessant struggles for mastery.

Recounting the Grievances

The master could write down his outrage in stereotyping stories of slave villainies. His diary narratives give copious access to the themes of the plantation slave system as he experienced it. Meanwhile, the slaves stored their outrage in their own memories and narratives which accumulated in time into a great collective memory. Exploring these themes in parallel is a way to uncover the two-sided character of the old plantation.

WORK

As the master's dependence on the slaves centered on the work he demanded of them, so the slaves' experience of the master was dominated by the work he extracted from them.

Landon's diary records much literal slave driving. More than half the recorded punishments in the diaries—nearly fifty out of some ninety—were for work judged too slow or careless. *Evident lazyness* or *neglect* were the phrases most readily used in these summary judgments. An overseer at a distant quarter might merely be said to have *whipped* a man *for not working*; but Landon's own record was usually more precise. Thus, if an inspection revealed *certain proof of villanous lazyness*, the diarist would declare that *all shall pay for it tomorrow*.

The master took for granted the long hours demanded of the enslaved. He only made a special record of night work when some delinquency rendered it noteworthy: *The people stemmed tobacco till the moon went down* accompanied a report on thieving after moonset. Once a planned tightening of surveillance occasioned the observation: *Where there is a large Crop which people are obliged to stem in the night—the Negroes in spite of our teeths will throw a good deal of their task away.* Landon resolved in future *to prevent it by making each person keep their stems by themselves till the morning for inspection and a proper correction.* On another occasion he noted that even his house slaves were *sent down to hang a prodigeous cutting of tobacco on Scaffolds at the Mangorike tobacco house.*

Collectively the 1930s ex-slave testimonies called forth searing memories of all their masters' and overseers' endless work enforcement. Feisty Elizabeth Sparks of Matthews County, just south of Sabine Hall in the Tidewater, saw the bad bargain in all the toil on short rations that the masters gave the slaves: "Gave them more work than they could do. They'd get beat if they didn't get work done. . . . They worked six days from sun to sun. . . . They get off jest long enough to eat at noon. Didn't have much to eat. . . . A woman with children would get about half a bushel of meal a week; a childless woman would get about a peck and-a-half. . . . That's the way the white folks was. Some had hearts; some had gizzards instead of hearts." And, "All them worked you like putting out fire," recalled the Reverend Ishrael Massie.

And there was the violence on top of the relentless demand. Rev. W. P. Jacobs carried memories both of pride in work and of cruel tasking. "My father often told me about his brother Charlie. . . . Father says he and Uncle Charlie used to work in the woods making rails. . . ." Uncle Charlie was one of the slaves that couldn't get his number finished. Almost every night he would get 39 lashes and that made him as sore as could be, and he couldn't work well the next day. . . . One day . . . he jumped on the nigger-driver . . . fought . . . and won. Uncle Charlie ran away." The same narrator told poignantly his grandmother's account of tasked field work. "Grandma said . . . she was small and just couldn't get her proper amount. . . . Lots of times she would come up short. . . . All the slaves who had fallen short had to stand in line with their backs bare for their whipping. Grandma said that often she was whipped until she could barely grunt."

Women's life stories mixed pride and anger in a special way. Eighty-six-year-old Amelia Walker recalled with pride that "Mama plowed with three horses. Ain't that something?" Hundred-year-old Simon Stoke, from Guinea—one river south of Sabine Hall in the Tidewater—had good and bad memories. He had enjoyed the work when it afforded the satisfaction of being in control; perhaps there was a parody of master-slave stand-over talk in his animal driving: "Me sure did like to get behind the ox-team in the corn-field, for I could sing and holler all the day, 'Gee there Buck, whoa there Peter, get off that there corn, what's the matter with you Buck, can't you hear, gee there Buck.'" But Simon had many bitter memories, such as "picking worms off the tobacco plants. . . ." The overseer's "hawk eyes" would see everything, and "you'd have to bite all the worms that you missed . . . or get three lashes on your back with his old lash, and . . . them lashes done last a powerful long time."

SILENCED SINGING

Simon Stoke recalled not only his hollering at the team of mules but also the way he would "sing" in the field. Their songs reflect their ambivalence. The work songs, and the manual skills and achievements they marked and celebrated, were a cherished part of the African American heritage, but the product of the work did not belong to those who labored under threat of the lash. The songs they remembered expressed both sides.

Teasing and binding her spell over the young interviewers, Mrs. Fanny Berry told them about the morning start of work for the plantation community: "They all start acoming from all directions with their ax on their shoulder, and the mist and fog be hanging over the pines, and the sun just breaking across the fields. Then the niggers start to sing:

> A cold frosty morning
> The niggers mighty good,
> Take your ax upon your shoulder,
> Nigger, TALK to the wood.
. . . . And when they sing TALK they all chop together. . . ."

There was, however, more than bright promising mornings recalled in the echoes of song. George White remembered his mother's singing and gave a snatch of a more ominous work song:

> Keep your eye on the sun,
> See how she run,
> Don't let her catch you with your work undone,
> I'm troubled, I'm troubled.

Landon Carter surely took for granted all the singing that filled his house, his fields, and above all his nights. Such singing had filled his ears from birth, and continued to through his whole life—save for the seven years of schooling abroad when it was replaced by the songs of English servants. Yet I can find no single reference to it in all his diaries. Perhaps he wanted to suppress it. The rational science that his library and diary were meant to introduce for the control of his plantation had no place for folklore. Southern gentry had not started to patronize and collect the songs and stories of those they later sentimentalized as their happy darkies.

Acknowledging the soundscape of the plantation in the diary would have been an explicit admission of how much Landon shared the domain he chronicled with the bearers of a culture profoundly alien to the literary ethos of the diary. And yet the diarist could, at need, draw on the intimate knowledge he had grown up with. In a memorable outburst, Landon projected the troubling exoticism of his own world onto the greatest of his English oppressors. A copy came into Landon's hands of "The King's Speech November 30th, 1774," calling for the American protesters to be forcibly crushed. The old man wrote on the back of it a bitter satire representing his sovereign as the leader of a black orchestra: "Father George Playing the

Celebration at the quarter. Painted by an unknown artist about 1800, it depicts a scene that must have been commonplace within earshot of Sabine Hall. The painting reveals a culture that Landon Carter's diary ignores. Dance, music, and liquor—a vigorous affirmation of life. *Colonial Williamsburg Foundation.*

American dead march on the Quaqua with Governor Hutchinson & the tarred & feathered man by way of Lion & Unicorn as supporters. With all his band in a kind of Platoon Concerto three drap Kneel, Stoop & Stand [?] Quaqua, Barafoo, Bangers [Banjers]. The Stooping Barafoo men excel everything. . . ."

Suddenly Landon reveals his diary's suppression of this African American cultural aspect expressed by the music and song on his plantation. But history in a book is itself unfortunately soundless. I have never heard a band with "Quaqua, Barafoo, [and] Banjers," but I wish I could at least provide a compact disc with this book to introduce some of the folksongs that have been the principle way of telling history for those who could write little or not at all.

SICKNESS

Henrietta King narrated a terrible equivalent to Landon's stories of extracting work from expectant mothers: "There was a young woman named Lucy lived on the next plantation that was [almost] in child birth and in the mornings was so sick she couldn't go to the field. Well, they thought . . . that she was just stalling so as to get out of working. Finally the overseer came to her cabin . . . and he dragged her out. He laid her across a big tobacco barrel and he took his rawhide and he whipped her something terrible. Well, sir, that woman dragged herself back to the cabin and the next day she give birth to a baby girl. And this ain't no lie, because I seed it, that child's back was streaked with red marks all criss-cross like. The next day Lucy died."

Claiming to be sick could be told in ex-slave reminiscences as both a kind of trickster-countertrickster tale and as clear instance of injustice. Listen to old Charles Grandy: "One day up here I was in the field hilling corn; [we all was] sowing peas and hilling corn all at the same time. When I got ways ahead of the boss sowing these peas I got tired and decided to get some rest. Then old boss come through the corn and say 'Boy what you doing lying down there?' Scared to death—had to think quick, then I say, 'I'se sick.' By that I is so bad off I didn't know what to do. Because I was lying to keep the cowhide off. Old boss say, 'Sick! You ain't sick. Get up from there and go on to the house.' I goes flying. When you gets sick, they give you some kind of medicine called ipicac. Look jest like snuff. You take that and drink water for to make you throw up. They make me take that and I got sick then sure enough. Got so sick I had to go to bed. Stayed there for three or four days too. So I got clear of that whipping."

Thus we hear from the other point-of-view both the master's dilemma whether to believe the suspected malingerer—and the master's use of such violent medicine as Landon's favorite treatment, ipecacuana.

ROGUERY AND VILLAINY

Landon's narrative impulse was most provoked by the conduct of slaves in which he could see thieving, drunkenness, and deceit. Defiance of authority in the form of lying and stealing found ready means of elaboration in the genres of gentry lore.

As the family were going to bed on the night of June 21, 1773, late as it was, a *Girl* (further identified as *old Sukey's Granddaughter*) appeared at the door of the great house. She had a *bloody ear* to show. It was part of a dramatic denunciation of the overseer John Selfe and his family. She said that, at his house, where she was assigned as a servant, his wife *had stuck pins* in her.

Nor was *the Girl* the only tale-teller that night. *My fellow Daniel came also up and said John Selfe was going to whip him about some corn which he said was lost out of the Landing warehouse.* He insisted that Selfe's wife had left the key in the warehouse door—*but he knew nothing about it.*

Landon reserved his judgment: *These 2 stories made me suspend my conclusion until I could hear further about it.*

The master was already commending himself on his cautious reception of perhaps villainous slave *stories* when, in light of his inquiries the next day, he wrote his report. (Once again, new stories and counterstories had tumbled out as the master pressed questions.)

This morning seeing no Pinholes in that girl's ear—only some blood about it, I asked her why she said the woman had run pins into it. She stood still for some time, and at last told me the overseer had whipped her about giving the Warehouse key to Jubas Harry: and her Granny bid her come and tell me that Selfe's wife had run pins into it. But she begged that Granny might not know that she told that she bid her say so, or she would whip her for it.

Landon made further inquiries:

After this I asked Selfe how he came to whip her over the ear.

He said that was an accident which he was sorry for, tho' she certainly deserved to be whipped, for he always kept that Key lock'd up in his chest, but that day left it with his wife to lock her soap tub—which she had just made—in the warehouse. And his wife going to the landing to catch a few crabs, the girl in the meantime took the key off the chest & gave it to Jubas Harry. And he went in with Daniel & took out corn enough for both them—he did suppose at least a week's allowance each of them.

Enter Granny Sukey as an archconspirator, if not a trickster! Now, it is part of the trickster's fabled attainments—amusing if you enjoy it—to set people at odds with each other. In this case the outcome may have been most satisfactory. As reports circulated and inquiries were pressed, Landon's whole family—especially his son Robert and his wife—were inclined to believe *every tittle of the above story as the Girl last night related it.* So they denounced the overseer John Selfe *and his prodigeous barbarity* to slaves. A blazing row ensued, in the course of which all the family took sides. Once more Landon felt betrayed by his family—even by his own daughter Lucy. (But that only confirmed his beliefs concerning the untruths called forth by *female resentment.*) He ended up salving wounded pride and unrequited affection: *Alas, how unfit are such good creatures—as women—to be judges of anything when once impregnated with resentment.*

After all this, the diarist found that *Jubas Harry & Daniel are run away.* Daniel had *pretended to be sick, but not so bad but he could run away.* How Granny Sukey, who had started all this, must have laughed! And she surely gave herself a further laugh. Landon learned that she had *turned out all my cattle last night on my*

Cowpen ground—which have done me a prodigeous mischief. Thus was she *revenged* on Landon because he would not take her granddaughter away from service with the Selfes, which was the original plot behind her sending the girl up to the great house. There had meanwhile been a confrontation between Landon and Granny Sukey, in which the old woman had *the impudence to say the child is poor and starved when I declare I never saw a finer, well, fat, nor healthyer child.* Assuming God's prerogative of vengeance, Landon fulminated: *I will repay this treatment.*

SECRET DRINKING

In August 1770, the master of Sabine Hall confronted Owen Griffith, his very knavish Welsh undermanager. Owen was charged that, *however the matter has been denied he certainly must have assisted Tom in getting the spare key of my bookcase and keeping it so long that my liquors might be at their command.* From this the diarist went straight into pronouncing a righteous squire's judgment: *Now such a circumstance carries the deepest die of iniquity with it—though but a trifling profit—unless the pleasure of getting drunk whenever they pleased can be satisfaction enough for the fraudulent method in which it was gained.* Suspected conspiracy was confirmed when Owen's attempts to avert blame were exposed, and *at last the key was found concealed in the lining of Tom's waistcoat.*

In a later period the English would develop a saying for escape from the slavery of their Industrial Revolution. The quickest way out of Manchester is a bottle of gin. As far as we can tell from the diary, Landon both knew and did not know of the *pleasure* (or relief) that his slaves found in drafts of rum. He surely denied himself any direct acknowledgment that they sought and found an escape. Drink was part not only of the conviviality but also of the sacred rituals of hospitality and solemn toasts at his own table. And yet the diarist only made scornful passing references to his slaves' indulgence. But what did the master really know of the realms of alternative reality opened to them by liquor? Could Landon imagine the forms of feasts and funerals in the Africa from which his people's culture derived? He would not acknowledge any communal experience of the sacred, generated in music, song, and dance at the quarters. He was only apprehensive of ill consequences because *with what are called holidays they run into great mischiefs & drunkenness.*

Travelers from Europe to America were more inquisitive than Virginians about plantation slavery. They were beginning to record observations of African American ways. The Englishman F.J.D. Smyth both saw and narrated exciting night occasions at the quarters. Stereotyping the exotic, he emphasized the intensity of the typical slave's involvement, leading him "six or seven miles in the night . . . to a negroe dance, in which he performs with astonishing agility, . . . keeping time and cadence, most exactly, with the music of a banjor (a large hollow instrument with three strings), and a quaqua (somewhat resembling a drum), until he exhausts himself . . . before the hour he is called forth to toil in the morning." Not having a master's controlling impulse toward moral censure, Smyth made no mention of liquor as part of the release into exuberance on such occasions; yet liquor was surely an indispensable ingredient of the celebrations he described.

Liquor was more to the slaves—and to the master, would he only admit it—than just a source of disorder and dishonesty. Liquor and its effects are subjects hedged by taboos in modern American culture. Joking references abound, and there is a prodigious clinical literature on alcoholism. But serious engagement with the social-cultural-religious transactions involved is rare.* And yet, is not drink very generally a sacred source of forms of altered consciousness at the heart of communal celebration? We know that in a long-ago time there were Dionysian rites and Bacchanalia. We sense that such forms of release may have been very general in the world's cultures. Certainly, the sharing of intoxicating beverages was a widespread aspect of accessing sacred realms in the Africa from which the ancestors of Landon's people had quite recently been forcibly removed. Understanding the master's tales of the colonial plantation world requires at least awareness of this background.

There are revealing contrasts in the historical sources. The ex-slave testimonies are almost as silent about liquor as this master was profuse in his denunciations. Nor is there anything surprising about such silence. Prudence and their own commitments made the narrators share the general American and modern-world shamefaced taboo against celebrating the positive aspects of intoxication.

Only two ex-slaves out of 153 recalled Christmas with the whiskey the master would supply at that season. Nancy Williams—who also noted how much pleasure her master had taken in his slaves' dancing—came near to breaking the tabooed silence surrounding drunkenness. Warming to her subject, she exclaimed: "Yes sir! We was walking and talking with the devil both day and night. Setting all round was them big demijohns of whiskey what master done give

---

* A history of the secularization of liquor, its construction into discourses of medical and social pathology, is an important one yet to be written. Wine is essential to the central Christian sacramental ritual. Sacred art, in earlier centuries, could still show the crucified Christ as God in a winepress—with the redemptive liquor flowing from his wounds.

us." The association of liquor with the devil—and the strong church connections of many of the ex-slave narrators—was no doubt a reason for the general silence about drinking. Only two weddings were narrated with recall of festivities; even then there was no mention of liquor. Teasing Fanny Berry recalled how "we could sing in there and dance." Vividly remembering, she could still "see them gals now on that floor, just skipping and a trotting." Levi Pollard told gleefully how, "That was where us kicked up fun . . . one good time."

Uncle Bacchus White was born, raised, lived, and died a little way up the Rappahannock River from Sabine Hall. He told, as an actual incident remembered, a folktale famous in the John-and-Master cycle; his story was unique in this Virginia collection for the importance assigned to liquor. He recounted a situation with the master suddenly away from home. (He had gone to "Philanewyork," according to one published version; that generic reference to an urban world beyond the plantation horizon is wonderfully rendered in this Virginia narration as "Flingamacue"!)

"I remembers this so well. There was a man named John who used to tend his Master. One day his Master told him he was agoing to Philadelphia for six weeks, so he told him to blacken up his boots. [John] got him all fixed up and after he left [John] went to the cellar and he told the man with him, 'Get bottle of A.B.C. whiskey, get number 3 whiskey' and he cooked up lots of victuals and invited company in. All of them was having a time when a ragged man come to the door. He looked just like a tramp. [John] asked him who he was, and he said I would like to have something for to eat. [John] said come in Toby Bob and I will attend to you. One of the friends said 'John, his fo't [forehead? foot?] certainly does look like Master.'

"No it ain't Master. I done black Master's boots by 'foreday morning star and he is gone to Flingamacue on 6 weeks joy trip.'

"They was having a big time, a-shouting and a-talking. This old ragged man just come right up and tooken his hat off, and there was Master.

"John didn't say nothing but he just fainted.

"Master said, 'I will see you tomorrow.'"

The coda to Uncle Bacchus's story intensifies the return to reality and gives a trickster's twist as John pretended to return stolen items as a gift to his master. The story concluded: "When they was a whipping him the next day his wife, Mollie, passed through the yard and he said to her 'Oh Mollie, woman no occasion for you to go with your head down making like you don't know me and don't hear me a calling you. Go throw those two hams down and tell Master I don't want them.'"

One might say that Landon Carter told this same story in his diary, but with very different meaning and imagined end: *Yesterday*, he wrote—more in sorrow than in anger—*by my being at Mt Airy all the servants left at home quite drunk.* He found his house a shambles. This was April 1777, and the diarist was beginning to suffer from his last illness. He was almost resigned to the ways of *servants*; he evidently inclined rather to blame his son and daughter-in-law as he ran his mind into the future: *I fancy when I am gone here will be great doings*—gone not to Philadelphia, but to the grave. "John," he obviously thought, would then have his day.

STEALING?

The descriptions of the way Landon ordered his extensive fields to be intensively plowed, dunged, turned, hoed, and weeded leaves no doubt as to how hard he worked his slaves. Readers of the diaries know how much he took from them. We see also from the gentry-lore stories about Manuel, Gardener Johnny, and others that Landon was obsessed with how much his slaves took from him.

In 19 out of 25 cases where the stolen goods are named, Landon's stories of theft were about pilfered food. The range was from the most petty cases such as the illicit harvesting of melons, to the level of indictable crimes such as sheep- or hog-stealing, and the robbing of granaries. But it was part of the master's conventional wisdom that the slaves' intention was always to trade this plunder for liquor. Maybe there was as much psychological defense in this as shrewd insight; if the planter saw the motives of the slaves otherwise, he would be condemning himself for keeping his people hungry.

Landon was indeed a hard master in regard to slaves' rations: he once wrote concerning a supplier of contract labor, that, *if Captain Tomlins chose to give his people meat twice a day—it was what I can't nor will not allow of.* In answer to a circulating rumor that he was mean to his people, Landon explained at once why he *allowed them but one shirt* (instead of the customary two): *My people always made and raised things to sell—and I obliged them to buy linnen to make their other shirts instead of buying liquor with their fowls.*

Needless to say, the ex-slaves in Virginia told it differently in their oral memoirs. Sharing the collective memory, these elderly and respectable persons told of stealing but not of trading to get liquor; for them the hard work and the short rations were the essential contexts for their stories.

Marrinda Jane Singleton of Norfolk told of being driven to kill and butcher a pig in the swamp. "We were so hungry, and had no food." But, "by some means the news got to Master about this pig. . . ." He then "took me to the Big House right there in the yard, stripped me stark naked and whipped me 'til the blood dripped to the ground." She broke off the story to explain whippings in general to the young interviewer. "Now this the way they whipped us slaves: Master or a Colored overseer would stand on one side or so, so he could lash the whips on you in a row across your back, then he would turn on the other side and cross them whips. They pickle you down with salt, then recross them whips again. When they got through with you, you wouldn't want to steal no more." She returned to her own story: "Yes sir, if you see a pig a mile off you'd, ha, ha, feel like running from him."

Faced with cunning thieves all around him, the would-be cunning master did not necessarily confine his response to harsh punishment. Beneath the cloak of his legitimate patriarchal authority he too might be scheming to counter roguery by turning trickster himself! The slave Harry came to tell Landon that *his tobacco house was robbed*, and a *full hogshead tobacco . . . opened & above 100 pounds taken out of it*. Landon both advertised a reward for the thieves if captured and set a trap for them. He wrote his name on *little tickets of paper . . . & tyed them up in the heads of many bundles*. Yet, even in this, the master could not escape dependence on the slaves. He could hardly sneak unobserved into the tobacco house to lay the snare. He must entrust Harry or another with that task—thereby, if not enlisting the thief, then letting the word get out on the grapevine.

The improbality of the master being more successfully cunning than his slaves is made very clear in this memorandum-style notation for a story not fully told:

Saturday, October 25, 1766
This day changed my lock on my wheat house door. A new lock cost me 17/6. Talbot has lain in that house every night and catched Smith's Johnny once; but this Owen—the undermanager—only left the key with Talbot & never locked him up as I ordered him . . . —so he may have made away with the grain—or the people may have got in when he went out at night to his wife.

All these contests were in a sense already scripted in the two opposed folklores: the master must keep striving to thwart his people in their nefarious strategems; but, since he had to rely on them in this, they would always find ways to outtrick his countertrickery.

MOCKERY AND REPRISALS

Cruelty could not destroy love of life among the enslaved; the air was often filled with the sound of laughter—exuberant, loud, and mocking laughter. That too went unrecorded in the Sabine Hall diaries.

Landon's gentry-lore narratives never show his slaves laughing, but often we can intuit that response. We see how difficult it was for the master—outnumbered as he was—to tell convincing stories that end in his own triumph. Typical was the 1766 story of Simon and Bart and their inside man, Gardener Johnny. As their conspiracies were uncovered, the master was already a laughing stock at the quarters.

The Africans who came to Virginia and the African Americans who were born there generation after generation brought and developed a stock of stories—like that of Lion, Tortoise, and Jackal—that were a rich resource for this aspect of slave defiance. And those African American stories have in them much mocking laughter. Sometimes we can be sure that the master's rage—like Lion's at Jackal—only amplified the laughter of his people.

Landon and his daughter had been to a neighboring gentleman's birthday entertainment. They rode there in the coach (*chariot*) driven by Nat the coachman. Nat's father, Nassaw—Landon's personal attendant—had meanwhile brought a riding horse around, because the master would not stay as late as his daughter. *Friday March 23 1770. . . .*

I came home but without Nassaw or Nat—a drunken father & Son. The . . . first mired my horse up to his Saddle in crossing a marsh that none but a blind drunkard could ever venture upon—and Mr Nat so ingaged with boon companions as never to get my chariot—by which means I was to plunge home 5 or 6 miles upon this mired horse without one person to assist me. I got home near sunset—and about 8 o'clock came the Chariot home with the drunken father and son.

Landon promised himself the last laugh: *This morning I ordered the son his deserts in part.* Over the head of Nassaw would hang a suspended sentence: *The father I shall leave till another opportunity—for though my old servant I am too old a Master to be thus inhumanely treated.*

Landon would not have let himself imagine Nat singing and dancing the story of his driving his own father back with the coach; but how could he not suspect that the sounds of merriment coming up on the night air from the quarters often included laughter at his expense?

There need not even be conspiracy. Incongruous mishap could make the master a figure of fun. Landon told his diary of an accident he had out riding on his horse. He had sustained a painful injury to his penis and was treating the injured organ for weeks. Earnest medical science, not wry self-mockery, inspired the master's narration; but his slaves—who assuredly knew all about it—were meanwhile undoubtedly telling it differently!

The most savored reminiscence of Mrs. Julia Frazier illustrates the liveliness of satire at the slave quarters: she joyously recalled the best entertainer in the quarter in her childhood:

Young Charlie had one day seen "old Master" riding home across the fields. His mount had stumbled, "and Master come tumbling off." But the master did not know Charlie had seen his fall; so when the master next—before a guest—asked Charlie (whose reputation evidently extended beyond the quarter) to sing his newest song, Charlie at first demurred. "Come on you black rascal, give me a rhyme for my company—one he ain't heard." So Charlie agreed, upon the promise of Master not to "whup" him when he heard it. "Master promised, and then Charlie sang the rhyme he done made up in his head about Master:

'Jackass reared,
Jackass pitch,
Throwed old Master in the ditch.'

"Well," said Mrs. Frazier, "Master got mad as a hornet, but he didn't whup Charlie, not that time anyway."

Predictably, this song was just beginning its life. Taken up in the quarter, it was a hit: "we'd swing all round the cabin singing. . . ."

Charlie soon had "a bunch of verses:

'Jackass stamped,
Jackass neighed,
Throwed old Master on his haid.'

Everybody sure bust their sides laughing . . ."—even when reminded of their danger by the last verse:

"Jackass stamped,
Jackass hupped,
Master hear you slave, you sure get whupped."

REBELLIONS

For the ex-slaves, the horrendous punishments were the proofs of the profound evil of the system. They did not speak of themselves as cared for and protected by a divinely appointed patriarch, nor did they recount their masters as acting out some good-shepherd parable. For them the evasions and stratagems of their people that Landon's 1770s diaries record so plentifully were the means to survival. But sometimes slaves saw an opportunity to fight back fiercely. An affront to pride and sense of justice could lead them to throw prudence to the winds and resist directly. There are such episodes recorded in the Sabine Hall diary.

Jamey had become foreman at the Fork Quarter where Jack Lubbar once had been; Billy Beale was Landon's apprentice steward-manager over all his operations.

Yesterday Billy Beale finding fault with Fork Jamy's slovenly weeding corn was answered a little impudently—which obliged him—Beale—to give him—Jamy—a few licks with a switch across his Shoulders, on which the fellow turned upon him—& Beale had a fair box with him; and then had him brought up. I enquired into it, and made my Home Quarter overseer *Selfe frighten him with a gentle correction for his being so impudent; but it seems nothing scared him, and he told the overseer he should not whip him without my orders.*

Of course, men like Jamey very rarely threw caution entirely to the winds. In defying managers and overseers in this case, he was playing on the incomplete delegation of patriarchal authority so usual on the plantation. Jamey was invoking the master against his deputies, and his violence was probably tempered by prudence. How, we might ask, was he actually *brought up* to Sabine Hall? How, for that matter, were Johnny and others who had been caught night riding overpowered by mere white boys? Jamey meant to show strong resentment, but he wanted to keep living in his community. This episode of forceful resistance ended in evasions. Landon recorded, perhaps implausibly, that he *did not hear* about Jamey's second defiant stand and had *ordered him to work, but he returned saying his Stomach pained him so much he could not work.* The master took this way out of further confrontation: now he could be the benign physician: *As we have had all the year bilious Complaints about—I ordered him a vomit which cleared a very foul stomach.*

Ex-slaves remembered a series of acts of fierce self-defense—their own, their father's, their mother's, their uncles' and aunts'.

Rev. Jacobs has already told us about his Uncle Charlie, who had run away to freedom in Canada after overpowering that driver; he was not forgotten. The tellers of these life stories celebrated defiant kinsmen—such as old Cornelius Garner's father, who inspired enough fear in the master to get special treatment.

Strong women were also remembered—and by men too. In 1937 West Turner was 95 years old; he still remembered himself as a child, "laying on the pallet listening" in the night to the whispered sounds of his runaway "Aunt Sallie" coming into the cabin to get food and shelter. Suddenly there was banging at the door. The master was onto them. "Then I heard old Master yelling for all the niggers and telling them to come there and catch Sally else he gonna whup them all." The trap seemed sprung. "Pa didn't know what to do," although he had the door wedged. "But Sallie ain't catched yet. She grabbed a scythe knife . . . and she pulled the chock out that door and come out a-swinging." She went; and her nephew concluded the telling with satisfaction: "Those niggers was glad because they didn't want to catch her. And Master didn't dare touch her."

RUNNING

Landon showed a wise master's caution in sometimes not pressing angry persons too hard. Irate slaves could and did run away, and he knew it. Once, on noting the whipping he had ordered for Ambrose, he simply added: *I suppose he will go off.* And there was not much the master could do about that—short of having *my runaways . . . work in chains.* But how much work could they then actually do?

Running could be quite casual—at first an unremarked withdrawal of labor or evasion of anticipated punishment. Thus, the complete surviving diary of 1770 has no mention of Ambrose's actual going. Only when he had been out a while did notes begin to appear: *No news of Ambrose yet.* But soon there was news; and it was of conspiracy: *Ambrose it seems by the Children's Account—is every day in Fork Jammy's house. It seems he brings his meal in there and bakes his bread.* What *Children?* The diarist's own grandchildren? They would be closer to the tattle in the yard—or enslaved children? They might be more easily pressured into talking. Either way, everyone once again knew more than the master about this matter. Landon organized a countercombination: *I have set a watch for him & shall send another in hopes to catch him.* And there was some success: *Mr. Ambrose brought home this morning.* He had been *catched getting in at his sister Franky's window.* The master took pleasure in the trap he had set: *I knew that bitch entertained him & there laid the scheme for Simon to watch for him—and he was accordingly taken. The punishment of him I will refer tommorrow and the whole week.*

A Brer Rabbit folktale tells how in life's contests "some go up, and some go down." In the big runaway episode of four years previously, Ambrose's captor, Simon, had himself been forcefully seized by Mangorike Will—another enslaved man ready to settle scores, or else just keen to win favors.

Most slaves, when they ran away, merely withheld their labor; they stayed nearby, drawing support from their kin. The ex-slave, Rev. Ivy, explained absconding to the young African American man who interviewed him. "There was two kinds of runaways—them what hid in the woods and them what ran away to free land." Negotiation was the norm with the runaways who lurked near the plantation. "Master would come down to the quarters and let out 'Guess Jim getting pretty hungry out in the woods.' Then someone say, 'Guess that nigger scared to come back, Master, scared you gonna whup him?' 'Who said I was gonna whup him?' answered Master. 'But I will whup him if he don't hurry back here.'"

Once slaves had been caught, then the freedom they had assumed by running was physically and ritually countered by strict confinement. But even then a further trick might defer punishment. We have already seen how Johnny, tied and imprisoned, contrived to escape again, and how, when Manuel's Sarah *was catched . . . and locked up*, the master's grip did not hold—*somebody broke open the door for her*. The reports in these cases were quite matter-of-fact.

Revolution and war, however, called forth a new kind of runaway. We have seen in the escape of the Eight in 1776 how Landon, faced with the prospect that some of his people ran away for freedom, became anxious and vindictive. In similar circumstances in September 1777, he reported of *Mrs Fork Judy*, that not only had he *kept her confined*, but he *had her whipped twice at 4 day's distance*, until, so he hoped, she *is resolved never more to stir*. His conclusion: *And so I shall do all runaways for the future. Confine them and every now and then a whipping.*

ULTIMATE MEASURES

In some degree all slave offenses were viewed as rebellions. Running away— even just to hide out—was a very overt sort of rebellion and was usually punished accordingly. We have seen how Landon punished runaways by whipping, imprisonment, and tortures like tying their necks and heels. Or he could escalate his response. If there was suspected aggravation—robberies and livestock killing—he could go to the law. He could arrange outlawry, trial for felony, and upon conviction, public hanging, at which point the public purse would, according to law, reimburse him the value that the court set on the slave. Thus, Landon had dealt with Manuel before he brought forth a pardon; thus, in 1766 he had threatened exemplary death for Bart if Simon could be made to turn evidence against him. He made the same threat against two sheep killers in 1777: *one shall be hanged to terrify the rest.*

There is, however, no diary record of Landon actually going through with the execution of one of his slaves. Perhaps the softer man-of-sensibility side of him may have shrunk from that ultimate penalty. On October 3, 1774, he wrote sadly: *Sent also poor Ned's Death Warrant to the Sherrif, a slave of Colonel Tayloe's before convicted of felony and on the Court's recommendation Pardoned; Again convicted and Condemned, now for Robbing his master.* He went on in a more matter-of-fact vein: *The first time he was only valued at £80; but now at 100£.*

The solemnity of the law may have served most to confirm in the masters their own sense of legitimacy; there are no Virginia ex-slave narratives about masters' due process for them under law. They silently rejected any claims of just treatment of that kind. In some 153 life stories there is only one courtroom scene, and that is as an occasion to tell a bawdy story! There were hangings in the collective memory—but these were lynchings with tar and flames to recall in horror the extrajudicial character of the killing.

We have seen repeated references to another form of ultimate punishment that was simply and absolutely in any master's power: he could sell slaves away. In his diary, Landon entered this threat against Johnny, Manuel, and Manuel's Sarah, but again the diary does not show an instance of Landon's actually casting out a slave in this way. Perhaps he could never bring himself to so complete a severance of the patriarch-dependent tie. Or perhaps he did it but kept the action out of the diary. Somehow, the latter seems unlikely; the diarist would have needed to justify his action to himself and to his posterity.

Of course Landon's patriarchal conscience experienced not a qualm as he sent away slaves all over Virginia in his settlements to cement the marriages of his own quite widely dispersed offspring. Only Lucy Carter Colston and Robert Wormeley Carter remained with their marriage settlement slaves in the same county as Sabine Hall. It may be that by remaining part of the extended Carter family, the inheritance slaves did not feel their severance to be so final: messages could surely be sent with attendants on every white-family visit; but for most, seeing each other would be at an end.

The diarist perhaps punitively sold away slaves in the time of his alarmed outrage at Lord Dunmore's promise of freedom. The chances were not good for the *runaways in Irons* in 1777. Landon darkly menaced: *I had them separately secured & confined—they shall be 'till I can sell them.* Meanwhile, Manuel's brother, Will, had helped two of his sons to escape; we have seen that entry in Landon's diary conclude: *to Carolina he shall go—if I give him away.*

In threatening Carolina, Landon was at the beginning of a fateful new development for slavery in Virginia. Tobacco profits were diminishing while the already large African American population was growing fast. More and more of the elderly were going to see their children parted from them. The experience of seeing loved ones sold away "down South" came to be the most frequently and bitterly recalled of any in the collective memory of Virginia's ex-slave African Americans.

Charles Grandy had a joking version of what the Richard Henry Lee Monument in Norfolk signified. He saw "the man on top there pointing south." "Know what it mean?" he asked—"'Carry the nigger down South if you want to rule him.'" Many others told of this doom without the least trace of mirth. They were haunted by images of slave coffles shuffling past, of mothers made to leave their babies, and always, always of families torn asunder. Often, it was remembered, the separation had been deliberately contrived to allow no chance of a farewell.

Words might make as forceful a resistance as ever that of Fork Jamey or Aunt Sally with her scythe knife. Mr. Beverley Jones, her nephew, told how Aunt Crissy presented her master with an ultimate defiance after he had sold away Lucy and Polly, two of her children. "She went to him and told him he was a mean dirty slave-trader." The master knew it; he "got sore, but he ain't never said nothing to Aunt Crissy." Then, when her second youngest, Hendley, sickened and died, "Aunt Crissy ain't sorrowed much. She went straight up to old Master and shouted in his face 'Praise God, praise God, my little child is gone to Jesus. That's one child of mine you ain't never gonna sell.'"

SEXUAL EXPLOITATION

Aunt Crissy's anger resonates through the collective memory of "them . . . terrible times." So did the plight of poor Lucy and poor Polly, mere girls wrested from their parents to be sent south to Carolina, Georgia, or away to the Delta. In an age when white ladies had few rights, young slave women lacked even a right to protection. Their parents saw these girls dragged out into a pitiless world of brutal racial and sexual exploitation.

The exercise of the white men's power over black women was a bitter theme in the ex-slave life stories—a cruel fact of life whose legacy was seen everywhere among their people. Many of the narrators wore the fact in the complexion of their own skins and felt it as their own shame. "I didn't have no father," Annie Wallace told one of the few white interviewers in Virginia. Her son explained "that her father was a Mr. Fields, a white man . . . but she was ashamed to say so." Virginia Hayes Shepherd told of her birth—"a white baby with a slave mother." Looking forward to the promised book of the slaves' stories, she told her two African American interviewers: "I don't know how you going to write that, but it's just the same true."

Stories of advances repelled were readily recalled. Minnie Folkes gave a terrible account of her mother being stretched, flogged, and pickled by the overseer, for "nothing other than to refuse to be wife to this man." Fannie Berry boasted how she resisted once—"The poor white man had his match." But after telling of wrestling off and badly scratching the would-be rapist, she added a line bearing on the frequency of the opposite outcome in so many cases: "Us colored women had to go through a-plenty, I tell you."

The ex-slave men remembered it bitterly too. In Robert Ellett's version of slavery times, "if you . . . had a good looking daughter . . . she was taken from you. . . . They would put her in the big house where the young masters could have the run of her." This was one source of the rage expressed by Rev. Ishrael Massie: "My blood is boiling now [at the] thoughts of them times."

Meanwhile, Landon's series of plantation diaries is almost silent about sexual relations between whites and blacks in his world. There were some indirect mentions, as in slaves designated mulattoes, but there were only two direct mentions of interracial coupling. In both cases however, it was not the sexual relationship in itself that occasioned the record; it was other associated disturbances of order in the extended household.

Landon's diary exhibits no concupiscent desires toward his slave women; if he harbored such feelings, he either deeply repressed or very skillfully concealed them. This matter could, however, be a casual one for fathers of the diarist's rank and station in Virginia. Philip Fithian was a tutor who kept a diary in the household of Councillor Robert Carter, Landon's nephew, living only ten miles to the north of Sabine Hall. Fithian was well aware that the eldest son was having a sexual liaison with a slave girl; but he sensed no instruction from the lad's father to watch and check such conduct, and consequently he did not interfere.

Whether or not they themselves exploited slave women sexually, masters like Landon knowingly presided over a system in which that was a routine occurrence. In this they contributed to the terrible stock of stories that was carried forward even as it was continually renewed. That was one part of the great ensemble of stories that called forth not only the repeated declarations that "Them were terrible terrible times", but also—even from the most Christian— the assertion that "God's going to keep punishing white folks . . . their children and their children's children."

JUDGMENTS?

Landon Carter saw himself as a pastor—a good shepherd—to his flocks and herds. He would pour forth his wrath on his workers when he thought they betrayed that charge. He also played pastor—one might almost say, played God— to his enslaved people, as we shall see in the attempted reclamation of Nassaw, Landon's slave surgeon and personal attendant.

In our age when authoritarianism is in disfavor—in literary-intellectual if not in corporate spheres—we readily condemn Landon Carter's bluster and his punishments, although we see him trying to be just. Now, the stories from life in the Sabine Hall diaries when read together with ex-slave remembered lives make it possible to see both sides of the master-and-slave world. In this two-sided way, we may attain greater understanding of the enduring legacies of pain and resentment that systematic exploitation and injustice begets.

To conclude this dialog of narrative, I shall give the enslaved the last word. Here is a folk story from among their descendants.

John was a trickster; he had contrived that his master should believe that he would find treasure on the seabed if he were dropped bagged and weighted into the ocean! "Good bye Massa," said John, as he pushed the sack overboard. "I sure hope you find what you looking for."

Landon was looking for moral vindication through the voluminous diaries he kept of all the most contentious dealings of his last years. Historical reading can now only reward him with a kind of understanding that he would have rejected if he could have imagined it; but perhaps there is treasure in this—if a two-sided understanding is of service in a world where terrible exploitations are no less rife than they were in "them back days."

Chapter 10

Duties Betrayed

Landon Carter's diaries come from a late moment of an ancient regime of knowledge and society. The diarist felt in his heart that he was chronicling decline. His own death could not be far off, and he sensed also the passing of the world which his altogether admirable father had bequeathed to him. And so he wrote affirmations of the old, the tried, and the true, along with his copious condemnations of the all-too-apparent trends of these latter days. The alarm—and so the affirmation and condemnation—grew ever more intense as defiance became armed conflict and then a republican revolution that cast out the king and the old constitution.

Though presented in diary fashion with little narrative scraps and occasional fully developed story episodes, Landon's account of his neighborhood presents and defends an entire worldview. It had to. How else could the diarist achieve his primary purpose in this chronicle: the justification of his stewardship under God. It is in this light that we must see the strong cast of characters from the parish and the county and beyond. There they all are—the women, the foolish young, and the seldom-wiser old. They appear individually and collectively, framed in the appropriate setting of dramatic weather narratives and of the reports of crops and sickness that still made up the staple of this plantation journal. The humans are God's creatures under the skies that were so continually monitored for signs of wrath or mercy. The characters are almost allegorical, as well as real-life figures. They are rich and poor, master and servant—all categories from the Bible as well as from life. Then there are also the tenant and the squire, and the smiling, vengeful baronet. There are the parson and doctor, and the lawyers and merchants. All should be in the service of

God, but the stories arise from the propensity of humankind to rebel against the father's law.

The great New England scholar Perry Miller made famous the Puritan preachers' denunciation of their times as sermons in the manner of the prophet Jeremiah. Prepare now to read the jeremiads of a Virginia Anglican.

A Rural World on the Brink

Landon's piety was not effortless or easy. The weather was God's constant manifestation to those who, like Landon, labored to get *food & raiment* for mankind. But the weather more often than not threatened or delivered disaster for those labors. Landon had therefore continually to school himself in the dutiful acceptance of disappointment and frustration.

The weather seldom got a favorable report, but Landon tried occasionally to correct that: *It is but fair that the good days should be observed as well as the bad ones. I would say this is a most glorious one—and I have enjoyed it in a comfortable ride.*

Mostly there was endless schooling in adversity. In 1772, on the first Monday and Tuesday of June, Landon had been doing his duty at the courthouse, but what was his reward? He recorded his disappointment and inner struggle:

June 3. Wednesday.

The 1st & 2d at Court extremely hot & fatiguing. On the 2d in the evening there fell at the Courthouse—& seemingly beyond the Courthouse and down to the Riverside—a most prodigeous rain indeed for near an hour—so great as to make a mere* River half-leg deep quite to the church; but beyond that it appeared less and less as I came home; and my Overseer tells me this morning there was not more rain below the hill than would water a plant patch well. However God be praised for this; Although an unprofitable one—I will not be an ungrateful servant.

The scene is complete: courthouse and church and plantation, master and overseer. Both master and overseer are servants in their degrees and in their places of service under the giving and not-giving heavens, which are ordained by their great master, God.

Two months later, Landon's entire entry for a Friday, August 7, was an an-

---

* "Mere" in eighteenth-century English was an intensifier of meaning. Landon used it often; we might say, an entire river.

guished question coupled with a high injunction: *Am I still to eat my bread by the severe sweat of my brows! And that without any moisture! Lord teach me humility, and patience, and let thy will be done.* We may smile, being more conscious than he of whose brows sweated most to produce Landon's bread. But he knew God had placed him in troublesome charge of those labors, and we should respect his pious self-chastening.

Landon believed that he had a duty of piety, prudence, and philosophy (science) to monitor the weather and to enforce on himself an acceptance of its divinely ordained decrees. It was Landon's further duty as a patriarch and senior judge in the county to monitor his own and others' performances of duty—or, more often, their delinquencies. Thence came the great recording of neighbor stories, for which, as much as for the domestic and slave narratives, the diary deserves to be famous.

Many of these stories seem comic—probably more so than was intended.

The great Greco-Roman literary tradition was the staple of Landon's school education; in that tradition, comedy comprised all narratives of simple folk, including their sufferings. Tragedy told the fall of the noble great. Christian traditions—always narrating events under the providence of God—varied this somewhat. Landon wrote naturally and unconsciously out of both these traditions. His solemn purpose—self-vindication as a servant of God—kept overt expressions of mirth to a minimum. But his ironies, often charged with scorn, frequently invite at least a smile from twenty-first century readers.

Being neighborly was a duty, and so therefore was visiting, especially to one's kin. Landon's diary is not a social record in the modern sense; it is demonstrable that he frequently omitted a record of a visit if nothing noteworthy was produced by it. It is equally clear that coming and going between houses (and the consequent hospitality) was incessant.

Talk was an essential part of the incessant visiting. Conversation was one of the most valued parts of hospitality, and table talk was one of the most valued forms of conversation. Of course, the diary itself, especially in its narrative turns, was a kind of written extension of table talk.

There was both duty and pleasure in talk, and so it was also a service to be rendered, especially by the young to the old. In the legendary world of the kings of yore, the vassals owed a duty of "paying court"; in one sense they owed talk to their lord. One of Landon's most constant complaints about his off-spring was that they did not keep him company. He craved their conversation, and expected genteel liveliness from them. Once Landon declared a doubt concerning one of his younger sons (it is not clear which). *I am mistaken if that son of mine lives long; he makes too much of every Circumstance in life—is quite dull with the weight of everything.* Landon was therefore much gratified when the Reverend Mr. Giberne wrote to cheer him by telling him that Mrs. Fauntleroy had said that she "would rather spend a day with Colonel Carter than with any of the young fellows."

Talk had its light moments, though they were seldom reported in the diary. A smile was surely intended in the 1771 gossipy report that Lord Dunmore (then newly arrived as governor) had a pack of dogs whose voracity had *raised the price of beef in Williamsburgh.* Certainly Landon was continuing in that vein when he mocked the fashionable rise of fine music in the town. *I do suppose they*—the dogs—*must make a great addition to the present modes of Concerts, for I hear from every house a constant tuting may be listned to upon one instrument or another, whilst the Vocal dogs will no doubt compleat the howl.*

There was usually a chuckle, albeit a scornful one, on the infrequent occasions when Landon reported talk about the mating game. Property considerations might be right up front, along with mockery of the youth of the day. *Who says that 2 or 3000 £ is not a great beauty? I'll answer for it—not one Youth of the Present age whose pockets are quite inverted with dissipation.* But Landon also made fun of his own age group:

Mr. Robert Burwell, the King's Counsellor, came here yesterday. . . . He is . . . a widower in his 52d year of Age, a Grandfather . . . too young to continue single; and too old for any lady but the aged to associate with—and as he has never been one given to much reading, he seems to have nothing to pass away his lonely hours with. In this situation, at present he is unhappy in not being able to think of anything but a wife—in which every man nowadays exhibits but an odd & foolish scene of life, and as he grows older he must be miserable; for without books or a desire to read how can the aged enjoy themselves when the Young—even their children—seem to despise them?

The married state was subject to a different kind of comment. A pair of opposites shows the extremes of bad and good.

It always ran in my head that my upland friend—who had a Vast estate now gone—has been not a little ruined by Madam his wife. . . . His mode of extravagance & want of care, has been owing to her; for now I hear she is so much of the mistress as to rule & keep him quite low. But must there not be some original defect in the spirits of such a man to be obliged for the sake of peace to have given her her way?

Just once we get a glimpse of an ideal realized. The perfect wife would be not weak and without will; she would combine strength with dutifulness. *Mr. Mills & his Lady came to see me, she is a good woman & I think I know her already, or I am much mistaken. James will grow richer & his servants better.*

Cultured table talk—or even an approximation to it—helped affirm the legitimacy of the rule of the gentry. If the circle included the parson, it was so much the more complete.

This dinner-time conversation happened on a sultry Saturday afternoon, while spectacular thunder and lightning played by turns in every quarter of the sky around Sabine Hall. Ralph Wormeley, Jr., Colonel Francis Lightfoot Lee, the Reverend Mr. Giberne, and the diarist's sons—Robert Wormeley (*Robin*) and John—were all at the table. Had one of the country doctors been there, it would have been even more appropriate, since the physiology of sex was the topic. Not surprisingly the talk profoundly affirmed a controlling male view of females and their libido.

We had . . . a very possitive though not a very learned Contest, about why some people's cows do not breed.

It was asserted that corn & hay would make any cow wanton & take bull.

I could not help observing that very hot weather would—notwithstanding fatness—prevent all those natural passions or cravings in brutes, that only answered the dictates of nature and did not run into the fancied pleasures of the human species tempted by lust, always—or very frequently—to be indulging.

I also told them That—although a ram full fed or a boar might teaze a female into a Compliance; yet observation had convinced me it was not so with fat bulls; They could not tempt a cow that was overheated by the weather to stand to their attempts. I added That—in the general—fatness produced sallaciousness, and that even Sallacious women are not esteemed breeders and that it was so evident to the Contrary that a woman in such a state never bred at all: which was the case of the most noted whores; for such a state would evidently destroy the Semen Virile, as every Physician I was persuaded could evidence from his practice.

But the young Gentlemen—Wormeley and my son John—were not to be convinced. However let them take their turns in life as others have done—and they will experience that no Corn or hay (which certainly cannot be often wanted in the usual bulling time of Cows) would always keep up a stock of calves.

Livestock and crops were, of course, a perennial topic of table talk—and churchyard, courthouse yard and tavern talk as well. There was such close over-the-fence inspection of each other's fields, such competitive talk about each other's prospects, and such anxiety not to be out of line that Landon was continually using his diary to affirm the rightness of his own distinctive methods. He knew it was his God-given duty to use his science-assisted reason to devise the best strategies. He owed that to the estate that was his family's inheritance and the source of food and raiment to all his people.

Landon himself held feasts; certainly, he publicly celebrated his birthday each year on August 18. He would usually set the tone with pious reflection and retrospection.

His 1772 record of the anniversary began with a resolution in favor of a combination of piety and sociability that was reinforced by a solemn example from history and literature. It ended with a notice of the toll taken by the acquisition of so much bookish knowledge.

They tell me this is my birthday when I enter my 63d year; and I will endeavour to keep it with all the prudent joy of a social Christian, and not with the Pompous sadness of a Roman Murderer; as being the best testimony that I can give of that prodigeous blessing of my creator who has suffered me to live to this period—& that with no other complaint than the usual Concomitants of old age. I am made a little infirm by a long continued Vertiginous disorder gotten by too great a desire for knowledge, an intense reading and observing upon all things.

Drawn from his reading of Dryden's own verse tragedy, "All for Love," the idea of the contrast between social Christianity and imperial pomp continued to haunt Landon; he returned to it in the gloom of what proved to be the last birthday of his life—now in time of war and of the republic he had dreaded. *Were I a Mark Anthony I . . . would keep it with double pomp of Sadness. But thank God . . . have . . . hopes in the Father of Goodness. . . . Therefore I will be as Cheerful with my friends as Society, decency, Justice, and a reverence to God . . . will let me.*

Service to God was, of course, the ultimate obligation that the diary must promote and record. Worship, prayer, thanksgiving, confession, and repentance were the direct acknowledgments of this obligation; and we have seen occasional prayers and a recurrent prayerful posture in the diary. Mostly, however, service to God must be translated into a duty to serve mankind.

Landon gave the benefit of his medical knowledge and his well-stocked apothecary shop to his poorer neighbors all around. His personal friends might get consultations and prescriptions over the dinner table on their visits, like it or not. Landon wrote on Tuesday, February 13, 1770: *On Sunday last Frank Lee came to dine with me. Poor fellow in a very low state but yet I think easy to be amended. It is my opinion that his whole intestines are smeared over with an acid slimy phlegm which should now and then be brought off by gentle pukes. . . .*

Landon instantly found fault with the medication given to his guest; he went into repulsive detail, that I shall spare the reader, as he proposed an alternative treatment. *Many Rhubarb purgative preparations . . . would cure this Gentleman. I could not but recommend to him this method—with a pill of mild soap every morning 5 grains in quantity.* And within two days Landon already had a grateful report: *He told me he had tried 2 pills—and had received their good effects.*

Poorer neighbors, clientlike, had to apply to Sabine Hall; and they found that Landon was a stern judge in matters of sickness and its outcome in life or death. He could indeed conclude that persons had been as good as killed by others. The following record is presented above dozens of others because it gives a sudden insight into Landon's dark folkloric wisdom concerning the nemesis of patriarchy, with the heirs waiting for inheritances:

Old Stanly Gower died Saturday last with a Pleurisy. It seems as if families desired their old Parents to dye, for ever before this I was always applied to when either that old gentleman or his family were ill—& I had been always so happy as to relieve them—but now I never so much as heard he was ill, though I lived so near him.

The country doctor is a strong icon of old-regime rusticity. Landon had an ambivalent relationship with these professionals who were both colleagues and rivals in the blessed work of healing. The stories that accumulated were more or less freighted with judgments as to how well each of these doctors served both God and man.

First let us enjoy a whimsical sketch that also shows what a figure familiar to everyone the doctor was. In the harvest season of 1772, Landon was amazed at the large size of the corncobs within meager-looking ears: *It puts me in mind of a Comparison made on Dr Jones's small Jemmy-coat. Take it off—and to look at his body occasions a wonder how such a Carcase could be contained in such a Coat.*

The doctors were university men. (At this time they had all trained in Edinburgh, even if Virginia born.) In over-the-dinner-table debates, the doctors were worthy sparring partners for the bookish squire. On one occasion both parson and doctor had dined at Sabine Hall; Landon relished that opportunity to exalt the great medical authority of his youth over a much-vaunted Scottish teacher of recent times.

Tuesday, May 26, 1772.

The Reverend Mr. Giberne & Dr Jones dined with me yesterday. We had much altercation about Theory & Practice.

I advanced the former but as the Grammar to Experience . . . as Grammars are made from language.

This was denied to be parallel, because all language was more perfect than Practice.

I answered . . . that from the Imperfectness of theory, there still was room for experience to improve it. These things led me into the defence of Boerhaave against a certain Cullen, the master of all the last imported pupils who—from a gratefull affection—joined the man in contradicting all the first principles of things.*

I was told Cullen had shone in those contradictions.

I answered so did the moon & stars when the Sun was set.

Many wild assertions filled up our arguments; but not one of them could be mentioned on Paper.

Landon had given a lesson in respect for the old order against those who made innovation a matter of principle.

Justice belongs to the king. So it had been in old England; and so it was in colonial British America. The remedying of wrongs in society was still an essential part of royal sovereignty; the public prosecutor was in fact called the king's attorney.

The service of justice was centered on the county court. Its magistrates were justices of the peace (JPs) named in a Commission of the Peace that was issued in the king's name by the colonial governor. Those commissioned were gentle-

---

* Boerhaave had been the preeminent clinical physician of Landon's school days (see notes to chapter 6). Cullen, a professor at Edinburgh University, was mentor to many of the young doctors in Virginia.

men of rank and wealth in their counties; mostly they were landowners, but a few merchants were named to the commission. These justices served without pay as a duty to the public—that is, to the king—and before they could be seated on the bench, they must take a set of solemn oaths. Like the newly elected members of the House of Burgesses, they swore the oaths of Allegiance, of Supremacy (acknowledging the king as head of the Church), and they took "the Test," vowing their abhorrence of the papist doctrine of transubstantiation. Thus, they repeatedly declared their loyalty to the king in person and to the institutions of the Protestant British monarchy. They met on an appointed day each month for a court in course. They could also be summoned at any time for a "called court" for criminal trial proceedings.

By the time of the 1770s diaries, Landon had become the senior member of his county court. He was named first in the commission, and he therefore regularly presided over the sessions. He took very seriously this duty as presiding justice, and he wished he could say the same of his fellow magistrates; but all too often he had to conclude that *the Public duty hardly seems to be any body's concern.* Indeed, just a week before this line of censure, Landon had recorded how, in poor health and with the weather bad, he had gone forth wearing the armor of God, as it were, to preserve him while doing the work of king, and community: *Still very cloudy, damp weather, and 'tis our court day. I must go there—though not yet recovered so well as I could wish. However by wrapping up warm I hope—in so good a cause as forwarding the Administration of Justice—I shall not receive any injury by it.*

Landon knew his duty, just as he saw a tendency in others to neglect theirs. That split imaging called forth some notable dramatic narratives that afford precious glimpses of scenes around the courthouse and its adjoining "ordinary" (or tavern) on court day. In May 1770 the diarist recorded considerable disappointment after two days of sluggish proceedings: *I had thought that by a kind of diligence . . . we should have been by this time able to have brought our Docket into a very small size—but I see each person concerned with the Court will reserve their lazyness. . . .*

There had been letters in the newspapers exhorting the courts to overcome the delay of justice; but the diarist did not see any good effects. *I believe every man of them shows not the least inclination even to incommode the least private concern for the sake of the public—and I wish I may not find a kind of surly obstinacy in some of them against doing this duty as he should.*

Obstinacy was once more apparent when a procedural measure that Landon moved from the chair was taken as a censure of the Clerk of the Court.

This motion was growled at by every member on the bench—and indeed Mr. Parker—
who seemed to be willing to show that he thought he had an influence—rose up in his
King's Attorney's seat & opposed it—pretending such an order would look as if the Jus-
tices were designing to lay the blame for every such omission from off their shoulders.

I could not help replying first to the growling bench . . . that I had been perswaded
from under the shelter of my own vine to take the chair in the court—*which* by seniority *I had lived into.* I told them *that I could easily retire & would do it if Gentle-*
men—instead of supporting me in the duty of the chair—should show themselves so
disposed as they had done in every instance to overrule my endeavours.

An angry Landon proceeded to instruct the court learnedly on a number of
points of law. He carried one motion with his casting vote; but it is not clear
from the diary whether or not his procedural motion was carried.

On rare occasions Landon had the satisfaction of recording that his zeal to
inspirit service did prevail:

Wednesday, December 4, 1771.

I went to Court the 2d—and by means of a most great endeavour I got the Court to set
the next day as well—so that besides some short causes / cases we got a pretty large Ap-
pearance list all docketed for some pleading—which certainly put the business so much
the forwarder. However some who waited to lounge by the fire would represent this as a
matter of no service.

Landon did duty for the court in many ways, including the supervision of
public works in the county. In July of 1770 he went to inspect a wooden bridge
constructed across Rappahannock Creek. (Roads were built and maintained by
the county courts out of an annual tax that they levied.) This was no ordinary
logs-between-the-banks bridge! The plan, Landon noted proudly, *was my*
own—taken from Vitruvius's bridge over the Rhine in Julius Caesar's days. He found
it *very substantially done*; with some prescribed reinforcement, *it will be a work of*
duration. The design had already proved itself during two recent floods when
the water rose at least three feet above *the crown of the arch*, without carrying the
structure away. *I was told there that travellers going by expressed a satisfaction at the*
Architecture—and Naval Officer Lee told me yesterday he believes it will be a model far
and near—for he never heard anything more spoken of.

Yet, Landon knew that he lived in a fallen world, full of pettiness, spite, and
mean contrivances. So, in the coda to this narration, he had to sound a sour
note: *But we—*the agents of the County—*will not receive it* as satisfactorily completed—*because it is built 20 foot above the old* crossing *place and on Sir Marmaduke*
Beckwith's land, who—although I heard he had directed the workmen to build it
there—from an ill natured principle—intends now to dispute it with the County.

Landon did not intend, however, that the malign baronet* should have his perverse will in this matter, since the court, when it met, had authority to legalize the new roadway and bridge— although, until it met, the baronet could legally tear down the bridge. *I said nothing to it—and—if he does not cut it down before next Court—I am determined to move to have the road turned over it.*

The Law and the Court existed—or so it was firmly understood at this time—to secure to each his own. The American patriots were to fight a war to defend this understanding of law: if a man could be taxed without his consent, then his property was not his own.

Landon was very fierce and exact about property. His fierceness and exactness often made him seem close and grasping; but he wrote the diary to show that he acted correctly. Assuredly Landon told the following story to affirm the rightness of precise reckoning. His exasperating eldest son had to be instructed with a proverb—perhaps coined for the occasion.

*In salting up the quantity of pork . . . —I found that in about a month it had lost near 2 per Cent. Ball—*the steward—*never considered this but paid Lawson his full compliment—*as though it was fresh meat—*for which I called him a foolish fellow, a word he stomachs much.* Landon was eventually able to secure the acquiescence of his overseer, *by representing a quantity of Corn under his Care—and asking whose loss the shrinkage should be—*his or mine. . . . *This so far satisfied him that he was ashamed of holding the dispute. But comes a blade—*my son—*that can't see right and justice because perhaps not wrapped up in £100 and he asks what use was the disputing about 12 lbs of pork.*

My answer always is—truth and justice have no virtue if it does not shine in a farthing as well as in a million. . . .

In other contexts this sort of dealing may have caused more trouble than the gains (or the principle?) were worth. Landon had to try to cope with extensive slanders down in Lancaster and Northumberland counties, because one of his overseers there, after having been dismissed with his wages withheld, had spread denunciations everywhere. But at least once Landon was prudent enough not to try such cheese-paring practices in a situation where a jury of farming folk would pass judgment in a case involving a poorer man. The diarist was in dispute with a former overseer, James Brown: *I had a mind to sue this*

---

* A baronet had the rank of a knight in the English system of honors. The baronet's title was inherited by his eldest son, in contrast to most knighthoods that were conferred only for life in recognition of service to the Crown. The only other baronet in Virginia at this time was Sir Peyton Skipwith, who lived farther south in Buckingham County.

man by a writ in County Court for my seventy-four barrels corn; but I considered it would be thought taking an advantage of him, which would be a plausible reason for juries finding for him . . .—because they fancy they themselves might be overseers. Though the value of the alleged debt was considerable (as such things were reckoned in the countryside), Landon decided to let it go, rather than be *any way the occasion* for some *willful Perjury in Juries.* Already in the winter of 1772, Landon had a sense of a mounting assertiveness on the part of the common man, although the uprising April of 1775 was a full two years in the future, when Virginia dirt farmers, guns in hand, rode forth in revolt against constituted authority.

At Sabine Hall, Landon had repeatedly to adjudicate out-of-court cases of trespass. Sometimes he would be invoking the law fiercely against those (usually poorer neighbors) whom he accused of letting their livestock damage his crops; sometimes neighbors, rich and poor, came to him in his role as a justice of the peace for writs to attempt to enforce their claimed rights.

The following examples give vivid glimpses of country life when, in the absence of wire fences, boundaries could only be protected with wooden rails or rough-woven wattle.

Robin Smith the younger some weeks agoe was seen by Williamson Ball, Walker Tomlinson and others feeding his hogs upon my land by my meadow—&—as they then told him it would teach those hogs to get into the meadow—so it has accordingly happened—for . . . they have rooted up a very large and very fine tobacco seedling plant patch.

Yesterday H. Hertford's cattle broke into my watled tobacco ground. I advertize them to be taken care of or I must kill them. This very man obliges Robin Smith to keep his own cattle from him, and yet he is a constant trespasser upon me.

When I went on tuesday last in my chariot to Hickory Thicket I observed some hogs had been rooting my tobacco up at the Gate of the watled ground & I sent Nassaw back immediately to tell Beale to order the boy Johnny . . . to go round to see where the hogs had got in. When I came home he told me he had done so, and had stopped every hole. I then sent to James Webb—the owner of the hogs . . . to keep his hogs out or I would shoot them.

Landon's fierce defense of his boundaries could call forth reprisals, he feared. *My guinea boar not to be found. I suppose Morgan, Colo. Tayloe's overseer, has shot him in revenge for my keeping his hogs out of my Corn field.* Squire Landon gave the legally required warning before he brought out the gun; overseer Morgan, it seems, did not.

Trespass was not a laughing matter, but these rural dramas could have their comic aspect—as in the following story that turned on an argument as to where geese seemed most at home.

Landon first gave the birds a place in his diary with an allusion to the famous geese that saved Rome: *I clearly see that the accident of the Fork geese—like the Roman geese—has saved my Capitol; for their work of destruction close at hand— and direct in my view—made me look upon the informations of overseers & negroes as a mere rascally falsehood.*

Of course, he did not know as he turned those phrases that in three months time the geese would involve him in a tougher contest—though one not so readily elevated by reference to epic ancient history.

Wednesday, August 19, 1772. . . .

Yesterday at dinnertime—during my birthday entertainment—my old henhouse woman wanted to inform me that one W Morgan had taken 18 of her geese from my barley and tobacco house at the riverside. And this morning she came again and let me into the story.

I sent for Lawson—the overseer.

He said that yesterday first a negro man came to fetch 11 of the geese from the yard by the barley patch, and also took 7 out of the tobacco house. . . . he drove the fellow away, and presently Will Morgan came and took the whole 18 away notwithstanding he forbid him.

I sent Beal to Morgan to tell him to bring them home to me or I would prosecute him for thieving.

The man came here. . . . He said he could swear to the geese.

My son said—then he must have marked them.

He said—no—but he knew them by their flash marks.

To be sure such an oath taken—as he proposed—would be making free with oaths to swear by the feathers—& the Colour of the feathers—especially of geese that had often been plucked in the summer.

I ordered him to bring them home or I would prosecute the theft.

Morgan brought them; and the moment they came the young brood went strait to the hole of the hen house and went in, and the old ones all associated and fed about with the gang at home.

Beale said that when he went to the man the geese were in a house—and as soon as they were let out they ran at once to the gate to come away.

Landon engaged in further demonstrations of how habituated to each other were all the geese in the reunited flock; but Morgan offered counter accusations; *so I bid him be cautious what he said as well as did.*

Beale went to reclaim another four geese, but Morgan, he found, was *away from home—I suppose to lay his deep schemes to get the rest of my geese, by getting others to swear to them as his, so that I did not get my 4 geese again; but have them I will— or will try if my right to my property can't be protected on my own Possessions.*

The greatest dramas of this rural world evolved from occasions when others brought their complaints of trespass to Landon's door in search of legal remedy against their own neighbors.

Out of what remembered piece of folklore, out of what story written and read, out of what comic play scripted for the stage did Landon write this narrative of The Smiling Baronet?

Sir Marmaduke Beckwith came here—a Gentleman of great age but with a declining look tho' chearful in spirits.

It seems Moore Bragg had purchased a Piece of land . . . part of which Sir Marmaduke fancied to be his—and although Bragg had got it in tending and sown with Oats, the Knight without any legal proofs ordered some of his slaves first to chop a line along that part which he fancied his—then to ditch it.

Bragg in support of his possession ordered the people away without any kind of violence—and filled up the ditch which they had dug.

I suppose they—the slaves—inflamed their master with many idle stories—for they came again & insulted Bragg very frequently up to his house. Upon which he got a re-straining warrant from me rather than carve his own preservation of the peace.

And the Knight came here to justifye his slaves. He brought papers to prove his right to the land.

I could not help telling him that as a Magistrate it was neither my business nor power to determine the disputed bound—but as a Magistrate—a justice of the peace—I was to preserve the King's peace—& as it was evidently infringed—I was sorry to see those ignorant creatures—his slaves—pushed on to such behaviour by a Gentleman who must know that the law—in preservation of the peace of the Community—had directed other methods for his recovering of his right.

But he would not distinguish between a man coming to dispossess him of his own possession and his going to dispossess the man by violence. In the first case he would have had a right to resist force by force, but in the second case the law would allow no force but would imploy or impute *every attempt not legally pursued—a violence in him to dispossess another.*

Therefore out of compassion to these Slaves I only ordered them 15 lashes apiece.

I am sorry to say that—from my first acquaintance with this old Gentleman to this moment—there is the same tendency in his disposition—he smiles even in the bitterness of his resentment—and whilst he seems most pleased—he is most earnest in calculating revenge. For he then wanted me to give an escape warrant against Jesse Thornton, one of the evidences or witnesses *in behalf of Bragg, who two years ago had broke jail. . . .*

I begged of him not to be so warm.

He laughed and smiled but was still resolute.

I told him that *upon the oath of the Officer*—then in charge of the jail—*I was ready to grant that warrant but that the Sherif said he was sure the Jailer had taken out one—and if he had not he himself would apply in a few days for one.*

*The Knight—in order to discover—*truly reveal—*himself then wanted a warrant against Bragg for stealing his two spades—which these* slave *ditchers had left there—& informed him* that *Bragg had taken.*

With great friendship I advised him against such a measure, but he was resolved to pursue it & told me he would get some other Magistrate and make this Thornton and Will Bragg . . . foreswear themselves if they would not own they saw Moore Bragg take the spades.

I told him, if they should so swear, *Moore was the Criminal—and, if not—Moore would be relieved in great damages by a civil prosecution for false imprisonment & a vexatious* lawsuit.

The English Common Law was strong in protection of a landowner, and yet Virginia law left enslaved persons unprotected. As we see here, a single justice of the peace, acting out of court, could summarily order a whipping. Furthermore, while Sir Marmaduke might quote his slaves' words in conversation, neither magistrate nor court could legally receive such reports as testimony from blacks against a white man. Moore Bragg, perhaps with his brother Will and Jesse Thornton to help, had readily driven off Sir Marmaduke's gang of slaves, in part because those slaves knew the penalties they would incur for resisting white men. When Bragg and his friends turned and laid a complaint against the slaves, they could immediately have them whipped. And yet the vengeful baronet would smile through it all.

The baronet's use of slaves to attack a neighbor was not an isolated incident, since half a year after Sir Mamaduke's visit, Landon had another visit from an aggrieved neighbor. This man was not a baronet but a dirt farmer. Just as with

Moore Bragg, no honorific "Mr." was written before his name. The difference made by class to the whole story is instructive.

Tuesday, November 28, 1770. . . .

This morning—wet as it was—came old William Northern thundering at my door whilst I was at breakfast.

As soon as I heard it was him I got up and went and saw him at my garden-fence *pails. I asked him to come in.*

He sent me—by my messenger—*an account of 54/4½ (£2/14/4½) against me, and an order of John Doleman's—my former overseer—for £3/2/2.*

I continued asking him in out of the rain.

He vowed or swore he would never come into my house again.

I asked him what was the matter;

He told me I wanted to whip him.

I asked him what *he meant by that.*

Sure he did then pretend to *arraign my opinion given in Court against his negro for killing Shackleford's hog. He said I then said it was a pity the court could not order him a whipping.*

I told him I said it was a pity the law would not countenance the whipping Masters for giving such orders to slaves to kill their neighbour's trespassing creatures before they had complyed with the law relative to trespasses.

I offered him a doubleoon to pay his account & desired he would come in & see it weighed for valuation by the amount of silver in it.

He said he could not change it and would not come in.

I offered to let him take it home & the balance should go in discharge of Doleman's note, which I would pay in a few days.

But he would not take it nor see it weighed.

I told him he had insulted me for my opinion I gave in Court and I would bring his Spirit down.

I had Billy Beale to see me offer the doubleoon—which he again refused.

At this point the last lines of the manuscript are broken and faded, but they clearly reveal Landon's indignation at how *insolent* the enraged Northern had been. Such refusal of proper deference to social rank and legal authority was yet another sign of these troubled times.

Service to God was the highest duty. In the well-ordered kingdom for which Landon yearned, there could be no higher duties than those of the parson, whose formal designation in the official Book of Common Prayer was priest. He was the appointed leader in worship; he was the interpreter of the word of God in his sermons; and he was pastor to his parish flock. Assuredly, the parson was as archetypal of the old-regime social order that Landon was affirming as the squire himself.

When the Reverend Mr. Giberne first came from England to the parish in 1762, he was given lodging at Sabine Hall. He proved himself very amiable. (Much later, Richard Henry Lee, in a letter from Philadelphia, would ask to be remembered to Dr. Jones and Mr. Giberne, declaring that, "he would not change an hour of the sensible conversation of the former and the facetiousness of the latter for an age of Congress wisdom.") The parson and Landon certainly became firm friends. But the friendship was always perilous. Landon's sincere pietism included a strong, almost uncontrollable, strain of anticlericalism. Exalting the holy character of the priesthood, he readily found its incumbents unable to live up to expectations.

There had much earlier been a controversy involving Landon and the then-rector of Lunenburg parish in Richmond County. The episode had highlighted issues arising from the clergyman's insistence on autonomy and the squire's claims to domination.

Back in 1747 the Reverend Mr. Kay had written the bishop of London, as follows: "I found to my sorrow that I had one wealthy, Great, powerful Colonel named Landon Carter, a leading Man in my Vestry, whom I could not reasonably please or oblige. . . . I soon perceived that he wanted to extort more mean, low, and humble obedience, than I thought . . . consistent with the office of a Clergyman, all his houts [hoots?] and insults I little noticed, until he publicly declared that I preached against him (which I did not), cursed and attempted to beat me, saying my Sermon was aimed at him, because I preached against pride. I replied that I was glad he had applied it, for it was against every one that was proud. After this he was my implacable Enemy and swore Revenge, that if he ever got a majority in Vestry against me, he would turn me out of the parish. . . ." Kay went on to narrate how Landon did get that majority, and then not only declared Kay ousted, but had arranged for both the churches in the parish to be nailed up to prevent him officiating in them. The aggrieved parson sued in the colonial courts and won; but Landon appealed the case to the King's Privy Council in London, where the rights of the clergyman were once more upheld.

It is very instructive to have a denunciation of Landon direct from the pen of a parson adversary who certainly could tell a parson-squire story every bit as vividly as the diarist. Alas, there was more to trouble Mr. Kay's ministry in

Lunenburg parish than Landon's imperious pride. The parson had been twice summoned before the county court and bound over to keep the peace; brought against him were allegations of domestic violence, of putting his wife in fear of her life. Nor may we assume these were charges trumped up to get rid of him; his tenure in the next parish, to which he escaped from this one, was sadly troubled by his continual drunkenness.

But let us return to the squire-and-the-parson stories in the diary. By 1770 the Reverend Mr. Giberne had married well and moved out from dependent status as a free-bed-and-board lodger at Sabine Hall. He and *his Lady*, as Landon called her, now had their own plantation; it was proudly named Belle Ville. Nevertheless, Landon continued to try to call the tune.

The first spat was recorded on Tuesday, March 27, 1770, when Landon wanted Mr. Giberne's agreement to christen a grandchild at Sabine Hall rather than at the parish church. Virginia custom was on Landon's side; but the Church's law, was for the parson, who insisted he must refuse to make exceptions. Naturally, Landon's protests turned into complaints about the exceptions Giberne had already made and accusations that he freely disregarded the law when it was in his financial interest to do so.

Nearly a year later there was still some good-humored tolerance—even in the face of the parson's scandalous disregard of his sacred duty:

Monday, January 21, 1771.

Yesterday as variable in its changes as possible. I went to Church but the parson—instead of 12 o'clock going in as he advertized—was better than half done by 30 minutes after 11.

Something similar happened barely two years later and on a more solemn occasion. Landon's patience was then more sorely tried:

This day being Sacrament day appointed by our minister, and as Church Warden, I had all the elements of bread and wine & plate ready. We had notice to begin at eleven.

The Parson came there about ten—read prayers—and was gone before anybody but a few was there—and said it was eleven minutes after eleven o'clock by his watch.

I got there twenty-five minutes after ten with my family and got back twenty-five before eleven.

Col Lee came to church after me and was at my house before eleven.

I am contented the Gentleman entertains/instructs me when he pleases to go into his pulpit, and I said nothing. God knows I went to commemorate the love and passion of my divine redeemer—and if his Servant was otherwise disposed, I hope it is to be imputed to some other cause than my neglect.

Then Landon registered his reflection that it was not only Mr. Giberne but the whole world that seemed to be falling into disorder. *I have had too much reason in my life to observe, that few think there is any kind of duty or trust in the offices they undertake of every kind. Thus does Social Virtue gradually die away—& always some imperious obstinacy succeeds.*

The initial good humored tolerance did not last. Mr. Giberne went out of his way to provoke; for a notable wit it must have been as easy as it was tempting to tease the old squire. Landon's vaunted scientific methods in agriculture provided ample opportunities. So, there came a prolonged wrangle about provocative boasts that the parson made about his own achievements: *I every day hear of great things done in the whipping out—threshing—of wheat. Mr. G told me 4 of his people in two days whipped out 37 bushels—which I calculated . . . was above 4 bushels each hand.*

What is more, the parson's wife was in this tease also. *And yesterday his Lady said they whipped out 48 bushels in two days—which was equal to 6 bushels a hand a day. Must these people really know what they say? I have not a hand that—by any invention of whipping or beating out on a cradle can do near 1 bushel a day—with the overseer constantly with them.*

Landon checked around—so the joke was probably going round also. *Brockenbrough says he never got above a bushel a day of wheat whipped out by any hand he had; and he declared those who boast otherwise must measure chaff and all.*

So, Landon renewed his own time-and-motion studies: *I have spent a day at it with my overseer—and it was as much as 8 hands could do to produce 8 bushels.* It went hard for his workers, of course: *Yesterday my people—8 of them—got to 10 bushels of wheat whipped out in the day, so that we mend a little.*

Landon sought the first opportunity to inspect Giberne's stack of wheat straw to see whether it matched the claims. Still taken in by the line that was being spun him, he remarked that for so small a quantity of chaff the crop must have been an exceptionally rich one: *I declare that twice the quantity of straw does not produce me as much wheat, and mine was very good.*

By the time that Landon was peering at Giberne's straw heap, he was already into a much more emotional contention with the parson. It had begun devoutly with anniversary pieties:

Sunday, August 18, 1771. . . .

It is my birthday, in which I am now 61 years old, and as to health very well the lord be praised; & indeed attended with very little more than what commonly is the lot of Old age. . . . Therefore Am I & will I with God's permission go this day into his appointed temple, and there with all humility acknowledge my unfeigned thanks & obligations for all his Mercies to me—which are many & daily. How wonderfully has he blessed me both with skill & inclination to assist my poor fellow creatures with success in their sickness! O may he continue that blessing unto me, and may I be always doing his will in Everything. And above all may I be so attended with a proper Portion of his divine grace as to resist every inordinate passion—that neither my tongue nor my lips offend against his majesty.

That last resolution was soon to be sorely tried. Landon went to attend divine service, and a dispute with the parson began outside the church door. It was recorded on the next day, Monday.

Yesterday I went to Church with a devout heart as I always do.

Many years ago upon asking the Rector in a very drye spell why he had not prayed for rain, he alledged that no one had mentioned it to him or he would have offered those prayers.

And yesterday I asked him to give me an opportunity of Joining in prayer for rain.

He seemed to think we could not want it, because he had a fine rain at his house.

*I answered so had I for about 10 minits—but after 17 days hot drowth so little presently all soaked in; and it did not even oblige the Coachmen on their boxes to leave my door—*during my birthday entertainment.

I was answered—he would pray for rain at my house if I went home.

I replyed if I had thought that—I would go home and not go into church.

I was answered I might for he would not pray for rain.

Everybody said nothing—& yet after he went away—everybody said that rain was much wanted.

*When I went in I bowed as usual to the desk—*where sat the parson—*but he never returned it.*

*I hate to go into the house of my God with a dissatisfied mind and therefore I did it—*made the bow—*otherwise I would not have taken notice of so capricious a man.*

There were two codas to this diary story; the first was a forward-looking one: *I go to see him this day out of complasance to my son Landon, but now if I see anything rude I will return immediately—for I will not indulge such an imperious pride.* And then came a retrospective one: *The gentleman however did pray for rain but introduced it as a particular desire of mine.*

Landon's judgment that the entire parish was in need of rain had been publicly disallowed; the affront was keenly felt. On Tuesday Landon wrote:

I went yesterday to Giberne's with my son—& found him & his Lady had gone out. I ordered my horses to be kept in the Chariot to see what this would turn out, And my son and I walkt to see his tobacco and corn, we found the former but mean & the latter but indifferent—and his whole plantation so drye that it was impossible for a man to say rain was not wanted even there.

In about an hour the good folks came home.

Giberne was very complaisant—& in a little while said he thought I wanted to be angry with him.

I told him he knew the art of crying whore first.

He then talkt of general prayers—as opposed to the particular request he had pointedly performed.

I told him that was confining the use of the word—when it only meant prayers to be in general use as occasion should make necessary. But though I thought I had a right to ask the prayers of the Congregation as to any distress I was sensible of—according to religion and notions of public prayer—yet I should never again ask him to pray.

He was very desirous to have no disputes with me in particular.

I told him that I should be careful to avoid them with him, but was determined to be cautious how I said anything to a person so capable of passion. And that I could not but think it a great ridicule of me that I should not know when our earth wanted rain to produce the fruits of the earth.

He mentioned the last rain—on the Saturday—had filled his Causeway pond.

I told him I had seen it only as full as the year before.

For all the anger aroused over prayers for rain, the diarist and Mr. Giberne remained friends and took journeys together. On a Monday in September 1772, the two of them set off to inspect Landon's down-river quarters in Northumberland and Lancaster counties. They made a social call at Landon's birthplace, Corotoman, and they crossed over the mouth of the Rappahannock to the Wormeleys' place at Rosegill. On return home, Landon noted simply that he had *Brought Giberne home, very sick with overeating and drinking.* Thus, in an unemotional way with no discernible censure, Landon foreshadowed his later portrait of the Reverend Mr. Giberne as a hard-living, hard-drinking country parson. But that switch was not made until Landon began to tell ever-more-dark stories of duty neglected and betrayed in a world sliding into disorder.

A parson is very vulnerable to censure because of his high calling in the service of God; but what of those manifestly in the service of Mammon? The lawyer and the merchant are vulnerable to caricature of a different kind.

Once only the caricature of lawyers could be whimsically humorous, even affectionate. Landon followed a rare two-word weather report—*more rain*—with
this snatch of saying, joke, or satire: *More rain—may it please your honor—as the
Lawyer said, by the Latin he met in the adjudged cases he was reading to the bench.*
Landon thought lawyers were mostly ignorant. This was a jibe at the country attorney's need to evade the Latin he supposedly could not read.

More often there was bitterness in Landon's lawyer stories. We have already
witnessed his high scorn for those who sought to profit from the law's delays,
especially when they obstructed his own efforts to do his duty by expediting justice. *Our court held three days but really our lawyers are merely averse to have their
business done.* Indeed, lawyers seemed to be experts above all in delay.

Disregard of duty reached new heights soon after, on a day when Landon
met with a most singular insult from Mr. Parker. Landon's hasty temper undid him
one more time. It was compounded by his sense of righteousness at calling
everyone to order. There had been fierce arguments and harsh allegations.
Apologies were demanded as might have been expected in this world where
honor was so important; Landon tried to mediate:

*Upon Which Parker told me I had no business to sit in the cause and that he did not
look upon himself obliged to pay* me *the respect due to a Judge.*

I answered I sat and would set to keep such impudent lawyers as himself in order.

*He boldly replyed that I was an impudent Judge, and he would not be browbeaten by
any man.*

I told him that I would show him that I would not either—*and that by and by.*

*I intended to make use of my own Authority and order him to the stocks—but seeing
the Court took no notice of this behaviour, the hero, upon being more respected than myself, rose—he was sorry for what had happened, because the wounds of a friend sank deep.*

*I made answer very Calmly—I was full as sorry—because the wounds of ingratitude
sank deeper.*

*I immediately removed home and resolved never more to go on to the bench till I had
satisfaction Publickly.*

Of course, apologies were offered and eventually accepted. Landon returned to the post of duty by which he set so much store; he would serve again
until the next time his quick-tempered zeal for order provoked more defiance.
Through it all, the squire's customary low opinion of lawyers was continually
confirmed.

Merchants were perhaps worse than lawyers; the system made for deep suspicion. Landon and his peers sold their tobacco in the top-end market in London. They consigned it via ship captains in the employ of (mainly London)

merchants, who then arranged for brokers to see the tobacco sold to advantage. The merchants received the proceeds; they then filled orders for all kinds of goods which they purchased for the planters and shipped back to Virginia, receiving commissions at every stage. These merchants were also the bankers, since bills of exchange drawn by the gentlemen planters on their merchants were something like modern-day checks; often the payouts exceeded the income and the planters were in debt—overdrawn at the bank. The planters needed to be able to rely on the merchant to conduct all these dealings to the growers' advantage; the danger was that the merchant would be in collusion with the buyers of tobacco and the sellers of export goods.

Landon's merchant stories varied from wry good humor to angry sarcasm. Once, when Landon learned that one of his London merchants had refused to honor a bill of exchange, but then had paid two subsequent ones, the diarist resolved to *tell him it was kind to do so, but at the same time he was something like the old Pirate—now about 50 years ago—who always whipped every unfortunate Prisoner—& afterwards gave them a ball on board.*

In March 1772 Landon entered this complaining story and commentary. *At last Mr. Molleson's ship Trimley is arrived. I think she should have been called the Trimmer—for after such pompous letters* from her owner *it is but a poor account to get but £9.15 a hogshead when but only now the Tobacco is found fault with. And what is the fault? The brokers say it is not in condition—otherwise very good. A happy word this . . . capable of any explanation that the maker out of the sales shall please to give it.*

There is one unhappy thing that strikes me—Molleson says he can send me abundance of depositions from the brokers as to this want of condition—in my tobacco. This Gentleman has been at depositions before. . . . And in this particular case I wish he may not be too fond of them—for by profession a broker is a villain in the very engagements he enters into. He must buy & must sell as cheap and as dear as he can—which is the very trade of a Jockey—and when a man becomes broker for both Merchant—the planter's agent—and Smoker—the consumer—it is the most villanous part of his roguish employment because he must be perpetually counteracting the interest of either one or the other—and therefore must add to his villany by doing it as secretly as he can. And . . . he substitutes these unfathomable words to justifye his breach of engagement to the merchant when he sells the poor planter's Tobacco for nothing to keep in with the Smoker. . . .

Is the Merchant then so stupid as not to see this?

Yes he sees it—but as he pays nothing for it he suffers it to go on & perhaps for the benefit of borrowing money—for the planter—of these brokers—that he may oblige the poor planter to make good the proverb that whenever he goes a-borrowing he goes a-sorrowing.

I wish this may not be Molleson, *my friend's case.*

Landon recorded a resolve to remonstrate with the merchant, but he continued to rely on him and is unlikely to have gotten better terms.

Landon's next reflection on the systematic cheating of merchants was finely developed and supported by the authority of that paragon of the old regime in Virginia, Landon's own father. It makes the preceding little narrative seem like only a rehearsal.

Friday, May 20, 1774. . . .

This day Capt. Dawson of the <u>Marlbro'</u> *delivered me my letters from John Backhouse— whom I used to call my friend; but I see that which I used to call friendship only subsisted when I lived low & kept myself within my Consignment; and ever since I overspent I have not in any sort received the least friendship from him—so that I must return again to a low & less expensive Prudence.*

My father always gave this lesson—not to trust any merchants—but I thought I had found two men who were otherwise—One was Molleson and the other this Gent, and both have deceived me. The former I have parted with & this—Backhouse—I must keep to through interest. He gives me rather more than others do; but that is vastly short of what I used to receive when I kept within bounds. And I think his prices of goods have been really rising ever since. One Man I knew, J Sydenham, . . . always gave me more than anybody & really broke an honest man to me. All the rest are much in trade—& I fear that is a Profession that kicks Conscience out of doors like a fawning Puppy. Perhaps they may have Charity to relieve a perishing object in their View, but as to friendship—they know it not in the least instance where their gains are concerned.

Six days later—with more whimsy—Landon wrote a kind of sequel to these musings. He had been reading reports of Captain James Cook's voyage to Australia; he decided that an honest merchant in the tobacco trade would be as rare in Virginia as the antipodean black swan.

To be sure, there may be a <u>Rara Avis</u> *in every land; and I wish I could once see a black Swan in a Virginia Merchant's Counting house. My old father used to say no man could be pronounced honest by another until he had bought & sold with him; for that is the Criterion of honesty in trade. A mere Solon—to be sure in all his responses, especially as they were always made with serious unaffected gravity.*

Landon the diarist of neighborhood was judge and jury—even sermonizing parson—to everyone around him. His impatience with dereliction of duty was intense. It is well that he can occasionally be discovered imposing judgments and penances on himself also.

Sorry indeed and very sorry I am ever to let anything whatever alarm me into indecencies. But the man who is of an hasty temper must be ever thinking of it if he intends to conquer it or it will for ever keep him under.

Words dropped in a Passion give greater wounds than can be expressed, not so much to the person spoken to as to the Speaker. I every day see the truth of this.

I laid down to sleep, but I could not. I felt myself quite disordered but knew not how.

In 1776, when war with the king's government had brought political divisions to a peak of intensity, Landon was going to a gathering where he knew there would be Tory-inclined neighbors:

I hope a little innocent Mirth will produce no harm—and I will entertain a most lively expectation that I shall be assisted according to my hearty and devout prayers this—that I may keep my tongue even from good words, rather than offend even the most perverse, most licentious and most inveterate guest, let he be whom he will—even my son. . . .

We shall now see how the tone of Landon's stories changed with changing times.

Over the Edge

When once peaceful protest against the king's ministers had turned into armed rebellion against the government, Landon's narratives of neighborhood that had formerly been tempered with satiric irony, sometimes even whimsy, changed to impotent expressions of outrage.

Richmond County court was the center of order and the chief post of duty for its presiding judge, Landon. Now it became the most alarming place of disorder, not least when it was the assembly place for the county's rebel army.

The military conflict was some four months old. Initially rebels formed "independent companies" under officers they elected. That had seemed too anarchic to the colonial ruling elite, and so they had imposed instead a system of minutemen—in effect, an adapted version of the old militia with discipline and parade-ground drill imposed from the top down. But even that was not top-down enough for Landon; he resigned his command.

Monday, September 4, 1775

I do suppose many will be angry at my giving up my Lieutenancy for this County because I will not be tried by a Court Martial of my under officers Who turn against me

*my reprehension of their accustomed idleness—which they never have taken kindly . . .
& I am persuaded will fall on some mode of resentment.*

Landon's unease continued to grow. He knew that the pressure for independence and a republic was mounting. The next narrative about contested
authority in the county began almost whimsically with a snatch of conversation.
*Yesterday on stepping occasionally behind our Court house I overheard a man amongst
two with their backs towards me desiring the other never to let Malice take possession of
his heart.* We must imagine Landon, having occasion to relieve himself, waiting
his turn as the speaker stands beside his companion, pissing into a pit. If there
was whimsy in the narration of the circumstance, there was no whimsy in Landon's application of the precept. The diarist made a sharp contrast with the
contentiousness that he thought prevailed on the bench and in Virginia at
large. The times were sweeping away due respect for rank, age, and seniority.
*I thought it great advice then; but what shall we say to see it this day so evidently disre-
garded? I now see the impossibility for meriting anything from the rising generation for
there will be some vain enough to fancy their knowledge exceeds experience, and ridiculous
enough to strike in with every opposition till at last they—through their ignorance—grow
mean enough to show their folly, and impudent enough to rejoice at the consequences.*

The proceedings in court had grown angry that day. Somebody had suggested that Landon was sitting in judgment on a case in which he had an interest. Landon considered the other judges inadequate in their defense of him.
Once more Landon declared that he would leave the bench forever, and he
was still strengthening his resolve the next day. First he responded to the slur
on his judicial rectitude: *If I wanted to wound my own character with suspicion, I
should not desire a better mode of producing that, than by going out of the way*—to
exert myself—*when a Public matter of my own agitating was to be determined.*

But for Landon there was insubordination in what followed.
Some people have a plaistered manner of carrying on their deceptions by advising others
not to be affected with the Public insults that are offered to them; but though they fancy
the optics of old age are dull—I believe they will in good time be convinced that my
glasses were clear enough to discern their artifices*

> *et manet quaq*
> *in tenera tam dira*
> *deceptio Forma*
> *English: Thus every smooth face is but the mask of a damnable deception.*

---

* "Plaistered" is a strong metaphor from Landon's medical practice: an ugly, suppurating
wound is covered smoothly over by a herb-scented plaster.

If the court seemed to go from bad to worse, the parson seemed to be scandalous and plunging deeper into excess.

Admittedly, the Reverend Mr. Giberne showed himself a strong supporter of
the patriot cause. With the renewal of the American defiance of Parliament
and king on June 1, 1774, he had summoned his parish to keep the appointed
fast and to attend church to join, as the burgesses had requested, in "Praying
that his Majesty and his Parliament may be inspired from above with Wisdom,
Justice, and Moderation." He then preached strongly in favor of *the just rights
and liberties of America*. So far so good, but the tease in Giberne had provoked
Landon once more. When he heard that Landon had stayed home from the
service to take medicine, the parson commented censoriously that the colonel
could have waited to take his dose the next day!

Scarcely two months later the parson began to be noted in Landon's diary
only for scandalously immoral ways. Soon Landon would find him altogether
unworthy of his cloth. (Surely, this is not a change in Giberne's conduct, but
rather a change in Landon's attitude.)

Sunday, August 14, 1774. . . .

*Mr Giberne came here on Thursday noon & never went away till last night. At cards all
the time but at meals & in bed.*

Two months later, Landon was more ironically severe; Giberne had promised
a visit to Landon but broke the promise for the sake of gaming at his own house.
It seems the fox—old Beale—*his cub and undercub is there. . . . A noble seminary this
for a rising genius. There is nothing like the sacrifice of a Gamester; all must enjoy a
table. . . .*

Who should not detest such connections?

To immorality had been added betrayal of friendship: the parson was in
league with old *fox* Beale, just when Landon's bitterness at the abduction of
daughter Judith was at its strongest. And the betrayal continued, especially as
Landon's heir, Robert Wormeley Carter, became more and more involved, with
his own son in tow.

The portrait of the card-loving parson continued to accumulate by episodes
great and small. There is no longer any indulgence of the foibles; there is only
an insistent monitoring of by-now-familiar signs that revolution is destroying
good order in the world.

The denunciation of Giberne was set to continue; the last episode was only
last because the diarist's strength was failing as his death approached. This reveals notable aspects of Landon's life—including the open-to-readers character of his diary

THE X·MAS· A CADEMICS.
A COMBINATION GAME AT WHIST.

A 1772 caricature of clergymen who loved card play and hard drinking. *Colonial Williamsburg Foundation.*

Tuesday, August 12 & Wednesday, 13, 1777. . . .

I sent notes of invitation to my birthday to all the neighbouring Gentlemen about. One of which—to the parson—produced a bill of fare in his inner Chamber.

He either encourages villains by believing them—or dresses off their untruths.

A certain Captain G T it seems . . . did swear to having read in my January diary that the rector was a disgrace to his Profession. . . .

I lookt for the book.

At last I found it; and this gentleman is in it but in one place—relative to some news from Hobbes Hole.

On this I plunged Christianity into him as it is his calling, with a question how he could credit him—the captain.

In answer, he . . . accuses me with haughtiness & rudeness.

*I was going to return that all things look Yellow to the jaundiced eye—and where the very medium looked thro' is pride itself, every object will be sullied with haughtiness and rudeness among such Visionary rays.**

---

* There seems to be a trace here of an ancient idea that the seeing eye emits rays as well as receiving them.

But I rather hope to practice Tolerance upon him, and leave him to bury his dead sentiments and cure his wounded Principles.

As to the birthday party . . .

Indeed, everybody came that I could expect,—for as to that monster—the parson—I neither expected him, Neither did he come—repleat with his usual lying excuses, too nefarious to be repeated. A mere Coiner of oaths which he takes Pleasure in emitting . . . to the injury of others. If this is clever in anybody, all hell must shortly be clever on earth.

Church and state in old-regime Virginia were the parson and the squire. So, in Landon's Lunenburg parish, this alignment was truly strained if not disrupted as the revolution arrived.

By the year 1778 the pall of gloom was deep; it was scarcely to be dispelled with efforts at piety and sociability. Perhaps war and the ravages of Governor Dunmore and of Generals Gage and Howe put Landon again in mind of the civil wars that had devastated the Roman world. The diarist again invoked Dryden's already-quoted narrative of the Emperor Mark Anthony's last birthday.

It is my birthday into my 69th year of life.

Were I a Mark Anthony I might say I would keep it with double pomp of Sadness. But I thank God I have lived so long as to experience that the hopes I have placed in the father of Goodness through the Merits of my dear saviour his only Son—are not in vain. Therefore I will be as Cheerful with my friends as Society, decency, Justice, and a reverence to God—through his interposition as to the pains of My Colic and old age—will let me.

Though last night—between the hours of 10 and 12—I could not promise myself life—much less ease with it.

And do thou my God preserve me in this resolution.

This was indeed his last birthday celebration: Landon died on December 22 of the same year.

The country doctor is another iconic figure of the rural old regime; but as it happened the doctors, unlike the parson, the justices, and the militia officers, did not feature as betrayers of the traditional social order. There was, however, one spectacular exception.

By 1775 it had been more than ten years since Dr. Nicholas Flood had ceased to be called to Sabine Hall for medical consultations. The rupture had happened before Landon's diary began to monitor rebellions and failures of duty. It seems there had been a blazing row in 1763 over money; probably there had been a dispute over fees said to be owing. Landon cut off communications with this prominent neighbor and, sometimes calling him *Old Nick*, began to equate him with the devil. There had been a standoff and they avoided each other; but, in time of revolutionary stirring, old rages and jealousies surfaced once more.

Monday, September 4, 1775, was court day. Landon had gone already with a familiar misgiving that the court *could only happen if indolence does not Prevent it*; and indeed there were early signs of insidious disorder. The gentlemen sat in the tavern during a recess of the court. We get a view of that scene—at once vivid and tantalizingly incomplete. Landon presided in the tavern as in the courthouse; he was seated at the head of the table and described the positioning of others in above-below terms. The entry reveals that the county's revolutionary committee was in the habit of holding at least some of its meetings in courtroom style, using the judges' bench for their seating. Landon wrote about all this the next day.

Yesterday there was a great discovery.

Boyd said he heard that on the Committee day I got drunk before twelve o'clock.

Colonel Peachey & Major Griffin said *that was not true because we did not leave the bench till dinner & that was near two.*

Another gentleman—Dr. Flood's son—said that might be a mistake.

I followed his eyes & travelled with them to my side of the table where the devil, Dr. Flood the father . . . sat below Captain Parker.

I asked Boyd his author.

He said he heard it coming up & he would tell me—but it might be a disturbance.

From hence the agent & his principal discovered themselves.

Landon believed that he had smoked out Dr. Flood once more. *Drunk before twelve o'clock!* This was not only a piece of slander against the old diarist's good name but also a subversion both of the old order passing and of the new revolutionary order taking its place. And *the devil*, Dr. Flood, was behind it all. He was using the instability of the times to launch a challenge. The only comfort for Landon was that he could tell himself he was well supported. *It seems the people are much disturbed at my going to resign the Lieutenancy of the County**; *and*

---

* The colonel commanding the county militia was called the "county lieutenant."

some of them are sure Old Flood's behaviour to me was entirely owing to his inclination to be Lieutenant.

I give him Joy on the occasion—and they too—that is the Committee.

But spreading slander had not been the most of old Flood's iniquity that day, and confronting the slander was not the sum of Landon's reported performance of duty. He had also tried as a Christian to forgive and to be reconciled—and so to restore order in the most profound way. Another scene began to be played out at that same tavern table around which sat the leading gentlemen of the county. The narrative here works almost like a video clip to show us circumstance, setting, the formal rituals of toasting, and even forms of dress, such as the wearing of swords. From an earlier order of an ear trumpet, we know that Landon was by then somewhat deaf!

Yesterday at dinner in the Ordinary Old Flood being therein—I had been endeavouring if I could to bring about a kind of reconciliation—being fully intent on a retirement as a Person who could not expect to live long. Accordingly I drank—a toast—to this devil & Colonel Peachey beside him but he would not take notice of me.

I passed it by.

Afterwards, drinking the healths, I drank a Hercules to clear the Augean stable of Britain.

He—Flood—drank a Hercules to clear all our Courts everywhere of the rascals.

Still I would not seem to take notice of him.

At last he got up.

I asked if he would not finish the bottle.

He said nothing, paid his reckoning, and—as I thought—went off.

After much cheerfulness with 3 or 4 more bottles I got up—ordered my chariot—& staid waiting for it at the door and saw him there.

As soon as the chariot came up, I went and put my foot in the Step—and the monster came and said he wanted to speak with me.

I went on the other side of the chariot—

*&—too low for me to hear—he talked of what somebody had told him—*of what I said of him.

I could not hear and told him so.

At which he spoke aloud.

I then told him he has been misinformed—for I always thought him too worthless a fellow to think of at all.

He said he did not know what Worthless meant.

I said—a scoundrel beneath anybody's notice.

On which he called me a damned lyar.

I said it was common for the devil to rebuke me.

He said he was but a Young devil.

I replied there was not one in hell while he was on earth.

He appealed to Sydnor—standing nearby—if everybody did not know me to be a lyar?

Sydnor said no—he never heard so or thought so.

I bid him ask if everybody did not know him to be a damned Villain, and that I would answer that any man that was not in his debt would tell him so.

At last somebody came and called him away.

I several times asked him if it was not cursed foolish for one man—a foot in his grave—and another following him—to be such fools.

He often talked of killing me.

I bid him use his tongue & not touch his sword—for if he did I would then be through his vile guts.

Thus did a scandalous affair end.

The scene with old Dr. Flood was an exceptionally dramatic episode very vividly recounted; but it was also a straw in the wind that was becoming a gale of disorder. Landon's neighborhood stories now showed a world that seemed to the narrator to be coming unhinged. We shall see in the chapters that follow how the menace of disorder and rebellion had its very center in the diarist's own household and in his close-kin family.

Chapter 11

Contests at Home

In the first almanac diaries of the 1760s, there were only occasional and brief notices of waywardness in Landon's eldest son, Robert Wormeley Carter, who after his marriage lived with his father at Sabine Hall. The presence of Robert's wife, Winifred, was becoming an added source of conflict between father and son. One sample reveals the tone. *Mrs. Carter was not well. . . . Robin was from home at his diversions. . . . His father, the old Slave doing a kind of duty in taking care of everybody.*

Then in 1765 came the Stamp Act and American rebellious resistance. We have already seen that, in the 1766 almanac-diary volume, the deep intention of this day-by-day record changed. Landon was increasingly haunted by the primal rebellion of his eldest son, incited by *Madam*, his wife. First came the great *domestick gust* of June 24, 1766; it was soon followed by a report of *another domestic storm*. The anxious patriarch would now use the diary to hold up the mirror to these rebels, these unnatural children. The result was the accumulation of an extraordinary set of passionate narratives, in which readers will find ironies, pathos, and unintended humor. These dramas are conflicts such as every family harbors to this day; but they are also historic since they carry reverberations of the disturbed times through which the diarist felt himself fated to live.

The high dramas of the early 1770s were so copious that they can only be presented here in summary overview. Two main sources of aggravation were at work. First, Robert, now approaching the age of forty, would continually challenge and criticize his father's agricultural management. Second, the father would rail against what he saw as a wastrel son's addiction to gambling. The bad situation was made worse by Landon's belief that his son was pushed into rebellion by Winifred, his demonic wife. It seemed that Robert and Winifred had even taught their children to disrespect their grandfather. The eldest grandson, Landon III, appeared to take on all the insubordinate ways of his parents.

The virtuoso narrations of father-defiance continue the authentic style of old Landon. Sometimes he wrote with a complex Latinate expression; more often he told the stories in the vernacular idiom of field, farmhouse, and marketplace that we have already met in the Judith story and in the narratives about slaves and outrageous neighbors.

Rivalry and mutual fault-finding in agricultural plantation management was a constant source of aggravation. The old diarist felt that his son always compared him unfavorably, praising every other plantation, and despising his experimental innovative ways:

I find I am not to act without fault to be found with me. My method of nursing up my tobacco plants when I weed, is condemned because some careless fellows throw now and then a clod over them—just as if the bad execution of anything was a proper rule for condemning the practice. A careless fellow, in the old way of weeding might cut up a plant—perhaps a more dangerous accident than the covering of the plant.

Let the old man, in an evening's conversation, promise himself a fine crop of peas—300 (or at least 200) bushels at 4 shillings the bushel—and his pleasure could be spoiled in a moment:

I was very tauntingly criticised upon last night—though these pease cost me but one day's work—of making pease at a dear rate. What was the matter? A large piece of Tobacco land not wed out. The son maintained that the peas cost dear, by reason of more important work neglected.

The next day Landon wrote a kind of little autobiography, spelling out his claim to high achievement in his most constant role in life. He eloquently summed up the obligations and aspirations of an old-regime agrarian patriarch.

Thursday July 19 1770

I cannot help taking notice that the long time I have lived—the care I have taken of my family, the paying off Children's fortunes—and putting out 3 sons with an Estate very well to pass in the world—still maintaining a large family at home—and all this without being in debt but a very trifle. I say I cannot help taking notice that these circumstances well considered as they ought to be—in a country almost universally enthralled by debt—do not preserve to me with my Son the character even of a tollerable manager. Everything that I do must be excessively wrong although vastly superior in the produce to any proportion of his profit—and much greater than better lands have produced for any number of years in my Neighbourhood. If this don't denote a perverse disposition either to quarrel with me or provoke me—nothing can.

There was at least on one occasion enough mutual respect for Robert to suggest a closer working relationship; but Winifred did not share her husband's need for rapprochement with his father and sought to protect her own immediate family's interests.

Monday, September 10th, 1770. . . .

My Son Robert . . . proposed our joining under one management.

I agreed but with the profits shared *as to the proportion of Slaves that each of us* had.

And, to my astonishment, his wife then said Then all the bargain should be off.

To which I replyed, With all my heart.

She asked if he was to have nothing for his trouble.

I could not help thinking he daily received a fuller reward for more trouble than he ever took for me.

In short this woman every day discovers—reveals—who is at the bottom of all the ill usage that I receive. The devil cannot be more busy. A mean spirited creature and sordid without remission, That cannot see her All already rising out of me, but unless I part with my all, she will not be satisfied. And I am certain then I should be turned agrazing, and by her means. And yet she finds a way after she has . . . raised a hubbub, to wonder at it, & show as if she was concerned at it.

I am certain she is always concerned in it.

Suddenly Landon discloses the nemesis of the traditional patriarchy: heirs awaiting their inheritances. Here also is the folklore of the heir's wife, the woman intruder in the family who wills her father-in-law to be gone into his grave.

Beside the recriminations about plantation management there always lurked that other source of aggravation: the gambling propensity of Robert Wormeley Carter. This issue could even strategically change Winifred into a figure of pathos in the diary narratives.

Sunday September 15, 1771

I cannot help taking notice of my young Squire—my son and grateful heir apparent. He knew it was beginning to be a sickly time, and that his own wife was in a bad way after her miscarriage; and yet he went off on Wednesday under pretence to go to eat Sheep's heads fish at Corotoman. But I see it was to game in Farnham that day, and to John

Wormeley's race on Thursday where I do suppose he was to game; and only *on fryday to Corotoman. All this I have heard since—notwithstanding the Gentleman wrote to me from Hipkin's store how uneasy he was at his going abroad when his wife was in such a way, and really begs of me to consult Dr Mortimer about her—and to have her taken care of. Thus am I constantly left alone in—I may say—the worst of times.*

But the antagonism between Landon and Winifred was such that a show of wifely loyalty from her might turn even his attempts to take her part into a row. When Robert had still not returned after the lapse of another three days, Landon resumed his carping:

Wednesday September 18, 1771.

I cannot conceive why my family are always so full of contradiction. They will not allow even a Sentiment of mine.

Yesterday Madam took upon her strangely, upon my imagining that my son should not come home till his pockets were emptied by gaming.

She said that would be presently, for he carried but little abroad.

I supposed maybe friends would lend, & perhaps Hipkin's had.

She knew he would not, & grew prodigious possitive.

I answered it was damned Possitive, and asked how she could know.

She knew—she said—and would say so; with many things extremely provoking, and as little respect as could possibly be shown to a parent and an old man.

I shall let folks see that such behaviour will work nothing on me.

The early 1770s saw a lull in the grumbling rebellion against the king's government. Landon seemed to be determinedly exculpating his son and heir by blaming his daughter-in-law. The next scene could be a comic one in a novel; but, knowing it to be a true story, we wince for the anguish it narrates. We surely wish Landon had been as good at promoting harmony as he was at recording quarrels.

Monday, January 13, 1772. . . .

Some people cheat the world by their tears; they first get into great passion, and then Pass off their crying as a tenderness in their disposition.

This day I saw mother and daughter smearing the butter they had helped themselves to over their plates:

I laught and took notice how exactly one imitated the other.

At which the old crying Pattern first got to bouncing at me;

I bid her not get into a Passion for she knew I never minded that.

At which she burst out into an alarming flood of tears, and cryed it away with abundance of impudent charges against my Partiality to Lucy—who by the by—I am always every day finding fault with for her thoughtless behaviour.

I cautioned her to keep to the truth and not to let her passion carry her out of the bounds of it; for she knew I was constantly reprehending Lucy for many things.

In short I too constantly see the obstinacy of this Lady in her eldest son and daughter. The first she entirely has ruined by storming at me whenever I would have corrected him a child; and the other has already got to be as sawsy a Minx as ever sat at my table. She can't eat brown bread, nor bread without toasting; She cannot drink Coffee, &c. so that at about 13 years she is a complete Lady Townley.*

Poor woman. Winifred's need to defend her young ones kept provoking scenes, and then the old patriarch would hold this against her. Here is another such intimate episode. It too is comic but painful, as the diarist records his reproof of the fussiness of an overly fastidious granddaughter:

Monday, April 6th, 1772. . . .

I think this morning at breakfast I saw as much impudence as could be shewn to a father & Grandfather.

Miss Prue kept Pearing about a plate of butter.

I could not avoid telling her that was a kind of nicety always disagreeable—because it generally gave occasion to others to suspect something.

*Upon which Madam, the constant and certain cause of all the ill usage that I ever receive from my son & all his family, brusseld up and said she hoped she—*her daughter—*would always be so nice.*

I replied I did not doubt it, because I had seen enough of her ill manners at my table, and was quite satisfied she had taught it to others.

Through Landon's diary, Winifred has a voice in history. But it is not her own voice; she is forever cast as the outspoken contrary woman in the patriarch's representation of the world. Not a line of writing has survived by which she may speak to us directly; and yet surely we know enough to reconstruct her own version of her story, including the sad, the infuriating, and the humiliating intimacies that Landon recounted in the enduring record.

Winifred had made a strong start as a fine-spirited young lady, queenly in her doting father's eyes. For that Virginia rural society in which she was raised,

---

* Lady Townley is a character in a remake by Colley Cibber of a satire by Vanbrugh (*A Journey to London*); the adaptation was published as *The Provoked Husband* (London, 1728). The play features a modern woman who would live a fast life in high society, disregarding her duty to her husband.

making a good marriage was the highest ambition a young lady might have. Winifred must have felt her whole family triumphed when her 1756 betrothal to Robert Wormeley Carter was announced. Hers was a county family; he came from a line of Virginia grandees. His lineage combined great wealth with elite status in the colony; by this match she would become kin to the Berkeleys, the Byrds, the Wormeleys, and other high-pedigreed families. Furthermore, her young man was amiable and high-spirited, popular among his peers. (We do not know just when he earned the soubriquet *wild Bob*, but it seems to have expressed affectionate admiration rather than any censure.)

Perhaps she was disconcerted when Robert, instead of establishing an independent household for the family he was starting, took the surprising step of arranging with his father to bring his bride home to live in the Sabine Hall great house that would only be his—theirs—when the old man passed away. At first it seems, civility, if not warmth, prevailed; she is referred to correctly as "Mrs. Carter," "my daughter Carter," or "my daughter in Law." Like nearly all the named references in the early plantation diary, it is her own and others' illnesses—her *very sharp ague all the time she tended the child*—that are noted. As late as January 1764 the diarist is partly her champion as he berates his *graceless son* for begrudging the wear on the livery uniform of Moses whom she needed to *ride postilion* before her carriage. She should be shown this *respect... as a Gentlewoman* who lived in Colonel Landon's house, but already this championing is offset by the old man's equally begrudging attitude over her use of his *chariot*, and his acerbic note that he did not *owe . . . particular respect to Madame because she has never deserved any of me.*

Tension was increasing. In 1766 Winifred's readiness to undermine the master of the house was recorded against her in the first fully told narrative of conspiracy and defiance at Sabine Hall. She supported her favorite maid and obstructed the inquiries into the affair of the concealment of the runaways Simon and Bart.

Then came the *domestick gust* of June 1766, the fierce quarrel as Winifred tried to protect the little boy Landon whom she saw old Landon attacking with his riding whip. Her outraged declaration that she and her husband and children presumably were leaving reveals the point to which she had been brought by the hostility of her father-in-law and the failure of her husband to provide a house of their own for his growing family. The arrangement of a three-generation household as at Sabine Hall was distinctly unusual among Anglo families in both Britain and America at this time. The misery of Winifred's entrapment can be fully discovered in the known sequels to that blazing row. Robert

Wormeley tried to work up sufficient resolution to leave, but he confided to his own diary that if his father carried out a threat to disinherit him, he would be ruined. There was more humiliation to come. Within ten days, the young wife and mother was thrown by an obstetrical emergency into intimate, humiliating dependence on the old man's medical expertise.

We can only gain access to this bitter experience through Landon's narrative; but we can readily imagine Winifred's anguish, as her husband had to summon her tormentor to intervene to save her from a painful death. He then came to inspect and prescribe for the most intimate parts of her woman's body. She faced in the same moments Landon's heavy disapproval and the knowledge that she had lost the child she had carried.

July 7 1766. . . .

I was just riding out . . . but was called back by my son to his wife then taken in labour the 3d time without a midwife—so punctual are women or rather obstinate to their false accounts. I found everybody about her in a great fright and she almost in dispair. The child was dead and the womb was fallen down and what not. I found her pulse good and even. . . . From the accounts I concluded it might be the Vagina swelled and inflamed. I therefore ordered it to be gently pressed up with Marsh Mallow decoction and milk. At last . . . a large dead child—much squeezed and indeed putrified—was delivered. An intire placenta but no lochial discharge. Another prodigeous alarm.

At this point Landon broke off the medical narrative to enter the resentment he felt at the couple's ingratitude. He must have been compounding Winifred's affliction when he railed at her for once again not having arranged for a midwife to be on stand-by at Sabine Hall.

One episode in the further expanded diary of the 1770s reveals clearly the hapless situation of Winifred, denied the role and authority of a wife who should be mistress of her house. Years before, during an early pregnancy, she had been asked to give the storeroom keys to the housekeeper, Mrs. Woods. Landon asserted that he had arranged for them to be returned; but it is evident that his daughter-in-law had not felt sufficiently supported in the role of household manager to accept them. Although a measure of female solidarity existed, the testimony of her sister-in-law Lucy in her support can have been only a small consolation to the disempowered wife as she listened, helpless in the face of a strident enumeration of her alleged shortcomings.

February 18, 1770. . . .

Somebody mentioned housekeeping. I said I hoped that term would not be used where nobody showed the least disposition to such a care. A person—Madam—then broke out that—until I sent Mrs. Woods to take the keys from her—every drop of Milk,

Spoonful of butter, of fat, every ounce of sugar plumbs, etc., passed regularly through her hands.

I laughed at the care we then experienced in Milk, butter, fat, sugar plumbs, soap, Candles, etc. Not one of these innumerations lasted my family half the year. New soap was obliged to be made in June. Fat gone by July. Sugar continually bought in—and old expended plumbs a large barrel of 300 weight bought of Grieg . . . all gone. No body knows how. Butter merely vanishing. I never listened to Negroes and therefore gave no ear to the pots of butter, the aprons of plumbs carried away. And when people grew too heavy to do anything but trust to thievish servants I directed Mrs. Woods to offer her service—and can be sworn when these inconveniences were removed the old Lady went by my direction of offer the keys again at the bottom of the stairs. I heard the insult she received. But Lucy remembered when Mrs. Woods went for the keys and said it was by my direction.

The pattern was by then set; we have witnessed it in the 1770s stories already told. Winifred was also increasingly vulnerable through her children and vicariously through the husband who more and more readily fled the house to be at horse races and card tables with his boon companions. He had an estimable life out there in the public world, where he gained election as a burgess for Richmond County and was commissioned, like his father, as a colonel in the militia; but that entailed expense, and his serious gaming losses exacerbated the economic dependence that imprisoned his family at Sabine Hall. As we shall see, when Robert brought his companions to "his" house to enjoy diversions, Winifred had the further humiliation of seeing him denied the role of host while his father banned gaming, exerted himself to regulate the flow of liquor, and insisted that the visitors must have come to converse with the old and only true master of the house.

Winifred, however, was developing ways to fight back. The tears that so infuriated Landon were one weapon, but she became more adept at stronger and more resourceful strategies. Landon perceived that she engineered his great defeat over his beloved Judith's forbidden marriage to Reuben Beale. She had in time regained the keys to the stores, and she simply fought back more and more vehemently, so that Landon was sometimes stormed down in the way that he had himself once prevailed. Let him now be sharply questioning her son, and he found that the mother answered, in contradiction. *And thus began that Storm which no trumpet could exceed Calling it her natural Affection for her child.* A bitterly negative comparison could only introduce another recorded defeat: *I have had 3 women to wife, but never one of them like Lady Fat, a Lady for lying & scolding. . . . Last night nobody was allowed to give evidence against her falsehood. She sees, and smells more than anybody can: Do you bring your negroe to contradict me?*

As he felt himself less and less able to prevail in face of *this prodigeous femail combination against me in this house,* Landon became more extravagant in the metaphors that registered his increasing impotence. Winifred became *her emperial Majesty,* or that menacingly powerful French virago, the king's mistress, *the sulkye, De Maintenon, who has long agoe determined the Sex of the infernals.* Indeed, in face of the fury he continually stirred up, Landon was impelled to invoke more and more explicitly the primal mythology of woman as the source of evil in the world: *Thus does the hypocritical She devil at unguarded time discover who first made Adam & all the male race rebel against God's commands.* In a sweeping statement the diarist once generalized the malign force he had come to feel in Winifred: *from the knowledge I have of some Ladies' tempers, I don't think there can be a more treacherous, interprising, Perverse, and hellish Genius than is to be met with in A Woman. Madam Eve, we see, at the very hazard of Paradise suffered the devil to tempt her; and of such a tendency has her sex been.*

So the balance of power was changing. Furthermore, Landon was painfully aware that the old fox Captain Beale, Winifred's father, could command special affection from Landon's own children. They readily went to the Beale house for parties but often shortened their stay when visiting Sabine Hall. Not in extenuation but by way of explanation, it must be said that for the last five years of his life Landon was in fairly constant pain from what he called colic. This probably did not improve his temper. But that still meant that Winifred was forced to fight all the way to his grave the aging patriarch who ruled the house that could never be hers and Robert's while he lived.

Robert Wormeley Carter, the husband, son, and wealthy patriarch to be, did have a direct voice in the historical records. Indeed, he too kept a diary of sorts at Sabine Hall—as a cash account book in which he occasionally sounded a more personal note.

In the turmoil of the day of the stillbirth crisis, he wrote: "July 7, 1766. . . . This day my Wife was delivered of a dead Child a fine full grown Boy; what occasion'd it's death I can't conceive." One week later, he wrote these words as a sad anniversary retrospect: "This day I have been married ten years. I have now living two Sons and a Daughter my Wife miscarried five times; brought a dead Child & lost a fine little Boy about 18 months old. . . ." Perhaps he could not bear to record, as Landon did, that the day before this stillbirth, he and his father had gotten into another blazing row—another domestic storm, his father called it—and he, Robert, had raged out of the house.

Six weeks after that, Robert wrote a still rather unemotional reflection on all this turmoil and the failure of the search he had meanwhile made for an arrangement that would give him a separate house on his own plantation: "I had determined somehow to live at Hiccory Thicket as soon as I can get myself and family to, as the only method to avoid the frequent quarrels between Father & me." He had talked to a family friend, the planter-lawyer Richard Parker, and "received from him some hints, that Father looks upon it in so heinous a light as to threaten to make an alteration in his will to the prejudice of me & my Children."

Robert had then turned to Landon for clarification: "Upon this I discoursed with the old Gentleman on the affair. I understood from him that he would take away the maids that tended my Children, & that he would not aid me but distress me." And so the younger man was deterred from continuing the struggle: "This prevailing reason obliged me to lay aside my design and with it bid adieu to all Satisfaction, being compelled to live with him who told me I was his daily curse; and who unjustly imputed to me his Negroes running away, &c but he is still my Father & I must bear with everything from him." The son resolved, "in order to live a quiet life; I have fully determined, therefore to avoid all Arguments with him; to converse little with any one in his Company; and never to find fault with any management on the Plantation—or to concern myself directly or indirectly with domestic matters. He concluded: "If I can keep these resolutions I am in hope things will alter from now—& that they may is the sincere wish of Robert Wormeley Carter . . ."

Since Robert almost certainly avoided reading his father's open letter diary, he probably did not know that Landon had come close to the same resolution in the immediate aftermath of that *domestic storm* on the July day before the trauma of the stillbirth. The "old Gentleman" had, in any event, soon changed his mind; on July 6, 1766, he wrote:

For my part—if my God will assist me—whether my son stays or goes—I will learn to destroy the right of a parent over his son—and give up—for I see he is too obstinate. And perhaps we are equally unhappy in temper. I am old but I should consider what becomes myself. . . . Nay Sons are determined against the least indulgence to the Grey hairs of a Parent.

And so they had remained locked in conflict in the same house, neither one able to live by their peace-keeping resolutions, as anyone who has been a witness to inveterate father-son conflict will readily believe.

"The Father's Curse, or the Ungrateful Son" (1777). The French artist Jean-Baptiste Greuze secured instant fame with his depictions of scenes of domestic life. Many were merely senti-mental; others, like this one, tapped into deep-seated fears concerning patriarchal authority in an age of advancing egalitarianism. *J. Paul Getty Museum, Los Angeles.*

Both the young parents, trapped in what continued to be the old patriarch's house, faced the vexed issue of how the children were to be raised. When Lan-don saw Winifred wronged by her own children, he did not express the least sympathy. In this narrative Landon again harked back to that day in June 1766 when he had been thwarted in his attempt to discipline the boy Landon III for being *sawsy to his mother.*

Thursday, June 25, 1772. . . .

It seems that my respectful Son's Son is going soon to the College; and I dare pronounce for what,—to make him the most outrageous scoundrel that ever appeared in human Shape.

I this day saw an instance of filial behaviour to his mother that would have shocked me, had I not most sensibly known that this woman—together with his father—has con-

tributed to ruin one of the most orderly boys of his time, by bellowing out to take him from under a very Just correction I was many years ago going to give him, for even an insult to that very woman.

This youth—going to the College—was in want of some necessaries such as hand-kerchiefs—which his parents had not.

I thought of some in my chest and offered—if they would do—to give them for his use.

It seems he had before seen them and wished I would give them to him, which I did not know of. But—now—upon seeing them making up, he dashed them down and swore he would not have them.

And on being asked what had entitled him to better, as they had them not, then immediately he asked his mother what had entitled her to better.

And upon her replying that she always was only upon a level with him . . . with warmth he asked what had entitled her to be any more than upon a level.

If from this Specimen the blade don't make good my Prophesy of his revenging all the ill usage I have received from his Parent, I will venture to be hanged.

A year later—after the college's summer recess—the grandfather saw no improvement. This time the blame fell on the boy's father:

Tuesday, June 29, 1773. . . .

My Grandson Landon after a 6 weeks' stay at home set off again to the College. I believe he has only improved his taste for trifling and lounging there. It is a Pity, a fine Genius ruined by a bad example at home; for his Father—well educated—hardly looks in a book—and his son rarely reads.

Rarely the conduct of the young Landon gave occasion for old Landon to control his urge to gloat and to sympathize with Robert Wormeley.

Sunday June 16, 1771

I was sorry to see what I did yesterday, and therefore sorry from the sincerity of my heart to say that if I wanted, or could be, gratifyed in knowing that my son would have a full measure meted to him of all the insults which he has frequently though imprudently offered me, and often confessedly for his diversion; for his son—not void of sense but void of all filial decency will—from a temper too visible in the appearance of it to be denied from whence he inherits it, in a very little time become the most outrageous of all children that ever lived. In short his indulgence of that temper is so constant and extravagant that I doubt not but in a little time he will turn everybody out of doors if he can. It is now above ten days since he began to unrein it, and except when he wants to be obliged in anything that he cannot get, he never behaves now with common decency to any one Soul, either to me, his Father, his mother, his Aunts, his sister, his brother, nay even to the smallest babies when out of temper, and that is now almost always.

Perhaps in this narrative we should hear echoes of one of the most famous passages in Thomas Jefferson's *Notes on the State of Virginia*. The short chapter on "Manners" (then a synonym for morals) is a tirade against the effects of slavery on the slave owners. "The whole commerce between master and slave is a perpetual exercise of the most boisterous passions, the most unremitting despotism on one part, the most degrading submissions on the other. Our children see this and learn to imitate it. . . ."

Sometimes the record did include cordiality and preparations for Robert Wormeley's time of inheritance, as when it was noted that:

Thursday, July 2, 1772. . . .

R. Callis—the builder . . . *this day begins to make the alteration in my house which My son desires may be done. As I am soon in all Probability to leave the world, I have consented to it.*

The father-son antagonism did not go away, however. Landon achieved great literary vigor in recounting this family storm about a summer storm. The two men had gotten into an argument about who knew best the amount of rain that had fallen on the Sabine Hall riverside fields—Landon, who was at the house, or Robert Wormeley, who was some miles away. Notice the archaic speech recorded in the finale. Is this from life, or from stage plays?

Tuesday August 18th, 1772. . . .

It is curious to hear . . . that . . . People at least 5 miles off will be knowing better how it has rained at another man's house. . . .

Thus my son at Captain Beale's all day yesterday—because he had rode by some puddles in a baked dry road—should violent suspect me of Untruth when I told him that at the house and further on from the river the rain was in some plenty—but towards the river where all my corn and tobacco lay—it was but moderate. . . .

And this bred almost the altercation of my telling a lie; such is his constant genius for contradiction—especially to his father. Certainly the most unnatural and most graceless of all behaviour.

His wife truely who must . . . have confined herself to her chamber in her heavy state; and could only see the rain going from the river, had the decency to join with him; to explain from whence this prodigeous vein of contradiction must have at first originated;

but I have long known this; and she will probably find that I do know it, in spight of all her Princesslike art; for I do believe women having nothing in the general in view, but the breeding of contests at home. It began with poor Eve—& ever since then has been so much of the devil in woman.

And the next day, having extracted from his overseer confirmation about the lightness of the rainfall, Landon triumphed exuberantly: *so that my bellow-*

ing 'Squire with all his God Zounzds! had he not come through . . . Puddles of water?—was vastly mistaken.

Sometimes the narration would turn to mild irony, with perhaps—just perhaps—a note of self-mockery. This next comment touched on gender, as well as age-related differences concerning the exercise of authority around Sabine Hall. Robert Wormeley is rendered for the moment as a young gallant:

Tuesday, May 10th, 1774. . . .

My rascals, none of them, in my garden did any work when I went out. . . . I am old— and my youth has resolved to please the Ladies by never correcting now.

But then Landon would resume the angry tone.

Thursday, May 26, 1774. . . .

I saw last night that either my son is a monster peculiar to himself—or that man is now grown altogether reprobate as to filial duty. This creature would not let me speak in my own house, which obliged me to avoid quarrellings—to remove to my bed chamber.

And the brute—after I was gone—set in to a mere halloing song.

I must separate from him, for he grows worse and worse in his treatment of me.

The renewal of Landon's unkept resolution to separate himself from his son was a coda to the last of the series of these stories belonging to the limbo time—the uneasy imperial peace—between the 1766 repeal of the Stamp Act and the new crisis that commenced in mid 1774. The patriots' defiance of the king intensified into a father-son conflict on a cosmic scale; the reverberations showed in the escalation of father-son clashes at Sabine Hall.

In mid-1774 there were new rounds of defiance. The conflict between colonies and mother country had been only grumbling along since king and Parliament had backed down in face of the Stamp Act rebellion of 1765–1766. In the aftermath of the Boston Tea Party of December 1773 and the imposition of military government on Massachussetts, effective June 1, 1774, American patriots—Landon amongst them—began once again to contemplate rebellion as an immediate possibility. The stories of family conflict and domestic rebellions began also to escalate.

This May-June period of 1774 was a troubled time for Landon's own sovereignty at home. True, he had an affecting reunion with his lost-lamb youngest daughter, Judith, on May 24; but it soon become apparent that Judith had only sought reconciliation with her alienated father in order to begin pressuring him to acknowledge her husband, Reuben Beale. By the middle of the next month, Landon was again suffering acutely from his stress-related colic.

Meanwhile, Robert Wormeley had gone to Williamsburg on the morning of May 26, 1774, following the lamentable episode when his father, feeling unable to speak in his own house, went off to bed to *avoid quarrellings* and then heard himself mocked with *a mere halloing song*. Robert had thus been away the whole time when Landon first learned of the ministry's outrages toward Boston. While away, Robert had signed on with the association for the boycott of imported British goods; and so he had done as his father would have had him do. But domestic aggravations recommenced as soon as Robert Wormeley returned home. The father continually saw undutifulness, and the son continually flared up in actual defiance.

Friday, August 12, 1774. . . .

If ever man can be truely said to be cursed with a Child it must be I; and with my eldest son too, for whom I have ever been doing the most tender of kindnesses; but ingratitude with him is a virtue—especially to his Parent.

(There follow reflections on how it all goes back to Robert Wormeley's marriage to a Beale, and how the avaricious patriarch of that clan had extorted a very generous settlement: *an old fox knew my tenderness to a child.* Then the usual complaints resume:

If he is not gaming away all and more than he makes, he is at Sleep on the Chairs or up in his bedchamber; and, at all times, if any company come to the house he endeavours to get them to cards; so that I hardly have the pleasure of a word's conversation of any one of them; for they play to bed time—and that to very late hours. In short if ever this brute did one complasant thing to his father I will agree that I have not common sense. Everybody must see even at dinner—he picks out all titbits, then asks everybody to have them—and at last asks his father. Such a creature I would leave to the Punishment of his God; but I fear I shall fall into some revenge for all this abominable ill treatment, as—to be sure—it is past all bearing.)

Nor could Landon's own generation be depended on:

Sunday, August 21. . . .

I went to see Colonel Corbin at Colonel Tayloe's, resolving/checking if he was silent about the present System of Politicks. At last he said he should not sign the association unless the Majority of the Council did, upon which I gave it to him & at last took my leave of him never more to consort—until I should hear he had signed it; and so we Parted.

Landon continued to get from all sides proof of the upside-downness of his world. Even traveling in a carriage was an occasion for the young to flout their elders.

Sunday, October 2, 1774. . . .

Perhaps I shall never be able to ride in a chariot again. But if I ever should & with any-one in it, he or she shall engage to be complasant to old age, and conform to the hoisting or lowering of the window Glasses as an old man Chuses. But instead of that, the aged is only to be complasant to the young Polites, and generally travel with every wind pouring upon them, because Squire Such-an-one would otherwise be suffocated. So it is— Spring & Fall—at most houses; the windows must all be open with the doors, or some indecent Coxcomb swears he is suffocated. Thus have I catcht a most deadly cold in my old & infirm state, by riding with Mr. Robert Wormeley Carter to Francis Lightfoot Lee's house and there setting with the windows open. A dear sacrifice indeed to as much ill manners as can attend a Young fool.

The young were out of control; their challenge had been felt ever since Patrick Henry's presumptuous usurpation of resistance to the Stamp Act. And Landon's son continued ever the gambling man. He was addicted; and since such practices were disapproved under the proposed austerities of the import-boycott association, his conduct seemed more disturbing and defiant than ever. The diarist extended one diatribe with striking reflections on the moral and political issues of the day:

Sunday, October 9, 1774. . . .

In short a gamester is only a person who keeps his wife as his Mystress, and only comes to see her from his tables when he wants her; & as to children he never shews he has any, and is ever treating them as bastards by a constant neglect of them. As to a father or any other relation, the gamester is too much of a brute to think of them—let them be ever so old—so infirm—or dangerous ill.

These are such fellows which talk of freedom, but no affrican is so great a Slave, as are such to their Passion for gaming.

How certainly has this monster made out his former most damnable position? When I gave up Part of my estate—I only desired him not to game; and he answered me before Colonel Thornton that ten thousand times my estate nor no consideration on earth should ever extract a Promise of the sort—it was so much a darling's Pleasure. . . .

I will subscribe to this, that I may be an evidence against such at the great day.

Conflicts involving patriarchal authority intensified also because of the un-curbed behavior of the seventeen-year-old namesake grandson. It was then with horses as it is now with motorcycles and sports cars. Old Landon had watched with dismay (but without surprise) as the boy became infatuated with riding out instead of showing the least studiousness. *I have repeatedly Pronounced that to give a young man a horse is to make him an ass . . .* Robert Wormely Carter *must indulge his son against this advice. . . . Instead of a book it is his mare to imploy him every moment. . . . with the inclination of admiring himself on so pretty a creature. . . .*

The grandfather also could be indulgent. When the lad needed a replacement mount, he supplied the want; but he covered himself by extracting a solemn pledge.

Tuesday, December 13, 1774. . . .

Yesterday a comical affair happened. I always saw that the desire for Pleasure would meet with one want or another in Master Landon. At last his mare was with foal . . . and GrandPapa had a horse. It is nothing uncommon for ingratitude not to blush; therefore, though every late behaviour was enough to produce a negative, I was merely teazed. At last the Gent began to expresss some desire of Amendment; and—as my horse was to be a condition—I entered into such a contract, being willing to make a small sacrifice to so good a Purpose.

The instrument was written by the Smart himself & signed: only Solemnly to restrain his temper that he might not disgrace himself or family; and to assist me all he could, and not to use that horse but as a riding horse—and then only when his Parents should give leave.

On this then was a delivery on both sides; but—later—some fit of laughter raised that temper he bound himself to conquer. I told him to return the horse & burn the writing, for it would be a terrible testimony against him *and so it was done.*

*I can make many deductions from his behaviour—but shall conclude them all in Horace's sentence—*Quo Semel est inebula recens Servatat odorum testes diu*—Where once was a bad smell the whiff of it lingers. That is, had this youth been Properly flogged when young—nothing of this would have happened—but* thank his *Mama for this. This Smart will ask advice about Sailing in a boat on a river of a man of experience—but with our bark of life, he places a confidence only in fellows as ignorant as himself—thus does the blind lead the blind.*

This youth is again in great confusion—such is his unhappy temper. He rode out with me on my bay Stalion, and seemed again ashamed & vexed about his odd temper; and I am persuaded will do anything to renew his obligation.

If the lad did once more bind himself, his grandfather felt he did not keep to the conditions for the loan of the horse.

By Christmas Eve matters had come to such a crisis that the old man declared it was actually a conspiracy to hound him to death. Landon began this diary entry in pious philosophic tone:

Saturday, December 24, 1774.

As soft and mild a morning as can be expected the day before Christmas. Wrote a letter this day in which I used this expression—Indifference carried too far often becomes a cornerstone to hatred. But affection is a noble base to build upon in every human System of Politicks.

Was he reflecting on the distance of a king and ministry who now revealed hatred where he would have them show affection? We do not know. Later that same day Landon was explicitly writing once more about his own domestic *System of Politicks.* He began with a report: *Landon Carter the fox hunter out again today, and so he has been ever since Tuesday & dined abroad on Sunday—and yet his graceless father says he is seldom abroad—which to be sure is an affected Lye.*

There it rested till *Past 1 o'clock* that afternoon. Then, something perhaps having inflamed the old man's anger, he resolved on yet another banishment decree and followed it with an almost whimsical reflection from Scripture:

*I sent for my horse and desired the person who rode him never to come to Sabine Hall any more while I lived; and so I told his temporizing parent who pretends to find out that young fellow can't be restrained. So that—*my son implies*—Solomon was a damned fool when he said spare the rod & spoil the child; for if a young fellow has not sense enough to be restrained, why should a child be expected to have more? Master Solomon must also have been barbarous.*

Old Landon now literally cried "murder" to justify his anger at the way his grandson seemed encouraged to defy him. He declared that it was Robert Wormeley's purpose to encompass the death of his own father. He raged on in this entry about those who wait to step into dead men's shoes!

But this is all stuff; this father knows even this youth can be restrained—& even by him if he would, but he knows it fluxes me to see so much dissipation—and rather than not injoy his hopes of my quietus he is willing to Sacrifice his son. It is not from his tenderness as a father or a master that he does thus; no, it is because he is fond of torturing his father. I never had a greater fondness than for this father & son, and both are going the same way. God send that those who wait for my estate may wait long enough, for I would willingly save a Soul or two alive before I die.

Perhaps the yuletide spirit softened old Landon. He began his entry for the December 25 with a note that, *Christmas Day . . . is the day set apart to remember the Nativity of our Lord & Saviour Jesus Christ.* Then he went on to record that *the letter I wrote desiring my Grandson not to come to Sabine Hall whilst I lived—was read with great concern by him—& at last by Mr Ball.* Landon gave reported or imagined responses:

One said—*Lord have mercy upon him;*

And the second said—Fie upon it, Sir, come no more a-hunting as it seems to be so disagreeable *to your Grandfather.*

The Youth came home, and when I was alone, came to me.

I asked if he had not seen the letter I sent by Nassau.

He said yes.

I asked him why he came here any more;

Tears & contrition then flowed and—upon a resolution to amend—

I welcomed him once more and shook hands.

God almighty send he may be thoughtfull—then he will do well—that alone can save *him.*

His own eighteenth-century sensibility, even sentimentality, had complicated old Landon's would-be stern patriarchalism; the grandfather was no longer speaking of God's law and the doom awaiting transgressors.

I told him he was welcome to ride the horse as usual—Provided he resolved to be advised—but not otherwise. I wanted nothing but to be happy in a good Prospect of his own happiness. He had Capacity and Constitution, & it would be a pitty that both should die away through dissipation; and as to estate—that might be a good one; but then he must make it one by deserving it.

I bid him to know, that I never would give over striving to save him whilst under my roof as it was—both from nature and Social tie—a duty incumbent on me; and if he would not be advised, he must leave Sabine Hall, where I wished him with all my soul to live long and happy.

He said he would alter, & hoped I would believe him.

But this grandfather was hard to please. His observation on the depression that gripped the humbled youth was not matched by insight into his own capacity (or incapacity) to admit mistakes. By the next day after Christmas, Landon had changed his mind:

I am sorry to see so much immovable seriousness in my grandson. He acknowledges he has done amiss & is resolved to amend, but yet he cannot cheerfully set about it. Certainly this is losing full half of the pleasure of correcting our errors—for with respect to myself there is nothing that I do receed from more joyously than I do from Error; and I cannot soon let the shame of having been in one in the least allay that joy. . . . What then are we to think of the dull serious Culprit? Is he in a true way of amendment?

If only these diaries were actually studded with Landon's rejoicing at his own errors pointed out by others!

⚓

The year 1775 was an in-between year for Virginia and for the Atlantic world. The reordering of the nature of authority had begun but was not concluded. The American patriots felt forced to take up arms when their boycott-backed protests failed to check the king, ministry, and Parliament. In April 1775 came on the clash of minutemen and redcoats at Lexington and Concord, which saw protest and confrontation turn into armed rebellion and war. Soon after, Williamsburg was occupied by patriot independent companies and abandoned by Governor Dunmore. When in June the Continental Congress appointed George Washington commander-in-chief of what was becoming the Continental Army, the war in Massachusetts had become a campaign of the United Colonies of America. Yet, there was a very widespread desire to stitch up the rending fabric. Many patriots in Britain and all along the seaboard of America still yearned to secure American liberties with a guarantee that would enable them to preserve the family unity of the free Greater Britain of which they were still such proud, though troubled, members.

PART V

KING LEAR
INTO THE STORM

Oh Lear, others have acted the same foolish part that you did, and have been as handsomely rewarded as thou wast by their Offspring.

—Landon's lament to the tragic king, written in the margin of an extract from Shakespeare's play.

Chapter 12

Primal Rebellions

In Boston on December 16, 1773, a band of ardent patriots had lit the fuse that would blow up the whole powder keg. Doubting that their fellow New Englanders would have patriotic virtue enough to continue the boycott of the taxed East India Company tea, these zealots had dressed themselves as Indians, boarded the company's three newly arrived ships, and thrown the hated cargo into the harbor.

The king's ministry in Westminster were watching closely: they saw that the elected authorities in the Massachusetts Bay Colony had not done anything to prevent or punish the outrage; the ministry therefore determined on a show of force. The British Parliament was easily persuaded to pass a set of Coercive Acts that would close the port of Boston and replace the government of Massachusetts with one imposed from the parent country. Parliament's rule would be enforced at bayonet point, if need be.

American patriots were brought to a crucial moment of decision. Many of them deplored the violence done to property by the Tea Party, but they also knew that the British Parliament was now decisively overriding colonial representative governments. Even tacit acceptance would crucially weaken all their claims to a sacred right to live under the forms of British constitutional self-rule; it would utterly destroy their capacity to be united in upholding those sacred rights.

So, American patriots went once more into strong defiance of their father king; once more they told themselves it was only the evil ministry that they were resisting. With greater or lesser alacrity, all the colonies reverted to the strategy that had served them so well in the Stamp Act crisis of 1765–1766. They formed associations to refuse all imported British manufactures; they foreshadowed a suspension of their own exports to supply British markets. They sent delegates to a Continental Congress to coordinate their resistance. The consensus was still strongly for American liberty under the British constitution. Had not all the wisdom of the age—including such French luminaries as Voltaire and Montesquieu—celebrated the British constitution as the most perfectly balanced form of government for the securing of liberty that mankind had ever, or could ever, devise?

At the start of their campaign these British American patriots believed that their boycott strategy would succeed again: the Parliament would heed them; the king would dismiss the hated ministry. This time, however, king and Parliament were determined to teach stern lessons; the patriots had either to yield or to increase their defiance. Both sides pressed on, producing a conflict that escalated until the Americans took the momentous step of declaring independence and casting out the father-king.

Into Defiance

Landon felt as much as any man the wrench of the impending break with the old regime. The strains showed strongly in the diary narratives. The diarist became more and more enraged at his own son's rebellions; he became less apt to blame his daughter-in-law for her husband's defiance. As he recorded the politics of the wider community, he bitterly denounced the king, the ministry, and the local Tories on the one hand and, on the other hand, he fulminated against radical patriots like Patrick Henry and the anonymous author of *Common Sense*.

When the diarist learned the news of Parliament's decision to subdue Boston, he was brought face-to-face with the crisis he had so long both dreaded and expected.

Friday, June 3, 1774. . . .
Great alarms in the Country. The Parliament of England have declared war against the town of Boston & rather worse—for they have blocked up their harbour with 3 line of Battle Ships & 6 others, and landed 8 regiments there to subdue them to submit to their taxation. As this is but a Prelude to destroy the Liberties of America, the other Colonies cannot look on the affair but as a dangerous alarm.

The House of Burgesses had responded to news of the Boston Port Bill with a resolution for a day of fasting and prayer throughout the colony. The governor imperiously dissolved them for this, but he could not stop the mounting protest. With satisfaction, Landon recorded the stirrings in his own parish as it assembled in its church; but that was before he heard that Giberne had publicly questioned whether he, Landon, had really been too sick to attend.

This Paper calling for a fast being Published—every Member sent a copy to the Clergy of his County. Accordingly our rector . . . appointed a meeting in his lower church on the 1st of this month—the day when Parliament's war against the town of Boston began; and it is said he did very Pathetically exhort the people in his sermon to support their Liberties, concluding with the resolve for the fast—& in the room of God save the king he cried out, "God Preserve all the Just rights and Liberties of America."

The diary carried a brief report of the substantive political action taken along with that symbolic fast. *An association was entered into on the 27th by 89 burgesses against all India goods whatever, but Saltpeter & spice—And a resolution to meet again August 1st to resolve farther against the use of any kind of Commerce with Great Britain. I shall be hearty in it, and I wish others may be also.*

Zeal for this cause sent Landon out into his community to instruct and exhort. *Wednesday, June 8, 1774. . . .*

I went to Court on Monday & there I endeavoured by my Conversation to Convince the People that the case of the Bostonians was the case of all America—& if they submitted to this Arbitrary taxation begun by the Parliament, all America must submit—and then farewell to all our Liberties.

I shewed them the resolutions entered into by the Philadelphians and Marylanders.

Then, in the spring of 1775 the Virginia patriots armed and formed themselves into "independent companies." In the spirit of the times, they elected their own officers. The royal governor, Lord Dunmore, after seizing the colony's stock of gunpowder, found himself forced to withdraw aboard a Royal Navy man-of-war. From that floating base he menaced the very vulnerable coastline of Tidewater Virginia. Meanwhile, the old establishment families of Virginia still tried to effect some mediation between the colony and the mother country. For them, the power of a people armed was no better than mob rule; they lost no time in disbanding the independent companies and instituted in their place a minuteman service that was under command of appointed officers. For the moment, the authority of the traditional leaders held.

Landon shared the concerns of the establishment that he was so much a part of. He believed that even the reinstituted militia discipline (when it came) gave too much to democracy. In July of 1775, when he went to a muster of the Richmond County Independent Company, he thought he saw the rough way discipline worked. The captain could only maintain himself against a self-promoting subordinate by telling him *if he was offended he knew where he lived—& that he would be always at home for him.* Was it a challenge to a bout of traditional country-style wrestling that the captain envisaged or was it the deadly pistols-dueling that was about to come to Virginia with this war? We cannot tell. But, as we have already seen, Landon had been outraged by concessions to the new democratic temper so evidently in the air and had already resigned his command of the armed force of his county.

The revolutionary disturbances of the times manifestly heightened Landon's alarm at Robert Wormeley Carter's expressions of defiance. The surviving diary fragments for 1775 record only one blazing row with the defiant eldest son. In this time of stress, Landon needed to know himself as a benign father, such as he longed for the king to be. He had already enacted this on his great day of forgiveness—September 11, 1775—when he had pardoned first Nassaw at the whipping tree in the morning and then Reuben Beale, the monster, his forbidden son-in-law, in the evening. Now he lamented the arbitrary willfulness that he saw in his son (and that his son so evidently saw in him).

Monday, September 18, 1775. . . .

I record only the extraordinary manoeuvres to let those who may be curious in my life, or after my death who shall Peruse these little books, see how surprizingly they have treated a Parent ever fond of them—and indeed kind to them. I am old—very old and infirm—and yet so seldom do any one of my children do anything to entertain me—or even keep my company, that were not my eyes yet to serve me to read—I should be miserable. Nay as it is—as my colic seldom allows me the pleasures of a night's sleep—I am often for want of company obliged to take to my room.

Yesterday old Stadler the musick master came here and dined.

He went into the Passage and there set to reading.

I was obliged to take my book for entertainment and at 3—for it had not struck till I got into the Passage—I was going into my room—but on seeing the old gentleman moving to Colonel Tayloe's—I asked him if he would not stay to Coffee*—it would be ready at 4.

He said he did not think of that, and set to reading again.

My son Robin then walkt downstairs—went towards the Mill dam.

---

* Tea was then politically incorrect in this house, of course.

Seeing all this I turned in to take a nap—and happened to sleep till past 4 about 20 minutes.

When I came out asking if Stadler was gone, the monster began to bellow at me for lying down &c.

I was immediately raised and could not contain myself at his prodigeous mouthing usage as well as absurdity in things that he knew were facts against him. At last I told him I had a good mind to throw the Coffee away. It came in—he would drink none.

I cannot suspect what he does this for; therefore am the more concerned at it; for—if it is mere temper—it is really a very bad one and must make him unhappy in time as it conveys to me his desire of being a sole determiner in all things—which is the worst disposition to be possessed of in the world.

Landon busily recorded also the outrage he felt at British plans to wear America down. The ministry, it appeared, had long stored in its arsenal a plan to cow the southern colonies by arming slaves against masters. At first the diarist had not been willing to believe it; yet suddenly Virginia lay under such a *Proclamation.* Lord Dunmore—as we know from the narrative of the departure of the Eight—had offered freedom to the slaves of rebels who would rally to the army he was gathering at Norfolk. Landon tried to reassure himself that only *some few thoughtless africans are sheltering themselves under the royal standard offered to them. And is it not to be doubted but the Standard bearer*—Lord Dunmore—*will meet his fate e'er long by some missive commission*—a bullet or cannon ball—*to Silence all his iniquities both male and female, and consign him to regions more suitable to his baseness.* Landon loved to invoke scurrilous stories that Dunmore seduced slaves sexually as well as politically.

But the diarist's greatest anguish was over the cruel and unnatural fatherhood of the king. His history had told Landon that, before any other part of the English nation, Virginia had declared for Charles II. *And though she did not long enjoy a gratitude suitable to the Loyalty, yet she continued his faithful people.* But now—*We see with the deep concern of weeping eyes that the present National Sun is no more permitted to shine on his grateful people than Charles II was. Has not one of his servants had the affront in Parliament to tell the nation that he*—the minister—*wrote that speech so displeasing to* the King's *Subjects?* . . .

There is a kind of brotherhood between the Ministers. . . . *As to the King—Indeed, I confess any man is to be pitied who cannot command resolution enough to drive such servants out of doors, that he must see are alienating the filial love of all his children from him.*

And this king would prohibit these loving American "children" from approaching him with petitions. *"Come unto me, all ye that are heavy laden, and I will give you rest . . ." Is not Petitioning . . . with decency and humility within the being's import of those words?*

Thus, in this crisis, did Landon invoke the familial-household model of kingly rule. He produced one of the passages in the Bible that most insistently asserts the loving care belonging to fatherhood and, in a different draft of this invocation—evidently intended for publication—Landon further reinforced the image of God and king as fathers, heads of great households. *How Lamentable must the situation of any man be who cannot—when he sees his very servants endeavouring to destroy his domestick Peace, his Parental respect—command resolution enough to order them behind him. . . .* Lord Dunmore and the ministry, seemed to Landon to be royal servants who destroyed the parental care the diarist still wanted from his king.

Revolution

King and Parliament had lost control; they could neither persuade nor coerce their North American subjects. A great revolution was in progress; the first democratic republic of the modern era was forming. It would be proclaimed on the momentous Fourth of July 1776 in Philadelphia. And it was during this time—the late winter, spring, and summer of this fateful year—that Landon's diary narratives of his son's disaffection and rebellion against his own patriarchal sovereignty at Sabine Hall went into a screaming crescendo.

As the old man faced the deeply unwanted consequences of all that fierce defiance of the royal sovereign, so his domestic paranoia intensified. A graph of moments of extreme conflict shows a peak during those months unmatched by any other time. With deep unconscious irony, Landon, in effect, took upon himself the role of King George vis-à-vis his subject son's claims to autonomy. His sense of the escalation of rebellion in his family even reached the point where he felt his son must intend a patricidal revolution at Sabine Hall. Only a small selection of the rich profusion of sometimes eloquent, sometimes passionately self-obstructing narratives, commentaries, and predictions can be offered in the series that follows.

Landon noted on February 14, 1776, that *the Philadelphia Pamphlet called* <u>Common Sense</u> *is much advertized . . . and it is Pretended to be written by an Englishman.* He feared, if that was so—*it is really much to be suspected of its secret intentions* *to fix an ill impression that the Americans are resolved not to be reconciled.* The whole thing seemed to be based on *the most absurd Arguments in the world.* Landon also suspected that this might be the work of some hotheads in the Continental Congress.* In that case, he deplored their perfidy: had they not repeatedly given solemn assurances that they did not aim at independence? Concerned for good faith and right order, Landon prepared to intervene: *I have written an answer to the extracts published by Purdie*—in his *Virginia Gazette, but . . . as . . . the new edition*—of *Common Sense*—*is to contain many Additions, I would wait to see what they are. . . . I would not have . . .* the American cause's *original justice*—*constitutional freedom*—*in the least sullied.*

Soon Landon would declare the author of *Common Sense* to be a *despot* who wanted to introduce dictatorship. Already the very next day he perceived his son to be such a despot at home. *And let me*—*since I am to be the constant butt of this man*—*remove out of his company or forever hold my tongue, for he is my most vexatious tyrant, & everybody seems to take pleasure that he is so.*

In the entry for the next day after that renewed resolution, Landon excelled himself in the way of old-man family narrative. He showed that, resolve as he might, he could not hold his tongue—or stay his pen:

Friday, February 16.

Elementary storms indeed are terrible; but what are the prodigeous storms within doors? They disquiet the mind, and by their strange effects torment the soul; and yet how few are so happy as either by nature or prudence to guard against them. I acknowledge my weakness in this; but I hope my God will assist me. But what will it be with those who Justify them? A Son—*because he is 40 years of age shall exculpate himself from his Abuses to his father because* his father *has been too harsh to him in his language; but at the same time he will not reflect on his eternal reprehensions, contradictions, and manifestly false assertions to his father's face as well as prejudice though he is near 70 years of Age, which are constantly thrown out to provoke this strange language? He shall acknowledge he cannot live anywhere else*—*and yet no gratitude inclines him to think of a better treatment to his father; a father . . . ever . . . doing him singular and frequent favours.*

No, none of these things have the least influence on his temper, nay he is a Son who has acknowledged he does these things to vex his father, although he can—*sometimes when conscience, though very Seldom, Pricks, call him Dear father &c.*—*yet put him in mind of these things, he either denies them solemnly, or argues like his monstrous behav-*

---

* It seems from a close review of all the ten references to *Common Sense* that Landon never did learn that Thomas Paine, an Englishman, was the author.

iour—they are all cancelled by mentioning them—when by his unnatural conduct he obliges the mentioning of them.

In a metaphor that would recur—perhaps because it expressed the changing epoch as well as the generational clash—Landon identified the deep source of the conflict. Kings and fathers were like the sun, whose warming rays should be gratefully received, *But this* Son, *like the rising Sun, has his votaries. It was but yesterday . . . this . . . appeared. A Storm was begun by the Son's Contradiction, and indeed Perverse conduct; and a Gentleman in company levelled all at the father. And because the father said, Every sun has its beams, and the setting is not quite so Promising & warm as those of the rising sun, this was called a reflection,* an insult.

Here was a hurtful accusation that Robert was gathering a young following to act as though he was already master of the house. Similarly, Landon had earlier referred to King Charles II as a "sun" that should have warmed Virginia with his rays but did not.

Common Sense continued to haunt and challenge Landon. Ten days after his first protest, he was out to dinner when a fellow guest introduced the topic of the pamphlet.

Saturday, February 24. . . .
I replied it was as rascally and nonsensical as possible, for it was only a sophisticated attempt to throw all men out of Principles—as I shewed . . . that it was as much the random of a despot as anything could be—for it declared every man a damned Scoundrel that did not think as he did—A coward & a Sycophant; and after reducing mankind to a mere brutish nature—that of an implacable and unforgiving temper—it tells us it is the image of God at first implanted on us. Just as if he who said "father forgive them . . ." in his expiring moments intended to instance himself on the Cross as an example of unforgiveness. This man writes for independency and is under the necessity of stating an independence in man at his creation—when it is evident he must be a social being.

Landon, still holding out for reconciliation and forgiveness, was sure he had vanquished the advocates of *Common Sense*-style *independency,* but he was in a steel-jawed trap. On the one hand, he rejected the antimonarchical, regicidal impulse in the emerging republicanism of *Common Sense;* on the other hand, he faced the atrocities committed by the representatives of the monarchy he wanted reestablished on a constitutional foundation. The day after Landon had so strongly rejected Paine's arguments, he heard of negotiations with the hated Dunmore:

If this is not one of the devil's vile tricks, the Devil must be now convinced that things are tending well; for a Ministry so resolute as they have expressed themselves—for rec-

onciliation—*would now have recalled this agent of their destruction, one so calculating—without any feelings more than a bull dog to Perpetuate their oppression.*

In March, as spring advanced, a sense of menace persisted in relation to Landon's own reign at Sabine Hall. Landon reverted to the metaphor that strongly expressed his sense of the waning of his own sovereignty as the old order passed, yielding place to new:

Friday, March 8. . . .

There is not a more seeming truth in the practice of moderns than that of worshipping the rising sun & disregarding the setting. Many have visited this house but my beams are too weak in my declining state to be regarded; and, lest in conversation *the knowledge attendant on a person of observation—& through a service of a long life—should give those beams strength in their decline, cards & every bewitching diversion are daily, hourly & momentarily kept up. So that there can be no plea (but a shew) of their coming to see me; and that because I own and keep the house. There is but one excuse for this treatment— and that is because it gives the unnatural pleasure to Colonel Robert Wormeley of shewing the utmost contempt to his father, such an abandoned & ungrateful fellow is he.*

Last night Proved this; everybody found fault with a card he played, & expressed the error without any reflection from him, but as soon as I joined, he . . . told me I was a fool & knew nothing of the matter.

Of course, Landon claimed to be a wise guardian of the future that their hedonism would put at risk. He wrote the next day: *It is a melancholly thing to think of; but at a time when there is the greatest occasion for sensibility and thoughtfulness, we see nothing but folly, idleness, and dissipation.* And he went on to read the malaise of his house as the malaise of the times:

Nothing so common as to hear Parents say, "to curb their children is to spoil their genius and tempers." But is not this, because those Parents have not yet forgot their own childish dispositions? Solomon was a fool—with his "Spare the rod and spoil the child." For he certainly said that this restriction on children, prevented their being rogues, Whores, & guilty of every species of immorality.

The Polonius, so strong in Landon, came out to defend himself in an imagined dialog:

I shall hear that old fellows when they have lost a taste for pleasure, are forever railing at it. Is not every man sensibly, from the Principles of nature—aiming to be old? Suppose then they have lived beyond those pleasures. Is it not kind and Prudent in them, to caution others from losing even those pleasures which old age might enjoy, if it had them in its Power to enjoy? Which is the certain intention—as well as good effect—of every old man's advice.

The next day was a Sunday; and Landon's reflection—still disturbing after more than two centuries—shows how deeply troubled he was in these times. Was he lamenting his own long-ago addictions, his act of begetting or his ways of child rearing? Was he holding himself responsible for the outrageousness of his son just turned 40? (Again, the weather is a metaphor.)

Sunday, March 10.

The fine day has given place to one of a very bad aspect, so that it seems to be in a foul way for more rain & wind.

I have lived to see many false steps amended; but I believe the indiscretion of 40 years past will never be recovered. It begot undutifulness and Cardplaying & every kind of dissipation—and I will acknowledge myself quite mistaken if it does not end in an entire mortification; for I do somehow see how the sins of the father are—by an inverted order of Punishment—in the direct road of extinction to the family. And it cannot be many generations to compleat the Catastrophe.

What can Landon mean by this dark reference to the time of his first marriage and the conception of his eldest son? The known dates of Landon's marriage and Robert's birth preclude an allusion to out-of-wedlock conception. But the anguish of his delving into his own past to predict doom in his family's future is unmistakable.

Two days later and it was the troubled scene of the larger world politics that preoccupied Landon. Squire Lee had come to the Hall.* He had brought news, and so this diary gives vivid glimpses of the circulation of news—or rumor mostly, which has to be assessed for credibility—in this time before instantaneous media. Lee's first report was of the excitement of a near mutiny of the militias in the environs of Williamsburg. It had arisen in response to the ruling group's sidelining of Patrick Henry in the military mobilization of Virginia. Landon detested Henry and did not believe a word of what *his friends, willing to give him a false praise,* were saying. The notorious seeker after popularity, Landon knew, would not have selflessly appealed to the mutinous soldiers to leave off protesting at his own ill treatment. Landon believed rather the squire's report

---

* No doubt it was something old-fashioned in his mannerisms—Richard Lee of Lee Hall was often quaintly distinguished from his more cosmopolitan cousins as Squire Lee.

that proper authority had forcefully restored discipline: *a party well disposed Clappt these two fellows*—the pre–Henry ringleaders—*under a close confinement.*

Squire Lee brought more disturbing news from the northward. The British authorities were going to try to talk the Americans into accepting terms. In this rumor, Landon saw the plots of radical conspirators:

We owe the credit of such reports to our famous Pamphlet "Common Sense" which has drove all who espouse it from the Justice of their contest—for American constitutional liberty—*into a Confusion, not knowing what to resolve upon. Therefore—as fear is ever the Product of Confusion—we embrace anything for truth; and I wish we may not at last be so Confused as to be intimidated into any mode of Concession . . .*

Landon had aptly expressed the dilemma felt by so many American patriots as they wavered between being lured into a reconciliation on unconstitutional terms or being forced into the independent republic that many dreaded. Landon revealed again his alarm at the ambitions of the republicans: *For my part, I am satisfied these authors intended this Confusion—and if they have not done it for the ministry, they have done it for themselves.* A reckless breach of faith would hurt the cause, as the fear resulting from confusion would render *Victoriousness in America extremely doubtful at last.*

In subconscious parody, the home-front confrontations reflected the power struggle in the political realm. The son's disempowerment, the crumbling of old standards, the defiance of customary authority, the withdrawal of privileges, and the predictable reactions among Robert's friends, all find ready parallels in the public sphere. Landon was indeed Sabine Hall's George III—but justified, as he saw it:

Friday, March 15.

Yesterday I think I never met with worse treatment in my life—headed by my son. The violence of the Present day—Joined with the ill manners of those who are Gentlemen (and would be so if they behaved as such)—is not to be endured. I have been glad to treat all who came to see me as well as I possibly could; but . . . wine could not be got in the same plenty as usual. I gave as much toddy, beers, and Cyder as could be drunk—and I believe the quantity used will shew it to be a full plenty. Besides this—that the house might not be quite without wine . . .—I only allowed one bottle after dinner, & now and then . . . two & 3 bottles. I thought I pleased; but it seems—because it was not as much as revelling throats could away with, an Opportunity was taken yesterday to resent it.

I have observed that people who came to see me would show an inclination sometimes to be in Conversation with me; but these Gentlemen were kept only at cards from after breakfast till late bed-time. . . . This was continued day by day for many days. I had as a committee man for the County Association *expressed my dislike—as being against the recommendation of the Congress.*

At last yesterday my house was to be again the Groom's porter's and I modestly protested against it and removed the table and the cards.*

This brought on the following behaviour—which I will appeal to the whole world if it can be called the behaviour of Gentlemen. Mr. Carter lay sulking on the chair—and another Gent got to sleep over his Chair; and at Coffee time it was refused.

I then told them I was glad to entertain those who came to see me—and did hope I had done so with hospitality.

I was answered I must then Judge for the world.

I replied—for the benefit of the Community I was obliged to Judge and he was no Proper individual who did not.

This Sulkiness continued.

I laughed & wished them better tempers—and Perhaps a few years would convince them they had treated me ill.

I was told by the 40 year old man—my son—he was not a child to be controuled; But I answered 40 ought to hear reasons.

*Another said every*body *ought to do as they pleased.*

I answered him some men were often disposed to kill themselves.

And this very wise man replied he did not see anybody had right to Prevent him.

This noble reasoner I immediately consigned to his own folly on a Position evident against the very Principles of Nature and society—telling him no madman shall be confined nor child Prevented then from going into the fire.

He thought they differed.

I said it was always a question with me whether an attempt to kill oneself *was not always the effect of great insanity. . . .*

And so it ends, they sulky and growling and I quite indifferent—except as to the Affront.

The next day brought an intensification of the anguish. The time of troubles was bringing on an extreme of imagined murderous violence.

I never saw, heard, or read of a more abandoned devotion to Cards than in my Son Robert. . . . This have they continued—paying no regard to me or any entreaty of mine; but every now and then can't you let us do as we will? But the monster does not consider

---

* "Groom's porter's"—a proverbial phrase for a gaming den, deriving from the location of that facility in the ancient royal court.

how far he must affect the gratitude of those entertained by me. . . . Everybody then must be a selfish monster with himself. Surely it is happy our laws Prevent Parricide—or that devil that moves to this treatment, would move him to put his father out of the way. Good God—that such a monster had descended from my loins.

On March 28, 1776, Landon was still trying to stave off impending revolution; he wrote: *There is abundance talked about independency, but as it is all from Mr. Common Sense, to decypher that Gentleman would be to shew the same tyrant disposition that he pretends to be wishing to avoid.*

Unease at developments filled the diarist with apprehension concerning the next day: *It is to be a general Muster of our Militia, and I do suppose it will be performed with no small degree of Confusion, . . . because everything in the shape of a soldier must be now raw and undisciplined.* His subsequent observations vindicated him: *I went to the General Muster of our Militia—and think I saw that the County Lieutenant nor his officers will never make any figure. The most busy man—that ought to be—seemed to know nothing about it—or if he did—to do nothing at all. The front rank more crowded with Spectators than I ever saw at a boxing match or a bull bating, and not above 3 or 4 Captains which seemed to be in earnest. Indeed elections have again got into their Old Channel, and of course the Public is to be neglected according as the People may be concerned.*

It was a small comfort at the muster to hear news that, although *Independency was thrice Proposed in the Congress, it was each time thrown out by a Vast majority, and that to the Northward 9/10 of the People are violently against it.* The advocates in the Continental Congress were thus embarrassed, *who not only denied their tendency to independency when they were charged with it by writers; but have over & over again told the whole British World that they only desired to be reinstated as they were in 1763.*

We see Landon's continued yearning for *the whole British World . . . as they were in 1763,* the year of British-American triumph.

Landon's bitter denunciations of his son's rebellion continued during April, while both democratic revolution and war came manifestly into the county. On the first day of the month there was an election to choose candidates for the Virginia Convention that must surely decide the great questions of the hour.

Elections were still very communal affairs in Virginia. The voters, who had to be white male owners of land in the county, came one by one to stand at a table set up in or in front of the courthouse, there to call aloud their votes. The sheriff presided, and the candidates sat beside him at the table; they were not just observers but active participants. They would thank voters who voted for them; they no doubt scowled at voters expected to support them who switched and called out their rivals' names. Landon's son, Robert Wormeley had to witness many such switches. He had been a burgess for Richmond County since 1769 and had then been continued as elected delegate to the extralegal conventions that had taken over management of Virginia's resistance in 1774, but he was rejected now in this overturn election.

Landon wrote an angry and alarmed narrative of the day's revolutionary politics. Its heavily ironic tone has become justly famous among historians because it reveals a lot about the Virginia gentry's conservative politics, about the interpersonal dynamics of these courthouse polling days, and about Landon's elitist sexism. The diarist's mind reviewed the longer-term erosion of respect that had occurred in these times. Now the 1766 ousting of Francis Lightfoot Lee, a high-gentry member of Congress, showed the trend to be accelerating. It was all the more disturbing since the unseated members were staunch patriots. Were they then penalized for being wealthy men of distinguished ancestry?

Monday, April 1, 1776. . . .

The election day—and I may say for the honour of Richmond County that she is no changeling.

I can well remember when I was turned out of the House of Burgesses. It was said that I did not familiarize myself among the People and . . . two elections after it was proved by my son's going amongst them and Carrying his Election . . . with . . . Francis Lightfoot Lee. . . . It was said by my son I should see that they would never be turned out.

But what has this day discovered? . . . My son has merely kissed the arses of the people and very servilely accommodated himself to others—and yet he has been shamefully turned out, and Colonel Lee—notwithstanding he was at Congress . . . he has been also turned out of Convention—although to the disgrace of his seat in Congress; and that by a worthless, though impudent, fellow. . . . I do suppose such a Circumstance cannot be paralleled. But it is the nature of Popularity. She I long ago discovered to be an adultress of the first order; for at any time—let her be most sacredly wedded to one man—she will even be grogged by her gallant over his shoulder.

But the worst of this day's discovery is the way unsteady Lukewarmness of even gratitude itself appeared in All its Proper Colours. And even relations as well as tenants all Voted against the shewy Professions of their Principals. One . . . curled Pate fellow—I was certainly told—was to come & Vote for them—old faithful servants of the community. I answered: if he did I would own myself mistaken in the man. He came—and *when it could do no good—he voted for one of the sitting members and at the same time he bowered his Vote by voting for his adversary.* *

No doubt tensions had been aggravated by Landon's censure of his son's attempted democratic political style and of the false assurances of success. The very next day Robert Wormeley was denouncing his father's attempted exercise of patriarchal authority, and he used the same strong rhetoric the American patriots used for the King's ministers; he once again likened the old man to the despotic pashas of the Ottoman Empire. The diarist meanwhile—as so often—tried in his narrative to mask his assertions of authority under the guise of the pathos of old age. (We have already witnessed Landon's identification with King Lear.)

Wednesday, April 3. . . .

The treatment I met with yesterday is not to be endured from my son. . . . Cards were proposed—I begged not & told them I should be ill used.

That most abandoned fellow abused me for it, calling me Bassha for not letting everybody do as they pleased—and so he continued for some time. I avoided altercation as much as possible—and I thank my God I did escape. But at supper I asked if there was not a bottle of wine brought up.

Yes, said that fellow my son let's have it—for last night the Colonel went to bed—carried the keys with him, and we could not have any wine.

To be accused so before company when, though I went to bed (being left alone for everybody went to dancing in the next room), I gave the keys to Parker—my apprentice manager—to get what they wanted. So this was really a falsehood—and it broke through my resolution of not speaking.

This fellow my son, then to conciliate the approbation of the Company says he was only in Jest. However he swore it was truth, and Justified it—and when I called Parker—he said he had locked the Keys up in my desk.

I asked this Pander—my son—if he never came into my room when I was in bed; He answered sometimes. Then the heroe told the company I denied him wine.

I did some months ago ask how he could waste the wine by Pouring it out on his

---

* In these two-member elections, candidates usually stood as pairs—in this case R. W. Carter and F. L. Lee were joined as defending candidates. The electors each had two votes; "bowering" was effectively cancelling your vote by supporting one of each opposing pair. (The metaphor comes from the card game of euchre.)

Pancakes, and he would not drink any; And this he has told of me almost to everybody, and yet pretends it is a jest.

An old father is a fine Subject to jest upon.

Landon's assertions of authority and his son's defiance continued. Four days later he wrote: *It seems after I went to bed*—last night—*Behemoth*—*though I publickly declared against any more Card Playing*—*got a gang . . . to cards.* As to the guests: *They must have in them some species of the devil, if so much ingratitude can denote anything of his infernal highness.*

Soon all his son's companions were showing joint resentment: *One looks as if his whole face had been just boiled in* Vinegar, *Another as sulky as the devil, & another as if his whole desire lay in severe wishes & insults against every kind of benevolence & hospitality. . . . How,* the old man asked, *is anyone to conduct himself in such a group? It is impossible to say, but with* the conduct of the *honest man who carries an even face on every action.* It seemed to Landon that they all were turning his house into *the Suburbs of Hell.*

With all this sullen defiance under his very roof, the diarist voiced explicitly his deep sense that the rebellion in the great kingdom fostered the same in his home domain. He revealed his pervasive *dread whether our own internal contentions will not again grow from this republican form we all seem to be hurrying into; for everybody wants to be ahead—& aims at it Neck or nothing—as it is commonly said.* His thoughts kept running to that great concern; the old order must somehow be preserved in spite of the revolution: *But if our form of Government is changed I hope some divine Inspiration will possess our rulers to establish the common Law of England amongst us.* This was the first explicit recognition that a great rupture with the past was unavoidably coming.

Dunmore was out there with his naval squadron; he could send in a raiding party at any time. Even the heavens above came to be read as portending hostile acts.

Thursday, April 11.

I had like to have rejoiced much at the clear sky and sunshine which the last night's thunder & lightning produced by the introduction of a Northwester—but that wind presently blowed itself quite out of breath, and—by carrying so many heavy wet clouds to the South—they possibly met with a fleet of clouds from the Sea—& here they all returned and again restored our rain.

Soon it was not just a metaphoric fleet of clouds but a real enemy strike force that came up the river. The next narratives give vivid glimpses of the circumstances of coastal Americans living in a theater of pirate-raid warfare. And, as is usual with revolutionary war, the population had divided allegiances. For a moment—but only a moment—family conflict at Sabine Hall was in abeyance. Landon wrote gripping narratives of naval guerrilla war on the Rappahannock. He told of the patriot endeavors to get their forces out onto the water to chase off the Royal Navy raiders and retake a captured cargo vessel. He execrated the treachery of antipatriot merchants at the little port of Hobbes Hole across the river. He cheered on his grandson, Landon III, in his zeal to join the fight; he deplored the defeatist talk of his son and others around him, especially when they sought to keep the would-be heroic grandson safely out of armed combat:

This is the language at Poor Sabine Hall now; at last nobody without terrible fears, except old age—and his courageous Namesake—who, though rash in ten thousand things without the least motive of duty in them, is hardly ever blamed for them. But now his Country beats in his Veins, why then he is a rash fellow! For God's sake what is Patriotism, if it is only to lie in a chamber, and provide against no danger, and run no risks? George III would be Glad of such Subjects in America, and he would Certainly Pardon them all.

The weakness of those around him appeared to the old man in other ways. His son was still *going on in the usual mode, complaining of his People, and never having them corrected.* . . . Two years previously Landon had suspected lenience came from a desire *to please the Ladies*; but now he supposed it came from a spirit of rebellion: *If I speak—except Striking me—I have every insult thrown out.* Such violence matched the hated governor's threats to the patriots of Virginia. *Certainly he—my son—has engaged with Dunmore to keep me in hot water this year—according to that Devil's expression.**

And there was no relief for the Richmond County patriots—unless Heaven might send it.

Friday, April 26. . . .

Nat returned from his Express.† General Lee gone—from Williamsburg. General Lewis is very sorry it is not in his Power to assist us. Colonel Dangerfield—across the

---

* Lord Dunmore, as he went to war against the patriots, had declared that he would "keep the Virginians in hot water."

† Nat—Nassaw's son, who carried this dispatch—could also report to his master on what he heard of the proceedings of the Convention with respect to the Tory, Ralph Wormeley; and so, suddenly, we see clearly how the politics of the revolutionary crisis were indeed being closely followed by the enslaved half of the population.

river—*is the nearest to us, and he is to give all the assistance he can if necessary. So it is—God for us all, and every man for himself. Amen, say I.*

The month of May only increased the tension until the breaking point was reached. News from Williamsburg convinced Landon that the de facto republicanism into which Virginia had fallen was bad. The ground of his reverence for the British constitution of a mixed, checked-and-balanced monarchy was clearly revealed in his comment that, *This only shows the inconveniency of the Legislative, the Judiciary, and the Executive Power arising out of the same body.* If all the branches of government came from a single assembly, then they could not be watchdogs on each other to prevent tyranny.

A democratic spirit—or, at least, a populist egalitarianism—was manifesting itself closer to home. On May 1 Landon rushed to his diary to record a shocking exclamation from a Richmond County small holder: *I have just heard that a certain G.R. when asked to lend his fire-lock—musket—to go against the* Royal Navy *tender—asked the People if they were such fools—to go to protect the Gentlemen's houses on the riverside—he thought it would be better if they were burnt down.*

Grand politics became more and more troubling to Landon. He despaired of Britain restoring its king and constitution as uncorrupted guardians of liberty, and he equally despaired of the American leadership patiently holding out for that moment. He heard rumors that the British were plotting to bring in the kings of France and Spain to help subdue the Americans in return for third shares each. But this he did not believe—if only from the impossibilty of any British accommodation to the *notorious Aims in france for Universal Monarchy.* More likely, he hoped, was a rescue that might be effected by a sudden rekindling of the spirit of liberty in Britain. If only the people would sweep away the false king as well as his evil ministers. (Landon seems now to have imagined a repetition of the Glorious Revolution of 1688, when a despot who was destroying the constitution was replaced by a new sovereign who was sworn to uphold it.)

I shall not be disappointed to hear the tyrant Hypocrite—George III—removed from his throne, and the People—through their grave necessities which must now be felt—rising to get a Peace and harmony restored. If this does not happen, they are not only fools but madmen.

Yet Landon's own American side seemed also bedeviled by plots:
Friday, May 3. . . .
I now see the pretence for Independency is compulsion—which I ever agreed to if Britain would be so mad as to compel us. But at first it was through choice agreeable to the Sophisticated nonsense of Common Sense—*a mere cookery among the Congress Republicans. It is enough to make anybody laugh to see the art in the Change.*

The world watched. A Continental European engraving of the Father King literally being pulled down. A crowd in New York City did indeed demolish the statue of George III, set up so recently to celebrate his repeal of the Stamp Act. *Colonial Williamsburg Foundation.*

And so the old man waited, watching from his riverside place, away from centers of decision making.

Then came the news that the leaders of Virginia had chosen the way of independence and the republic. With all the shock it gave him, Landon could relish the drama of his own triumphantly patriotic response.

Saturday, May 18.

Yesterday was our fast day, and I went to church and . . . endeavoured to join heartily in our Public Prayer Against our enemies, and with sincere gratitude for all the mercies of heaven. But oh! when I came home and after a composed nap of sleep, how was I unguardedly agitated in a moment almost!

A paper from our Convention came to me declaring unanimously, with 112 members, for a direction to our delegates to represent this colony in their endeavours in Congress for an independent government—independent *of the Crown of Parliament of Great Britain. . . .*

It was really very well penned, and—*except as to the hurry of declaring the thing until there could be no hopes of a reconciliation, it was not reprehensible.*

When the matter was discussed at Sabine Hall, old Landon was angered by a tendency to question the sincerity of his acceptance of the revolution. Nevertheless, he still scolded against the hot-headed republicans—*the peculiar genius of some folks.* And he kept up his strong patriotic commitment. He expressed his defiance of the military reinforcements that Britain was said to be sending.

But suppose those 45,000 should come, can they be more dreadful than the number of blood-hounds whom we have lately vanquished, though fed with all the despotic food of Parliamentary statutes. Indeed it is a pure contrivance for weak minds to bring about Independency, and it has done it in Virginia, God help us all.

The revolution was accomplished and accepted—almost. The father-king was cast out; but then George III was turned *tyrant Hypocrite.*

Virginia moved boldly into the new relationships—actual and symbolic—of a republic. "Commonwealth" was the name Virginians soon gave to their brave new regime. In this they were using the literal English of the Latin, *res publica.* Ominously, it was the same name as Cromwell had used for his regicide republic.

It is very hard now for people in the twenty-first century to realize the radicalism of this step and so to understand not only the agony that Landon felt, deep-dyed patriarchal monarchist that he was, but also the kind of collective anguish of the colonists, long so proudly British. That anguish was manifest in the repeated declarations of ultimate loyalty that Landon still dwelled upon; it was manifest in the long fifteen months of bitter warfare that had been waged by and upon the Americans before they could bring themselves to opt for independence.

Casting out the king and founding the republic was a patricidal act; and the father killing was cosmic. It profoundly changed the order of the world. The principle of patriarchy within the institution of monarchy had been comprehensive; it had given coherence to the whole system. We saw, in the frontispiece to this book, how the new Commonwealth of Virginia designed its "great seal" to express the violence in its founding. We have seen the armed female figure wearing the insignia of Liberty. She stands in the center, with her right foot pressing down a fallen tyrant; the crown that has rolled away declares him a king cast down. The image committed all those who now swore allegiance to the republic; it had to be deeply disturbing for those who could not forget the old allegiance.

Landon knew he had lost on the constitutional principles at stake; but he maintained a rear-guard action against the republicans. He could vigorously affirm the rightness of the patriotic stand he had joined in, and he could fiercely declare what ought to have been the limits—and still should be as far as possible. *Thursday May 23.*

I cannot avoid observing on a most outrageous inconsistency governing between those who have unanimously declared for an Independency, and all the half pay writers on that side of the present question, from the famous author of Common Sense *down to the E. F.—who wrote in the* Gazette—*of the 17 of May inst.—said to be Dr. Jones. They all declare against the English constitution, as a form of Government which freedom can't exist under—from its arbitrary tendency. . . .*

On the same day, a wartime measure to requisition the arms of Virginians provoked an outraged response from Landon:

Why then is a limited monarchy objected to on account of some possible arbitrariness that may be introduced into it? . . . An evil begot how it will is still an evil—and necessity is no better plea in a Republican form than . . . in a monarchical form. In both it is bad, and is such a payment to extravagant power that I dread its effects wherever I hear it mentioned.

But in the lines that followed, we clearly see how much Landon was still caught between opposed attachments: he was devoted to the British constitution, but he detested those currently claiming to rule under it. He expostulated concerning a rumor of "Commissioners" sent by the Crown to try to stave off the impending rupture. According to this report, the emissaries were armed with money to bribe, as well a new army of soldiers to coerce.

But I can't believe one word of the report, or at best it is some ministerial scheme to deceive America. . . . I cannot think that the King—with so foul a mouth as that with which he opened Parliament in his last speech—can ever desire or design or grant America her reasonable demands now, or that his accursed ministers—with his more damned Parliament—would now propose such a thing. . . . Possibly they have at last seen that they cannot conquer us; and certainly we cannot receive them with their Bayonets thus fixed. In short I cannot believe the tale the more I think of it.

The war on the Chesapeake continued. On May 27 Landon heard of a fierce engagement between a Virginia force and the defenders of Lord Dunmore's stronghold near the entrance to Chesapeake Bay, at Portsmouth. After heavy casualties, the governor and at least 55 vessels had sailed off no one knew where. *It seems Dunmore said—as the country had declared for Independency—there was no occasion or business for him here.*

By the next day, Tuesday, May 28, Dunmore was said to have been sighted on the Sunday. He was moving in on the Piankatank River, close to the mouth of the Rappahannock River. Landon asked whether it could *be possible this chief could be so great a fool as to burn his place of resort in Portsmouth . . . only to remove to another place; and to have got no farther than the mouth of two rivers up this bay from Wednesday to Sunday?* Surely this was *a mere Baltimore*, that is, a report, like those in the newspapers of that town, without the least truth in it. But then, was not Dunmore *a human creature abandoned to barbarity and inhumanity and so deprived of senses. Whom God wishes to destroy he first drives mad*.

The Wednesday brought confirmation that Dunmore's force had indeed made a landing on *Gwin's Island*. It was to this encampment that we saw the Eight direct their journey after arming and leaving on the night of June 26–27. It was an unpromising place; Landon remembered it from many years back as small, with *not more than half a dozen hutts merely . . . on it*. A bad choice it might be as a stronghold for a fighting force, but now his lordship's camp was there, and revolutionary war had come close to work its subversions on Landon's extensive nearby plantations.

Meanwhile, the master of Sabine Hall was advised to clear his plunderable property (slaves and livestock) back out of reach of possible raiders; he declared he would not—*even if Dunmore should come on shore and order me to do it*.

Landon, the old die-hard, argued himself one more time to the viewpoint he now held.

I can with truth say, and bless my God for it, that although I from the beginning abominated this present contest—which Great Britain certainly began with America by attempting to tax her out of the constitutional road, yet I was so convinced of the Romanticness* of her intention to come 3,000 miles and subdue above 3 million of her People to her arbitrary rule of enslaving, that I never once entertained the least possibility of her success. . . .

Since the revolution had by now subverted the household at Sabine Hall, Landon had to grapple with the challenge to inequalities that the struggle had invoked. He had to acknowledge new controversies arising from *the rights of nature—impressed on all mankind at their creation*. We saw, as we followed the search for the Eight, that he did not yield the point, asking rhetorically how else the work of the plantations could be done. But, in his sudden need to address this subject, he was already getting caught up in the imagined new order that the Revolution was evoking.

The month of July saw all the revolutionary disturbances in the psyche of the old patriarch continued and intensified. He was mainly obsessed with get-

---

* Landon's self-revealing word for an unreal, impracticable project.

ting news of the defecting Eight. Would vengeful justice overtake them? Would misfortunes of war overwhelm them? Or would they, as told in his yearning dream, come back to be forgiven—so that the old regime, in which they had been raised under their master, would be restored?

During this time, Landon ceased to fight and refight the contest over independence; instead, he fretted over the signs that the Revolution had opened the door on chaos. There was Patrick Henry winning election as Virginia's first republican governor—this upstart who had usurped Landon's claim to be *the first who opened the breath of liberty to America*. Then temporary relief came in a double report—of Patrick Henry's death and of *our battery's beginning to Play on Dunmore's gang and they being routed*. These were *two glorious events, Particularly favourable by the hand of Providence*. But both proved to have been false rumors.

Always, however, Landon's rebellious son seemed to menace his rule of his own house. In this time of regicide, any defiance—be the cause ever so trivial—seemed to become a menace of revolution at home, of patricide even.
Monday, July 22. . . .
However incredible this relation may be of any animated part of the creation except the brutes, I hereby call God to witness the truth of it. Colonel Robert Wormeley Carter who surely has been somehow changed since born of his mother, though this day at dinner, though at my own table and with my own victuals, seeing me take a little vinegar out of the cucumber plate—called out to his daughter to put some more vinegar & pepper in, for his father had taken it all out—as he always does. I vow to God I had not more than half a teaspoonful to acidulate some oyster broth.

I have dreaded what this filial disobedience will get to. I must be provided with pistols.

Thus, a commonplace form of family conflict was rendered overt and made cosmic in its resonance by this time of crisis of monarchy. Readers who have been themselves maturing sons to aging fathers, or who as women of the family have watched the common patterns of unwanted but seemingly unavoidable aggression in the father-son relationship, will surely believe that there was a deeper underlying drive to all this conflict: the lurking form of rage Sigmund Freud called oedipal.

No monthly book diaries survive for the later summer and fall months of the inauguration of the new Commonwealth of Virginia. We have therefore mostly to imagine Landon's response to the energetic revolutionary reform program entered upon by zealous converts to republicanism and a new order.

During this time of remaking, Thomas Jefferson led the charge in the first General Assembly convened under the new constitution. There are some clues as to the contempt in which Landon held this assembly. The elections to choose its members were further manifestations of the general disorder. Thus, on July 22 Landon noted that, *The first Monday in April was April fool day . . . at our Court house—And the first Monday in next month will be a second day of the sort in this new government.*

In Landon's Daybook there is a vigorous polemic against the proposed law abolishing entails in Virginia. This, indeed, is the clearest sign of his resolute rear-guard defense of the old regime, whose decay he had so long been lamenting.* This was a draft in preparation for a denunciation to be published in one of the *Gazettes*. Either it was never published or the issue it appeared in has been lost. Landon wrote that, *Those who fancy entails of any injury to a republic must be monsters of an Agrarian cast. . . .* And then he turned from secular Rome to sacred Israel; he went on to declare that *Moses' injunction against the alienating the inheritances of the fathers* was probably *one of the laws of Nature or at least inspired into the minds of the People before they were established into Government.*

In this matter Landon was also roused by his own dilemma with respect to his enduring love-hate vendetta with his own *son and heir.* On this topic he lectured to himself under the guise of an address to the readers of the *Gazette.* Into his essay, the embattled father wove much of his troubled conscience as to whether he was a wise patriarch or a tyrant; he also placed in the foreground the vexed issue of "independency" from sovereign fathers.

No, reader, Let not the disobedience of your heir incline you to conclude it—disobedi-

---

* "Entail" was the term in English Common Law for devices whereby a landowner could leave his estate not just to his next heir but as a secure continuing endowment of the greatness of the elder male line of his family. It was profoundly patriarchal in an old aristocratic mode. Land entailed must pass on down the line—so it could not be sold or mortgaged away by he who was technically not owner but "tenant for life." Landon knew his history. He knew how the brothers Gracchus, in ancient Rome, had proposed their notorious "Agrarian Law" that would have seen dispersed the very large concentrations of land then in the hands of a few great patrician families (like the Carters). And so the old man knew with dread certainty that the worst revolutionary excesses of that old Roman popular party were now being attempted in Virginia.

ence—proceeds from an expectation of independency, and incline you *therefore to Punish him for what you can but guess at. But if that*—independency—*is his motive to disobedience, leave him to the judge of every unseen cause, and let . . . God punish him according to his commandment. . . . Otherwise the question may be frequently asked how came you by those entailed Possessions? Those who seek their own revenge—on* their sons—*in such cases of this imaginary cause of disobedience, can be but despots in their hearts, and Cowards to boot. The latter because they fear the Judgements of men, and the former in seeking their own justice, as every Tyrant will do, through an arbitrary Principle.*

The assault on entails was an assault on the principles of orderly succession in the hereditary monarchy of the landed estate. Landon's anguish over the threatened republican abolition of entails drew together all his long-endured anguish over the primal rebellions that he felt were pulling down the order of the world he most desired to see continued. At stake also was his view of his own reign as a benign patriarch-protector. This was the role that his diary narratives continued to affirm.

Landon's sense of outrage at this measure caused him to pen an extraordinary image, which strikingly lampoons Thomas Jefferson. Landon wrote to George Washington at the time when his indignation was at its greatest height. He adopted the tone of a kind of admiring uncle, addressing the younger man as "my dear George" and, later, "my chum." Landon sought at least the General's moral support: "Was any man in your camp to say, who is the greatest drunkard, and most pernicious to society, he who only drinks in the night, and is perhaps ashamed of it in the morning, or he who gets drunk . . . at midday? . . . I dare say the midnight drunkard, would be the most to be respected." Landon had seen all this coming—the young republicans intoxicated with revolutionary new ideas. He went on to name the bearer of this radical attack on the forms of inheritance that preserved the property of ancient lineages as "the famous T. J——n."

The fateful year of 1776 had begun with Landon's dreading the already inevitable declaration of independence. He feared the rupture with ancient forms of authority that would accompany the separation from the mother country and its revered constitution. We see how soon he felt that his worst fears were being realized.

Chapter 13

Landon and Nassaw

Nassaw was a man of about Robert Wormeley Carter's age. He was not a son to Landon; he was an enslaved African American attendant. He was also the surgeon assistant in the master's active healing practice and, as such, physically closer to the diarist than any son or daughter. In his contrariness he provided, almost as much as Robert, occasions for Landon to affirm order in a world turning upside down.

The intensity of conflict in this relationship was evidently also synchronized with the phases of revolutionary breakdown of the old authority system. A series of crises with Nassaw erupted in the time of the crisis of the monarchy in America. But there is more to it. The diarist, led on by his sense of a master's power and responsibility, formed now a great project of redeeming Nassaw from the fires of hell. The tales of Nassaw—and the larger story that we are compelled to construct as we collect those tales—give intimate insights into the unequal enslavement of both master and man within the plantation system. In this story we approach an end: Landon's striving to bring light into his darkening world intensified as he felt his own death draw near.

We take up the story of Nassaw in the fall of 1775. Landon already knew in his heart that he would be reconciled with his rebel daughter Judith and her forbidden husband. By that time, however, the armed revolt against His Majesty's Government had been in progress for almost half a year.

The complex narrative that Landon entered in his diary begins with troubling sickness of the body, but, in the culmination of the telling, it arrives at the anticipated cure of a soul.

Monday, September 11.
A fine day but still in the heat of bilious complaints. . . . At last perhaps strong bitters restores a patient or two out of the numbers that are laid up. I have hardly a servant to wait on me; and the only one *to assist my endeavours after humanity is drunken Nassaw who has not been sensibly sober one evening since this day fortnight.*

But yesterday—Sunday—*my overseer at the riverside—perhaps frightened to death with his disorder—sent up to desire some assistance. I sent this fellow—Nassaw—down to him with possitive orders that if the man was very bad to come directly and inform me: but he—though at Church—gave money to a negroe of Corrie's to get him some rum and to meet him somewhere. . . . The fellow*—Nassaw *pretends he did not know his name—was true to his trust—and though he was not soon enough to meet him, yet Nassaw went to this man—whose name he says he does not know—and there took such a dose that Just held him to get to the overseer; and what he did then God only knows; but I do hope He was graciously Pleased to prevent the drunkard's doing wrong and to bless my endeavours in this humane way with success.*

But what should I not do to Mr. Nassaw? Nobody could find him. At last Tom Parker on horseback found him at sunset—asleep on the ground dead drunk. As soon as he was got home I offered to give him a box on the ear and he fairly forced himself against me. However I tumbled him into the Sellar & there had him tied Neck & heels all night—& this morning—Monday—*had him stripped & tied up to a* tree *limb—and with a Number of switches Presented to his eyes—and a fellow with an uplifted arm.*

He increased his crying Petitions to be forgiven but this once; and desired the man to bear witness that he called on God to record his solemn Vow that he never more would touch liquor.

I expostulated with him on his and his father's blasphemy of denying the holy word of God in boldly asserting that there was neither a hell nor a devil, and asked him if he did not dread to hear how he had set the word of God at naught—who promised everlasting happiness to those who loved him and obeyed his words & eternal torments to those *who set his goodness at naught and despised his holy word.*

After all I forgave this creature out of humanity, religion, and every virtuous duty—with hopes—though I hardly dare mention it—that I shall by it save one soul more alive.

Landon's precipitate change of tone from threatening master to forgiving father seems to have been triggered by the oath that, in extremity, Nassaw uttered. Landon chose to believe that the solemn promise to God would commit Nassaw to the path of salvation, and that he, as master, might indeed have managed to *save one soul more alive*. Again we see the neediness of the master of Sabine Hall in his craving for success in this endeavor.

"The best bleeder about." An eighteenth-century engraving of a surgeon preparing to let blood. But what if the practitioner was drunk? *Colonial Williamsburg Foundation.*

No work on the plantation was dearer to Landon than that of healing. In this he put his Enlightenment study of the reason of things directly to the service of God and man; these were his *endeavours after humanity*. Nassaw's life had therefore run in close, but profoundly unequal, parallel to Landon's for nearly two decades by 1775. And when the diaries began to fill up with stories of named protagonists, Nassaw cumulated more than 50 mentions, including a rare commendation of him as *the best bleeder about*. There was some limited mutuality in this regard. On the one hand, Landon complained that Nassaw took all the credit for successful physicking: *on every recovery it is his doings*. On the other hand, Nassaw, faced with life-threatening illness in his own family would call on Landon to effect a cure. Thus, he *waked* Landon *in the night* to see to his little son, Meredith, *concluding him dying* from the way *the child's pulse sunk*. The master could then boast of doing a cure by a *very bold Practice but yet a rational one*.

As the one who always accompanied the diarist on his tours of inspection, Nassaw had learned enough of the business to be a second opinion. Sometimes his authority might be confirmed when that suited the moment: indeed, the gentle mockery in one entry suggests that the master and he could even share a laugh about Nassaw's claimed expertise: *I walkt about in these home fields . . . and sent Nassaw all over them. I thought the tobacco stood—as the planter means—very well indeed, and Doctor Nassaw says he has seen much tobacco, and never saw any stand better.* But Dr. Nassaw, the consultant, might also serve as sparring partner: *I believe both my colt and John Carter's . . . will dye; though Nassaw differs, mine he says will live—but Jack's must go.*

Nassaw was expected to be the immediate extension of the master's eyes, ears, and arms; he was constantly involved in the conflicts and aggressions of the master's exercise of authority on the plantation. The psychological and social cost of this to Nassaw would never be reckoned in the diary. It is taken for granted that Nassaw must check tallies to expose livestock losses that fellow slaves—Talbot, and Johnny's shepherd-daughter—had tried to conceal. Nassaw had to go down into the home field to verify his master's suspicion that his own sister, Maryan, was engaged in deception about the rate of progress of the work gang she led. Later, in what was probably a very stressful confrontation, Nassaw had to—while Landon stood by—*strip* the *cloaths off* Tony, a fellow home-quarter slave, to show that the master's blow upon Tony's arm had not really disabled him from carrying on his fencing work. Sometimes Nassaw's own antagonisms may have been gratified by these enforced aggressions; at other times his friendships and alliances may have been strained. His master's unconcern was part of the way it was within the world of the slave plantation.

Many of the narratives involved Nassaw but scarcely featured him. A story recorded for July 13, 1777, is directly concerned with the threatened dismissal of Billy Beale—the apprentice steward—but the occasion of it was that the master had *yesterday . . . ordered* Beale *to whip Nassaw naked—he it seems only gave him a stroke or two over his cloaths. I told him I would be obeyed—and he was to go. He said he had all along intended it. Joy go with him—an ungrateful fellow.*

A month later the little drama was about a man who came to Sabine Hall to visit a slave woman there. He brought liquor for *this whore's father,* as Landon scornfully phrased it. Nassaw was that father, and he became incapably drunk with the liquor. As it is told, Nassaw was prostituting his own daughter in return for the indulgence of his craving for drink; but the point of the story for the diarist was the disturbance of routines. For the sake of order, Landon *was obliged to threaten to shoot the fellow before he would go.* We simply do not know Nassaw's story here, nor yet his daughter's; all we have are Landon's judgmental phrases.

In some more fully told stories Nassaw was assigned a pronounced role. These divide into a few distinct but related types which give varied insights into the master-slave relationship. Derived from an old folklore theme, one recurrent type is the story of the servant as bold knave and even trickster. One of the most developed of these narratives was the conspiracy of Nassaw with other knavish members of the Sabine Hall staff to shield yet another knavish servant, Simon the runaway ox carter. Also, we have already smiled at the tale of how Nassaw—heedless of duty and matters of safety—had left his master with a muddy horse to ride home on unaccompanied, while he and his son, having partied well, came home in Landon's coach. Landon had then resolved that the delinquent son should be flogged, and that Nassaw should have that retribution hanging over him: *Though Nassaw is my old Servant I am too old a Master to be thus inhumanely treated.*

Far more disturbing for the diarist and evidently for Nassaw himself was a different story that had to be repeatedly told. It is the dark and troubling tale of the drunken surgeon.

On one notable occasion, after an elaborate contrivance to secure a horse on which to ride out in search of liquor, Nassaw was too intoxicated to bleed his master. And there were even more unpardonable threats to life. Nassaw, on Saturday, November 24, 1770, was *most inhumanly drunk and what is worse blooded a two year old child & his father in that fit.* For that—together with the lies he was said to have told about the treatments he had administered—he was *clapped . . . in irons to lye all night & feel his drunkenness.* Another time his drunkenness prevented him *giving a just account* of his physicking. Even when Nassaw was actually too sick to minister, his sickness was blamed on his having *by drink . . . grown stupid.*

When Nassaw was on the job, it was perhaps worse because the master, intent on the healing work, felt he had been constantly thwarted in it: *I have nobody but him to bring me account* of the sick, *nor to give what medicine I order; and when he gets drunk he lies and only remembers to do so, by telling me he has done what he has not done.* On the occasion of this complaint, the master felt obliged to give Nassaw a severe whipping; but that was only after the drunken surgeon had himself been purged and blooded to ease the effects of drinking on his own health. So Nassaw's body was the object of the master's practice in multiple ways—purging, bleeding, and then flaying with the rod or lash. The case seemed hopeless. And yet, the scolding diary continued: *he will drink; he can't say he can't help it, because he could help sending for liquor.*

Landon and this drunken slave surgeon had a long history, as did this diarist's way of entering dire threats that he did not carry out. Back in 1768—a time for which no diary survives—the irate master had made his dissatisfaction very public. On March 3 of that year, Rind's *Virginia Gazette* carried this advertisement:

"My man Nassau, who I have with much care bred up to be of great service amongst my sick people, having fallen into a most abandoned state of drunkenness, and indeed injured his constitution by it, is become now rather a prejudice to me, as he cannot be trusted in the business he has been long practiced in. As I intend to indulge his appetite, which he cannot be cured of by any persuasion, I will, as soon as I can, send him to some of the islands, where no doubt he may get his liquor with less pains than he now seems to take: Therefore I advertise, that I am in want of a young man with a good disposition, that can shave and bleed well, and I am satisfied such a person will find it so much his interest, by pursuing my directions, amongst the sick, that, with the wages I shall give him, he will think the place nothing disagreeable to him. —LANDON CARTER"

As we know, Nassaw did not go to the West Indies, whence, bearing such a name, an ancestor had surely come. The cycle of transgression, sentence, and reprieve continued.

In the time of rebellion at home and abroad, Nassaw's delinquencies came to enmesh themselves with his master's own deepest anguishes. From that complex interaction, we get an otherwise unmatched insight into Nassaw's own misery and into the very nature of plantation-household enslavement. Through some of those no longer casually told stories, we find ourselves glimpsing into the depths of the desolation of an enslaved man and his longings for an end to the burden of life itself.

As the master intensified his drive to dominate, violent attacks upon Nassaw's body seemed insufficient. A different kind of cure must be sought, one that was even more invasive than the physicking and flogging. Evidently disturbed at the whipping of the surgeon on whom he relied, Landon inscribed his justification for what he was doing in a mode that transcends the gentry-lore stories told about this undutiful servant. Suddenly Landon was engaged for Nassaw's soul: *I have threatened him, begged him, Prayed him, and told him the consequences if he neglected the care to one of these sick people; that their deaths . . . must be an evidence against him at the great and terrible day, I have talked a great deal to him in a most religious and affectionate way.*

Here Landon's narrative has become something else; it invokes explicitly the ultimate truths of salvation and damnation. The master tells that he had kept up this pressure *day by day;* we might suspect that he was thereby aggravating the problem. This appeared at least dimly to Landon himself: *And yet all will not do; he seems resolved to drink in spight of me, and I believe in order to spight me.* A stern patriarchal idea of justice still prevailed in the master's mind over any search for understanding: *He knows he never gets a stroke but for his drinking, and then he is very sharply whipped; but as soon as the cuts heal he gets drunk directly. I am now resolved not to pass one instance over—and think myself justified both to God and man.* Having thus put his resolve in a religious frame, the diarist continued: *I confess I have faults myself to be forgiven—but to be every day & hour committing them,—and to seek the modes of committing them—admits of no Plea of frailty.* Relentlessly Landon concluded: *I hope then I may still save his soul.*

Landon's project to reform Nassaw brought slave and master very close, restricting Nassaw's chance for any escape. The diarist's son Robert Wormeley was also the object of an incessant patriarchal moral reform campaign, but he could answer back fiercely or travel away in search of his diversions. Nassaw, on the other hand, could only seek refuge in the bottle or occasionally abscond for a time—and thereby cause an intensification of his master's oppression.

The master's straining past the slave's body to claim his soul, and the guilt that this approach was intended to induce, surely took its toll. A week after the whipping and the intense daily sermonizing, Nassaw, in the middle of being interrogated about the symptoms of his patients, was *accused . . . of being drunk.* That may have been for the moment too much: *at dark he went off,* leaving his master to fulminate on what *a cursed Villain he must be,* since *he knows his own Father, his sister Marian, a child of his, another of Nelly's,* my nephew, *Billy Beverley,* and grandson, *Johnny Carter—are all sick—and yet he gets drunk & goes off.* But Nassaw was not without conscience in this. Perhaps he was making a heartrending plea for acceptance as a caring healer: *Having the key of the* physic *Shop—he came back in the night & laid that down on the steps of the Narrow Passage.* He was gone some time: *Somebody must harbour him,* the narrator surmised, *as it has rained ever since he has been out.* Meanwhile, the results of his drunken doctoring were meticulously noted.

In the summer of 1775, it seems that the bonds of enslavement to drink and to a master who kept at him about it drew unendurably tight about Nassaw. A first indicator in the surviving diary is a story of demotion and banishment whose casual telling itself belies the painfulness of what was done: *Talbot—Nassaw's son—proved more of a drinker than he was of a fool; therefore I made a plowboy of him, having catched him asleep with a Piece of a bottle of Grog in the Closet window,—and for his father's sake I will have no more of such creatures, as he—*Nassaw, the boy's father—*is as unhappy a drunkard as can live.*

The master has sententiously redirected lives—*I made a plowboy of him*. It is punitive; Landon assumes the boy and his father wanted Talbot to remain in the house, rather than be sent to toil in the fields away from his father and his mother. Perhaps this assumption was well founded; Landon knew all these slaves personally. Certainly, from this high-handed determination of the enslaved son's destiny according to an inscribed judgment of what was known to be good for the enslaved father, the strains in the relationship intensified.

Six weeks later, Landon Carter was himself deeply troubled in his own fatherhood. He was in armed rebellion against his King, and simultaneously his daughter Judith was ostracizing him for disinheriting her husband. The diarist played out his patriarchal dilemma on Nassaw. This was the scene with which this chapter on Landon and Nassaw opened; so, we have already followed the detailed narrative of the drunken surgeon apprehended, *tied Neck & heels all night*, strung up in the morning, menaced with the whip, and forced into confession and penitential promises. We have watched the master recounting his assumption of the role of father in the divine manner, as—*After all I forgave this creature out of humanity, religion, and every virtuous duty—with hopes—though I hardly dare mention it—that I shall by it save one soul more Alive.*

The menacing, yet still mundane, stories of the drunken surgeon have now given way to an intense dramatization of Landon Carter in the role of the cosmic father who reclaims his lost children. Possibly the master was enacting a kind of rehearsal with the slave Nassaw for the mighty culminating act of clemency that would bring daughter Judith's husband, Reuben Beale, to Sabine Hall as an acknowledged son-in-law. Perhaps Landon subconsciously hoped that a season of forgiving and reconciliation would see a restoration of harmony between king and subjects, colonies and mother country.

By his actions to this point, Nassaw's own story was one of rebellion against domination, escape from oppression; now he was coerced into engaging himself in a redemption story. He had at some time denied the reality of hell and the damnation of the soul; tied, threatened, and admonished, he now recanted. We sense Nassaw's anguish and scarcely doubt that he longed for a release from the bondage of drinking bouts, repeated failures, and the hell of the stern preaching of his master.

The way for Nassaw was yet deeper into the pit—with his master still looking down on him there.

∞

Nassaw, of course, had a life of his own, apart from what his master could or would script for him in the course of their unequal intimacy. Perhaps that other life was also becoming unsustainable under the pressure.

The enslaved surgeon effected some cures in an intervening time during which he was trusted again; but two weeks and three days on from the ostentatious pardoning, Nassaw was overcome once more with drink. The newly acknowledged son-in-law Reuben Beale was at Sabine Hall to receive medical treatment; but Nassaw was *so very drunk he could not Assist me. At night he crawled about the room and did not know a chamber pot from a botle of water.* In consequence, his master renewed his resolution to be sternly punitive; he *ordered him to be tied and imprisoned.* By the next day, however, the diarist reported, *he will not eat. . . . He desires to die.* Landon does not convince us when he declares, *I don't care.* Perhaps it would have been better for Nassaw if the master had not cared, for surely that obsessive care was an added affliction. The following lines are on a damaged page of the diary, but the gist of their ambiguous treatment of the agonized man who is to the master part resource and part human soul is quite clear: *I say he may* die *but he is so far* damned . . . *he certainly has forfeited his solemn promise before heaven. . . . If he goes, I shall be rid of a Villain, though a most capable servant.* And there follow some largely illegible words about ingratitude.

Life, however, dragged on for Nassaw. The drinking and the punishment, the abscondings and the returns to duty continued. His daughter died after childbirth in the sequel to an alarm caused by a snake at her mother's *cabbin door.* With unusual attention to the feelings of his enslaved assistant, Landon had noted that snakes were *her father's aversion to an amazing degree.* After that it is related that Nassaw was *for the last time excused on a most solemn Promise never more to drink. It seems he says he got drunk with the rattlesnake drink for Dinah.*

Perhaps Nassaw had charm that made others give him comfort and support in this long contest between himself and his master. The July 13, 1777, entry recorded that the overseer Billy Beale, himself endlessly tyrannized over, acted as a protective ally when he whipped Nassaw not naked as ordered but over his clothes.

Then there is the last story. It is last in a profound sense because the diary will soon cease with Landon's death. The ailing Landon had prepared some mulled wine with cinnamon to ease a bowel condition. But the next day the master found that, when he needed more of the wine-based potion, Nassaw had *drank up most of the rest* and had *run off on the discovery of it.* The comment was: *This fellow is proof against his oaths never to drink—and gets so drunk every morn as to contradict every time I speak.* It seems as if this painful, destructive relationship could only be ended by the separation of death, and so it was, when the old master died some four months later.

Fully told stories of Nassaw cease in the record with that last quoted entry in Landon Carter's diary, but the life of Nassaw can be traced a little beyond that. In Landon's will of September 4, 1770, he arranged that "Mulato Betty . . . and her Children, Coachman Nat and Tom in the house, and my man Nassaw" should all be included together in the half of the slaves assigned to Robert Wormeley Carter. This bequest was never altered; but, on October 6, 1778, old Landon, preparing to leave the world, wrote a codicil to his will. We have seen how he at last gave Reuben Beale his due as an acknowledged son-in-law, but he made also a significant new arrangement for some of his enslaved house-hold staff. Landon would inflict a last punishment from beyond the grave:

"Item: My desire to reward the deserving impells me to take notice of my Coachman Natt and my Wench Mulattoe Betty, therefore I hereby direct that on every Christmas day they shall have liberty to make choice of which one so-ever of my . . . sons and daughters they shall desire to live with—and that each of them . . . shall have an annuity of Ten pounds per Annum paid to them. . . ." Nassaw's wife and son were specially noticed, but the errant Nassaw was excluded in silence.

Landon's relationship with Nassaw appears as the most intimate of all in his later years. The master could dominate Nassaw as he could not command his children, especially the challenging eldest son. Landon struggled to enact a redemption story combining the stern old patriarchal imperatives and the new humanitarian sensibilities. But what of Nassaw? Was it Landon who drove him to drink? After all, we know he was accomplished enough to be admitted to practice his surgical and apothecary skills on persons who could have refused the service.

Relieved at last from the tyrannical surveillance of his long-time master, Nassaw lived on, employing at least his veterinary expertise. Seven-and-a-half years after Landon's death, Robert Wormely Carter's matter-of-fact account book-diary has this record: "1786, May 22: Nassaw cut 18 Lambs, turned out 2 Rams & marked 15 Ewes."

And the rest is silence? But no—most persons expect to live on in their children and in the remembrance of their names. We do not know their relationship to old Nassaw, but there were three young Nassaws in Robert Wormeley Carter's 1783 list of taxable property.

Chapter 14

Toward Death

Four little diary books survive from the year 1777. Only the months of February, April, July, and August are covered. The whole Landon as we have come to know him is still there, however. He wrote still as an angry observer of wide-world politics; he continued as a testy reporter of his own domestic scene. More or less reconciled to independence, Landon was now more concerned at what he thought was the unjust disregard of his own historic role in the great political struggle of his age.

The following charming narrative of an evening of *sensibility and friendship* was contrived so as to conclude with a celebration of the diarist's greatest patriotic moment.

On Friday, February 23, 1777, the aged master of Sabine Hall had been notably gratified. Feeling that his grown-up offspring shamefully neglected him, he was starved for company. A new acquaintance had been more attentive. One Captain William Dennis—it was recorded with a revealing repetitiousness—*came to see me again a second time.* The visitor was a paroled British prisoner of war, a ship's captain whose vessel had been *taken* on the high seas by a privateer out of Baltimore. The diarist had been charmed from the first; here was *a well behaved man, and too genteel to accept any commiseration* upon his misfortunes. The English captive so enchanted Landon that he forgot the wrongs of his country and the brutal wartime logic of privateering. *Indeed I do think had I been an adventurer in the Privateer that took him, I would, out of my part of the cruise, have given him back all his own adventure capital—though I should have then got nothing by the capture.*

Perhaps Captain Dennis was also charmed. We may suspect, however, that he was bored at Parson Giberne's house where he lodged and that he was ready to amuse himself a little by visiting and observing the ferocious American patriot who held court as an old-fashioned gentleman in the great house overlooking the Rappahannock River. The visitor found he was especially welcome as *a Gentleman whose whole application has been to obtain knowledge in every science almost; and as such has rendered himself a most agreeable companion.*

At the time of this second visit from the captain there was much excitement at Sabine Hall. Landon's namesake grandson, *having had an offer of a Lieutenancy by General Washington in Colonel George Baylor's regiment of horse—was Preparing to set off.* He would carry with him his grandfather's letters to the general and to Colonel Baylor, for everyone should know that, *it was through my recommendation he became so respected.* The sea captain prisoner of war was perhaps committed on the other side in this war, but how could old Landon be sure of that? Any true Briton, after all, might support the British constitution which was still, according to Landon, what the struggle was about. Anyway, the patriotic grandfather could record how *this Captain* had undertaken to do a portrait to commemorate the occasion. He had *offered to take* the grandson's *Picture,* dressed and ready to go to war; and *he really effected it on blue Paper with Chalk and Charcoal in a very natural & masterly manner.*

Perhaps the portrait captured a boy's bravado in his rush toward battle; perhaps too much of her child was in the likeness. *The mother could not any longer contain her grief—and after having employed the whole night in tears, she discovered a greater willingness to leave the world than part with her son.*

Old Landon so far overcame his usual hostility to Winifred as not only to record her distress sympathetically but also to indulge her wishes. (Perhaps he was for the moment led by the sensibilities of his guest.)

Of course, as nobody can know those feelings so beautifully expressed in Scripture, which makes a woman to forget the pains she endured in bringing forth a son—with a joy that she has brought a man child into the world—the whole scheme of his going into the army was laid aside; and I accordingly wrote to General Washington and to Colonel Baylor.

Landon gave his excuses *for soliciting* the commission in the first place. He expressed the mood of his house at that moment, *desiring it to be laid in the Scale of sensibility and friendship.*

The portrait of the grandson about to leave for the war must now have become slightly embarrassing. Old Landon tried to distract the English visitor from the momentary triumph of women's *sensibility* over manly patriotic valor at Sabine Hall; his own vanity also became involved. The diary narrative continues:

At last I proposed to this captain to do me the favour to take my figure in the same manner. This he performed . . . and has produced a serious, thoughtful old gentleman—holding in his right hand a paper thus inscribed:

"America, Freedom
supported
Against the British Stamp Act.
*Merui, sed intus tantum fruor"**

It alludes to my having first of all in America opened the door of freedom against the Supremacy assuming in the British Parliament to make laws for America. . . . This she attempted in the . . . Stamp Act which I had the honour Publickly and indeed openly to oppose—and obtained a Majority great enough to Petition the King . . . , the House of Lords, . . . and the House of Commons. . . . But of what avail was reason, Justice, and proper language—where folly grown mad with Power was resolved to be absolute or nothing?

This *agreeable companion* seemed both to understand the American cause and old Landon's need for more public recognition; but the episode did not end on such a happy note. The pastel drawings had been produced in the course of that February time of *sensibility and friendship*. In April the captain had been allowed to return to his countrymen in a ship appropriately named *Albion*. Five months later on September 2, the vain and so-often-disappointed diarist recorded news that the befriended prisoner had, in some undisclosed way, dishonored the hospitality accorded him. Landon's outrage extended once more to a condemnation of the times: *I heard Yesterday of Captain Dennis' Villany. A monster beyond expression because Hypocrite in all the modes of gratitude in Pretence. But it is nothing to meet rascals nowadays.* The diarist went on—bracketing the captain and Parson Giberne, with whom he had lodged: *Indeed he staid where he did belong, the temple of Hypocrisy.*

The pastel drawing with its celebratory English and Latin inscriptions has not been found—and yet it would be hard to believe that Landon tore it up in rage.

---

* I have deserved my country's honours, but only inwardly have I enjoyed satisfaction.

In the surviving books of the 1777 diary, Landon is still engaged on a wide front: he is found fighting the king and the ministry; he keenly follows the fortunes of Washington's Continental Army; and he expostulates on the politics of the war at every opportunity. In February, the British commander, Lord Howe, was said to be surrounded and on the point of being overwhelmed. Landon, eager to believe this (untrue) report, heard that Howe had sent a flag of truce, requesting to go into winter quarters, which Washington denied. Landon was outraged that Howe could *make such a request of the most extraordinary favour imaginable from the Oppressed, the dishonoured, the barbarously used* Americans *in an hour of Presumptive Victory. And of a people too who only desired to continue to enjoy the same Constitution with their fellow Subjects; for which daring request of freedom from such supreme Lords, they first sent their fleets and armies among us. To be sure they do think us beasts of burden & fools only fit to be enslaved. . . . But however absurd the request, it is just like Lord Howe desiring everybody to come to his temple—Peccavi*—saying I have sinned—*and asking Pardon for petitioning to be as free as other Subjects.*

Two and a half months later, Landon's refighting of the old battles turned his attention right to the top: *I every day see more and more of the unhappy base tendency of that George the Third . . . O! he'd hazard his crown but he would subdue. Who for God's sake? The only virtuous friends he ever had. . . . They still revered him, and gave as far as they could . . . and no People ever asked with more humility, fidelity and good Order 'till by his taking away almost the very shadow of freedom, they were compelled to take care of themselves. I mean the American subjects. But men can't be kings but they must be tyrants indeed.*

Landon was dragging himself clear of his lifetime devotion to the British constitution and its monarchy. He was no longer *astonished so many fine speeches should be uttered in parliament—and neither the King, the Ministry, nor the People should listen to them. Just as if it was any Surprize that a monarch should incline to be a despot—or that he would not bribe men enough to sell themselves and Country to him. It is no surprize that Corruption once tasted should continue.*

Finally on July 15, 1778, Landon wrote out the terms of the broken contract between himself and his former king—the terms of his right to participate in a new regime succeeding the old. George III had destroyed the reciprocity upon which obedience to him must be based. *Allegiance was mine—& the condition for it was Justice and freedom—together with a Paternal affection. If that is broken or denied me—I am absolved.* Those words "paternal affection," that he had once written in affirmation of loyalty as new burgess in 1752, were now brought forth in the deliberate disavowal.

Learning to accept the new regime was more difficult, however. Even the weather seemed republicanized, freighted with the disaster of the times: *It came from clouds really alarming with blackness. . . . What an alteration do I know in this Climate? Formerly it used to afford us these blessings in all the mildness of its creation. . . . But very rarely was it ever disgraced by any Storms. But . . . it never rains now but it pours.*

The year 1778 was the last of Landon's life. The only complete surviving monthly book from the veteran diarist's last year is for August, and it contained no valedictory inscription to end this long-kept diary series. The little book ran on (as was not unusual) into the beginning of the next month, and the September 2 entry ends in a broken sentence at the bottom of a page. There was evidently at least one more leaf, but whatever more there once was is now lost. We can only surmise that—some time before December 22 when Landon died—the colic, the shakes, and the puffy swellings that indicated the failing of his heart combined to prevent him from rising from his bed to write more entries.

Although the last surviving monthly book sustained the strong voice of Landon and his distinctive ways of recording the life around him, its scope was already contracting as his powers failed. The diarist was no longer inclined to fight George Washington's campaigns with him, or to refight the battles with the king and the ministry, or even to continue his complaints against the republicans who had taken charge of Virginia. The diary's horizons had shrunk to the bounds of the estate, but Landon still recorded that plantation world with vigor. His weather narratives had lost no power: *July finished as she began— a very wet Slushy month with more rain than a planter could possibly tell what to do with—or indeed the earth without immediate drains could dispense with, but by drowning many of its grassy herbages and plants.*

Landon's plantation tableaus still had great descriptive force. The example that follows developed a playful tone. The diarist sarcastically personified laziness and neglect as unwelcome trespassers on his property.
Grace and her three hands Yesterday finished Manuring, chopping the dung in, and sowing between the Upland corn rows. . . .

Grace is got into the Lucerne Patch to weed. . . . Note: I had before ordered all the weeds . . . to be cut up both root & branch. But it seems it was left to be done After the rest was wed.

But now I resolve that Mr. After & Mr. By and By shall never be again suffered to be on my plantation without *taking the rascally twin brothers up and giving them condign punishment. They were begot by indolence & Sloathfulness; and walk more in their Sleep than they do awake. I never yet saw either of them—though I have hunted for them for years in most fences—till the very stakes and riders they were left to put up—had rotted or were burnt. Nor in Cornfields could they be seen—though the very bushes which they were to have cut down had grown to mere spreading trees. Accordingly Grace is to catch these fellows if they are to be found.*

The outbursts against Robert Wormeley Carter were less extreme but they did not cease.

Is it not a Strange thing in a Son—always complaining of his father's temper, to be so singularly Provoking as to encourage even his father's Servants, before his face—to disobey him.

No longer ago than last night—when that hell-born Coachman Ben was getting a pass to go to Captain Ball's—at which place he pretends he has a wife—I ordered the fellow to be sure to come to me at ten o'clock this day.

This Devil—my son—to his father said aloud, Then the fellow need not go at all.

Sir, I want to teach him subjection to orders, and this is the way to accustom such a Villain to it?

Therefore I bid the fellow at his peril to appear to me at ten o'clock: though I knew from what this Colonel intended, he would not.

And 'tis now 11 & he has not been seen. If he is not gone off, I will make him repent Colonel Carter's Advice. So that his humanity, as he corruptly calls it, is a designed barbarity either against his father or that fellow.

In the last complete surviving diary entry, Landon rehearsed his entire grievance at Robert's insubordination and his wife's worse than complicity:

I don't know how it happens, but I can't give a slave an order about anything but this devil driver—my son—grows into high reprimand just as if I was a fool.

I this day called for all the small young cucumbers to be got for pickling—and the monster . . . merely stormed at my folly in giving such an order—A man perpetual intending to affront his father will devil-like be at everything. Certainly as this Creature with his large family must have a great deal to deserve—it is time for him to begin to deserve: but I do leave him to perdition—and he has paid dear for his sulkye De maintinon—who has long ago determined the sex of the infernals.*

---

* Madame de Maintenon was the second wife of King Louis XIV of France; a malign, Protestant-persecuting influence on the policies of the *Grand Monarque* was attributed to her.

❦

Landon recorded his growing infirmity. The second paragraph of his August 1778 book announced: *I can give no favourable account about my Colic. . . .* Two days later he wrote, *my Colic so bad last night from 9 to 4 I never got a wink. I am very thin, legs & feet swell much.* And by August 7 he was lamenting that, *Last night more like the night of my death than any recovery.* Soon he would have an inflamed skin condition—a *Nettle rash* he called it. He identified it from a medical manual, but that gave small comfort, since *the faculty*—of medicine—*cannot reason upon it—which comes & goes . . . without one visible Cause.* Landon feared that the recommended remedy was too strong. *I would try it, but am too old to venture without knowing how the decoction affects the body.*

There were consolations, however. On August 11 he wrote that *Mr Reuben Beale and his Lady my dear daughter got here yesterday—a comfort to me indeed.* Next day he was able to write—*Betsy to be here on Saturday.* His eldest daughter, long married and settled to the south, was coming at last to see him.

Meanwhile, the fight had certainly not gone out of Landon. He angrily took on a problematic overseer's family: *Freshwater and his mad bitch began their tricks this day.* Two of his other overseers, *going to see the Peach orchard, found in it a daughter of that rascal's getting a large basket of unripe ones; and upon reproving her for it Mrs Brimstone begun a Vile strain of Abuse—and the old rascal joined her.* Landon took reprisals, and then was talked out of it. *I sent immediately to turn them away & had all their things out of doors. George Carter says he cried much—was sorry for what had happened & begged to stay the year out. On promise of no more such—& . . . a readiness to Submit to my orders sent by anyone—my humanity became ready to indulge the fool: but as to the wife, the least movement to such a behaviour would oblige me to have her whipped off the Plantation.*

The next day: *Freshwater is again abusively outrageous. He, his wife, and daughters shall be this day drove off, and Mangorike Will placed there to take care of everything. But perhaps he may turn a rogue.* Three days later Landon learns that an overseer on a neighboring property, *has given harbour (a tobacco house) to this Gang of Devils of Freshwaters—whose wife and all his daughters by his 1st wife—who lie there to do Me all the mischief they can—Stealing away my chickens . . . quarrelling with people because negroes. . . .* That neighboring overseer was warned by Landon against harboring the marauders—*I let Mr Greenlaw know I hoped his wife would not again want my assistance in lying in. . . .* He was also advised *to caution those creatures against coming on my land—for I had ordered both Griggs*—the overseer—*and the people to tie them, whip them & bring them to me.*

By the last of the month Landon professed to be surprised at the reluctance of overseer Griggs to submit to reproof. The diarist declared that, when persons were employed by him, he *would reserve the power of finding fault; and if they would not mend, then of turning them away.* Learning on the same day that neglectful workers had left countless caterpillars on his crop plants, he resolved that *the brutes who suffered my tobacco to be so eaten shall be severely punished, by every method not barbarous that I can devise. A set of Monsters to leave such an enemy behind them—which it seems they did last week. Indeed, Slaves are devils—& to make them otherwise than slaves will be to set devils free.* Even as he disavowed "barbarity," old Landon was impelled to justify slavery now that the Revolution had called its legitimacy into question.

In late entries, the disgruntled patriarch renewed a familiar complaint; he was aggrieved both at Robert Wormeley's family living in his house and at his other children whose visits were too brief and perfunctory: *I see it is vain to expect much of my Children's company who come to see me. Some* of my household— *quite inconsiderate on such an occasion of a sick old father—are for pressing these* visiting family *abroad on Visits. Others take all the pains they can to draw them into diversions; and Some—out of pure malice to a regular family—are for inventing every mode of Avocation.*

Landon had already lamented that Judith, his *daughter Beale*—whose arrival had given him so much pleasure—would now cut short the length of her promised visit: *This child chose to go out of the world from her father. Farewell fondness. I hope in God.* So there was still some bleeding from the wound ostensibly healed after Judith's forbidden marriage.

The theme of neglectful children still haunted Landon in the last lines of his diary that survive: *A backwoods Visit*—from son John—*to see an aged Very sick almost unto death, and very infirm father—whose constant care has been to provide well and the best he could for his children—besides a most uncommon concern and expence for their education.* But John was not assiduous enough: *This the most respectful visitor calls seeing his father—and all could only equally . . .* Here, with the final word unclear, ends the torn last surviving page of the diary.

Three and a half months after that half-lost entry, Landon died. Eldest son Robert, with whom he had such bitter quarrels, entered an obituary in the family Bible: "My honoured Father Coll Landon Carter departed this life the 22nd Decr. 1778 about eight o'clock at night, he died of a Dropsy. He would have been 69 years old had he lived to Augst 1779. He was born in 1710." He also wrote a Latin lament; its sincerity need not be questioned because real love as well as constant antagonism had bonded the pair: "Eheu, mortuus est quem nunquam obliviscor."*

There was another, later sign of filial affection that is the more moving because it was evidently spontaneous. On April 26, 1780, sixteen months after Landon's death, Robert Wormeley Carter wrote into his account book–diary an acknowledgment to a companion of the old man who had perhaps kept closer to him at the last than any of his pleasure-seeking offspring. "This morning our old Cat Coorytang died . . . near 17 years old. He was a favourite of my Fathers—and I have taken great care of him on that account—tho' very troublesome."

So we have a parting image of Landon as an old man writing his diary with an old cat on his lap.

---

* "Alas he has died, whom I shall never forget."

Last Words

Since the invention of the diary, this form of expression has been one of the most varied and powerful genres of writing to catch, hold and transmit to posterity personal experiences of time passing.

Landon Carter's long-kept record is truly remarkable among diaries. The imprint of its angry keeper is so intense, and his outrage resonates with the deep family drama embedded in one of the most momentous revolutions in the history of the world. Through all his experiences he gives us an unequaled view of a man, like many of his contemporaries, divided within himself. He clung to his British constitutional heritage, but his heart was given to the cause of American liberty.

Above all, Landon's diaries record his stories. They are in every way his stories, but between the lines of these vivid accounts of action other points of view can be discerned. It is this richness of context that I have attempted to sample for readers of this book. Within his accounts, many counteraccounts can be found of the revolutionary genesis of the United States of America. To us that beginning is so massive an accomplished fact that we feel it as inevitable, but it was in its time an unprecedented act of political daring and very uncertain of its outcome. Indeed, for Landon and countless numbers of his generation, it was not a glorious dawn but the toppling of an old order whose crumbling he had long been lamenting.

∽

The output of stories was broken off, never to be resumed, some days, weeks, or months before December 22, 1778; death then gave a quietus to Landon's otherwise indomitable spirit.

Here is a narrative sketch from that near-the-end monthly book of August 1778. In this late performance, we follow one more time the observing eye of the old master of Sabine Hall; we hear his sharp commentary and sense again his neediness, his craving to show himself so right where those who would make light of his authority were so wrong. This little vignette should serve to start reflections on what Landon has revealed to us of himself in his diary of troubled times. Our reflections should challenge us to know ourselves better in a world that is as much caught up in revolution, violent demands, and violent denials.

August 30, 1778. . . .

A Surprise to some people happened here last week. A humming bird catcht sheltering itself from the weather was kept in a cage for more than a fortnight on honey & water from a wooden spender spoon. At last it got out & went away.

After much labour to catch it in Vain I said—great Chance but it comes tomorrow to the cage.

Lord how the improbability was laughed at by the greatest Ass—my son—in sacrifice to his cursed Malice and revenge.

But the next day—as I said—it came, was catched & fed voraciously indeed—and continues in confinement by hunger, the only passion every Man is subject to, that must inevitably enslave.

We all are most revealed when we least intend it. As he penned those lines, Landon could not have known how much of his grasp on life, his patriarchal mode of self-assertion, becomes manifest in them. It is not just the tiny bird that is ensnared but Robert Wormeley, and Winifred and her children, and all the rest of the master's "dependents" who must submit to him for whatever succor and sweetness they might get. Ultimately, Landon too is caged by this disposition of the world.

How much has changed? So much and yet so little. In theory we reject the top-down model of legitimate power that gave point and moral to Landon's hummingbird story. The revolution in which the master of Sabine Hall was so conflicted a participant declared the equality of "all men." During the long-delayed continuation of that revolution, which we call the Civil War, Abraham Lincoln proclaimed the emancipation of the slaves. In the aftermath of the Second World War, the victorious leaders emerging from that revolutionizing struggle comprehensively expanded Jefferson's immortal dictum: they adopted a "Universal Declaration of Human Rights" to affirm the equality of

A detail from the engraved plate of the hummingbird in Mark Catesby's great 1730s Natural History of the Southern colonies. *Colonial Williamsburg Foundation.*

all persons, women as well as men, blacks as well as whites. Subsidiary charters have canvassed the rights of the child in subversion of the ageism that is as strong as sexism in the forms of patriarchal pretension. Very vocal groups seek to extend the principle to animals, and to the varieties of living species, and to the planet itself.

We have made momentous strides in proclaiming equality. The benign principle has reached and uplifted countless millions; their lives can be lived with a sense of opportunity, free of the kinds of tyranny that Landon assumed were the rightful exercise of patriarchal power. But what of the countless millions—surely it is billions globally, and millions within the wealthiest nations even—who are still trapped in the cruel cage of *hunger*, their needy lives lived in squalor?

Perhaps we think that the issues that so preoccupied Landon are historical, belonging to time past. Have we not transcended sexual servitude and race-based slavery? May we not alternately frown our disapproval and smile our condescension at Landon's attempts to enforce those codes? But the struggles he recorded are really timeless: we are all Robert Wormeleys, all Winifreds, all Nassaws—and, above all, every one of us is Landon himself, forever telling ourselves stories of ourselves and of those around us, mostly to show how right we were, and how wrong they were. From Landon's extraordinary feat in writing down so many such stories should we not strive to learn to examine our own? Do we, in our own worlds, abuse our power and, worse still, turn into a tyranny the love out of which we believe we act? What do we, who so readily disapprove of Landon, actually do to advance freedom and equality? Have we schooled ourselves to seek and to augment signs of hope rather than portents of doom in the troubled, revolutionary world in which we too live?

"Il faut cultiver son jardin"—one must tend one's own garden—Candide concluded, when he had at last acknowledged the extent of evil and misery in what he could no longer tell himself was "the best of all possible worlds." Voltaire breathed the same revolutionary air as Landon. He was scarcely more optimistic about outcomes, though he did journey to Paris in 1778 for that ecstatic moment of the eighteenth century when he embraced Benjamin Franklin, the fellow philosopher who had snatched lightning from the sky and the scepter from the tyrant. Later in that same year, both Voltaire and Landon breathed their last. Perhaps Voltaire's Candide, with his maxim that might translate as "revolution must begin with self and home," is our best guide for the reading of Landon Carter's diaries.

Chronology

YEAR	POLITICAL HISTORY	LANDON'S DIARY
1752		Newly elected burgess starts diary
1754	Start of war with France for North America.	Landon chronicles struggle to fund war against the French and Indians.
1755	British force under General Braddock defeated on the Ohio.	
1756–58		Landon's notebook plantation diary.
1757	William Pitt begins to infuse new energy into war effort.	Eldest grandchild, young Landon III, born to be raised at Sabine Hall.
1758	Capture of Fort Duquesne (later Pittsburgh) secures the West.	Death of Susannah (little Sukey).
1759	Capture of Quebec secures North America for English speakers.	
1759–62		No surviving diary.
1763	Comprehensive British victory; surge of loyalty but Wilkes-ite agitation sows seeds of doubt.	Plantation diary resumes in Virginia Almanack.
1765	February: Stamp Act to tax Americans passed by Parliament and King. May: Patrick Henry calls for rebellious defiance of the King's government. America becomes ungovernable.	No diary for this year May: Patrick Henry calls for rebellious defiance of the King's government. America becomes ungovernable.
1766	Stamp Act repealed; paeans of loyalty to King George III; New York erects a statue of him.	Landon's diary begins to carry narratives of rebellions in his own plantation kingdom.

1766–73	Uneasy peace; colonists constantly reaffirm loyalty to the King and the constitution while protesting taxes.	
1768		Landon unseated in election, ceases to be a burgess.
1770		Series of "monthly books" commences. Gardener Johnny demoted.
1771		Gardener Johnny restored.
1772		Daughter Judith banished.
1773	Boston Tea Party; armed rebellion.	Judith marries Reuben Beale.
1774	Virginia supports Boston rebels; calls for Continental Congress.	Landon elected Chair of Richmond County Committee to organize resistance.
1775	April: Battle of Lexington & Concord—full armed rebellion begins.	
		September: Nassaw forgiven. Landon reconciled to both Judith and Reuben.
	November: Virginia's Governor Dunmore proclaims freedom to slaves who will fight rebel masters.	November: Virginia's Governor Dunmore proclaims freedom to slaves who will fight rebel masters.
1776		January to May: Landon dreads independence and a republic without benefit of the British constitution. June: The Eight go armed from Sabine Hall to Dunmore—a slave rebellion.
	July: After 15 months of waging war, Congress (prompted by Virginia) votes for independence; monarchy disowned; world's first secular republic.	
1778		The dying Landon is reconciled to revolution, and he has ceased to fight the war in his diary.

Annotation

In these notes I aim to supply (1) references for quotations, information and ideas, and (2) a review of the most important writings that have guided my reading of Landon Carter's Diary.

Abbreviations

CFP	The Carter family papers, 1659–1797, in the Sabine Hall collection, Paul P. Hoffman, ed. (Charlottesville: Univ. of Virginia Library, Microfilm publications; no. 3, 1967), cited as "CFP, microfilm"
CUP	Cambridge University Press
DNB	*Dictionary of National Biography*
LC 1779 Inventory	Inventory of Landon Carter, 1779, Richmond County Courthouse Records, microfilm at Library of Virginia, Richmond
LCD	Diary of Landon Carter, mss in CFP
LLC	Library of Landon Carter, Special Collections, Alderman Library, University of Virginia, Charlottesville, Va.
OED	*Oxford English Dictionary*
OIEAHC	Omohondro Institute of Early American History and Culture
OUP	Oxford University Press
RWC	Robert Wormeley Carter
RWC diary	Robert Wormeley Carter, "Diaries, 1764–1792," transcripts in Special Collections, John D. Rockefeller, Jr., Library, Colonial Williamsburg, Williamsburg, Va.
RWC 1783 list	"Robert Wormeley Carter 1783 Taxable List," in "CFP, microfilm."
UNCP	University of North Carolina Press
UPVA	University Press of Virginia
VMHB	*Virginia Magazine of History and Biography*
WMQ	*William & Mary Quarterly*
WTBC	Winifred Travers Beale Carter

GENERAL

Early in my Virginia researches I discovered *The Diary of Colonel Landon Carter of Sabine Hall, 1752–1778* edited by Jack Greene (Charlottesville: UPVA, 1965). The introduction to that edition was subsequently published as Jack Greene, *Landon Carter: An Inquiry into the Personal Values and Social Imperatives of the Eighteenth-Century Virginia Gentry* (Charlottesville: UPVA, 1967). This is both a powerful appreciation of the diary and a penetrating interpretation of the Virginia political culture in which Landon operated; and it has been an inspiration to me in my own exploration of Landon Carter's world.

As a historical anthropologist I intended using Landon Carter as my "informant." In the 1980s historians had begun to ask questions about the hidden agendas of history; we self-consciously examined our methods. Encouraged by the linguist Alton Becker, I delved into the study of stories—narratology as it is infelicitously called. Much of my thought on the subject as it relates to historians (together with applications to Landon's diary) has been published in Rhys Isaac, "Stories of Enslavement: A Person-Centered Ethnography from an 18th-Century Plantation," in Bruce Clayton and John A. Salmond, eds., *Varieties of Southern History: New Essays on a Region and Its People* (New York: Greenwood Press, 1996), 3–21; and in Rhys Isaac, "Stories and Constructions of Identity: Folk Tellings and Diary Inscriptions in Revolutionary Virginia," in Ronald Hoffman, Mechal Sobel, and Fredrika Teute, eds., *Through a Glass Darkly: Reflections on Personal Identity in Early America* (Chapel Hill: UNCP for OIEAHC, 1997), 206–37.

I came into the field of American Revolution historiography much under the influence of R. R. Palmer, *The Age of the Democratic Revolution: A Political History of Europe and America, 1760–1800*, vol. I, *The Challenge* (Princeton: Princeton Univ. Press, 1959). I understood the American Revolution as the first great wave in a series of waves that changed forever the ways we view politics and society. Later, Jay Fliegelman, *Prodigals and Pilgrims: The American Revolution against Patriarchal Authority, 1750–1800* (Cambridge: CUP, 1982), introduced me to the interrelationship between the personal and the political in the unfolding of this revolutionary age. This important book also presents its subject matter in an Atlantic world perspective; it reviews the stories that colonial British Americans learned to tell themselves out of the literature of the day; and it showed how those stories must be related to the history we now tell of the coming of the American Revolution. Fliegelman's revelations merged with the insights I had already acquired from my early mentor, Gordon Wood, about the vitality of a gentlemen-dominated "old regime" in pre-Revolution America, see Gordon S. Wood, *The Radicalism of the American Revolution* (New York: Knopf, 1992). Long ago Winthrop D. Jordan, "Familial Politics: Thomas Paine and the Killing of the King," *Journal of American History* 60 (1973), 294–308, suggested there was a psychodrama little attended to in the historiography of the American Revolution. Finally, as I arrived at a fuller historical appreciation of the phases of the Landon Carter diary, I saw how distinctive were the diaries in the years after the Stamp Act rebellion—how they entered compulsively into repeated tellings of rebellions in the diarist's domestic kingdom. More recently Nancy Armstrong and Leonard Tennenhouse, *The Imaginary Puritan: Literature, Intellectual Labor, and the Origins of Personal Life* (Berkeley: Univ. of California Press, 1992), has greatly enhanced my understanding of the ways written stories of the self were reshaping consciousness and identity from the late seventeenth century onward. Although largely ignored by historians, this must be one of the most important books yet written on the mode of identity formation of the emergent bourgeoisie of the modern age, and so on the deep sources of the Atlantic Revolution—of which the American Revolution was the first wave to break.

In the long search for adequate readings of Landon Carter's plantation chronicles, the subject of diaries as such has inevitably fascinated me. The most inspiring historical treatment of a diary that I know of is Laurel Thacher Ulrich, *A Midwife's Tale: Martha Ballard from Her Diary, 1785–1812* (New York: Vintage, 1990); and yet I have not taken it as a model, since I see Landon's diary as a kind of unedited masterpiece, where Martha Ballard's journal was nearly all terse memorandums. The most instructive work I have found on great diaries is by a literary scholar: Robert A. Fothergill, *Private Chronicles: A Study of English Diaries* (New York: OUP, 1974). It demonstrates the way long-kept personal journals tend to become part of the author's very being—a "book of the self." The archetypal instance of this phenomenon has recently been the subject of a fine new biography by Claire Tomalin, whose *Samuel Pepys: The Unequalled Self* (New York: Viking, 2002), establishes a clear basis for the comparison with Landon Carter. Tomalin's Pepys, in contrast to Landon Carter, is a curiously detached observer of himself. His outlines of very urban days, enlivened with detail and arresting language, have proved immensely appealing to readers, perhaps because they are not shaped as "stories" and so match the one-thing-after-another quality of everyday life. Landon Carter's days, on the other hand, are profoundly rural, and for all his sense of scientific vocation, there is notoriously in the stories no self-observing detachment. There is, however, a historical symmetry between the Pepys diary, which began in the anxious time of the collapse of Cromwell's Commonwealth—the first English-speaking republic—and Landon's diary, which came fearfully to chronicle the American inauguration of the next such republic.

Just lately the subject of eighteenth-century diaries has been further illuminated by an author who has been an inspiration to me for most of the time I have been engaged in this project. See Patricia Meyer Spacks, *Privacy: Concealing the Eighteenth-Century Self* (Chicago: Univ. of Chicago Press, 2003), and her earlier *Imagining a Self: Autobiography and Novel in Eighteenth-Century England* (Cambridge: Harvard Univ. Press, 1976).

REFERENCING

The sources of quotations (unless indicated in the text itself) will be annotated by the page on which they fall. Extracts from the diary will be referenced by their date, since the original manuscript is the cardinal source; but readers can thereby trace them also in Jack P. Greene, ed., *The Diary of Colonel Landon Carter of Sabine Hall, 1752–1778* (2 vols., Charlottesville: UPVA for the Virginia Historical Society, 1965, reprinted 1987)—cited hereafter as Greene, ed., *Diary*. The original manuscript diary has been published in microfilm format: CFP, microfilm, reels 2 to 4. This collection, which contains many other papers associated with the diary, will be cited hereafter as "CFP, microfilm." The letters and other papers are in chronological order on reels 1 and 2. There is a convenient, though incomplete, review of the papers in Walter Ray Wineman, *The Carter Papers in the University of Virginia Library: A Calendar and Biographical Sketch* (Charlottesville: UPVA, 1962).

On occasion I have cited the manuscript diary of Robert Wormeley Carter in the Carter Family Papers, Library, College of William & Mary, Williamsburg, Va. The Rockefeller Library of the Colonial Williamsburg Foundation owns a typed transcript.

Note: I have given brief profiles of persons named when they first appear in the text of the book. The index to this book should enable those mini-biographies to be retrieved at subsequent mentions.

Annotation is supplied for each page (annotation and page number in **bold**). Quotations from Landon Carter's diary—hereafter LCD—will always be first; they are all from the original manuscripts and are indicated by the date of the entry only. A first-words tag is supplied for each quote for ready identification.

iii   **Great Seal:** On July 5, 1776, as the last act of the Fifth (and final) Convention, George Mason, speaking for "the Committee appointed to devise a proper seal for this commonwealth," secured the adoption of the design that had been agreed upon. See Brent Tarter et al., eds., *Revolutionary Virginia: The Road to Independence*, vol. 7 (Charlottesville: UPVA, 1983), 708–709. See also Edward S. Evans, *The Seals of Virginia* (Richmond: Virginia State Library, 1911).

First Words

The best biography of Landon, albeit brief, is in Greene, *Landon Carter*, 1–11; or Greene, ed., *Diary*, "Introduction." See also Rhys Isaac, "Landon Carter (1710–1778)," in *American National Biography*, John A. Garraty and Mark C. Carnes, eds. (New York: OUP, 1999), vol. 4, 491–492. With a few exceptions, the surviving Landon Carter diary notebooks are among the Sabine Hall Papers in the Alderman Library of the University of Virginia. The almanac diaries for 1764, 1766, and 1767 are, however, in the William S. Clements Library of the University of Michigan, Ann Arbor. On the Carter dynasty, see Greene, *Landon Carter*, 1–4.

PAGE NOTES

xv   *Virginia Almanack:* Two of the three Almanack diary volumes (for 1766 and 1767) are in the William L. Clements Library, University of Michigan, Ann Arbor. All the other originals of the diary are held in Special Collections, Alderman Library, University of Virginia, Charlottesville, Va.

xv   *these little books:* Sept. 18, 1775; June 23, 1770; July 28, 1777.

xvii   **12 wealthiest men:** For a ranking of Virginia property holdings, see Jackson Turner Main, "The One Hundred," WMQ 11 3 (Oct. 1954), 355–384.

xvii   **competing for his place:** For the birth order, see Florence Tyler Carlton, comp., *A Genealogy of the Known Descendants of Robert Carter of Corotoman* (Irvington, Va.: Foundation for Historic Christ Church, 1982), 2.

xviii   **Solomon Lowe:** This schoolmaster published enduring works on language, grammar, and composition in English and Latin.

xix   **my first book:** Rhys Isaac, *The Transformation of Virginia, 1740–1790* (Chapel Hill: UNCP, 1982; 2d ed. 1999).

xxii   **Latin writers:** See Leo M. Kaiser, "The Latin Attainments of Colonel Landon Carter of Sabine Hall," VMHB 85 1 (Jan. 1977), 51–54.

PART I: REVOLUTION IN HOUSE AND HOME
Chapter 1: Morning of Revolution

The most recent, comprehensive, and persuasive account of the political situation and the threats facing the Virginia leadership from many sides is Woody Holton, *Forced Founders: Indians, Debtors, Slaves, and the Making of the American Revolution in Virginia* (Chapel Hill: UNCP for OIEAHC, 1999). On the commencement and course of Lord Dunmore's campaign against the Virginia patriots, see ibid., 143–163. For a narrative history of this time and place, see John E. Selby, *The Revolution in Virginia, 1775–1783* (Charlottesville: UPVA, 1988). Dunmore's armed encampment just near the mouth of the Rappahannock River has been carefully documented and strongly narrated in Peter Jennings Wrike, *The Governor's Island: Gwynn's Island, Virginia, During the Revolution* (Gwynn, Va: Gwynn's Island Museum, 1993). The engagement of African Americans in the struggle was first comprehensively treated in Benjamin Quarles, *The Negro in the American Revolution* (Chapel Hill: UNCP, 1961); more recently the subject has been enlarged in Sylvia R. Frey, "Between Slavery and Freedom: Virginia Blacks in the American Revolution," *Journal of Southern History* XLIX (1983), 375–398; and, for all the colonies, in Sylvia R. Frey, *Water from the Rock: Black Resistance in a Revolutionary Age* (Princeton: Princeton Univ. Press, 1991). The entire historiography of this subject, led no doubt by an unconscious reluctance to acknowledge the British as liberators where the America patriots were enslavers, has told the story of this exodus as a futile flight to disease and death. Cassandra Pybus is currently completing research on the long journeys of some into the wider world and on the continuing struggles for freedom that begin with revolutionary departures from Virginia plantations.

PAGE NOTES

3   **Postillion Tom:** The departing eight will be profiled in chapter 2. Their names have here been silently corrected from "Postillion John" and "Tom, Panticove," as they appear in a manifestly mis-transcribed text. The original manuscript at this point is now missing, and the only surviving text of the diary for January 9–21, May 18–31, June 4–29, and July 3–26, is therefore Lyon G. Tyler's transcription, published in *William & Mary Quarterly*, 1st Ser., vol. 15 (1906–07), vol. 16 (1907–08), vol. 18 (1909–10), vol. 20 (1911–12), and vol. 21 (1912–13). This copy was modified and printed in Greene, ed., *Diary*, and I have taken the June–July 1776 quotations that appear in this book from the Greene edition, making essential corrections as necessary. For Landon's own careful listing of the Eight in his own hand, see July 10, 1777.

3   **my grandson Landon:** Landon Carter III (1757–1820) was the eldest son of Landon's eldest son, Robert Wormeley Carter, and Winifred Travers Beale Carter, his wife, hereafter RWC and WTBC. He was actually the fourth person known to have had this as a given name, since Landon I had a namesake younger son, and a brother, Charles, who also gave this name to his fourth son, Landon Carter of Cleve (1751–1811). Since the eighteenth century the English family name of Robert "King" Carter's second wife has proliferated in the South. Grandson Landon later married Catherine Griffin Tayloe (1761–1798), granddaughter of Landon's friend Colonel John Tayloe II of Mount Airy. They in turn had a son named Robert Wormeley Carter II (1792–1861) of Sabine Hall, and, since this bearer of that name left no male heir, the house and estate passed through his daughter, Elizabeth Landon Carter, into the Wellford family by way of her marriage to Dr. Armistead N. Wellford, whose heirs are still its proud owners. Carlton, *Descendants of Robert Carter*, 352, 372.

3   **Petty Auger:** Various forms of this word circulated in North America—Landon usually wrote "periauger," which is close to the Caribbean "perigua"—a large canoe or a flat-bottomed sailboat. See OED.

3   **Mr. Robinson:** Perhaps Maximilian Robinson (d. 1777), or William Robinson (d. 1777), both planters up-river from Sabine Hall in King George County, and sons of William Robinson (d. 1742). See Greene, ed., *Diary*, 1051.

4   *my Riverside field:* July, 11, 1770.

4   **My grandson George:** He was a younger son of RWC and WTBC. Landon secured him the name of his own deceased younger brother, George (d. 1741), who had left his siblings a considerable estate. Bearing the name, young George was then given an extra inheritance to go with it (see Aug. 12, 1774; Aug. 9, 1777). George was also, it seems, informally taken on as a gentleman apprentice plantation manager (see July 19, 1776; July 14, 1777; Aug. 18, 30, 1778). He married Sarah Carter, a descendant of Landon Carter's oldest half-brother, who established the Shirley Plantation, that is to this day a Carter estate on the James River (see Carlton, *Descendants of Robert Carter*, 372).

4   **Tom Parker:** A gentleman apprentice plantation manager at Sabine Hall, the son of Richard Parker, a lawyer and fighting friend of Landon (see below, chapter 10, and Greene, ed., *Diary*, 169).

4   **piazza:** April 25, 1770; Daybook, April 17, 1773; see also LCD July 2, 1772.

8   *Scheme for:* notes from 1775 in the "Daybook, 1772–1777," in CFP, microfilm, reel 3, hereafter cited as Daybook. (These notes, not locatable in the microfilm by date, have been reproduced in Greene, ed., *Diary*, 744–745; 785–790; 909–917; 953–963; 1067–1070; and 1135.)

9   *with ten stout men. . . . were killed.:* June 29, 1776; *we heard. . . . I don't know:* July 3, 1776; *hearing so many. . . . Stay home in.:* July 5, 1776.

9   **King and Queen:** This county was some twenty miles to the south of Sabine Hall on the York River side of Virginia's middle peninsula.

9   **Billy Beale:** A nephew of LC's third wife. For his family connection, see Frances Beal Smith Hodges, *The Genealogy of the Beale Family, 1399–1956* (Ann Arbor, Mich.: Edwards Brothers, 1956) 32, 34; and Greene, ed., *Diary*, 400.

10   *Much is said:* July 6, 1776; *so Just a cause:* Feb. 23, 1777; *Moses. . . . refused to give it up.:* July 9, 1776.

11   **Captain Berryman:** A member of the Lancaster County Battalion, later sheriff of Lancaster County. His death is recorded in 1787; see Greene, ed., *Diary*, 1055.

11   *Some returning runaways. . . . Could get off.; our Gloster county. . . . not born to.:* July 13, 1776.

11   **Guthrie:** Small traders such as he were comparatively unsettled persons; there is no record of his remaining in Richmond County for a will to be probated; see Robert K. Headley, Jr., *Wills of Richmond County, Virginia, 1699–1800* (Baltimore: Geneological Publishing, 1983), passim.

12   *illumination:* July 15, 1776; *told me last night:* July 16, 1776; *A strange dream:* July 25, 1776. Six dreams are recorded in the extant diary. In addition to this one, there was one about blighted crops (Jan. 30, 1771); one about Reuben Beale, his outrageous son-in-law (Sept. 11, 1773, see chapter 3); one about Judith, his daughter married to the son-in-law (Feb. 21, 1774, see chapter 3); one about *entertaining dead people* (Oct. 9, 1774); and another about runaways and a vengeful former overseer (Feb. 13, 1777).

12   **Judy:** Judith Carter Beale (1749–1836), Landon's youngest daughter, married Reuben Beale, 1773. She too had come to him in a dream, also as a delinquent craving forgiveness. That was recorded February 21, 1774 (see chapter 3). For birthdates, etc., see Carlton, *Descendants of Robert Carter*, 427.

13   *two of the slaves:* undated entries, "Daybook," 1776.

14   *old Will . . . terrify the rest.:* July 9, 1777; *I am glad:* July 10, 1777.

14   Old Will, Ben and Molly: There are three Wills and three Bens among the 74 Landon Carter slaves listed in Northumberland County, but no Molly—only a Milly. (See "An Inventory of the Estate of Landon Carter Esquire deceased taken February 1779," in CFP, microfilm, hereafter LC 1779 Inventory.)

Chapter 2: The Egypt of This Exodus

The most recent and comprehensive account of the enslaved population of Virginia—living and working conditions, culture and community—is to be found in Philip Morgan, *Slave Counterpoint: Black Culture in the Eighteenth-Century Chesapeake and Low Country* (Chapel Hill: UNCP for OIEAHC, 1998). Briefer and perhaps more available to general readers are Gerald W. Mullin, *Flight and Rebellion: Slave Resistance in Eighteenth-Century Virginia* (New York: OUP, 1972), and Isaac, *Transformation of Virginia*, 22–32, 80–87; or, very simply, Rhys Isaac, *Worlds of Experience: Communities in Colonial Virginia* (Williamsburg: Colonial Williamsburg Foundation, 1987). On the religion of the enslaved African Americans, the essential starting point is Albert Raboteau, *Slave Religion: The "Invisible Institution" in the Antebellum South* (New York: OUP, 1978); see also Lawrence Levine, *Black Culture and Black Consciousness: Afro-American Folk Thought from Slavery to Freedom* (New York: OUP, 1977). On the Revolution as religious ferment among the enslaved, see Sylvia Frey, *Water from the Rock: Black Resistance in a Revolutionary Age* (Princeton: Princeton Univ. Press, 1991); also Sylvia Frey and Betty Wood, *Come Shouting to Zion: African American Protestantism in the American South and British Caribbean to 1830* (Chapel Hill: UNCP, 1999). See also James Sidbury, *Plowshares into Swords: Race, Rebellion, and Identity in Gabriel's Virginia, 1730–1810* (Cambridge: CUP, 1997) a work to be celebrated for its constructive attempt to access revolutionary Virginia not as it was known to Thomas Jefferson but as it was shared by the associates of the enslaved rebel blacksmith Gabriel Prosser. A longer perspective is opened in Eddie S. Glaude, Jr., *Exodus!: Religion, Race, and Nation in Early Nineteenth-Century Black America* (Chicago: Univ. of Chicago Press, 2000).

PAGE NOTES

17   *Captain Moses*: July 13, 1776.

18   *going very fast*: June 26, 1776; ***1st, Mr. Moses*:** July 10, 1777; ***postilion ... graceless ... his Grace's Portmantua.*:** Jan. 14, 1764.

19   *his man*: Sept. 21, 1773; ***to their place*:** June 26, 1776; ***An inhuman. ... to Moses.*:** June 26, 1776; ***Captain*:** July 13, 1776; ***gang*:** June 29, 1776.

19   Winifred: Winifred Travers Beale was a daughter of William Beale of Chestnut Hill, Richmond County. She was the wife of Landon's eldest son, Robert Wormeley Carter. As a major protagonist in the dramas unfolded in the diary, she will be more fully introduced in chapters 3 and 11. (See Frances Beal Smith Hodges, *The Genealogy of the Beale Family, 1399–1956* [Ann Arbor, Mich.: Edwards Brothers, 1956] 38, 39.)

20   *howling*: July 13, 1776; ***that Moses*:** June, 29, 1776; ***2d Mr Manuel*:** July 10, 1777; ***plowing my Fork land*:** Nov. 12, 1756; ***I went*:** June 3, 1774; ***I saw Manuel*:** Aug. 21, 1770.

21   *I find that*: May 6,1766; ***Mr Manuel has. ... sell Mr. Manuel.*:** April 26, 1770; ***He was once. ... part with him*:** April 26, 1770.

21   1744; the record of the case: "Two Negro men slaves Names Ralph and Imanuell Belonging to Landon Carter Esq." were charged and convicted that "on the Fourth day of September in the night of the same day in the year of our Lord one thousand Seven hundred and Forty Seven with force and arms the Mansion House of the said Landon

Carter at the parish of Lunenburg . . . Felloniously and Burglariously did Break and Enter and two hundred and thirty three Ells of Dreheda Canvas . . . did Steal Take and Carry away against the peace of our Lord the King his Crown and Dignity." Peter Charles Hoffer et al., eds., *Criminal Proceedings in Colonial Virginia* (Athens: Univ. of Georgia Press, 1984), 236–238. Another form of the name—Manuell—is also used. Landon still had a slave carpenter named Ralph in 1757, so probably both these men were reprieved after being sentenced to be hanged. See LCD, June 5, 1757. Two Ralphs are listed in the LC 1779 Inventory.

22   *my long taken resolution:* July 7, 1770; *I thought. . . . in Manuel.:* July 12, 1770.

23   *the Oxtree:* Sept. 20, 1770; *No News:* Sept. 23, 1773; *cowkeeper . . . on his revells:* April 26, 1770.

23   **Manuel's Sarah:** She appears in the diary plantation record only as a persistent claimant of pregnancy privileges, who ran away to make her point. See LCD, March 22, 1770, and chapter 9 for more about Sarah and others who acted like her. There are two Sarahs among the persons listed in LC 1779 Inventory under the heading "In Richmond County—Negroes," but then there are also a Joe and two Peters, and a Manuel, who was probably a namesake—unless the old recalcitrant did come back by choice or coercion. (See LC 1779 Inventory.) There were still two adults of this name in a list made four years later. (See "Robert Wormeley Carter Taxable Property in Richmond County in March 1783," in CFP microfilm, hereafter RWC 1783 list.)

23   **Sicely:** She is only recorded in the diary for this one episode. A "Scicily" is listed in the LC 1779 Inventory. Sicely was gone from Sabine Hall by 1783, dead or sent away to one of RWC's younger siblings (see RWC 1783 list).

24   *3d Mr Pantico:* July 10, 1777; *laying off:* Feb. 18, 1770; *expressed great apprehensions:* Oct. 19, 1772; *the great Pox:* Feb. 4, 1777.

24   **Dr. Jones:** Walter Jones (1745–1815) was an active practitioner of medicine. He was on the Richmond County [Patriot] Committee designated to enforce the 1774 Non-Importation Association in the precinct of Naylorshole (RWC Diary, September 22, 1774). With Robert Wormeley Carter he represented Richmond County at the December 1775 Virginia Convention (William G. Stanard and Mary Newton Stanard, *The Colonial Virginia Register* [Baltimore: Genealogical Publishing, 1965, orig. 1902], 205). Dr. Jones participated keenly in intellectual and political debates (see LCD, May 26, 1772, May 23, 1776, and chapters 10 and 12). A native of Virginia, he graduated from Edinburgh University in 1769 and commenced practice in Richmond County the next year. See Elizabeth Ryland ed., *Richmond County, Virginia: a review commemorating the Bicentennial* (Warsaw, Va.: Richmond County, 1976), 197.

25   *the wench Nelly. . . . the worst.:* April 5, 1770; *be done:* May 20, 1772; *Last night. . . . when she is well.:* Oct. 5, 1774.

25   **Nelly:** She was a strong fieldworker, see LCD, May 20, 1772; but, as shown in this chapter, it was as a fiercely protective mother of her sick children and as a wayward, sexually charged woman that she most featured in the diary; see LCD, Oct. 5, 1774. A "Nell" is listed in the LC 1779 Inventory; but she was not there four years later (see RWC 1783 list).

26   *She is a jade:* Oct. 5, 1774; *4th Mr Peter:* July 10, 1777; *Black Peter:* Aug. 4, 1774; *Peter the plowman:* July 8, 1771; *a night Walker:* July 8, 1771; *catched Mulatto Peter:* July 25, 1775.

26   **Black Peter:** Only appears once in the diary under this name, when he was accused of disposing of stolen goods in a complex episode of the kind that typically brought slaves attention in the diary; see LCD, Aug. 4, 1774, and chapter 9. Two Peters are listed in the LC 1779 Inventory, but only one four years later (see RWC 1783 list).

26   **Gardener Johnny:** An older African American patriarch on the plantation. He is profiled in chapter 9. Two Johnnys—probably father and son—are listed together in the LC Inventory. There were still two of this name in a list four years later (see RWC 1783 list).

27   *Mulatto Peter has. . . . all to no purpose.*: January 24, 1770; *The evening before. . . . to satisfye that.*: Jan. 24, 1770.

27   *delivation*: Clearly written as such in the manuscript. I can find it in no dictionary, but since Landon was aiming to draw blood from upper to lower body, he probably meant either the opposite of elevation, or else deliveration (delivery).

27   **Dr. Mortimer:** Charles Mortimer was much employed by Landon. He was a successful physician and married well (into the prominent Peachey family). He later moved to Fredericksburg, where he became mayor. See Gwenda Morgan, *The Hegemony of the Law: Richmond County, 1692–1776* (New York: Garland, 1989), 61; and Greene, ed., *Diary*, 244.

27   **Dr. Fauntleroy:** George Fauntleroy (d. 1770); see Robert K. Headley, Jr., *Wills of Richmond County, Virginia, 1699–1800* (Baltimore: Genealogical Publishing Co., 1983), 137. Landon hoped to buy some of his medicines when his estate was put up for sale; see Greene, ed., *Diary*, 348, 504.

28   *Peter & two horses*: May 15, 1772; *Manuel and Peter*: Sept. 5, 1772; *Because there had been*: Sept. 5, 1772; *5th Mr Joe*: July 10, 1777; *maid*: April 8, 1758.

28   **Winney:** Mother of freedom-seeking Joe, and wife to his father, Joe Sr., she is much in the diary since she had been an attendant and nursemaid and perhaps wetnurse to the diarist's younger daughters, and then also to his grandchildren. Like so many in this diary, she is recorded when sick or deemed delinquent. Landon noted that he sent for a doctor to attend her, *as she was useful (though careless) among my children* (April 10, 1758). She was mother to children of her own, but we only know about that through their reported sicknesses and deaths; see LCD, April 17, 1758; Nov. 24, 1770. She also acted as a nurse to sick persons, including the enslaved (Feb. 9, 1772). Two Winneys are listed—widely spaced—in the LC 1779 Inventory. There was only one among the adults listed four years later (see RWC 1783 list).

29   *little Abraham*: Sept. 3, 1773; *This day*: April 17, 1776; *Ironed in them. . . . behind the Kitching.*: Aug. 4, 1774; *great passage. . . . and her son, Joe.*: Daybook, April 17, 1773.

29   **Abraham:** A younger child of Winney's, he was in training as a house attendant (Sept. 3, 1773). He was at least once enlisted to give testimony to protect his brother Joe, for which he was whipped (Aug. 4, 1774). An Abram is listed in the LC 1779 Inventory; and again in RWC 1783 list.

29   **Tom Beale:** Probably a son of Thomas Beale, the son of old Captain William Beale of Chestnut Hill, and so oldest brother of Winifred and Reuben, Landon's daughter-in-law and son-in-law. Thus, he was a cousin to Billy Beale, the gentleman apprentice whom we have already met. Thomas Beale, the father, represented Pantico precinct on the county Non-Importation Committee (RWC Diary, September 22, 1774).

30   *I laid aside. . . . liquid laudanum*: Daybook, April 17, 1773. See also LC to Mr. David

Jameson, Secretary to the Society for Propagating Useful Knowledge, *Virginia Gazette* (Rind), April 14, 1774.

30   *paragoric. . . . I then indulged:* Daybook, April 17, 1773.

30   **Betty:** Usually named as "Mulatto Betty," she was or had been, wife to Nassaw—at least, Nat the coachman is said in Landon Carter's will to be her son; elsewhere he is identified as Nassaw's son. Betty lived at Sabine Hall long enough to be assigned a role something like that of the "Black Mammy" of the antebellum era. Landon was always most attentive to her in illnesses: *She is a nice Lady and only wanted to be made much of.* In his impatient way, Landon was indulgent of her refusals to follow his medical directions (Sept. 14, 1775; March 5, 1776). Later we find the diarist worrying over her aged frailty and arranging for her to be *walked out* in his carriage to get air (March 3, 1776). She was for long a responsible housekeeper, tending to supplies, etc. (Sept. 8, 1767; Feb. 13, 1770; April 25, 1777). It is sadly in character for the diarist and his relationship to those he loved that his last surviving reference to her was of an alleged failure in this role: *Betty is a fool*; she had for some time given over weighing incoming supplies, as she should have (Aug. 5, 1778). But she was not cursed out; she and her son were endowed, in a last codicil to Landon Carter's will, with a pension of £10 per annum, and the right to choose each year with which of Landon's offspring they would live for the ensuing year (Will of Landon Carter). For these family provisions in the will, see also chapter 14. Three Bettys are listed, widely separated, in the LC Inventory; and again in a list from four years later (see RWC 1783 list). Betty lived until Feb. 28, 1790, when Robert Wormeley wrote a kind of obituary in his account-book diary. Like his father, he mixed pathos and medical report: "This morning I was informed poor old Betty, the washer woman was dead. Death was a great relief to her, one of her feet had rotted, and her leg rendered quite useless." (RWC diary, Carter Family Papers, Library of College of William & Mary, Williamsburg, Va.).

30   **Nassaw:** He was Landon's close attendant, both valet and surgeon-assistant in the medical practice that was so cherished a part of the diarist's identity. Landon had a troubled, emotionally intense relationship with this man, who was probably about his son's age. We shall meet Nassaw often in tracing the history discoverable in the Sabine Hall diaries; the special relationship, which became tormented in later years, is the subject of chapter 13.

31   *Clyster on Clysters; Reader, whoever thou art. . . .:* Daybook, April 17, 1773; *6th Mr Sam:* July 10, 1777.

32   *7th Mr Tom:* July 10, 1777; *Mr Tom in irons:* March 12, 1771; *was a rogue:* July 12, 1770.

32   **Lancaster County Court:** *Virginia Gazette* (Dixon & Hunter), Jan. 6, 1776.

33   *unwilling:* March 12, 1771; *too impudent:* April 7, 1771; *most wretchedly meager:* July 25, 1776; *8 Mr Billy:* July 10, 1777.

33   **Will:** Manuel's brother must have spent his long years as a slave working for Landon at outlying quarters downriver from Sabine Hall, since this passage, with its vindictive conclusion, is the only mention of him in the diary. Three Wills are listed, widely separated, in the LC 1779 Inventory, under the heading "Northumberland County." There is a Manuel listed in first place; so dynastic naming may have been well established there. We cannot know whether Will, the contriver of escapes, was indeed sent to Carolina.

34   *that I have no:* July 10, 1777; *with conduct like this:* March 9, 1770.

35   **"Imanuell":** See Hoffer, *Criminal Proceedings*, 237.

35   **For cases clearly linking the Revolution to biblical promises:** Frey, *Water from the Rock*, 62.

Chapter 3: "All for Love"

Jay Fliegelman's *Prodigals and Pilgrims: The American Revolution Against Patriarchal Authority, 1750–1800* (Cambridge: CUP, 1982), is the best introduction to the underlying relationship between changing ideas of familial authority and those concerning the government of the state. Making full reference to Samuel Richardson's very successful novels (especially *Clarissa*, published in London in 1748), he shows how large in imagination loomed the issue of fathers and their daughters' marriages. My understanding of these issues has also been assisted by Terry Eagleton, *The Rape of Clarissa: Writing, Sexuality and Class Struggle in Samuel Richardson* (Minneapolis: Univ. of Minnesota Press, 1982); Patricia M. Spacks, *Desire and Truth: Functions of Plot in Eighteenth-Century English Novels* (Chicago: Univ. of Chicago Press, 1990); Lisa A. Freeman, *Character's Theater: Genre and Identity on the Eighteenth-Century English Stage* (Philadelphia: Univ. of Pennsylvania Press, 2002); and Julie Ellison, *Cato's Tears and the Meaning of Anglo-American Emotion* (Chicago: Univ. of Chicago Press, 1999). It has not been usual to discuss novels under the heading of "the consumer revolution," but I am here suggesting that these commodities, the stories they contained, and the intense identifications that they invited of persons with fictional characters were among the most potent products of this new commercial capitalism. For a brief and witty account of the consumer revolution by one of the historians who first identified the phenomenon, see Cary Carson, "Consumption," in Daniel Vickers, ed., *A Companion to Colonial America* (Oxford: Blackwells, 2003), 334–365. For an earlier treatment of the subject of Virginia patriarchs and the marriages of their daughters, see Kathleen M. Brown, *Good Wives, Nasty Wenches, and Anxious Patriarchs: Gender, Race, and Power in Colonial Virginia* (Chapel Hill: UNCP, 1996), especially pages 344–346, where Landon's impulse to control his offsprings' marriages is compared to similar ones of earlier generations of stern parents including Landon's own father, Robert "King" Carter.

PAGE NOTES

37   *I see in her:* June 27, 1766.

37   **Nat:** He was the enslaved coachman son of Nassaw and Mulatto Betty. Nat was an important figure in the household. He had care of the fine carriage and riding horses, which he could issue to the young gentlemen apprentices (May 28, 1772; Sept. 21, 1773; June 3, 1773). He was a go-between who might be engaged in locating wandering daughters, or gathering news of the volatile politics of the revolutionary crisis. His special reward under Landon's will is explicable: of all the often-mentioned slaves he was the least blamed—drunk twice, and lazy once—in some forty references. There was one of his name in the LC 1779 Inventory, but none among the adults at Sabine Hall four years later. He had died, or, more probably, exercised his option to live with one of Landon's offspring elsewhere (see RWC 1783 list).

37   **Pittsylvania:** Then a comparatively new county in Virginia's southwest; Landon Carter thought it was wilderness, with no genteel inhabitants. In 1768 it had been named (as is Pittsburgh) for William Pitt, the national hero of the British and American struggle against France (see chapter 7). Its nearest points were at least 150 miles from Sabine Hall.

37   **Reuben Beale:** (1751–1802) was brother to Winifred, wife of Landon's eldest son, Robert Wormeley Carter. He was a younger son of William Beale of Chestnut Hill, Rich-

mond County, the seat of the elder line of a long-settled upper-class gentry line. (See Frances Beale Smith Hodges, *The Genealogy of the Beale Family, 1399–1956* [Ann Arbor, Mich.: Edwards Brothers, 1956], 38, 39; and Florence Tyler Carlton, comp., *A Genealogy of the Known Descendants of Robert Carter of Corotoman* [Irvington, Va.: Foundation for Historic Christ Church, 1982], 2). See also diagram above on p. xxiii.

37   **Elizabeth Beale:** She married Landon Carter in 1746; her exact date of death in the mid-1750s (before the plantation diary commences in 1756) has not been determined. She bore three daughters: Susannah (d. 1758), Lucy, and Judith. See Hodges, *Beale Family*, 32, 33, 34; and Carlton, *Descendants of Robert Carter*, 2, 372.

38   *would have murdered me:* May 8, 1774.

39   *only Claiming a right:* Aug. 30–31, 1772; *Those who never:* Feb. 19, 1774; *the wound:* Oct. 13, 1774; *the cause:* Feb. 19, 1774.

39   **Captain Beale:** William Beale of Chestnut Hill, Richmond county (1710–1778), was brother to Landon's third wife, Elizabeth, and father to Winifred and Reuben. See above, and Hodges, *Beale Family*, 37–38. In 1822 the last Beale in possession of Chestnut Hill died without a male heir, and the family name no longer features so prominently in the county. Through marriages of old Captain Beale's siblings and his offspring, many of Landon's most eminent neighbors also had connections to this clan. See Elizabeth Ryland ed., *Richmond County, Virginia: a review commemorating the Bicentennial* (Warsaw, Va.: Richmond County, 1976), 86–90.

40   *I dreamed last night:* Feb. 20, 1774.

40   **Francis Lee:** Francis Lightfoot Lee (1734–1797) was a son of Thomas Lee of Stratford, Westmoreland County (1690–1750). He was one of the formidable brood of Lee brothers (including Richard Henry, William, and Arthur) who made their mark on Revolutionary Virginia and America. Francis was a delegate to the Continental Congress and a signer of the Declaration of Independence. From 1769—the time of his marriage to Rebecca Tayloe—the couple lived in Richmond County on the Menokin estate, where they built a handsome mansion house that is currently under careful conservation (Ryland, ed., *Richmond County*, 86–90, 104–108). Assisted by the influence of his father-in-law, Colonel John Tayloe II, builder of Mount Airy, Francis Lee was able immediately to secure election as a burgess for the county. (His partner at the poll was Robert Wormeley Carter.)

41   *I do suppose. . . . courage had not failed him.:* May 8, 1774; *I answered her:* May 16, 1774.

41   **Williamson Ball:** Mr. Ball was a judge on the Richmond County bench and represented Lunenburg Parish on the county Committee to enforce the Non-importation Association, positions also held by Landon (RWC Diary, Sept. 22, 1774). He too was an in-law to the Beales and would soon also be in dispute with them. In November 1778, just five weeks before he died, Landon signed a statement supporting Ball's claim against the estate of old Captain William Beale, lately deceased, for the dowry of Anne Beale Ball (by then deceased also); it had been promised at the time of his marriage. (Robert Wormeley Carter was one of the defendants, in respect of his own wife's entitlements under her father's will.) The suit dragged on; eventually it was terminated by the death of Williamson Ball in 1793 (Hodges, *Beale Family*, 39). Ball's Creek (formerly Williamson's Creek) seems to be the main vestige of this family's time as important property owners in the county (Ryland, ed., *Richmond County*, 34).

42   **Genre painter:** The most apposite examples for the purpose of this story are Francis Hayman's fine set of scenes for Richardson's novel, *Pamela*. From across the English Channel, one might cite Jean-Baptiste Greuze.

42   **Solids:** By an update of the ancient humoral theory of health and sickness, attention was now paid to the ducts, the "solid" vessels whose condition promoted or obstructed the flow of the blood (see chapter 6).

42   *Tristam Shandy:* An anonymous polemic against the Stamp Act was unquestionably by Landon; it invokes the witty and sentimental novelist in a concluding paragraph. See *Maryland Gazette*, May 8, 1766. There was a horse at Sabine Hall named for the character Corporal Trim in Sterne's *The Life and Opinions of Tristram Shandy, Gentleman*, first published in London in parts between 1759 and 1762. This book, now thought of as a comic classic, was in its time also a handbook of sentiment.

42   **Patriarchal regime:** On the husband's ownership of property due to their wives, see Marylynn Salmon, *Women and the Law of Property in Early America* (Chapel Hill: UNCP, 1986).

43   **Sally:** Old Captain William Beale had a younger daughter named Sarah (familiar form: Sally), later Mrs. James Evans (Hodges, *Beale Family*, 39).

43   **"All for Love":** In this play by Dryden, the emperor Mark Anthony forsakes his civic and familial duties to indulge his amorous passion for Cleopatra. We shall later find Landon contrasting himself with that corrupt Roman emperor.

44   *She made no reply:* June 15, 1774.

44   **The uncouth Germans:** This reference is obscure. Tacitus's history—which Landon read—holds up the Germans as a positive example compared to the decadent Romans. The ancient historian Cornelius Tacitus (c. 55 BCE–c.117 CE) fascinated the American patriots because he wrote such lurid accounts of political corruption and the failure of a state once dedicated to liberty.

44   **"The Wedding Day":** a poem in Aaron Hill, *Collected Works* (London, 1753), 3: 175. Landon's copy of this book is in Landon's library (LLC).

45   *On Tuesday:* Oct. 6, 1774; *which I minute:* Sept. 3, 1774; *let those:* Sept. 18, 1775.

45   **Namesake grandson:** Landon Carter III, son of Robert Wormeley Carter and Winifred Beale Carter.

45   **Had to cope with furor in the county:** Aug. 12–13, 1777. For other evidence that the diary was an open document usually left out to be read, see the note about the visit of an impertinent young kinsman, whose comments would not be welcome: *Many sensible observations would have been made, but we have had rather too much Curiosity to visit here, and therefore this* monthly *book has been removed from view the whole time* (March 28, 1776). The young gentleman was Harrison Randolph, son of William Randolph (1719–1762) and Ann Harrison. Landon's oldest full sister, Ann (d. c. 1743), had married Benjamin Harrison IV, of Berkeley Plantation on the James River. (See Greene, ed., *Diary*, 988; and Carlton, *Descendants of Robert Carter*, 2.)

46   *A second letter. . . . flatulency:* Oct 13, 1774.

46   **Weakness in solids:** See note on p. xxx.

46   **consumer revolution:** See Carson, "Consumption," in Daniel Vickers, ed., *A Companion to Colonial America* (Oxford: Blackwells, 2003), 334–365.

47   *right to dispose:* Aug. 30–31, 1772.

47   **characteristically young women:** This important topic was opened up for me—and will

be for readers who follow up on it—by Jay Fliegelman's milestone book, *Prodigals and Pilgrims*, and more recently by Nancy Armstrong and Leonard Tennenhouse, in *The Imaginary Puritan: Literature, Intellectual Labor, and the Origins of Personal Life* (Berkeley: Univ. of California Press, 1992).

47   **"Father George":** For a bitter satire in which Landon explicitly gave this name to the king, see, William Dennes (?) to The Revd. Mr. Giberne, n.d., in "CFP, microfilm." Landon wrote the satire as an endorsement on the letter, which remained among his papers. It is fully discussed in chapters 9 and 10.

47   **Laurence Sterne:** See above for reference to Sterne's *Tristram Shandy*, that great source of sentimental education (as well as whimsical mirth) to Landon's age. On Jefferson's delight in Sterne, see Rhys Isaac, "The First Monticello," in Peter S. Onuf, ed., *Jeffersonian Legacies* (Charlottesville: UPVA, 1993), 82, 101–102. Landon recorded a "dispute" with Henry Fielding, who was not sufficiently pious in his moral essay "Of the Remedy for Affliction for the Loss of Our Friends," in *The Works of Henry Fielding . . . in Four Volumes* (London: 1762), see LCD, July 15, 1771. A collected edition remains in Landon's library.

48   *drunken Nassaw. . . . save one soul more Alive.*: Sept. 11, 1775.

49   *Yesterday I walked up. . . . if possible*: ibid.

50   *Thus my God*: ibid.

51   *I could not but*: ibid; *Yesterday my daughter*: Sept. 13, 1775; *This evening. . . . I take to be acidity*: Sept. 27, 1775; *really drunk. . . . I administered to him*: Sept. 28, 1775.

52   *discovered how. . . . easily draw.*: Jan. 9, 1775. See Greene, ed., *Diary*, 965–966.

52   **Lucy:** Born in 1748, she had been betrothed (or at least spoken for by one of the Fitzhugh brothers) in 1769 and had—perhaps in the aftermath of disappointment—proposed to go on a jaunt to Philadelphia. See Robert Beverley to LC, Dec. 30, 1769, Sept. 24, 1770, in "CFP, microfilm" We do not know if Landon refused the young Fitzhugh as he had the young Beale as a partner for Judith. (I am indebted to Cathleene Hellier of Colonial Williamsburg for drawing this episode to my attention.) In 1775 Lucy did marry William Colston. They had a son, William Travers, and two daughters, Susannah and Elizabeth (Florence Tyler Carlton, *A Genealogy of the Known Descendants of Robert Carter of Corotoman* [Irvington, Va.: Foundation for Historic Christ Church, 1982] 2). Will of William Colston: Robert K. Headley, Jr., *Wills of Richmond County, Virginia, 1699–1800* (Baltimore: Genealogical Publishing Co., 1983), 155.

52   **Blane . . . Hamilton store:** in Westmoreland County, on the Potomac, run by Scots factors (agents) for the Glasgow merchant, John Ballentine. See *Virginia Gazette* (Purdie & Dixon), Sept. 23, 1773. Such stores had become very important exchange points in the Virginia export-import trade (see Isaac, *Transformation of Virginia*, 137).

52   **William Colston:** (1744–1781?) of Richmond County (Carlton, *Descendants of Robert Carter*, 427). The Colstons were among the first gentry settlers of Richmond County. They were intermarried with the Hornby family and in 1750 Hornby Manor was left for young William Colston when he came of age, subject to the entail provision that concerned Landon Carter (Ryland, ed., *Richmond County*, 97). Colston's will was probated May 1, 1781, with RWC as executor; see Headley, *Wills*, 99, 155.

52   **Settlement:** The legal system whereby a married woman's property was wholly at the disposal of her husband could be counteracted by concerned fathers and others if they

arranged a "settlement" in a legal document that reserved rights to her, and very often to her children. It was usually her dowry that was so protected.

53   *The gift. . . . easily draw*: Jan. 9 [7?], 1775; *little boy*: April 13, 1777; *My daughter*: April 17, 1777.

54   *Mr. Reuben Beale*: Aug. 11, 1778; *My daughter Beale*: Aug. 21, 1778; *it was sending*: Aug. 21, 1778.

54   **"Item. . . .":** Quotation from codicil to Landon's will, probated in Richmond County, February 1, 1779. Conveniently abstracted in Headley, *Wills*, 151–152.

PART II: ENLIGHTENMENT CALM

It is usual to refer to the Enlightenment as a French phenomenon, which it was in its mid-eighteenth-century, aggressively anticlerical phase; but, like their famous Revolution the French moment had its origins in the English-speaking world. The advent of the Enlightenment in France may be dated to Voltaire's return in 1729 from his three-year exile in England with a zeal to publicize the works of Newton and Locke. My thinking on this subject was long ago directed by Alfred Cobban, *In Search of Humanity: The Rise of Enlightenment in Modern History* (London: Jonathan Cape, 1960). The English Enlightenment is currently being profoundly reassessed in a many-volume work: J.G.A. Pocock, *Barbarism And Religion*, vol. I, *The Enlightenment of Edward Gibbon, 1737–1764* (Cambridge: CUP, 1999). For the Enlightenment on the western side of the Atlantic, the best brief background account is Henry F. May, *The Enlightenment in America* (New York: OUP, 1976). Regrettably the author's northern bias results in small coverage of the Anglican South. Landon Carter's diaries may be the most comprehensive day-by-day record anywhere of a life lived according to what May identified as the "moderate Enlightenment," but they received no mention in the book. The most delightful reading on eighteenth-century American gentlemen's engagement in fashionable science (or "philosophy" as it was called) is Garry Wills, *Inventing America: Jefferson's Declaration of Independence* (Garden City, N.Y.: Doubleday, 1978) recommended also for its insights into mid-eighteenth-century sensibilities.

The eighteenth-century obsession with measurement is wonderfully illuminated in Greg Dening, *Mr. Bligh's Bad Language: Passion, Power and Theatre on the Bounty* (New York: CUP, 1992), especially 133–140. My own attempts to situate Landon in broader intellectual traditions have been published in two essays with more detail than this comprehensive reading of the diary can accommodate: Rhys Isaac, "Communication and Control: Authority Metaphors and Power Contests on Colonel Landon Carter's Virginia Plantation, 1752–1778," in Sean Wilentz, ed., *Rites of Power: Symbolism, Ritual, and Politics Since the Middle Ages* (Philadelphia: Univ. of Pennsylvania Press, 1985, repr. 1999), 275–302; and Rhys Isaac, "Imagination and Material Culture: The Enlightenment on a Mid-18th-Century Virginia Plantation," in Anne Elizabeth Yentsch and Mary C. Beaudry, eds., *The Art and Mystery of Historical Archaeology: Essays in Honor of James Deetz* (Boca Raton, Fla.: CRC Press, 1992), 401–423.

Chapter 4: Plantation Pastoral

I have read extensively in the primary and secondary literature of eighteenth-century agriculture. Landon commenced his diary just as the English landed aristocracy's long engagement in improving agriculture was going into crescendo. He had clearly read Jethro Tull's celebration of the "pulverization" of the soil (through repeated deep cultivation), and he manifestly drew his terminology and sense of expertise from seminal studies of plant physiology and "English husbandry" that he acquired and studied in the 1730s, as he started to develop his estate in Richmond County. See Jethro Tull, *Horse-hoeing Husbandry, or, An Essay on the Principles of Vegetation and Tillage*, 3d. ed. (London: 1751). All this was modern practice against an esteemed background of the writings of such revered ancients as Virgil, whose celebrations of work on the land the diarist could quote from memory (June 6, 1773; Feb. 2, June 25, July 25, 1776). The diary does not show Landon much engaged in scientific agricultural discussions with his neighbors, although there are repeated mentions of his proudly showing off the quality of dunged fields and the resulting crops. Sometimes there was implied debate with others over sound practice; perhaps this dialog aimed to refute the criticisms of more persons than just his hypercritical son, Robert Wormeley Carter. Especially relevant is the defensive little discourse on "my method of introducing the English husbandry," July, 28, 1757. See also Timothy H. Breen, *Tobacco Culture: The Mentality of the Great Tidewater Planters on the Eve of Revolution* (Princeton: Princeton Univ. Press, 1985).

The secondary work that I have found most useful to prepare my reading of Landon's agricultural diary is: Joan Thirsk, ed., *Chapters from the Agrarian History of England and Wales, 1500–1750* (New York: CUP, 1990). I was greatly helped through access kindly granted to an unpublished portion of the draft for Roger D. Abrahams, *Singing the Master: The Emergence of African American Culture in the Plantation South* (New York: Pantheon, 1992); in it he explored the Georgic tradition and changing ways for educated English speakers on both sides of the Atlantic to experience the working countryside. I have been instructed on the historic forms of landscape perception also by John Barrell, *The Idea of Landscape and the Sense of Place* (Cambridge: CUP, 1972), and by his *The Dark Side of the Landscape: The Rural Poor in English painting 1730–1840* (Cambridge: CUP, 1980). See also Joan Thirsk, ed., *The English Rural Landscape* (Oxford: OUP, 2000).

I have felt that I must treat the Landon of his agricultural days as though he were a landscape painter. I then found that he depicted an old-world more than a new-world exotic rural scene. To better grasp what is involved here, readers can look at a powerful diary depiction of an exotically "other" landscape: Douglas Hall, *In Miserable Slavery: Thomas Thistlewood in Jamaica, 1750–86* (London: Macmillan, 1989). This record of the daily life of the manager of a Jamaica plantation is replete with exotica: a mansion house fortified against attacks by maroons (descendants of fugitive slaves), encounters with extravagantly dressed maroon chiefs, and the sense of the profoundly African life and culture of the slave laborers among whom the diarist lived. For a direct comparison of the styles of dominance of Carter and Thistlewood (with a South Carolina slave owner included as middle term), see Philip Morgan, "Three Planters and Their Slaves: Perspectives on Slavery in Virginia, South Carolina, and Jamaica, 1750–1790," in Winthrop D. Jordan and Sheila L. Skemp, eds., *Race and Family in the Colonial South* (Jackson, Miss.: Univ. Press of Mississippi, 1987), 37–80. On the extravagant otherness of mid-eighteenth-century Jamaica, see Kathleen Wilson, *The Island Race: Englishness, Empire and Gender in the Eighteenth Century* (London: Routledge, 2003), 146–168. A gradient of exoticness as perceived by a mid-century British geographer of the Empire can be followed in the characterizations of colonies from New England southward through Virginia to Barbados and Jamaica in [John Oldmixon], *The British Empire in America* (New York: A.M. Kelley, 1969, orig. 1741).

PAGE NOTES

57   *Rain yesterday:* Jan. 31, 1757.

57   **Georgics:** This is now understood as an important classical model for the eighteenth-century protobourgeois concern with "the civilizing capacity of labor, the vindication of empire, [and] an ideal of progress": see April London, *Women and Property in the Eighteenth-Century Novel* (Cambridge: CUP, 1999), 5.

57   **Horace:** He was a satirist as well as a great lyricist. I have found satisfying the translations in *The Esssential Horace: Odes, Epodes, Satires, and Epistles*, Burton Raffel, trans. (San Francisco: North Point Press, 1983).

58   **"hall":** see John E. Crowley, *The History of Comfort: Sensibility and Design in Early Modern Britain and Early America* (Baltimore: Johns Hopkins Univ. Press, 2001), 8–14.

58   **Virginia estate houses:** Landon had at least three "halls"—Sabine, Bull, and Rippon; his brother Robert had a Nomini Hall; and Squire Richard Lee of Westmoreland County had Lee Hall. See Moncure D. Conway, *Barons of the Patomack and the Rappahannock* (New York: Grolier Club, 1892).

58   **William Byrd II:** The quotation is from William Byrd II to Charles, Earl of Orrery, July 5, 1726, in Marion Tinling, ed., *The Correspondence of the Three William Byrds, of Westover, Virginia* (Charlottesville: UPVA, 1977), 1:355.

59   *my people:* Aug. 8, 1757; *my out & in doors family:* Aug. 25, 1757.

59   **The number . . . between 40 and 50:** This estimate is based on Landon's work allocations. In 1773 the number was recorded; it had grown to 69 slaves over 16 years of age. See "Tithables belonging to Landon Carter in Lunenburg Parish in Richmond County, June 10, 1773," in Carter Family Papers microfilm. (Tithable slaves were those of both sexes over the age of 16, but only white males over 16 were counted for the poll tax—based on a convention that blacks of both sexes raised tobacco, while only white males, supposedly, were in the fields.) See LC 1779 Inventory.

60   **401 slaves:** see LC 1779 Inventory.

61   *We are still turning:* March 5, 1757; *Began this day. . . . Joe's illness:* April 14, 1758; *4 last:* Jan. 18, 1758.

61   **Farming in the English manner:** see LCD, July 28, 1757.

61   **Joe:** Surely Joe, the husband of Winney, and father of the young Joe who was one of the Eight, see chapter 2. Perhaps this handler of draft animals succumbed to that illness, or to a later one, for he was gone from the diary record by 1763.

62   *I can see no prospects:* April 5, 1758; *let the rains:* April 28, 1758; *Very cold:* April 30, 1758.

63   *Mole destroying. . . . grain well down.:* May 3, 10, 1758.

63   **Two-Penny Act:** Tobacco was money in Virginia. Taxes were paid in it, and contract payments were expressed as so many pounds of tobacco. By compelling cash payments in lieu of tobacco, the act was interfering in such contracts in a way that the U.S. Supreme Court would certainly now disallow; the government in London saw it the same way. Landon, however, showed his prowess as an author in a satiric pamphlet defending the act and the Assembly that had passed it. For this complex dispute, see Rhys Isaac, "Religion and Authority: Problems of the Anglican Establishment in Virginia in the Era of the Great Awakening and the Parson's Cause," *William & Mary Quarterly*, 3d ser., 30, no. 1 (Jan. 1973), 3–36.

64   *I began:* May 10, 1758; *that it:* March 3, 1758; *cockling:* March 25, 1758; *My wheat:* April 10, 1758; *ears:* May 27, 1758; *overdone . . . were done before this.:* March 3, 1758; *owing to:* March 20, 1758; *very Cold:* April 18, 1758.

64   **rust. . . . fly weevil:** see May 27, 1758; April 22, 1758.

65   *had begun to lay by:* July 14, 1757; *abundance:* July 18, 1757; ***Thus the Farmer:*** June 29, 1757; ***The poor Farmer:*** July 7, 1757; *Am I always:* July 24, 1757; *The first:* Aug. 8, 1757; *Rain all day:* Aug. 12, 1757; *but very few:* June 30, 1757.

66   *yesterday's Sun:* Aug. 29, 1757.

66   **Tatham:** Quotations from William Tatham, *An Historical and Practical Essay on the Culture and Commerce of Tobacco* (London, 1800), facsimile reprint included in G. Melvin Herndon, *William Tatham and the Culture of Tobacco* (Coral Gables, Fla.: Univ. of Miami Press, 1969), 24–25.

66   **Jefferson:** Quotations from Julian P. Boyd, ed., *The Papers of Thomas Jefferson*, vol. 7 (Princeton: Princeton Univ. Press, 1953), 210.

67   *Yesterday's cutting:* Sept. 19, 1770; *tobacco stick:* July 10, 1777.

67   **Mangorike Will:** He was a strong worker. When he fell ill soon after his first appearance in the diary, Landon wrote: *I can't tell what to think as he is a most principal hand* (June 16, 1766). But six years later, Will's claimed sickness was said to have been cured by a whipping—*got clear by a revulsion to his back* (Oct. 19, 1772). The last appearance in the diary is typical of Landon vis-à-vis slaves he must empower. A very unsatisfactory overseer is to be driven off from his quarter, *and Mangorike Will placed there to take care of everything. But perhaps he may turn a rogue* (Aug. 5, 1778). Will's first appearance in the diary was as the captor of Simon (see c. 9). In this there may have been some intercommunity hostility in his action against Simon, he being of the Mangorike Quarter, while Simon and his allies were of the Home Quarter, see Isaac, *Transformation of Virginia*, 328–339.

68   *very giving foggs:* Sept. 17, 1757; *cold at night:* Nov. 5, 1757; *in cure:* Sept. 26, 1757.

69   *1¾ pounds:* Nov. 2, 1757; *the people:* Dec. 15, 1757; *2 hogsheads:* Oct. 24, 1757.

69   **Tatham:** op. cit., 38.

69   **Bulked:** A process Landon has following immediately on "striking," although both Jefferson and Tatham say it follows bundling.

69   **Jefferson:** op. cit., 210.

69   **Deaf ear:** The diary is silent; but we know that Landon observed the music of "his people," for when he wanted to satirize King George III, he mocked him as the leader of a Negro band, equipped with "quaqua, barafoos, and bangers [banjers]" (see chapter 9).

69   **Jefferson:** op. cit., 211.

70   **Toney:** A.k.a. Tony. He was one of the conspirators in the Simon and Bart episode. Otherwise he is known to us almost entirely through the reports on his work as a carpenter, his alleged misconduct at work. His religious conversion will be noted in c. 9. If his father was a carpenter, as he well may have been, then a reference in the 1750s diary may be to himself as his father's "boy": *Toney's boy ill* (April 12, 1758). By the 1770s, however, he himself had an apprentice for three years (March 12, 1770). There was no Tony in LC 1779 Inventory under Richmond County; so both father and son were gone by then. There was a Tony (or Tory? Or Tovy?) listed for the Loudoun and Prince William county quarters.

71   *The last day. . . . as yet.:* Dec. 31, 1770; *Had all:* Feb. 9, 1757.

72   *Care & protection:* April 15, 1758; *God is Mercyfull:* Feb. 14–20, 1757.

72   **"cursed is the ground . . . ":** Genesis 3:17.

72   **Each quarter:** For the naming of the quarters, see Aug. 22, 1757; for the 10-hand gang,

the 10,000-hill task, and the 1¹/₂ share overseer's allowance, see March 4, 1757; on the 300,000-hill total expectation, see Aug. 28, 1757.

73   *my farm*: July 12, 1758; *I see*: March 1, 1758; *Smart rain*: June 24, 1757.

73   **John King**: The elder King died in 1771; a young man of the same name, whom Landon referred to as John King the Younger, later worked for Landon's nephew, Charles Carter of Corotoman (Sept. 13, 1771).

73   **Varro**: Marcus Terentius Varro (116–27 BCE), an early Roman writer on agriculture.

74   *We began*: Oct. 26, 1756; *Began to put*: Oct. 15, 1757; *It is necessary*: Dec. 13, 1757; *the Lazyness*: Nov. 23, 1756; *not owing*: Nov. 27, 1757; *but a Chattering fellow*: Feb. 9, 1757; *more care*: July 28, 1757; *disobeying*: Sept. 6, 1757.

75   *My threshers*: Jan. 21, 1757; *I am greatly surprized . . . a wench.*: Feb. 28, 1757; *I observe*: Feb. 28, 1757.

76   *George was*: April 17, 1758; *Farming Observations etc.*: Sept. 21, 1756.

76   **George**: The words quoted on this page seem to be all there is from which to reconstruct the life of this George. He probably died soon after this. There is only one George in the lists for 1773 and 1779, who is certainly Foreman George, whom we shall meet in chapter 9.

76   **Engineering designs**: for a discussion of the implications of reengineering the traditional work of the plantation, see chapter 9. On Landon's "reveries," see Isaac, "Imagination and Material Culture," 401–421, esp. 407–408.

77   *I have discovered*: Feb. 23, 1757; *Constitution*: Oct. 3, 1756.

77   **Thermometer**: June 28, 1766. For Jefferson's fascination with temperature measurements, see Thomas Jefferson, *Notes on the State of Virginia*, William Peden, ed. (Chapel Hill: UNCP for OIEAHC, 1955), 73–81.

77   **Jefferson**: On Jefferson as measurer, see Garry Wills, *Inventing America: Jefferson's Declaration of Independence* (Garden City, N.Y.: Doubleday, 1978), 118–131, 145–148, and Isaac, "The First Monticello," 91–93.

78   *mud & mire*: July 28, 1758; *baked*: June 6, 1758; *mere mortar*: July 8, 1757; *well pulverized*: June 16, 1758; *merely dust*: April 5, 1758; *It began to rain*: May 5, 1758; *if it proves*: March 3, 1757; *My stiff land*: Oct. 20, 1757; *I dread*: June 6, 1758; *My method . . . our profit*: July 28, 1757.

78   **Earth agreeably entertained**: Compare a Maryland planter's pronouncement that "all my fields smiled on me." Charles Carroll of Annapolis to his son, June 11, 1772, in Ronald Hoffman and Sally D. Mason, *Princes of Ireland, Planters of Maryland: A Carroll Saga, 1500–1782* (Chapel Hill: UNCP for OIEAHC, 2000), 243.

79   *enimy*: Oct. 25, 1757; *the hornworm*: July 18, 1757; *as well as a hog*: May 15, 1758; *flye Weavel*: Oct. 25, 1757; *the weavel would*: Oct. 25, 1757; *I have frequently. . . . grainery floor to cool.*: Oct. 25, 1757.

80   *See the drafts*: Oct. 25, 1757.

80   **Réaumur**: See [René Antoine Ferchault] de Réaumur, *The Art of Hatching . . . Domestick Fowls . . . At Any Time of the Year. . . .* (London: 1750). The book is still in Landon's library (LLC).

81   **Botanical paper**: see "Carter Family Papers," reel 1.

81   **Francis Lightfoot Lee**: see chapter 3.

82   *that in me. . . . so generally acknowledged.*: Oct. 18, 1774; *tall punchiond place*: Dec. 15, 1756; *experiments*: Oct. 3, 1756.

82   **Communicated the paper:** Landon Carter to Colonel [Francis Lightfoot] Lee, n.d., read at the American Philosophical Society, Nov. 15, 1768, in *Early Transactions of the American Philosophical Society.* . . . (Philadelphia: American Philosophical Society, 1969); *Virginia Gazette* (Rind) Nov. 19, 1772.

82   **Peritrochio:** The mechanical advantage system now known as the "differential pulley." Landon probably found it in an encyclopedia—John Harris, *Lexicon Technicum ; or, an Universal English Dictionary of Arts & Sciences* (London, 4th edition, 1725)—that is still in his library; March 5, 1757.

83   *a line of Cowstalls. . . . next year's ground.*: March 5, 1757; *As to dung. . . . not rotten.*: March 9, 1757.

84   *I am much pleased*: Dec. 14, 1757.

Chapter 5: Landon's Library

In order to "read" Landon Carter's surviving library with its extensive annotations, I have had to enter the special field of book history, or *histoire du livre*, as it is known to the French, who more or less invented it. My inspiration in this endeavor has been the work of Robert Darnton; all of his writings I commend to the readers of this chapter, but most especially *The Great Cat Massacre, and Other Episodes in French Cultural History* (New York: Basic Books, 1984) and the essay "Readers Respond to Rousseau: The Fabrication of Romantic Sensibility," 215–256. On Landon's side of the Atlantic, there are many works to learn from—beginning most appositely with Louis B. Wright, *The First Gentlemen of Virginia: Intellectual Qualities of the Early Colonial Ruling Class* (Charlottesville: Dominion Books, 1964, 1st pub. 1940). See also William Joyce et al., eds., *Printing and Society in Early America* (Worcester, Mass.: American Antiquarian Society, 1983), including my own essay: "Books and the Social Authority of Learning: The Case of Mid-Eighteenth-Century Virginia," 228–249. For an important early American case study, see Edwin Wolf, *The Library of James Logan of Philadelphia, 1674–1751* (Philadelphia, 1974). None of these works, with the partial exception of Darnton's essay, go into the "stories" told, beyond the subject classification.

My use of the concept "cosmology" matches, I believe, the definitions to be found in dictionaries and reference books. My use of "myth" is more the result of long-running discussions within the Melbourne Group of ethnographic historians. This is best accessed through Greg Dening's engagement with Marshall Sahlins's brilliant exposition of the "mythical history" according to which the Hawaiians knew and remembered their actions in killing Captain Cook. Dening was moved to ask: what, then, was the "mythical history" according to which the English knew and recalled the death of their own hero? See "Sharks That Walk on the Land," in Greg Dening, *Performances* (Chicago: Univ. of Chicago Press, 1996), 64–78.

For the same reason that we have great difficulty identifying the myths on which our own knowledge of truth is founded, it is difficult to find a satisfactory brief account of the essentials of the orthodox Christian cosmology that framed all knowledge from the Middle Ages until the rise of modern scientific secularism. I have been guided and inspired by the work of a great literary critic, who was historical enough to push past the insistent disaggregation of the Bible in modern Scripture scholarship, and to ask what stories (and what metanarratives) the Bible told for all the centuries when it was diligently read as a single book by a single author, namely God. See Northrop Frye, *The Great Code: The Bible and Literature* (New York: Harcourt, 1982). On the Enlightenment revision process see Henry May, *The Enlightenment in America* (New York: OUP, 1976); Garry Wills, *Inventing America: Jefferson's Declaration of Inde-*

pendence (Garden City, N.Y.: Doubleday, 1978). I learned gratefully from Norman S. Fiering, "Irresistible Compassion: An Aspect of Eighteenth-Century Sympathy and Humanitarianism," *Journal of the History of Ideas*, vol. 37, 1976, 195–218. I received early assistance from Fiering in my coming to grips with Landon's library as a topic.

For a comprehensive catalog of Landon's library, prepared shortly before the books were relocated to the University of Virginia, see Carol Edith Curtis, "The Library of Landon Carter of Sabine Hall, 1710–1778," thesis presented to the Faculty of the Department of History, 1981, in the Library, College of William & Mary, Williamsburg. Gayle Cooper was most helpful as I worked through Landon's books in the Alderman Library, University of Virginia, Charlottesville Va.

PAGE NOTES

85   *The History of Herodotus*: trans. Isaac Littlebury, 3d ed. (London: 1737), vol. 2, end leaf; 1:152, in the Library of Landon Carter (LLC). Unless otherwise stated, all the eighteenth-century editions cited in the annotations to this chapter are items in LLC.

85   **Meager list:** See LC 1779 Inventory.

86   **Tillotson's sermons:** *The Works of the Most Reverend Dr. John Tillotson, Lord Archbishop of Canterbury*, ed. Thomas Birch, F.R.S. (London: 1752). On Tillotson, see Norman S. Fiering, "The First American Enlightenment: Tillotson, Leverett, and Philosophical Anglicanism," *New England Quarterly* 54:3 (Sept. 1981), 307–344.

88   John Locke, *Essay Concerning Human Understanding, in Four Books*, 4th ed. (London: 1700). Landon admired Locke, but the annotations show him ready to debate points with "this great man" (see, for example, p. 63).

88   *An Universal History, from the Earliest Account of Time.* . . . , 20 vols. (London: 1747). This publication, attributed to no author or compiler, is an impressive storehouse of knowledge; these are twenty 8-by-5-inch octavo volumes, leather-bound with lines and lettering in gilt work.

88   **Works of husbandry:** G.A. Agricola [Bradley], *Experimental Husbandman and Gardener.* . . . (London: 1726); [Stephen] Switzer, *Practical Husbandman and Planter.* . . . (London: 1734).

90   Robert Carter to John Dawes, 1724, in Louis B. Wright, ed., *The Letters of Robert Carter, 1720–1727: The Commercial Interests of a Virginia Gentleman* (San Marino: Calif.: Huntington Library, 1940).

90   **Lily's Grammar:** William Lily, *A short introduction of grammar.* . . . This was a long-time favorite that went through many, many editions.

90   **Comenius:** I have consulted the first English edition of this pedagogic work: [Johann Amos Comenius], *The Gate of Tongues Unlocked.* . . . (London: 1631), reproduced in facsimile reprint under the title *Porta linguarum trilinguis reserata* (Menston, England: Scolar Press, 1970).

92   **Herodotus's . . . chronology:** see Herodotus, *History*, 143, 163.

93   **Asia-Minor tree frog:** the description occurred in Charles Thompson's *Travels through Turkey, . . . the Holy Land, . . . and Other Parts.* . . . (2 vols., 1754).

93   **Herodotus:** *History*, 1: 375.

93   **Aaron Hill:** *The Works of the Late Aaron Hill, Esq.* . . . . 4 vols. (London: 1753), 1: 175.

94   **Shakespeare's tragedy:** extract in [John Hawkesworth, comp.], *The Adventurer*, 3d ed. (London: 1756), no. 113, 67.

94   Pliny: John [Boyle], Earl of Orrery, trans., *The Letters of Pliny the Younger* (London: 1751), 3: 219–220.

94   [George] Buchanan's *History of Scotland. In Twenty Books. . . .*, 3d ed. (London: 1723), 349.

97   Aaron Hill: *Works*, 1: 164

97   Alexander Pope: [William Warburton, ed.], *The Works of Alexander Pope. . . .* (London: 1751), 3: 93.

97   Warburton: William Warburton (1695–1779) was a learned English cleric who took it upon himself to make a stand against the increasing skepticism of the Age of Reason, and—in his *Divine Legation of Moses* (1737–1738, with many subsequent editions)—to demonstrate the divine inspiration behind the Bible. He was consecrated Bishop of Gloucester in 1759.

97   Aaron Hill: *Works*, 1, end flyleaf.

98   Quotations from William Warburton, *Principles of Natural and Revealed Religion. . . .* (London, 1754) 2: 14; and John Milton, *The Works of John Milton, Historical, Political, and Miscellaneous. . . .*, 2 vols. (London, 1753), 1: 156.

99   Pious refutations: See Landon's William Warburton, *A View of Lord Bolingbroke's Philosophy. . . .*, 2d ed. (London, 1756). For Jefferson's intense reading of Bolingbroke's works, as he reasoned himself out of dogmatic Christian faith and into a viewpoint close to deism, see Douglas L. Wilson, ed., *Jefferson's Literary Commonplace Book. The Papers of Thomas Jefferson*, 2d ser. (Princeton: Princeton Univ. Press, 1989).

99   *Universal History* 1: 43.

99   Herodotus, 1: 145, end flyleaf.

101   Bible: *A Dictionary of the Holy Bible. . . .* (London, 1759) 3, at "Zoheleth."

101   Griffith Hughes, *The Natural History of Barbados* (London, 1750), 245.

102   [Switzer] *Practical Husbandman*, 1, no. 4: 58–59.

Chapter 6: Plantation Medical Science

A short illustrated outline of the medical practices of Landon's time and place has just been published: Sharon Cother, Kris Dippre, Robin Kipps, and Susan Pryor, *Physick: The Professional Practice of Medicine in Williamsburge, Virginia, 1740–1775* (Williamsburg, Va.: Colonial Williamsburg, 2003). Older standard texts in medical history are largely replaced by a fine recent compendium: Roy Porter, *Blood and Guts: A Short History of Medicine* (New York: W.W. Norton, 2003). My access to a large overview of the history of medical knowledge and understandings in the Western tradition was long ago informed by a set of brilliant television programs that became a fine book: Jonathan Miller, *The Body in Question* (New York: Random House, 1978). More focused on the eighteenth century, and much more profoundly authoritative, are two strong interpretive essays: Charles Rosenberg, "Medical Text and Social Context: Explaining William Buchan's Domestic Medicine," *Bulletin of the History of Medicine* 57 (1983): 22–42; and Charles Rosenberg, "The Therapeutic Revolution: Medicine, Meaning, and Social Change in Nineteenth-Century America," *Perspectives in Biology and Medicine* 20:4 (Summer 1977), 485–506, especially 485–497, which describes the state of medicine in the late eighteenth century. In addition, Andrew Wear, "Medical Practice in Late Seventeenth- and Early Eighteenth-Century England: Continuity and Union," in *The Medical Revolution in the Seventeenth Century*, ed. Roger French and Andrew Wear (Cambridge: CUP, 1989), 294–320; and Anita Guerrini, "Isaac Newton,

George Cheyne and the Principia Medicinae," ibid., 222–245, were invaluable for identifying early eighteenth-century trends in medical thought that found expression in Landon's casebook diary entries. Both these essays trace the complication of humoral theory by the rise of hydraulic and mechanical models that derived from William Harvey's 1628 demonstration of the circulation of the blood and from the immensely prestigious *Principia Mathematica* (1687) of Isaac Newton, which revealed the universe as a single system of matter in motion according to calculable principles of mass, gravity, and momentum. For some background information on the therapies that Landon employed, see Guenter B. Risse, *Hospital Life in Enlightenment Scotland: Care and Teaching at the Royal Infirmary of Edinburgh* (Cambridge: CUP, 1986).

Readers may want to know what would be the modern diagnoses of the ailments recorded in Landon's diary; this is very difficult to determine now. "Worms" is a term that covers a range of intestinal parasites; but where it is specified (as Landon sometimes did) that the creatures were working their way into lungs and throat, we know that the invasion has been by *Ascaris* lumbricoides, a worm that has been proved to have infested the population of colonial Virginia. There was an even greater presence of the human whipworm. (I am grateful for advice on this point and many others to Robin Kipps and her colleagues at the Colonial Williamsburg Apothecary Shop.) "Flux" is dysentery, with the specific pathogen now unknowable. Malaria is comparatively easy to pick among the fevers and agues, because the attacks come at very predictable intervals; so we know that the "quartan," a common form, was the variant on a four-day cycle, and similarly the "tertian" and the "quotidian." See *The Encyclopaedia Britannica*, 1st edition (Edinburgh, 1771), under "Medicine—Fevers." This whole topic as a challenge to biomedical history has been reviewed in K. David Patterson, "Disease Environments of the Antebellum South," in Ronald L. Numbers and Todd L. Savitt, *Science and Medicine in the Old South* (Baton Rouge: Louisiana State Univ. Press, 1989), 152–165. Patterson identifies malaria, as well as typhoid, worms, and tuberculosis, as very prevalent according to the 1850 census (152–156, 160–161). See also Darrett Rutman and Anita Rutman, "Of Agues and Fever: Malaria in the Early Chesapeake," *William & Mary Quarterly*, 3d. ser., vol. 33 (1976), 31–60.

PAGE NOTES

106 **Hippocrates and Galen:** See Porter, *Blood and Guts*. In the course of the seventeenth century, these great ancients had been ostensibly superseded by newer theories. A recent study of William Byrd II, who was a Virginia diarist a generation older than Landon, shows how he recorded his ailments and medical theories using Galen's terminology. This makes it clear what paradigm shifts had been made between the seventeenth and the eighteenth century (see Trudy Eden, "William Byrd, Transmutation and the Promise of Early Modern Medicine," paper presented to the Society of Early Americanists, Providence, R.I., April 2003, kindly communicated by the author). There was, however, a lot of continuity both in underlying assumptions and in applied therapies; the ancient theorists are the essential starting point for making sense of eighteenth-century medicine.

107 **Malaria:** The fit between the symptoms that Landon (and others) described and the patterns of malarial infection known to modern medicine is minutely examined in Rutman and Rutman, "Of Agues and Fever."

107 **Pulvis Bazilicus:** The Royal powder, a laxative and worm destroyer.

108   *Note*: Feb. 25, 1757; *at night. . . .3 bilious stools.*: Feb. 24, 1757.

108   **Ipecacuana:** Said to be among "the mildest and safest emetics." See *The New Dispensatory: Containing: I. The Theory and Practice of Pharmacy . . .* (London, 1753), 143.

108   **Spiritus Mindererius:** Sal ammoniac and vinegar, a great "deobstruant and diaphoretic [sweat inducer] . . . diuretic . . . loosens the belly . . . [and for] attenuating viscid humours" (*New Dispensatory*, 195).

108   **Dr. Nicholas Flood:** Dr. Flood (d. 1776) has gone into the annals as "an eminent practitioner and Consultant," see Wyndham B. Blanton, *Medicine in Virginia in the Eighteenth Century* (Richmond, 1931), 382.

109   *His vomit*: March 9, 1757; *Samson easy*: March 10, 1757; *but Just recovering*: May 3, 1757.

109   **Scientific revolution:** See Wear, "Medical practice," Guerrini, "Newton and the Principia Medicinae." For the first two-thirds of the eighteenth century the dominant theorist who had made a new synthesis of the new science as applied to medicine was a Dutch professor at Leyden, Herman Boerhaave (1678–1738). See Lester S. King, *Medical Thinking: A Historical Preface* (Princeton: Princeton Univ. Press, 1982), 192–193. (I am grateful to Robin Kipps for this reference.)

111   *Hepatic duct*: March 9, 1757; *requiring*: April 8, 1758; *the Season . . . regular intermittant*: Aug. 21, 1757; *period . . . a vomit*: Nov. 8, 1757; *a load*: March 9, 1758; *relieved*: Feb. 23, 1757; *The bile discharged*: Aug. 21, 1757; *the middle & last*: Aug. 25, 1757; *thicker*: Aug. 21, 1757; *Green & Yellow*: Aug. 21, 1757; *a prodigious difficulty*: April 22, 1758.

111   **Crocus wine:** A decoction of saffron flower parts that "exhilarates, raises the spirits," says the *New Dispensatory*, 119.

112   *yellow bile*: March 6, 1758; *green bile*: March 8, 1758; *attenuating . . . juices*: April 17, 1758; *3 bilious stools*: Feb. 24, 1757; *upwards or downwards*: March 9, 1757; *purgative*: Nov. 27, 1757; *exhibit*: April 22, 1758; *break its viscid state*: April 12, 1758; *produced a*: Oct. 20, 1756; *breathing moisture*: Feb. 24, 1757; *breathing Sweat*: Oct. 20, 1756; *powerfull sweat*: March 9, 1757.

112   **Rattlesnake root:** Used as a sweat-inducing diuretic, sometimes purgative and emetic (*New Dispensatory*, 206).

113   *endeavoured*: March 9, 1757; *moisture over him*: March 8, 1757; *the Nervous coat*: March 10, 1757; *dangerous ill*: Dec. 12, 1757; *lost her pulse. . . . to recover.*: Dec. 13, 1757; *mad*: March 17, 1758; *low state*: April 17, 1757; *proper Nervines*: March 11, 1757.

113   **Cordial:** Says *New Dispensatory*, 9: "Whatever raises the spirits . . . , is termed cardiac or cordial, as comforting the heart."

113   **Pulvis Cantian:** The Duchess of Kent's powders, to induce sweating (Greene, ed. *Diary*, 189).

113   **Pulvis Castor:** A "capital nervine" (*New Dispensatory*, 206, 279).

113   **Ginseng tea:** Then a mild purgative (Greene, ed. *Diary*, 205).

113   **Agua Mirabilis:** a multiple infusion including cinnamon, Angelica, and balm leaves—to ensure "cordial and carminative" properties (*New Dispensatory*, 384).

114   *being more composed*: March 10, 1758; *with child*: April 22, 1758; *Hysterick Symptoms*: Feb. 22, 1757; *bitters to brace*: Aug. 8, 1747; *I was obliged*: Aug. 28, 1757.

114   **Rhubarb purge:** Turkish or Russian rhubarb was used; it has a purgative action not produced by the garden variety.

115 *inflammatory:* Feb. 27, 1757; near 4 ounces: Feb. 24, 1757.

115 **Royal Infirmary:** See Risse, *Hospital Life,* 203, 210.

116 *check:* Sept. 2, 1757; *found worms:* March 16, 1758; *slimy gourd seeds:* March 17, 1758; *many Children who swelled:* Oct. 3, 1756; *many negroe Children:* Aug. 8, 1757; *emolient:* Sept. 15, 1757; *correct:* Oct. 29, 1756.

116 **Occasion of all the coughs:** Evidently an invasion of *Ascaris* lumbricoides.

116 **Mercurius Dulci:** Also known as calomel; a chloride of mercury, only slightly more poisonous to worms than to humans.

116 **Joint worm:** Here he is observing signs of the tapeworm.

117 **African American healing arts:** See Sharla M. Fett, *Working Cures: Healing, Health, and Power on Southern Slave Plantations* (Chapel Hill: UNCP, 2002).

118 *dear Sukey:* April 22, 1758; *Dr. Flood:* April 16, 1758; *gentle evacuations:* April 8, 1758; *My dear Sukey. . . . very little time.:* April 22, 1758.

119 *This morning:* April 25, 1758; *Severe stroke. . . . God Omnipotent.:* April 25, 1768; *Could it have:* April 25, 1768.

120 *She dyed:* April 25, 1758.

PART III: POLITICS, WAR, AND REBELLION

The period and many of the issues treated in the pair of chapters that comprise this part are covered in some detail (and also as a superb overview) in Fred Anderson, *Crucible of War: The Seven Years' War and the Fate of Empire in British North America, 1754–1766* (New York: Knopf, 2000). Anderson writes expertly as a military historian, but he has profound understanding of the political cultures involved. His treatment of the changing identities among the Indians and the British Americans is particularly apt.

Chapter 7: Landon, Legislator

There are four classic works on the political culture of eighteenth-century colonial Virginia. I shall list them in order of first publication: Charles Sydnor, *Gentlemen Freeholders: Political Practices in Washington's Virginia* (Chapel Hill: UNCP, 1952), later reissued as *American Revolutionaries in the Making: Political Practices in Washington's Virginia* (New York: Free Press, 1965); David John Mays, *Edmund Pendleton, 1721–1803: A Biography,* 2 vols. (Cambridge: Harvard Univ. Press, 1952); Jack P. Greene, *The Quest for Power: The Lower Houses of Assembly in the Southern Royal Colonies, 1689–1776* (Chapel Hill: UNCP, 1963); and Lucille Griffith, *The Virginia House of Burgesses, 1750–1774* (University: Univ. of Alabama Press, 1970). None of these works, however, has used Landon's diary to explore the strong role he assumed for himself in his first session as legislator. Nor do they trace the way he enhanced that role in the crisis of the coming French and Indian (or Seven Years') War. For general accounts of Virginia in this time, see Isaac, *Transformation of Virginia;* and Warren M. Billings, John E. Selby, and Thad W. Tate, *Colonial Virginia: A History* (White Plains, N.Y.: KTO Press, 1986). On the country ideology (and so the role of the independent country gentleman), see Bernard Bailyn, *The Ideological Origins of the American Revolution* (Cambridge: Harvard Univ. Press, 1967). It is incomparably the best introduction to the forms of political theory and practice behind the Revolution. An excellent account of the combination of sincere monarchical loyalty with jealous contending for local rights is to be found in Richard L. Bushman, *King and People in Provincial Massachusetts* (Chapel Hill: UNCP, 1984).

On America's crisis during the French and Indian War, I found myself greatly instructed by Fred Anderson, *Crucible of War*. On Virginia in particular, I found James Titus, *The Old Dominion at War: Society, Politics, and Warfare in Late Colonial Virginia* (Columbia: Univ. of South Carolina Press, 1991) to be a work of very fine scholarship, yielding remarkable insights.

As I grappled with the issue of British nationalism in America during the time of the 1750s titanic struggle for continental and global dominance, I realized that the nation that threw itself against France was not simply an island population offshore from Europe but a sprawling pan-Atlantic people conscious of themselves as an empire kingdom, a greater Britain. I then found that a fine appreciation of strong attachments to a "greater Britain" is developed in Eliga H. Gould, *The Persistence of Empire: British Political Culture in the Age of the American Revolution* (Chapel Hill: UNCP for OIEAHC, 2000), xvii–xviii, 66 and passim. Gould's attention is focused, however, on the view the Britons of the British Isles had of themselves. He traces the ways the conflicts of the Revolution contracted the boundaries of the islanders' imagined nation—though not of their empire. I, for my part, am here engaged with the tragic predicament of the "Britons" in continental America, who had painfully to detach themselves from their proud Greater Britain national identity. In revolutionary struggle, the Americans had to forge from their old libertarian British nationhood an equally proud, new American one. More of awareness of an expanded nation, roused to a stronger sense of kindred ties in its love of liberty, is captured in Kathleen Wilson, *The Sense of the People: Politics, Culture and Imperialism in England, 1715–1785* (Cambridge: CUP, 1995), 200–201.

In a recent review essay, Jack P. Greene has emphasized the origins of the American Revolution in the Britishness of the colonies—Britishness as to both institutions and identity. He emphasizes the shattering effect of "metropolitan measures that seemed to challenge settler control over local affairs and to deny settler claims to a British identity." His focus is on the measures of the 1760s and 1770s leading to rupture. My intention here is to focus on the 1750s and the intense experience of shared nationhood that emphasized Mr. Pitt's wartime role. In my view, the topic of conflicted American identity needs to begin at least with those years immediately preceding the "metropolitan measures" of the 1760s that so outraged the rebel patriots. Those measures were always repudiated by Pitt. See Jack P. Greene, "The American Revolution," *American Historical Review*, vol. 105 (2000), 93–102; quotation, p. 100.

On William Pitt's career, I have chiefly been guided by Marie Peters, *Pitt and Popularity: The Patriot Minister and London Opinion during the Seven Years' War* (New York: OUP, 1980); I have, however, resisted the "let's-get-to-the-facts" debunking tendency of most modern historiography. (The limitations of Winston Churchill as wartime leader have been much demonstrated of late.) The problem with this is that mystique and charisma get short shrift. Readers who want to get a sense of the Elder Pitt, a legend in his own time, would do well to read his entry in the old *Dictionary of National Biography*, ed. Sidney Lee (London: 1896), 45: 354–366, where they will find appropriate hyberboles such as the statement that the years of his life belong to the history of the world after he took charge of the war effort. For a very readable account of this tempestuous figure, see Stanley Ayling, *The Elder Pitt, Earl of Chatham* (London: Collins, 1976). See also Stanley Ayling, *George the Third* (London: Collins, 1972).

Indispensable is Fred Anderson's account of Pitt's charisma as national leader in America at large (Anderson, *Crucible of War*, 231). Illustrating the specific application of this for Virginia is difficult. Very few numbers of the *Virginia Gazette* survive for the period of William Pitt's triumphant rallying of Britons on both sides of the Atlantic. American response can be traced in some measure from newspapers of other colonies. These showed "the Patriot Minister," or "great commoner," fearlessly in his role as "the minister of the people." He was held up to admiration as—with "Roman greatness"—he purged a "corrupted state" that was centered on a court whose favoritism entrusted fleets and armies to effete commanders. A survey of the American press alone, however, ignores the volume of British printed material that was still so strong a presence in forming colonial consciousness. (The quotations above are from the following newspapers: *Pennsylvania Gazette*, Dec. 10, 1761, 1; *Boston Evening Post*, Oct. 23, 1759, 1; *Boston Gazette*, May 30, 1757, 4.) The American press's reporting of the great man's wartime leadership is reviewed in Carol Lynn H. Knight, "A Certain Great Commoner: The Political Image of William Pitt, First Earl of Chatham, in the Colonial Press," *Proceedings of the American Philosophical Society* 123: 2 (April 1979), 45–67.

On the press and the emergence of the nation as the prime aggregate unit of modern politics (including insights on the American Revolution), see the instant classic, Benedict Anderson, *Imagined Communities: Reflections on the Origins and Spread of Nationalism* (New York: Verso, 1983, revised edition, 1993).

PAGE NOTES

124 **Byg man:** March 13, 1752; **Bashaw:** March 14, 1752.

124 **Law of Parliament:** Landon's *History and Proceedings of the House of Commons. . . .* (London, 1742) has annotations that indicate how closely he studied it (in LLC).

124 **Speaker of the House:** John Robinson (1704–1766) was well connected in England and in Virginia; he was nephew to a bishop of London and was elected a burgess at the age of 23. He became speaker and treasurer in 1738 and retained these posts until his death. In 1749 he secured for the Loyal Land Company a very large grant of land on the upper waters of the Tennessee River and, soon after that, another grant for his Greenbrier Company. (There is a theory that it was these interests that made him seem indifferent to the French encroachments on the Ohio; but readers will find this chapter arguing that Landon's diary offers a different interpretation.) In 1765 he survived moves led by Richard Henry Lee to impugn his integrity, but, at his death the next year, it was revealed that he had indeed applied large sums of public money in private loans to his political associates. See John E. Selby, "Robinson, John," in John A. Garraty and Mark C. Carnes, eds., *American National Biography* [hereafter ANB], vol. 18 (New York: OUP, 1999), 662–664. Selby does call attention to the insights into Robinson's political style that are given by Landon's journal.

124 **King's Privy Council:** The colonies were regulated by the Board of Trade, a committee of the King's executive advisory body, the Privy Council.

124 **The General Assembly:** A fuller (but still brief) account of the colonial government is given in Griffith, *Virginia House of Burgesses*, 3–21.

126 **Quotations from Dinwiddie's speech:** H.R. McIlwaine, ed., *Journal of the House of Burgesses of Virginia: 1752–1755; 1756–1758* (Richmond, 1909), 58, 5–9.

127 **All the best:** March 2, 1752.

127 **"King and common Father":** John Pendleton Kennedy, ed., *Journals of the House of Burgesses of Virginia, 1766-1769* (Richmond, 1906), 166–68.

128 **Attorneys:** April 4, 1752; **Mr. Attorney:** March 11, 1752; *for the restraining:* March 4, 1752; *a great debate:* March 6, 1752; *the Dogg bill:* March 16, 1752; *I told Waller:* March 16, 1752.

128 **The older brother:** Charles Carter of Cleve (1707–1764) was an older full brother of Landon. He was a burgess for King George County on the upper Rappahannock.

129 *I got the blanks:* March 19, 1752; *I hear'd:* March 21, 1752; *if the Praise:* March 10, 1752; *standing order. . . . with the Speaker:* March 3, 1752.

129 **Mr. Martin:** John Martin (d. 1756), lawyer and burgess for Caroline County, south of the Rappahannock and a little west of Sabine Hall. (See Greene, ed., *Diary*, 71.)

130 **Tobacco Act:** Under a statute passed in Virginia in 1733 (and continually revised thereafter), tobacco could not be exported until it had passed an inspection by a government-appointed inspector at one of the many publicly maintained warehouses on the great rivers. Since tobacco (once it passed) was effectively money—Virginians bought, sold, and paid taxes with the inspectors' certificates of approval ("tobacco notes")—the appointment and control of these officers was a matter of concern to everyone, especially big planters like Landon. For a slightly fuller outline, see Isaac, *Transformation of Virginia*, 29–30.

131 *The House. . . . whatever he Opposed dropt.:* March 12, 1752; *he beckons:* March 12, 1752.

131 **Carter Burwell:** Colonel Carter Burwell (1716–1756) was senior burgess for James City County. He was a very wealthy planter, and a nephew of Landon, whose oldest half-sister, Elizabeth, had married Nathaniel Burwell. The nephew had been raised outside Williamsburg at Carter's Grove—so named to this day because Landon's father, Robert "King" Carter, had made that name a condition of his deeding the land in the marriage settlement!

131 **William Randolph (1719–1761):** He was a planter, son of William Randolph of Turkey Island, one of the founders of this great James River dynasty (see Greene, ed., *Diary*, 73).

132 *I waited. . . . all in All:* March 13, 1752.

132 **Benjamin Waller (1710–1786):** He was a Williamsburg lawyer who represented James City County in the legislature and, as clerk of the colony's high court, was part of the establishment (see Greene, ed., *Diary*, 68). Landon thought him too subservient to Speaker Robinson.

132 **Colonel Thornton:** Presley Thornton (1721–1769) was a gentleman planter, burgess for Northumberland County in the Northern Neck, where Landon had sizeable plantations, down-river from Sabine Hall.

132 **Mr. Woodbridge:** Representing Richmond County from 1734 to 1769, John Woodbridge (1706–1769) was in every sense the "senior burgess." At the election for this Assembly, he had ranked first in the poll, having secured more votes than Landon, the next candidate, who was then elected as the second or junior burgess. (See chapter 10 for a fuller account of the voting practices at the courthouse.) Since there was antagonism between the two men, it must have been satisfying for Landon that he topped the poll at the next election (Griffith, *Virginia Burgesses*, 164). Woodbridge, who was for years the presiding judge on the Richmond County bench, was a resident of neighboring North Farnham Parish. Woodbridge seems to have served in more capacities than just the legislative and the judicial, for a contemporary report attributed to him a string of illegitimate children in the county (see Gwenda Morgan, *The Hegemony of the Law: Richmond County, 1692–1776* [New York: Garland Press, 1989], 82).

133 *as he could not attend. . . . whole House.:* March 14, 1752; *so Cunning. . . . was overruled again:* April 7, 1752; *As Councillors. . . . like Bowls:* April 11, 1752.

133 **Ralph Wormeley:** He was an in-law of Landon. Ralph Wormeley II (1715–1790), squire of Rosegill, across the Rappahannock in Middlesex County, was brother to LC's first wife, the mother of Robert Wormeley Carter. There was friendship and antagonism between the two old gentlemen, especially when Wormeley, by then a councilor, exhibited Tory leanings in 1775–1776.

133 Richard Bland (1710–1776): a veteran burgess (1742–1776) for Prince George County, south of the James River, Bland (1710–1776) was a prominent Virginia lawyer and a Randolph on his mother's side. In 1764 and 1766, he published two much admired pamphlets in support of colonial constitutional rights, and was a delegate to the first two Continental Congresses (Greene, ed., *Diary*, 67).

133 Edmund Pendleton: A person of comparatively humble origin who made good, Edmund Pendleton (1721–1803) was a lawyer and man of business useful to the leaders in the House. By 1775 he was a leader himself and came to chair the Committee of Safety, making him the de facto chief executive in the interim government of Virginia. Under the Commonwealth he became a chief justice. See David J. Mays's superb biography of Pendleton.

134 *In the God Sped. . . .Yesterday Reddick*: April 7, 1752.

135 *By the by. . . . Bribery &c.*: April 8, 1752; ***to his Majesty*:** April 9, 1752; ***Many methods*:** April 11, 1752; ***This Representation*:** April 14, 1752.

136 *resolution for £500*: April 18, 1752; ***Then the Governor*:** April 20, 1752.

136 A fee: The notorious pistole fee.

137 Narrative overview: See Billings, Selby, and Tate, *Colonial Virginia*; Anderson, *Crucible of War*; and Titus, *The Old Dominion at War*.

142 *I was . . . seized. . . . the River Ohio; Some Compliments. . . . River Ohio*: Preamble to the memoir of the Assembly session of August 1754. (In the manuscript, this preamble appears as a passage in the notebook on the bottom portion of a page facing the last of the journal quoted above. Next are three pages of a record of 1753 proceedings in Richmond County court, and then, as a heading across the page following: *Session assembled August 22, 1754 Journal privately kept*. The background narrative continues with the completion of Landon's inquiries into Washington's campaign; then comes the text of what certainly is a memoir rather than a journal or diary, beginning with the words: *Under these circumstances were we when our Governor called us together in August. . . .*)

142 Peyton Randolph (1721–1775): He was king's attorney (equivalent to an attorney general) for the colony. He was very much part of the Robinson network, and at Robinson's death in 1766 succeeded him as speaker, though not as treasurer. (That office was split off to reduce the concentration of patronage and power, and Landon's nephew, Robert Carter Nicholas, became the next treasurer.) In chapter 8 we shall meet this Randolph as a conservative restrainer of the colonial revolt led by Patrick Henry. Perhaps continuing that role, in 1774 Peyton Randolph, a Virginia delegate to the First Continental Congress, was elected its first president. His death the next year freed him from the necessity of embarking on the "regicide" revolution into which he would no doubt have been drawn in 1776. Peyton's brother was John Randolph (1727–1784), Clerk of the House of Burgesses, 1752 to 1756, and then King's Attorney General for Virginia, in sucession to his brother Peyton. He was a Tory who went into exile in Britain in 1775.

142 A pamphlet: This was published anonymously—as was then quite usual—as *A Letter from a Gentleman in Virginia, to the Merchants of Great Britain, Trading to that Colony* (London, 1754) (see Greene, ed., *Diary*, 108).

143 *only a Skirmish of a few. . . . in the engagements.*: memoir of August 1754. Greene, ed., *Diary*, 108.

143 *The Facts appeared. . . . French from the Ohio*: Greene, ed., *Diary*, 109. (Since diary citation by date will not work here, I shall give page references to Greene, ed., *Diary*, although the quotations used here have been made to conform to the original manuscript.)

144 *Under these Circumstances*: Greene, ed., *Diary*, 111. (Here commences the session memoir proper.) *'Tis hard to point out. . . . a seeming Harmony*: Greene, ed., *Diary*, 111–112.

145 *After this Bill was prepared*: Greene, ed., *Diary*, 112; *Against this Tack. . . . should pass above.*: Greene, ed., *Diary*, 113.

146 *Accordingly. . . . much specious reasoning for it*: Greene, ed., *Diary*, 113–114; *And in a few day. . . . much Applause*: Greene, ed., *Diary*, 114.

147 *at home*: Memoir of the session commencing October 17, 1754. Greene, ed., *Diary*, 114.

148 *And so the busines. . . . Lords of themselves.*: Greene, ed., *Diary*, 115; *We received*: Greene, ed., *Diary*, 115.

149 *I will now Comprehend*: Greene, ed., *Diary*, 123.

150 *It may be said*: Greene, ed., *Diary*, 123.

150 **"Anti-expansionists"**: See Marc Egnal, "The Origins of the Revolution in Virginia: A Reinterpretation," *William & Mary Quarterly*, 3d. ser., 37: 3 (1980), 401–428.

151 *the Speaker. . . . willing to help us*: Greene, ed., *Diary*, 111–112.

152 **"An Epistle . . . a sinking Land. . . ."**: see Moncure D. Conway, *Barons of the Potomac* (New York: The Grolier Club, 1892), 139–140.

153 **"So illustrious an Example."**: Fauquier to LC, June 30, 1760. Colonial Williamsburg Foundation, Rockefeller Library, Miscellaneous Manuscripts.

154 **"Wilkes and Liberty"**: See chapter 8.

155 **Save Great Britain**: For Landon's sense of being British, rather than English, see his annotation of his copy of Aaron Hill, *Works*, vol. I, 211, where he crossed out "English" and wrote in "British." The eminent historian of the Revolution Pauline Maier considers that during the 1760s the name "American" was, for the patriots who used it, a component identity of the compound, "British"—equivalent to Scottish, Irish, Welsh, or indeed, English. (Personal communication.) See also Pauline Maier, Merritt Roe Smith, Alexander Kessar, and Daniel J. Kevles, *Inventing America: A History of the United States* (New York: Norton, 2002), 153.

155 **George Grenville**: Prime Minister, author of the Stamp Act of 1765. His role, and his image are discussed in chapter 8.

156 **"One of the great occasions of the century"**: Peters, *Pitt and Popularity*, 27–28.

157 **"It was like a torrent"**: Quoted in Ayling, *Pitt*, 168–169.

157 **"This whole summer"**: Pitt quoted in Ayling, *Pitt*, 173.

157 **"It is an high style"**: Quoted in Ayling, *Pitt*, 189.

157 **"a despicable electorate"**: Pitt, quoted in Ayling, *Pitt*, 80.

158 **"Pitt was . . . "**: Anderson, *Crucible of War*, 229, 231. Fred Anderson, a military historian, rejects the parochial American name for this war, which was, he insists, not just American but a European-based struggle for global empire and naval dominance. He offers an important reassessment in relation to the Revolution and the whole century's history; but he does not engage with the ideological aspects of Pitt's eminence in America,

nor, explicitly, with the nationalism arising from the imagined pan-Atlantic British-and-American nation, which the last lines of the quotation above implicitly invoke.

160 **"His power . . .":** *Annual Review*, vol. 4 (1762), 47. See also, Peters, *Pitt and Popularity*, 265.

160 **nationalism:** See Linda Colley, *Britons: Forging the Nation 1707–1837* (New Haven: Yale Univ. Press, 1992). Concentrating on the forging of shared British identity among the nations that have remained "British" to this day (the English, Scottish, Welsh, and some of the Irish), Colley does not review the aborted beginning of this process in British America. For a brief, very lucid account of the colonists' pride in being British at the climax of the war with France, see Jack P. Greene, "The Seven Years' War and the American Revolution: The Causal Relationship Reconsidered," in Peter Marshall and Glyn Williams, eds., *The British Atlantic Empire before the American Revolution* (London: Frank Cass, 1980), 85–105.

Chapter 8: Rebellions Begin

This chapter comes to the turning point in the narrative trajectory of the diary. The Stamp Act rebellion of 1765–1766 so changed the circumstances of Landon's life that he began to chronicle rebellions in his own home environment. As background for the Stamp Act I recommend Edmund S. Morgan and Helen M. Morgan, *The Stamp Act Crisis: Prologue to Revolution* (Chapel Hill: UNCP, 1953). It is still the "standard" history, but it is out-of-date and is written with a New England bias that tends to show Patrick Henry's debut—Williamsburg's immortal May 1765 moment—as a humiliation rather than as the triumph it really was. For an account that is lucidly put together with closer attention to the intricacies of Virginia politics see J. A. Leo Le May, "John Mercer and the Stamp Act in Virginia, 1764–1765," VMHB, vol. 91 (1983), 3–38. Billings, Selby, and Tate, *Colonial Virginia*, gives a very readable outline; it is without notes but has a useful bibliography. David John Mays, *Edmund Pendleton, 1721–1803: A Biography*, 2 vols. (Cambridge: Harvard Univ. Press, 1952) is one of the best works on late colonial and Revolutionary Virginia; pp. 156–173 for an excellent account of the Stamp Act rebellion in Virginia. (See the readings for part III and for chapter 7 for the particulars of these two books.)

Addressing the sudden eruption of domestic stories in the diary at this turning point, the second half of chapter 8 takes us back into that microcosmic kingdom of the pre-industrial household. Even a summary bibliography would be a very long list. The readings that have guided me most are, first, the overview contained in John R. Gillis, *A World of Their Own Making: Myth, Ritual, and the Quest for Family Values* (New York: Basic Books, 1996); and then a work that is deeply insightful on Landon's region, Jan Lewis, *The Pursuit of Happiness: Family and Values in Jefferson's Virginia* (New York: CUP, 1983). I also refer readers again to Jay Fliegelman, *Prodigals and Pilgrims*, on the interaction of big-world politics and familial relationships; and to Armstrong and Tennenhouse, *The Imaginary Puritan*, for the deep significance of the modern impulse to render one's story in writing.

PAGE NOTES

163 **"Dying Speech":** The account given here follows the one published (presumably by Richard Henry Lee) in the *Maryland Gazette*, Oct. 17, 1765. The details concerning the composition of the procession, the wearing of Wilkes's colors, etc., come from an extremely hostile and satiric report that was later published from secondhand reports by

George Mercer's father, John Mercer—*Virginia Gazette* (Purdie & Dixon), Oct. 3, 1766. Historians have usually preferred the colorful report but have not declared the bias in it. Furthermore, the indication that Lee himself wore the Wilkes colors is omitted (see, for example, Morgan and Morgan, *Stamp Act Crisis*, and Billings, Selby, and Tate, *Colonial Virginia*, 304).

163 **Richard Henry Lee:** He has already been noted as one of a formidable quintet of brothers, see notes for ch. 3. He emerged as a fiery young revolutionary, but there lurks a suspicion that he was compensating for a near fatal error of judgment. During heated controversy, the Mercers revealed that he had allowed his name to be put forward as a candidate for the same Stamp collectorship that he assailed George Mercer for accepting. (This combines with much other evidence that the Stamp Act was generally seen as a law that would be enforced, however unwelcome—until Patrick Henry's cry of defiance rang out at the end of May 1765.) Living at Chantilly, just across the county line in Westmoreland, Lee was a neighbor and correspondent of Landon, but Landon was wary of his radicalism (see below in this chapter, and in chapter 12).

163 **George Mercer:** Born 1733, died in exile 1784, he was badly hurt by this episode that checked a career that included gallant service in the Seven Years' War. (His brother had been killed in that service—hence, some of the father's bitterness at the dishonoring of his family.)

163 **George Grenville:** The prime minister, who proposed the stamp tax and arranged its enactment, was a very important figure not only in active politics but also in the psychology of the shadow drama that was commencing here. The execration of the evil ministers, Grenville and Lord Bute, at first enabled patriots for British liberty in America to avoid attacking the king himself; he was represented as enthralled by evil ministers. Landon, we shall see, singled out Grenville as the villain when he celebrated William Pitt as one of the heroes.

163 **Pageant:** On street theater English radical traditions, see David Waldstreicher, *In the Midst of Perpetual Fetes* (Chapel Hill: UNCP for OIEAHC, 1997).

164 **John Wilkes (1725–1797):** He had a stormy career in radical politics. In 1763 he was known as a libertine who partly lived by his scurrilous journalism, but he sensed the role he could adopt as a champion of endangered liberty. He had to go into exile over the prosecution of the *North Briton*, number 45, but returned in 1768 to face trial and imprisonment, while huge crowds gathered at the prison, chanting "Wilkes and Liberty," only to be fired on by troops in the St. George's Field Massacre, in which seven were killed. In 1769 Wilkes was three times elected to represent the county of Middlesex, an electorate on the edge of London, with many artisan voters. Each time the Parliament declared the election invalid; the third time they declared the defeated candidate to have been elected. The watching Americans saw in all this manifest signs that the constitution was being subverted by rank corruption. In 1774 Wilkes's popularity with urban radicals saw him elected lord mayor of London—but then, in this time of the second English Civil War (known to Americans as the War of Independence), the same alignment of politics had in 1773 seen William Lee, brother to Richard Henry, then a merchant resident in the city, elected sheriff of the City of London.) Wilkes sat in Parliament through the years of the American War, championing the cause of liberty in this struggle. He espoused other radical causes—religious toleration and reforms to make Parliament more democratically representative—but, growing

more conservative through the 1780s, he was rejected by the still radical Middlesex electorate in 1790 and went into political retirement.

164 **Lord Bute:** John Stuart, third Earl of Bute, had been tutor to the young heir to the throne. For a time he seemed to his royal ward to be the fountain of political wisdom. Popular satire depicted him scurrilously as the paramour of the dowager Princess of Wales, the new king's mother. Eventually the youthful attachment wore off, but politics were personal and passionate while the king insisted on heeding this Scottish outsider to the circle of leaders in Parliament.

165 **Quotations regarding Wilkes article:** See Ayling, *George the Third,* 111.

168 **Quotations from the three documents:** John Pendleton Kennedy, ed., *Journals of the House of Burgesses of Virginia—1761–1765* (Richmond: Virginia State Library, 1907), 302–303.

168 **"Sons of Liberty":** Quoted in E. S. Morgan, ed., *Prologue to Revolution: Sources and Documents of the Stamp Act Crisis* (Chapel Hill: UNCP, 1959), 32.

168 **Britannia . . . and her alternates:** A striking shadow play of the implied age-and-gender family drama was enacted in a number of Stamp Act mock funerals, in which English Freedom, an old man in a coffin, was taken to be buried; but, at the moment of interment a young female spirit figure rose up—Liberty. (I am much indebted to Jason Shaffer for this example and for the insights he and other colleagues in the Society of Early Americanists shared with me. See Jason Shaffer "'Great Cato's Descendants': A Genealogy of Colonial Performance," *Theatre Survey* 44, vol. 1 [May 2003], 13–15.) For accounts of these mock funerals, see Philip Davidson, *Propaganda and the American Revolution, 1763–1783* (Chapel Hill: UNCP, 1941), 176–177; and Peter Shaw, *American Patriots and the Rituals of Revolution* (Cambridge: Harvard Univ. Press, 1981), 180. The celebration of the figure of Britannia had been intensified with the 1740 publication of the poet James Thomson's song, "Rule Britannia." She figured greatly in the iconography and caricatures of the revolutionary struggles, until—in the same way that British nationalism was transformed into a newborn American nationalism—she metamorphosed into a look-alike Columbia. Specimens of both these figures can be found in Linda K. Kerber, *Women of the Republic: Intellect and Ideology in Revolutionary America* (Chapel Hill: UNCP for OIEAHC, 1980). A full-length study of these figures and their transformations through this time of the birth of nations is now overdue.

169 **Patrick Henry (1736–1799):** The great patriot orator was probably the most admired man of his generation among Virginia's lesser gentry and plain farmer folk. (He was elected Governor of Virginia as often as he was eligible under the new republican constitution.) He came from middling gentry (not grandee) stock in the Piedmont county of Hanover and, like many, turned to the law for his fortune. Learned lawyers belittled his reputed small stock of knowledge, but he knew how to sway a jury and became one of the greatest trial lawyers of his day. After the tempest aroused by the audacious Stamp Act resolutions narrated here, he was the hero of rank-and-file patriots and legislators for decades while the establishment leaders tried consistently to curb his influence. His next great moment was the March 1775 declaration of a time to turn from seeking political accommodation to all-out arming for a fight: "Give me liberty or give me death"—a line from the play *Cato,* which Washington would stage at Valley Forge in the winter of 1776–1777. In April of 1775, Henry began to enact this militancy with his threatened march on Williamsburg, leading a company of volunteers intent on con-

fronting the royal governor. He had no possible rival in June 1776, when the Virginia Convention came to elect the first governor of the commonwealth. For an excellent short biography, see Richard R. Beeman, *Patrick Henry: A Biography* (New York: McGraw Hill, 1974).

169 **"A Committee of the whole House . . .":** see, Kennedy, ed., *Journals of Burgesses: 1766–1769.*

170 **A motion including the whole proposal:** It is a puzzle to work out just how it could be that Governor Fauquier's report implies debate only on five of the seven resolutions, while the only eyewitness account written at the time makes it clear that the most inflammatory seventh resolution was before the House in the course of the public session on May 30th. The best published account to date is Le May, "Mercer and the Stamp Act," but his close concern is not with these burgess sessions.

170 **The sixth and seventh resolutions:** reprinted from the *Newport* [R.I.] *Mercury*, June 24, 1765, in Morgan, ed., Prologue, 49–50.

171 **Governor Fauquier's report:** quotations from Lieutenant-Governor Fauquier to the Board of Trade, June 5, 1765, in Morgan, ed., *Prologue*, 47.

171 **Thomas Jefferson:** See his "Autobiography," in Adrienne Koch and William Peden, eds., *The Life and Selected Writings of Thomas Jefferson* (New York, 1944); Jefferson to William Wirt, Aug. 1814, in Paul Leicester Ford, ed., *The Writings of Thomas Jefferson*, vol. 9 (New York, 1899), 468.

171 **An unnamed eyewitness:** "Documents: Journal of a French Traveller in the Colonies, 1765," *American Historical Review*, vol. 26 (1921), 745.

172 **Established leaders everywhere:** For the assumption that, like it or not, the act would have to be accepted, see Le May, "Mercer and the Stamp Act," 12–13, 19–20.

173 **"They are men!":** Morgan and Morgan, *Stamp Act Crisis*, 134–135.

173 **"Honor and obey the king":** See *The Book of Common Prayer*, introduction by Diarmaid MacCulloch (London: Everyman's Library, 1999). This edition reprints the 1662 version of the prayer book that was legally required to be used in the established Anglican churches in every parish in colonial Virginia.

174 **Landon announced:** The quotations are from a paper dated June 3, 1765 in CFP, microfilm.

175 **Lee's letters:** RHL to LC, June 22; and Aug. 18, 1765, in CFP, microfilm. For a brief account of the forms of resistance that Lee led, and for a violent riot in Norfolk, see Billings, Selby, and Tate, *Colonial Virginia*, 305–306.

177 **HONEST BUCKSKIN:** *Virginia Gazette* (Purdie and Dixon), April 4, 1766. From this time onward, the gazette has to be identified by printer. In 1766, dissatisfied patriots persuaded a Maryland printer, William Rind, to establish an independent press in Williamsburg. Both the rival newspapers called themselves the *Virginia Gazette*. The pseudonym "Honest Buckskin," signifying a countryman with no budget for tailored clothes, was one that Landon used from time to time. See Greene, ed. *Diary*, 8. This polemic, and others attributed to Landon, are printed with an introduction in Jack P. Greene, "'NOT TO BE *GOVERNED* OR *TAXED*, BUT BY . . . OUR REPRESENTATIVES': Four Essays in Opposition to the Stamp Act by Landon Carter," VMHB 76 (1968), 258–300.

178 *This Almanack:* The manuscript of the diary for 1766 is in the William L. Clements Library, University of Michigan, Ann Arbor.

178 **suspected slave robberies:** For a fuller account of this episode, see chapter 10. See also Rhys Isaac, *The Transformation of Virginia, 1740–1790* (Chapel Hill: UNCP, 1998), 328–344.

179 ***Madam pretended:*** Landon often used this word in an archaic sense. The OED shows pretended as having a long early usage (in line with its Latin root, to hold forth or "give out") in which deception is not affirmed. We might say that she "came on" like a mad woman.

180 **Nearly all the work was still done in somebody's household:** The appropriate historical emphasis on this profound difference in the organization of the pre-industrial world was dramatically supplied in a milestone book—Peter Laslett, *The World We Have Lost* (New York: Scribner, 1966).

182 **The sentimental novel:** See again Fliegelman, *Prodigals and Pilgrims;* and Armstrong and Tennenhouse, *Imaginary Puritan.*

183 **"subject" . . . "citizen.":** See Samuel Johnson's *Dictionary of the English Language* (London: 1755). "Citizen" then had a very restricted meaning: an inhabitant of a city (then a town that was the seat of a bishopric). "Subject" was the all-purpose word for members of the political community, defined, as already noted, by their obligation to obey. Of course, the new use of "citizen" had been creeping forward unremarked by Dr. Johnson; but it only truly burst in with the coming of the American republic in 1776.

184 ***I made it my business:*** June 16, 1771.

PART IV: A TROUBLED OLD REGIME
Chapter 9: Master and Slaves

This chapter is written in two voices. On the one hand, its principal subject and its principal source is one master's version of the endless set of derogatory stories that lords of the soil have always told about their field hands and household attendants; on the other hand, I have invoked the memories of that tyrannized experience as collected from the survivors of the last generation of the enslaved to grow up in Virginia.

Ancient literary archetypes of the scheming slave can be found in the Roman comedies of Plautus and Terence that were certainly known to Landon from his school days. When, however, we turn to more modern times, the subject of the masters' tales (unlike their counterpart, the folk tales) has not been much addressed. Neither the folklorists nor the literature scholars I consulted could identify for me any defining studies of what must be a persistent topic in early modern fiction and stage plays: the wayward servant. The historians who write of lord and peasant busily document the "social facts" of conditions of life and the relationships between the two classes. The ways that the lords represented their laborers in narratives seems not to have been studied. There is, however, a very lively appreciation of English forms of the consciousness of masters and mistresses during the eighteenth century, in Paul Langford, *Public Life and the Propertied Englishman* (Oxford: OUP, 1991), 500–509, the section entitled "The Fifth Commandment."

The situation is quite different when we turn to the experience of the enslaved Africans and the folk culture created and sustained by their new world descendants. Lawrence Levine's *Black Culture and Black Consciousness: Afro-American Folk Thought from Slavery to Freedom* (New York: OUP, 1977) was a milestone work in the new culture-oriented social history. More recent, and immensely instructive about culture and living conditions, is Philip Morgan, *Counterpoint: Black Culture in the Eighteenth-Century Chesapeake and Low Country* (Chapel

Hill: UNCP for OIEAHC, 1998). The topic of the rich exchanges between white and black was brilliantly explored in a very relevant regional study: Mechal Sobel, *The World They Made Together: Black and White Values in Eighteenth-Century Virginia* (Princeton: Princeton Univ. Press, 1987). (She has followed this up with a daring work that has been inspirational for me, because it deals searchingly with unconscious undercurrents and vortices in the multiracial American colonial world as it went through traumatic revolutionary changes; see Mechal Sobel, *Teach Me Dreams: The Search for Self in the Revolutionary Era* [Princeton: Princeton Univ. Press, 2000].) Also inspirational on the long history of cultural interactions is Shane White and Graham White, *Stylin': African American Expressive Culture from its Beginning to the Zoot Suit* (Ithaca: Cornell Univ. Press, 1999). For a finely researched study of the creation of the plantation-quarter settlements and their material culture, see Lorena Walsh, *From Calabar to Carter's Grove: The History of a Virginia Slave Community* (Charlottesville: UPVA for CWF, 1997). Walsh's work is focused on the Burwell plantation, which stood on land given by way of dowry to one of Landon's half sisters. Since slaves were also part of the dowry, that land was being worked by people who were kin to the persons whom Landon wrote about in his diary. Also attentive to Landon and other members of the Carter family as slave owners interacting with their people is Gerald W. Mullins's path-breaking little book, *Flight and Rebellion: Slave Resistance in Eighteenth-Century Virginia* (New York: OUP, 1972). On a topic of pervasive importance, I have already cited Albert Raboteau, *Slave Religion* (New York: OUP, 1978). Although its protagonists came a generation later than those in Landon's narratives, James Sidbury's *Plowshares into Swords: Race, Rebellion, and Identity in Gabriel's Virginia, 1730–1810* (Cambridge: CUP, 1997) is too important an engagement with the lives and culture of enslaved African Americans in revolutionary Virginia not to be recommended again here.

On the folk culture generally and the storytelling traditions it sustained, I have constantly been instructed by Roger D. Abrahams's work; see especially his *African Folktales: Traditional Stories of the Black World* (New York: Pantheon, 1983), and his *Afro-American Folktales: Stories from Black Traditions in the New World* (New York: Pantheon, 1985), each with a very instructive introduction by one who has devoted much of a lifetime to such studies.

The memories of Virginian African Americans who began their lives in slavery were recorded under the auspices of the New Deal's Works Progress Administration, and its Federal Writers' Project (WPA, FWP). The history of this great work of memory conservation is briefly traced in two valuable magazine articles: Ronald L. Heinemann, "Alphabet Soup: The New Deal Comes to the Relief of Virginia," *Virginia Cavalcade* (1983), 28:5–19; and Nancy J. Martin Perdue and Charles L. Perdue, Jr., "Talk About Trouble: The Virginia Writers' Project," *Virginia Cavalcade* (1997), 46: 227–238. The subject is also enlarged upon in the introduction to the collection of all the known surviving FWP transcripts, published in Charles L. Perdue, Jr., Thomas E. Barden, and Robert K. Phillips, *Weevils in the Wheat: Interviews with Virginia Ex-Slaves* (Charlottesville: UPVA, 1976). In the notes that follow, this volume will be referred to as *Weevils*.

PAGE NOTES

187 **Lawson:** William Lawson was one of Landon's overseers at Sabine Hall at this time. Billy (as he is often called) was a young man when he came to Landon; lately he had been working for his father. At first he showed himself tough on delinquents; he would catch runaways and was entrusted with the administration of severe punishments. He evidently set out to impress Landon with what he could achieve; and the old man was

pleased for a time to write into his diary the glowing prospects promised, but soon Landon preferred to set his doubts down beside the boasts and began a game of catching out Billy Lawson—as appears in this June 12, 1771, entry. Eventually this young man came to stand for all who served in his station—*In short care is only in an Overseer's mouth, but never in his thoughts* (April 4, 1772). Already Landon had written: *I do imagin he is under some diabolical influence. Perhaps some Bitchington* (Sept. 21, 1771). Lawson, however, was trusted enough to be sent to take over the Park quarter up-country in Stafford county. At this time it was also noted that *Lawson is to marry and go up immediately* (Oct. 24, 1772). He then vanished from the diary and has not been found among the records of Richmond County property owners.

188 *I walkt out. . . . earth up.*: June 12, 1771.

188–

190 *I must not. . . . I cannot do.*: June 27, 1774.

190 *I should have cured*: Aug. 24, 1774; *Farewell*: June 25, 1774. The Scripture adaptation is from Matthew 25:21.

191 *though everything*: April 20, 1764; *all rooted up*: May 4, 1766; *that would have kept*: May 16, 1766; *too easy*: May 23, 1766; *no hills turned*: June 4, 1766; *drunkard*: June 4, 1766; *the more particular*: May 4, 1766; *Even the most aged*: May 5, 1766; *this old fellow*: May 5, 1766; *Old Jack*: May 23, 1766; *All is my own fault*: June 4, 1766.

192 *meat from my Smoak house. . . . prospect in corn*: June 28, 1770; *Having nobody but women*: Aug. 14, 1770; *lazy*: June 4, 1766; *my very old and honest*: June 12, 1771.

192 **George:** His recorded career is revealing of the unenviable position of the foreman, between the contrivances of his own people and the demands of his master. George was for a long time one of Landon's most approved slave foremen. He first appears, however, as the father of a namesake son who died (June 8, 1757). The record onward from this earliest first outburst is characteristically mixed. Satisfied notes of the work team George led are interspersed with notes such as this: *I have ordered him to be whipped for thinking to disobey orders* (June 17, 1771), and *him I almost barbecued for giving orders to his gang without doing the things himself* (Nov. 6, 1771). During the time of the missing monthly book for May 1771, Landon must have been induced to replace George with Simon (see below). But Simon immediately disappointed, and so we read for June 14, 1771: *Simon . . . shall have a good whipping and George take his place again.* And then, fifteen months later, Landon decided to install a white overseer at the Fork, since *my dog of a foreman is grown a lazy villain* (Oct. 19, 1772). George then drops out of sight for five years—until: July 18, 1777. . . . *Mr. George run away for bursting a meal bag.* And eleven days later, his last appearance, an entry for being AWOL: *George . . . still out.* He seems to have returned, however, for there was a George listed in LC 1779 Inventory.

193 **Interview quotations from Patterson, Berry, Folkes, and Brock:** See Perdue, *Weevils*, 219–20; 36; 94; 62.

193 **Roscoe E. Lewis:** Lewis (1904–1961) was a professor of chemistry, until 1942, when he moved into the Social Science Department. Appointed to supervise the preparation of a "Negro" contribution to the state's reporting, he initiated the direction of the effort into gathering ex-slave narratives. He did not live long enough to complete the book, "Oh, Freedom," that he intended to develop from all this work (*Weevils*, xvii–xx. This book is most appropriately dedicated to his memory). He was head of the only all African American unit of the WPA in any state, and at least the beginnings of a public

acknowledgement of his great achievement appears in Perdue and Perdue, "Talk About Trouble." There is a photo portrait of Professor Lewis in Ronald L. Heinemann, "Alphabet Soup," 5.

193 **Mrs. Jennie Patterson; Mrs. Fanny Berry; Mrs. Minnie Folkes; Reverend John Brown:** the compilers of the transcripts published in *Weevils* were not able to trace the informants, all long dead by 1976.

193 **Miss Susie Byrd:** She was a resident of a neighborhood in Petersburg, close to the dwellings of some forty known ex-slaves. She was a dedicated interviewer and left a very informative memoir of her work and those with whom she worked (see *Weevils*, 383–388).

194 **Shepherd quotation:** Ibid., 257.

194 **Collective . . . memories:** Slowly we overcome the myth that "the individual" is the atom from which all society is constituted. Psychologists are recognizing the extent to which each person's memory is very largely a social creation; we recall what it would be relevant to share with others. Our memory is shaped by the narrative conventions of our culture. See David Middleton and Derek Edwards, eds., *Collective Remembering* (London: Sage, 1990).

195 **Muse quotation:** *Weevils*, 257; 215–217.

195 **Horace Muse:** Muse was a slave-owner name in Richmond County; RWC was defeated at the polls by a Hudson Muse in the 1776 "April fools election"; see chapter 12.

195 **Master Riles:** I have not been able to trace this name in Richmond County records.

196 **Myth:** See chapter 5 and notes.

196 **Gentry lore:** This is a term I have coined. Concerning the lack of an identifiable literature on this important subject, see the notes at the head of this chapter.

197 *My honest ones:* July 13, 1771; *He was once:* April 26, 1770.

197 **Hogarth's famous print:** The hanging at Tyburn is the final frame in the "Rake's Progress" series, first published in London in 1738.

198 *For a while:* April 26, 1770.

198 **His former master's power:** There are two Manuels and an Emanuel in LC 1779 Inventory, but none of these need be the Manuel who was one of the Eight.

198 **The Amaxhosa:** adapted from Abrahams, *African Folktales*, 178–180.

199 **Johnny:** See note to chapter 2.

199 **Simon the ox carter:** A heavy man, as was noted when he trod the tobacco down well before the prizing completed the packing (Oct. 20, 1770). His skills gave him the care of valuable hauling teams and yet he appears remarkably few times in the diary. We know he had a brother, Sawney, who would cover for him when he was in hiding (April 27, 1766). Probably he died, or found a way out after the last entry about him on August 4, 1772: *Simon Whipped for killing a hog.* He was not listed in LC 1779 Inventory.

199 **Talbot:** He was a resourceful man with many skills and was young rather than old in 1766, since he is not named in the 1750s diary. He probably lived on, appearing as one of the two Talbots in the LC 1779 Inventory; but he was gone—with only a youngster bearing his name in the RWC 1783 taxable list. He was a sower of seed on the land that he also plowed or drilled. He sheared sheep, weighed goods and crops into and out of storage. If he had any specialty, it was as a boatman, as he frequently did errands on the river. It was he who was angrily blamed when the periauger was found to be badly out of repair. He is often mentioned just by tasks he is performing satisfactorily;

but, with so many responsibilities and Landon as master, he is not infrequently denounced as a lazy villain or dog. In 1766 he had an unnamed wife early on since he neglected guard duty to visit her (Oct. 25, 1766), and on May 20, 1774, *a Sucking child of Talbot's* was in danger from measles, and the unnamed mother was blamed for not alerting the master.

199   **Tom:** This was almost certainly Postillion Tom, one of the Eight. See chapter 2.

199   **Will:** He was a strong worker whom we have already met when he testified to the size of the tobacco plants in the 1770 crop. See chapter 4. When he fell ill soon after his first appearance in the diary, Landon wrote: *I can't tell what to think as he is a most principal hand* (June 16, 1766). But six years later, Will's claimed sickness was said to have been cured by a whipping—*got clear by a revulsion to his back* (Oct. 19, 1772). The last appearance in the diary is typical of Landon vis-à-vis the slaves he must empower. A very unsatisfactory overseer is to be driven off from his quarter, *and Mangorike Will placed there to take care of everything. But perhaps he may turn a rogue* (Aug. 5, 1778). There may have been some intercommunity hostility in his action against Simon; he was of the Mangorike Quarter, while Simon and his allies were of the Home Quarter. See Isaac, *Transformation of Virginia*, 328–339.

200   *I shall punish:* April 24, 1766; *Bart broke. . . . Gardiner Sam:* April 25, 1766; *wench Betty. . . . harbourd them.:* April 27, 1766.

200   **Bart:** His series of entries is very short for a man with his skills and evident inclination toward rebellion. He is noted as staying out committing robberies on May 23, 1766. Four years later he would be punished by being made to work with a hoe (March 27, 1770); and he was around though sick in the spring of 1773. After that he must have kept healthy and learned to obey or to conceal transgressions, for he lived on without further notice save that he was counted in LC 1779 Inventory and in RWC 1783 taxable list.

200   **Gardiner's boy Sam:** Of this young man we know nothing personal. He had a recurrent presence in the diary because he became, like Talbot, a busy messenger. Later Landon referred to him as *postboy Sam*, or *postilion Sam*—although he was sometimes sent walking not riding (Dec. 10, 21, 1770; Oct. 24, 1774).

200   **Kit the Miller:** Also a tanner with a son called Sam who, having been apprenticed to his father, rebelled against being sent to hoe in the field (April 24, 25, 1770): *because put to work with the people he has taken himself off.* The special skills did not protect Kit from being hired to an up-country neighbor (Oct. 24, 1774). Kit lived outside Sabine Hall, but was prepared to raise the house staff to get help for a fellow slave, Daniel, who was in agony and feared to be dying (March 31, 1771). There was still a Kit listed in LC 1779 Inventory, and he was still there in RWC 1783 Taxable Property List.

200   **Outlawed . . . militia:** If runaways were marauding in their neighborhood, they could be proclaimed outlaws. There was a reward for taking them dead or alive; and the militia could be called out.

200   **Lansdown Old Tom:** The quarter whose name is used to distinguish this Tom from others had been assigned to RWC in his marriage settlement. This is the old man's only appearance in the diary.

200   **Betty:** There were six persons of this name in LC 1779 Inventory. This one, wife to Sawney, was evidently the personal attendant of daughter-in-law Winifred. She perhaps came to Sabine Hall as part of the dowry; she is named this once only. She is not to be

confused with Mulatto Betty, who is the Betty who did tailoring and storekeeper duties throughout the time of the diary.

200 **Sawney:** He was husband to Winifred Carter's Betty, and brother to Simon. He was evidently also the property of RWC, for he is named as a *villain* in his service and brought bulletins from RWC's nearby Hickory Thicket plantation (July 5, Sept. 3, 1775). Eight years later, he was gone from Richmond County, probably dead, for he is not in RWC 1783 taxable property.

201 *making away. . . . few of them:* April 27, 1766.

201 **Adam:** The grandson can only be identified through Lansdown Old Tom.

201 **Moral . . . tendency:** see Patricia Spacks, *Desire and Truth: Functions of Plot in Eighteenth-Century English Novels* (Chicago: Univ. of Chicago Press, 1990), 4–5.

202 *One lamb:* March 17, 1770; *now convinced:* April 12, 1770.

203 *Gardner Johnny. . . . for a greater villain cannot live.:* April 26, 1770.

203 **Postilion Tom:** He was one of the Eight.

203 **Robin Smith:** Landon made repeated accusations against this neighbor, Robert Smith, that he traded liquor for goods stolen from the Sabine Hall estate. (Robin was then an affectionate—or diminuitive—form of Robert; Landon sometimes called his eldest son Robin; one wonders if an allusion to Robin Hood does not lurk in it all.) Robert Smith was a small-holding or tenant farmer, living near Landon. In 1774, "for fatherly love," Smith transferred slaves to his daughter, Margaret Ingram. By November 1778 he was dead; no will is recorded, but the court ordered an inventory of his estate. See Headley, *Wills,* 135, 151.

204 *last month. . . . with Johnny:* July 12, 1770; *I fancy:* Feb. 28, 1771; *Mr Tom says. . . . old in peace:* March 11–12, 1771.

204 **Frederick Douglass:** See Deborah E. McDowell, ed., *Narrative of the life of Frederick Douglass, an American Slave, Written by Himself* (New York: OUP, 1999), 66–67.

205 *many little Children:* March 31, 1770; other quotations from Robert Williams *Weevils,* 324; *the cattle:* Nov. 6, 1771; *that fellow:* June 25, 1774; *abundance of trash:* Aug. 4, 1774.

206 *about these runaway people. . . . belonging to me:* July 25, 1776; *The two Johnnys:* July 25, 1777.

206 **My grandson:** Probably RWC's son Landon, who was by then an eighteen-year-old college student. Even so, his ability to capture very strong working men seems to imply some complicity on their part in order to mitigate consequences of their transgressions (see the section of this chapter on "Rebellion").

207 **Engineer or works manager:** The subject of the intellectual imperialism of the colonization of the workplace by the mathematically and scientifically educated bourgeoisie is vast. The most relevant treatment, showing what significant beginnings were made in American colonial plantation work places, is in Sidney W. Mintz, *Sweetness and Power: The Place of Sugar in Modern History* (New York: Viking, 1985), 46–52.

208 *Mr. Toney. . . . this impudence.:* March 15, 1770; *I think. . . . such a rascal.:* March 31, 1770.

209 *I thought:* March 31, 1770; *I visited. . . . tomorrow.:* June 19, 1770.

209 **"New Light" Baptist preachers:** One of the profound changes revolutionizing old Landon's world from what he had known in his childhood was the rise of evangelical preachers and the congregations they gathered outside the established Church of England. The church, and the traditional deferential authority it sustained, was dear to Landon. For a short account of Virginia's first stage of the passage into southern Bible Belt Christianity, see Isaac, *Transformation of Virginia*, 161–177.

210 *My Chariot:* Aug. 16, 1770; *Toney had a great flogging:* April 20, 1771; *Toney shall make his own Coffin:* June 14, 1774; *Yesterday Toney's son:* Feb. 3, 1777; *It takes.:* April 4, 1777.

211 *his correction. . . . Cows in the night.:* March 22, 1770.

211 **Manuel's Sarah:** The section of this chapter contains all that we know of Sarah. She was of child-bearing age and had already given birth when she appears. The property records do not resolve the doubt as to whether she was sold away; there are five Sarahs in LC 1779 Inventory and one was probably her, but we cannot be sure.

211 **Wilmot:** All that is known of this courageous woman is in this reflection. She was listed in LC 1773 Tithables, but does not appear in LC 1779 Inventory. Probably she died between those two dates.

211 **Criss:** She had a difficult birth on October 19, 1770. That is all we know—beyond her continued presence in LC 1773 Tithables, LC 1779 Inventory, and RWC 1783 Taxable Property.

212 *Manuel's Sarah:* Sept. 22, 1773; *No News:* Sept. 23, 1773.

213 *Evident lazyness, neglect:* Jan. 21, 1757, April 26, 1770; *whipped:* Feb. 14, 1757; *certain proof:* June 22, 1770; *The people stemmed:* Dec. 15, 1757; *Where there is:* Feb. 15, 1770; *sent down:* Sept. 21, 1770.

213 **Quotations from Sparks, Jacobs, Walker, Stokes, Berry, and White testimonies:** *Weevils*, (Sparks) 274, 276, 206, 156–157, (Jacobs) 292, (Stokes) 281, (Berry) 39, (White) 309.

215 **Father George . . . dead march:** The King playing state-funeral music.

216 **Governor Hutchinson & the tarred & feathered man:** Thomas Hutchinson (1711–1780) was a native-son Governor of Massachusetts (1771–1774). As a stern upholder of crown authority, he became very unpopular and went into exile in 1774. The other figure in this mock substitution for the heraldic beasts must be taken as a reference to Boston's way of disciplining persons who were deemed to have betrayed the cause of American liberty.

216 **Quaqua, Barafoo, Bangers [Banjers]:** The first is a kind of drum; the second is like a xylophone; and the third refers to an early banjo, with its *g* to be sounded like a *j*. (Personal communication from Dr. Rex Ellis of the CWF.) See also Morgan, *Slave Counterpoint*, 583.

216 **Folksongs:** Readers can go to the web site of the Blue Ridge Institute, Ferrum College, Ferrum, VA 24088, and order BRI-001-007.

216 **King and Grady quotations:** *Weevils*, 190, 115–116.

217 *old Sukey's Granddaughter. . . . each of them.:* June 22, 1773.

217 **Old Sukey:** She lives in history only through these pages of Landon's diary. There is no individuality for her in the three Sukeys listed in LC 1779 Inventory.

217 **John Selfe:** He was from a family that had placed itself in client relationship to Landon. (Selfe's father, John Selfe, Sr., was already overseer to Landon at Rippon Hall in York County.) Like most overseers, he did not stay long at Sabine Hall—two years only. Landon evidently enjoyed straightening out the young man, *this puppy* (May 6, 1774). When the youthful appetite of Selfe made him crave two meals during the day, Landon gave him instruction on what every *Poor housekeeper* must expect to endure and insisted that he limit his meal breaks or leave his position (June 27, 1774). He was next given a distant quarter, but Landon's grumbling disapproval continued.

218   *every tittle. . . . Jubas Harry & Daniel are run away.*: June 22, 1773; *turned out all my cattle. . . . this treatment.*: June 23, 1770.

218   **Jubas Harry:** Presumably Juba's Harry. His father had been a laborer at the Fork in 1757, and all that is known of Harry personally is in this story. There were four of his name in LC 1779 Inventory.

218   **Daniel:** He lives mainly in this story. He returned voluntarily after a another running away episode (April 4, 1776) and was one of the six slaves delivered to Reuben Beale at the time of Landon's death (LC 1779 Inventory).

219   *however the matter. . . . Tom's waistcoat.*: Aug. 25, 1770; *with what are called holidays*: July 20, 1775.

219   **Owen:** Truly a knavish fellow! Owen Griffith (b. 1746), was a Welsh indentured servant, who was employed as bookkeeper and storeman to the plantation. His service at Sabine Hall now seems like a caricature hyperbole of all Landon's trickster servant experiences. Landon said he had great ability but doubted his honesty, yet succumbed to his charm. The diary is peppered with the usual denunciations of his *roguish care*—his neglect, his evasions and deceits, and (as here) his seeming connivance with the enslaved (April 24, 1770). Nevertheless, he was able to end his time in style by contriving to get a false letter sent that declared him an heir to a substantial inheritance in Britain. On the strength of this he induced Landon to advance him £30. But the wide Atlantic was a small world; Owen had hardly left when reports came back from persons who had seen his father alive. Landon smarted sorely from the advantage taken of the generous disposition that was the complementary side of his irascibility. On the one hand, he recouped what he could by selling to Billy Beale the shirts, etc. that arrived for Owen after his departure; on the other hand he wrote in the diary and to the newspaper defending his kind actions against the prevailing ridicule. To make matters worse, Owen wrote a letter defending himself by denouncing Landon in an apt phrase, as a "boisterous Tyrant" (CFP, microfilm, Dec. 21, 1771).

219   **Communal experience of the sacred:** This is a complex issue, and my suggestion will be controversial. Anthropologists have dealt with this topic, where historians, it seems, have not. The subject is usefully opened up in a theoretical way and with reference to cultures around the world (although with more emphasis on the power plays than on experience of the sacred) in Michael Dietler and Brian Hayden, eds., *Feasts: Archaeological and Ethnographic Perspectives on Food, Politics, and Power* (Washington, D.C.: Smithsonian, 2001).

219   **Africa:** For very relevant studies that engage specifically with alcohol and the ancestral realms of the slaves, see Michael Dietler, "Theorizing the Feast: Rituals of Consumption, Commensal Politics, and Power in African Contexts," ibid., 65–114; and Gillian Feeley-Harnik, *A Green Estate: Restoring Independence in Madagascar* (Washington, D.C.: Smithsonian, 2001). Pages 36 and 454 show how indispensable alcohol is for the safe burial of the dead; pages 43–46 show how necessary it is in order to safely keep in touch with the dead. A classic early study that presents the special meanings and bonding power of the people's millet beer is Audrey I. Richards, *Land, Labour, and Diet in Northern Rhodesia: An Economic Study of the Bemba Tribe* (London: OUP,

1939 [repr. 1961]), esp. 77–80. I am immensely grateful to Dietler and Feeley-Harnik for their generous response to my requests for help on this topic. I have also received guidance and counsel on this (and so many other matters) from Roger D. Abrahams.

219   **Night occasions:** F.J.D. Smyth, *A Tour in the United States of America* (London: 1784; facs. repr. New York: New York Times, 1968), 46.

220   **Christ as God in a winepress:** This theme recurred in folk art. For a fifteenth-century example, see Hugh Johnson, Dora Jane Janson, David Revere McFadden, *Wine: Celebration and Ceremony* (New York: Cooper-Hewitt Museum and Smithsonian, 1985), 62. The images in this book show clearly how the ancient wine cult has haunted western art at least since the Renaissance.

220   **Quotations from Williams, Berry, Pollard:** *Weevils* (Williams) 318, (Berry) 36, (Pollard) 231.

221   **"Philanewyork":** See Abrahams, *Afro-American Folktales*, 291–292.

221   **Quotations from Uncle Bacchus White:** *Weevils*, 307.

222   *Yesterday:* April 4, 1777; *if Captain Tomlins:* July 14, 1777; *allowed them:* Sept. 8, 1770.

222   **Captain Tomlins:** He is not readily tracked in the Richmond County records, though his surname is associated with a mansion once called Bloomsbury, that has a colorful history; see Elizabeth Ryland, ed., *Richmond County, Virginia: A Review Commemorating the Bicentennial* (Warsaw, Va.: Richmond County, 1976), 76–77. The little history in Landon's diary is also colorful. The passage here quoted begins with typical irony: *The great Captain Tomlins . . .*, and develops into a memorable piece of Landoniana: *I heard lately the above Captain bought a house in New Castle—40 miles away—to remove to. I expressed concern at it. . . . Depend upon it, said he, the man who wants to leave a neighborhood can only do it on his own Account. Certainly, certainly, then a person so selfish ought to go—said I—for if he stays the same proper love as the french call self love will elevate his self Sufficiency and at last he will become intolerable. Old Solomon used to say a fool is wiser in his own conceit than ten men can render a reason. Indeed it is difficult to accommodate yourself to the restless soul. If You Press him to stay, he becomes supercilious—and if you shew an indifference as to his going— then he is sure to stay to torment you* (July 14, 1777).

222   **Quotation from Singleton:** *Weevils*, 266–267.

223   *his tobacco house:* Dec. 15, 1757.

224   **Painful injury to his penis:** Feb. 13, and Feb. 26, 1764. Landon noted that the doctor laughs at me and pronounces me in a good way.

225   **Quotation from Frazier:** *Weevils*, 98–99.

226   *Yesterday Billy Beale. . . . a very foul stomach.:* June 4, 1773.

226   **Jamey:** His name was variously spelled. He was a man of abilities, skilled and trusted. Most of the references in the diary are to the quarter that he operated for Landon in the mid-1760s, and then to the house on its own that was set up for him, that became a landmark for other observations. He was in demand also to be hired out as a mason. Only once—and then in company with others—did he attract such a usual phrase from Landon as: *Cursed villains indeed* (June 14, 1771). Yet, he had been a two-month runaway before his recorded foremanship. He was a troublesome prisoner to the overseer of Landon's son, who had to make a special journey from up-country to return him (Landon Carter, Jr., to LC, Jan. 1, 1763, in CFP, microfilm). Once he harbored a

runaway (Jan. 7, 1764; July 20, 1770). Nothing is recorded of him having a family. Since there are no Jameys and seven Jameses in the LC 1779 Inventory, it is impossible to trace him further in the estate records.

227 *I suppose:* Sept. 22, 1773; *my runaways:* March 5, 1757; *No news:* July 18, 1770; *Ambrose it seems catch him.:* July 20, 1770; *Mr. Ambrose. . . . the whole week.:* July 22, 1770.

227 Quotations from West Turner: *Weevils,* 289.

228 *was catched:* Sept. 22, 1773; *Mrs Fork Judy:* Sept. 2, 1777.

228 Quotation from Rev. Ivy: *Weevils,* 153–154.

229 *one shall be hanged:* July 9, 1777; *runaways in Irons. . . . give him away.:* July 9, 1777.

229 Ned's Death Warrant: Landon's colleagues on the bench did from time to time prosecute their own slaves and have extreme penalties imposed; see Gwenda Morgan, *The Hegemony of the Law: Richmond County, 1692–1776* (New York: Garland Press, 1989), 113–114.

230 Quotation from Grandy, Jones, Massie: *Weevils,* 115, 183, 207.

231 Quotation from Wallace, Shepherd, Folkes, Berry, Ellett, Massie: ibid., 293; 255, 93, 36; 84; 207, 206.

231 Philip Fithian: See H.D. Farish, ed., *Journal & Letters of Philip Vickers Fithian, 1773–1774: A Plantation Tutor in the Old Dominion* (Charlottesville: UPVA, 1968), 184–185, 187, 188. The tutor was reluctant to believe that the young heir to Robert Carter's Nominy Hall estate was seeking sexual encounters with slave women, but rumors (and evidence) strongly suggested he was.

232 Trickster John: This story was collected and published by Zorah Neale Hurston. It is reprinted in Abrahams, *Afro-American Folktales,* 270–274.

Chapter 10: Duties Betrayed

This parish and county world, according to Landon, is quite evidently constructed from rural archetypes, and yet it has proved very hard to relate to an available literature about narrative representations of manor house life. A lot of the problem is tone: Landon was mostly writing out his indignation while most of the literary matches tend toward mocking humor, see Oliver Goldsmith's play, *She Stoops to Conquer,* for a strong example. Henry Fielding's *Tom Jones,* is another classic by an author contemporary with Landon, whose complete works were acquired and assuredly read by the squire of Sabine Hall.

I must also give access to nonmocking accounts, see Part I of Isaac, *Transformation of Virginia.* Important aspects of neighborly cooperation and rivalry are very well rendered in Timothy Breen, *Tobacco Culture: The Mentality of the Great Tidewater Planters on the Eve of the Revolution* (Princeton: Princeton Univ. Press, 1985).

PAGE NOTES

234 *food & raiment—; It is but fair:* March 3, 1776.

234 jeremiads: See Perry Miller, *The New England Mind: From Colony to Province* (Cambridge: Harvard Univ. Press, 1953).

235 *Am I still:* Aug. 7, 1772.

235 Comedy: See Natalie Zemon Davis, *The Return of of Martin Guerre* (Cambridge: Harvard Univ. Press, 1983). For the Scripture tradition as literary model, see Northrup Frye, *Great Code: The Bible and Literature* (New York: Harcourt, 1982).

236 *I am mistaken if*: Aug. 31, 1774; *raised the price*: Aug. 21, 1771; *Who says*: March 5, 1776; *Mr. Robert Burwell*: Sept. 2, 1772; *It always*: Feb. 8, 1776.

236 **Quotation reproduced in Walter Ray Wineman:** *The Landon Carter Papers in the University of Virginia Library: A Calendar and Biographical Sketch* (Charlottesville: UPVA, 1962), 226.

236 **Present modes of Concerts:** The cultured Lord Dunmore was a great success with high society in Williamsburg—as long as he gave concerts and balls and attacked Indians, not patriots. See John Selby, "Murray, John," in *American National Biography*, vol. 16, 154–155.

236 **Robert Burwell:** Robert Carter Burwell, whose home was near Norfolk in Isle of White County, had been a member of the King's Council since 1764. He died in 1777. See William G and Mary Newton Stanard, *The Colonial Virginia Register* (Baltimore: Genealogical Publishing Co., 1965), 50.

237 **Mr. Mills:** Sept. 16, 1772. These persons have not been identified; *We had*: May 17, 1772.

238 *They tell me*: Aug. 18, 1772; *Were I a Mark Anthony*: Aug. 18, 1772. Landon refers here to Dryden's play "All for Love."

238 **Over-the-fence inspection:** see Breen, *Tobacco Culture*.

239 *Old Stanly Gower*: April 6, 1772; *It puts me*: Oct. 10, 1772.

239 **Frank Lee:** Francis Lightfoot Lee, one of the Lee brothers; see note to ch. 3.

239 **Old Stanly Gower:** He was, it seems, a man of small property, who left no will to be proved in the county court. Landon gives him no honorific "Mr." nor any militia rank, though he refers to him as an "old gentleman." Gower did witness a will in 1766, but that is the last entry in the county's will and deed book for a family that had been long settled. Perhaps he was survived only by daughters, and it is they and the sons-in-law whom Landon suspects of wishing him dead. See Headley, *Wills*, 136.

239 **Dr. Jones:** see ch. 6.

239 **Jemmy-coat:** This was a colloquialism when Landon used it. "Jemmy" is not in Samuel Johnson's famous *Dictionary of the English Language* (London: 1755), but the great *Oxford English Dictionary* explains that it meant fancy-worked fabric or garments. The earliest traceable usage is 1750.

240 **Boerhaave and Cullen:** see headnote to ch. 6.

240 **County court:** For a brief outline of the rituals of the court and its day-to-day work, see Isaac, *Transformation of Virginia*, 88–94. For a much fuller account, see A. G. Roeber, *Faithful Magistrates and Republican Lawyers: Creators of Virginia Legal Culture, 1680-1810* (Chapel Hill: UNCP, 1981).

241 *the Public duty*: June 14, 1772; *Still very cloudy*: June 6, 1772; *I had thought. . . . overrule my endeavours.*: May 9, 1770.

241 **Transubstantiation:** It is a dogma of the Roman Catholic Church that in the ritual of the Mass the substance of the bread and wine mystically become the body and blood of Christ. Catholics could be thus excluded from public life if anyone about to take up office had first to swear their detestation of this doctrine.

241 **Clerk of the Court:** This important and remunerative position was held by Leroy Peachey from 1768 to his death in 1793 (see Greene, ed., *Diary*, 405). He was also appointed clerk to the Richmond County Committee that enforced the Non-Importation Association of 1774 (RWC Diary September 22, 1774).

241 **Mr. Parker:** Richard Parker (1729–1813), of Westmoreland County was a lawyer and planter and fighting friend of old Landon. He was a member of his county's committee during the time of rebellion and became a judge of the General Court in the new republic (see Greene, ed., *Diary*, 169).

242 *was my own. . . . road turned over it.*: July 30, 1770.

242 **Vitruvius:** The reference is to Marcus Vitruvius Pollo, a Roman writer on architecture of the first century CE, whose works were reclaimed and emulated in the Renaissance.

242 **Naval Officer Lee:** This was Squire Richard Lee (1726–1790). The coast of America was divided by the British customs authorities into "naval districts," each under a "naval officer," who had the responsibility to check the papers of arriving ships and to issue clearance before they departed again.

242 **Sir Marmaduke Beckwith:** Much more on this character further in this chapter. The old gentleman, the son of Sir Roger Beckwith, was born in England in 1687. He had lived in Richmond County for a very long time, and was clerk of the county from 1708 to 1748. He resided in the other parish of the county—North Farnham—where his children had been baptized (see George Harrison Sanford King, *The Registers of North Farnham Parish, 1663–1814, and Lunenburg Parish, 1783–1809, Richmond County, Virginia* [Fredericksburg, Va.: private publication, 1966], 13.) Landon viewed Beckwith and most of the "Pharnamite" gentry with suspicion.

243 *In salting up*: Jan. 25, 1770; *I had a mind*: Daybook, Dec. 5, 1772.

243 **Ball:** William Ball was an apprentice manager at Sabine Hall. It is possible that he was a son of Williamson Ball, who had married Ann, a sister of Winifred and Reuben Beale; see notes for chapter 3.

243 **Lawson:** See notes for chapter 9.

243 **James Brown:** His family appears in the Richmond County will and deed book. He was a younger son who would only inherit if his older brothers, first Christopher, then Thomas, should die without heirs (see Headley, *Wills*, 142–143).

244 *Robin Smith*: April 13, 1770; *Yesterday*: Sept. 15, 1771; *When I went*: July 18, 1771; *My guinea boar*: Dec. 13, 1771;

244 **Robin Smith:** See notes for ch. 9.

244 **Hertford:** Henry Harford (d. 1776) was a neighboring farmer (see Greene, ed., *Diary*, 630).

245 *I clearly see. . . .*: May 22, 1772.

245 **Beale:** Billy Beale, the apprentice manager; see ch. 1.

245 **Morgan:** Perhaps the William Morgan who claimed the geese (see below). The name was common in the county, so it is impossible to identify this man further.

245 **Roman geese:** In an episode that entered legend, it is recounted that the Gauls, climbing the rocky ramparts of the Capitol by night, would have surprised and overwhelmed Rome had not the sacred temple geese cackled and aroused the watch.

246 *Sir Marmaduke. . . .& a vexatious lawsuit.*: April 26, 1770.

246 **Moore Bragg:** He lived in trouble with the law. Four years after this episode, Landon recorded that Bragg was under legal process, together with his brother Benjamin, on suspicion of felony for stealing a slave (March 1, 1774). Bragg survived that; his will was proved in Richmond County court in 1792. He left a modest estate to be divided between five children after his wife's death (see Headley, *Wills*, 174).

246 **Jesse Thornton:** There is no will from this man in the Richmond County will and deed book, so he was very likely a tenant farmer. His movable property was ordered

inventoried on Jan. 12, 1779, so most likely he died late in 1778 (see Headley, *Wills*, 151).

246 Will Bragg: possibly a brother to Moore Bragg.

248 William Northern: Evidently a poor tenant farmer. There is no will from him in the Richmond County will and deed book, but he is noted there in marginal roles only—as a witness or as the recipient of a kind gift of fishing rights at Accaceek Point in Lunenburg parish. (See Headley, *Wills*, 158–9; 179; 139). Persons of this name were, however, still to be found in the county in the early nineteenth century (see Ryland, *Richmond County*, 199, 201).

248 John Dolman: This man does not appear in the Richmond County records. He was a married man with a child, but we only know this through complaints about alleged misappropriation of cows and milk. His full record in the diary epitomizes the relationship of Landon and his overseers. Dolman was a young overseer whom Landon hoped to teach before, as so often happened, he grew angry and impatient. The record is puzzling. Dolman had been on the job already in 1769; there are frequent entries about work done, to be done, or not done well through 1770. In late spring, Landon sputtered: *John Dolman is a fellow of such determined laziness that I ordered him away yesterday. . . .* There followed a list of his costly neglects; but then, on the same day, came the typical Landon compassionate relenting: *The pitiful puppy has been this morning crying about the unhappy situation that he is in—so that I have been obliged to try him a little further. He has promised to amend.* He served the summer through, and into the fall; but then he is gone from the record until mid-1774, when he appears as if without interruption—*no more use than a pecking turkey*—but there are no regular complaining reports, only the dismissive: *It is impossible to imploy Dolman—he can't be made diligent.* And the final word, declaring a fraud supposed typical of all overseers: *I believe it is a scheme—not one of these fellows can be honest*—Quotations: May 15, 1770; May 12, 1774; July 17, 1774.

248 Shackleford: Richard Shackleford was a smallhold farmer in Lunenburg parish. He died in late 1794, leaving land in two counties, but no slaves (Headley, *Wills*, 179).

248 Doubleoon: A doubloon was a Spanish gold coin, worth 2 pistoles, or £1–14s approximately.

249 Reverend Mr. Giberne: He came to Virginia letting people know how well connected he was; he therefore expected to return to a promising ecclesiastical career in Britain. Maybe this was in his dreams, or for show. He married a Fauntleroy, became a well-to-do planter, and cast in his lot with the rebel patriots. He came with sufficient recommendation at least to lodge at the Governor's Palace in Williamsburg on arrival. His first parish was St. Thomas's in Orange County, where he even baptized one of the siblings of the later President James Madison. On coming to Lunenburg parish, Richmond County, he lodged with Landon—a sure way to begin a stormy friendship. How could he possibly show sufficient gratitude? He evidently cut a figure from the start. At one moment William Fitzhugh exclaimed about the misuse of horses by "my lord Giberne," and then Giberne pictured himself out walking, carrying a special "Tuck stick" for "defence against snarling biters." (See Fitzhugh to LC, May 13, 1763; and Giberne to LC, Nov. 1764; both in CFP, microfilm.) He established himself in this society in the best available way, by marrying a widow with property, one who was born a Fauntleroy and had been a Beale (see below, and Ryland, *Richmond County*, 70–71). For the Madison family connection and a fund of information about Giberne and all the worthies of Richmond County and beyond, see also William Meade, *Old Churches, Ministers, and Families of Virginia*, 2 vols. (Baltimore: Genealogical Publishing Co., 1966; 1st pub. 1857), 2: 97, and passim.

249 **Quotation from Lee's letter:** James Ballagh, *The Letters of Richard Henry Lee* (New York: Macmillan, 1914), 2: 50–51.

249 **Quotation from William Kay** to the bishop of London, June 14, 1752, in William Stevens Perry, ed., *Historical Collections Relating to the American Colonial Church*, vol. 1, *Virginia* (Hartford, Conn.: 1870), 389. This case and the position of the church in Virginia are discussed in Isaac, *Transformation of Virginia*, 143–157. For Mr. Kay's subsequent history, see 143–145, and 379. For Landon's appeal to the Privy Council, see LCD, May, 14, 1752. There is an informative review of the Kay episode in David John Robinson, "Roots of Anti-Clericalism in Colonial Virginia down to 1750," PhD Thesis, University of Southampton, 1980, 471–476.

250 *his Lady*: Aug. 15, 1771; *This day. . . . imperious obstinacy succeeds.*: Oct. 25, 1772.

250 **His Lady:** Mary (b. 1725), daughter of Major Moore Fauntleroy and Margaret Micou (of French Huguenot descent), was first married to Charles Beale, who left her a widow, bequeathing the Belle Ville estate to her. When she married Giberne, this estate became his.

250 **Belle Ville:** There is a colorful history of the house, that still stands close by what had been the site of the church in present-day Warsaw, Va., see Ryland, *Richmond County*, 70–74, 158.

250 **Church law . . . canons:** As an established church, supplying the religion of the state, the Church of England was heavily bound by law. Its Book of Common Prayer, for instance, had to be used in the services with no variations—at least in principle. (For a brief introduction to the forms of Anglican worship in colonial Virginia, see Isaac, *Transformation of Virginia*, 58–65.)

250 **Church warden:** Each parish was managed by a Vestry, or committee, presided over by the rector (minister). This body too was created and sustained by laws of the state; it was required to levy taxes to pay parish expenses, including the minister's salary (16,000 lbs. tobacco per annum). Vestrymen, by turns, would act as church wardens to organize the provisions for the communion service and support the minister in the actual services at the church.

251 *I every day*: Aug. 15, 1771; *Brockenbrough says. . . . mend a little.*: Aug. 18, 1772; *I declare*: Aug. 20, 1772.

252 *Yesterday I went. . . . imperious pride*: Aug. 16, 1771; *I go. . . . desire of mine.*: Aug. 19, 1772.

252 **The desk:** So called because, in this prayer book form of service, it supported lecterns for reading. It was an elaborate structure in three tiers: lowest was the clerk's desk, from which a lowly officer would read announcements; the middle level was for the appointed Scripture readings in the service; and the highest was the level from which the sermon was preached. There was no cross-adorned altar in these churches—that came in with the Oxford Movement, which turned back toward Roman ritual in the nineteenth century—so bowing to the altar (now quite usual) would then have been unthinkable.

253 *I went yesterday. . . . as the year before.*: Aug. 20, 1772; *Brought Giberne*: Sept. 20, 1772.

253 Corotoman: This was the place where Robert "King" Carter had set his great house. Situated at the tip of the Northern Neck, it was both the seat of a gentleman's estate and a wonderful lookout point for this great import-export merchant to see the coming and going of ships into the Rappahannock River or onward toward the Potomac and the upper Chesapeake. Its importance was amplified by the axis of the avenue that connected it to a beautiful high-walled church nearby. (Carter had secured for himself what is known as a "proprietary church" by undertaking the building of the parish's house of worship at his own private expense.) There may be material for solemn reflection in the situation today—where the church, wonderfully preserved and maintained, still stands in its green glade, but Corotoman, the proud house of the Carters, is vanished without any trace above ground.

253 Wormeley . . . Rosegill: see notes for ch. 7.

254 *more rain*: Feb. 27, 1776; ***Our court*:** Aug. 6, 1772; ***met with. . . . satisfaction Publickly.*:** Sept. 9, 1772.

254 Returned to the post of duty: Landon did not make an extended withdrawal at this or any subsequent time; but he had done so on three previous occasions. He had refused to sit with his offending colleagues from 1742 to 1748, 1756 to 1758, and again from 1762 to 1769. He continued to be listed in the Governor's Commission of the Peace for the County, however, and so by seniority, with the death of Colonel John Woodbridge in 1769, he became the presiding justice. See Morgan, *Hegemony*, 76.

255 *tell him*: Feb. 27, 1774; ***At last. . . . my friend's case*:** March 23, 1770.

255 Old pirate: There had been a famous trial of Blackbeard's captured pirates in Williamsburg in 1718, just when Landon was an impressionable eight-year-old.

255 Molleson: Willam Molleson was a London merchant. William Lee unsuccessfully tried to get Landon's custom for his own London-based tobacco importing business, so the Lee brothers shared a view that Molleson kept Landon's custom "chiefly by flattery." See Greene, ed., *Diary*, 51. For a brief explication of the tobacco consignment trade as engaged in by the wealthy planters, see Isaac, *Transformation of Virginia*, 15, 137.

256 *To be sure*: May 26, 1774.

256 Captain Dawson: By the time the ship was turning around to return to England, Landon was impelled to write: *Captain Dawson of the Marlbro' sent for my tobacco to get it to the* inspection *Warehouse. I don't like this man, though he may be diligent*—June 16, 1774.

256 John Backhouse: He was a Liverpool merchant through whom Landon had marketed tobacco and purchased goods over a long period. The sums of money that Landon drew by way of credit were substantial, e.g. £100 on May 5, 1766.

256 J. Sydenham: He was a London merchant from some way back in Landon's long life as an exporter. This is his only mention in the diary.

256 Captain James Cook's voyage: There were a number of publications from the voyage that brought Cook to Terra Australis, the land of the kangaroo and the black swan; the official one was *Accounts of the Voyages in the South Seas . . . by . . . Captain Cook . . .* (London, 1773).

257 *Sorry indeed*: Sept. 20, 1775; ***Words dropped*:** Sept. 21, 1775; ***I hope*:** April 18, 1776.

257 "Independent companies" . . . minutemen: A revealing account of the determined attempts to manage the democratic urges expressed in the revolutionary mobilization is given in Michael A. McDonnell, "Popular Mobilization and Political Culture in Revolutionary Virginia: The Failure of the Minutemen and the Revolution from Below," *Journal of American History* 85 3 (Dec. 1998), 946–981. This is an important corrective to the account too much derived from a top-down perspective in Isaac, *Transformation of Virginia*, 248–260.

258 *Yesterday on stepping. . . . at the consequences.*: Feb. 6, 1776; *If I wanted*: Feb. 7, 1776.

258 **Into a pit:** The expert on colonial courthouses doubts whether they were relieving themselves against the back wall, as I had supposed. He was sure there was a latrine pit or necessary house of some sort. (Carl Lounsbury, CWF, personal communication.)

259 *the just rights*: June 3, 1774; *It seems the fox*: Oct. 5, 1774.

259 **Old Beale:** Captain William Beale, father of Reuben and Winifred. For more particulars and the jest about the fox, see ch. 3.

260 **Captain G T:** Cannot readily be identified. With the war on, many officers from different parts were passing through.

260 **Hobbes Hole:** Now Tappahannock, a small river port in Essex County, across the Rappahannock from Sabine Hall.

261 *Indeed, everybody*: Aug. 31, 1777; *It is my birthday*: Aug. 18, 1778.

261 **Generals Gage and Howe:** British commanders in the war at this time, whose ferocity against the Americans impressed Landon.

261 **Mark Anthony:** Again the reference is to Dryden's verse play, "All for Love."

262 *Yesterday there was a great discovery. . . . affair end.*: Sept. 5, 1775.

262 **Boyd:** Probably David Boyd (d. 1781), lawyer and planter of Northumberland County. He had incurred Landon's indignation three years before by the way he imposed on the court to bully a jury into changing its verdict (July 4, 1771).

262 **Major Griffin:** The Griffin whom Landon distinguished as Major could at least ingratiate himself with Landon, as when he came back to Sabine Hall—*behaved very pleasantly as he always does*—and tried to dissuade Landon from withdrawing from the bench in response to a supposed insult from Colonel Peachey (March 5, 1774).

262 **Dr. Flood's son:** The implication is strong that *the devil, the father* in this narrative was Dr. Flood, and so the one termed *another gentleman* must be his son. I find no record of a son, however. If the usage is extended to a son-in-law, then this must be Archibald Mc-Call, a Scot, who was about to withdraw from Virginia until after the war (Ryland, *Richmond County*, 80).

264 **Sydnor:** Probably this was the John Sydnor who is named as a member of the Richmond County 1774 Non-Importation Committee (RWC Diary).

Chapter 11: Contests at Home

We again trace the world out of joint, with respect denied and authority defied, but we are in the domain not of the plantation work force or of the parish and county neighborhood but of the intimate circle of the diarist's closest family. The bibliographic essays for chapters 3 and 8 took note of works that have described the changing forms not only of family life but also of the stories told that helped condition domesticity. Those readings also apply to this and the next chapter, which continues the family theme into times of intensifying crisis. For the political crisis running parallel to the familial conflict, see again, Warren M. Billings, John E. Selby, and Thad W. Tate, *Colonial Virginia: A History* (White Plains, N.Y.: KTO Press, 1986), and David John Mays, *Edmund Pendleton, 1721–1803: A Biography*, 2 vols. (Cambridge: Harvard Univ. Press, 1952).

PAGE NOTES

265 *Mrs. Carter:* Sept. 21, 1764; *another domestic storm.:* July 6, 1766.

266 *I find:* July 7, 1770; *I was very tauntingly:* July 18, 1770.

267 **Farnham:** North Farnham parish.

267 **Corotoman:** See notes for ch. 10.

268 **Hipkin's store:** Samuel Hipkins was a local Richmond County merchant trading at To-tuskey Bridge, a landing place on a creek a short way down-river from Sabine Hall. He extended credit as loans to such as RWC and could be drawn on by Landon to pay substantial amounts (March 12, 1771). RWC had assisted in his selection to the 1774 Richmond County Non-Importation Committee (RWC Diary, Sept. 22, 1774).

268 **Mother and daughter:** Judging by age, the daughter in this and the next episode must be Betsy (Elizabeth) Carter.

268 **Crying Pattern:** that is what the manuscript clearly reads. The word "bouncing" that follows suggests that he meant "bittern," a metaphor from a ground-nesting bird that will attack those encroaching on its nest.

268 **Lucy:** Since Winifred and RWC's daughter of this name was born a year later, this must refer to LC's own daughter (see June 21, 1773, and ch. 3).

269 **Miss Prue:** A mocking nickname for granddaughter Betsy.

270 *wild Bob:* Feb. 12, 1774.; *very sharp ague:* Aug. 8, 1757; *graceless son. . . . respect . . . deserved any of me.:* Jan. 14, 1764.

271 **Lochial discharge:** Medical terminology for fluid produced after the birth.

271 **Mrs. Woods:** She was already housekeeper at Sabine Hall when the diary resumed in 1763; she evidently left soon after (see Dec. 22, 1763; June 14, 1764).

272 *And thus began:* April 23, 1776; *I have had 3 women:* July 7, 1777.

272 **Grieg:** This was Johnson Gregg, captain of the ship patriotically named "Admiral Hawke" (Feb. 18, 1770). Through him, Landon had trade and correspondence with London merchants Russell and Molleson (see ch. 10). He was made to feel the force of Landon's dissatisfaction with the latter.

273 *Do you bring your negroe:* It is not clear whether this is Landon's protest at the witness she called, or hers at testimony he had invoked.

273 *this prodigeous femail combination:* Aug. 9, 1777; *her emperial Majesty:* Aug. 8, 1778; *sulkye, De Maintenon:* Sept. 2, 1778; *Thus does:* Aug. 15, 1778; *from the knowledge:* April 27, 1777.

273 **De Maintenon:** This famous Frenchwoman, a strict Catholic, was the second wife of Louis XIV and a petticoat influence on a tyrant king, according to the legend, who persuaded him to persecute the Protestant Huguenots.

273 **Quotations are from RWC Diary,** July 7, July 14, 1766; August 25, 1766.

274 *For my part:* July 6, 1766.

275 **College:** College of William & Mary (founded 1693) in Williamsburg. The college records for this period are very incomplete. Young Landon may have been the only Sabine Hall Carter to attend in colonial times; the claim that old Landon himself was an alumnus cannot be substantiated.

277 **Jefferson's *Notes*:** See Thomas Jefferson, *Notes on the State of Virginia*, William Peden, ed. (Chapel Hill: UNCP), 162.

277 *R. Callis:* July 2, 1772. Robert Callis was a builder, originally from across the Rappahannock in Gloucester County (see Greene, ed., *Diary*, 646).

279   *old fox*: Captain William Beale, see ch. 3.

280   **proposed austerities:** The Virginia Association of August 1774 and then the Continental Association (1774) prohibited not only British imports, but all extravagant pleasures, in which were included gaming (whether in card-play, horse-racing, or cockfighting), and assemblies or balls where dancing would take place.

281   *I have repeatedly Pronounced*: Oct. 8, 1774.

282   **Mr. Ball:** It is not possible to determine who this was. Young William Ball had been an apprentice manager at Sabine Hall.

283   *I am sorry*: Dec. 26, 1774.

Part V: KING LEAR INTO THE STORM

285   **Lear quotation:** Landon's inscription in the margin of an extract of Shakespeare's *King Lear*, in a periodical, *The Adventurer*, ed. J. Hawkesworth et al. (London, 1756), no. 113, 67.

Chapter 12: Primal Rebellions

The politics of Virginia's war in league with the other colonies against the mother country can be followed in more detail in Warren M. Billings, John E. Selby, and Thad W. Tate, *Colonial Virginia: A History* (White Plains, N.Y.: KTO Press, 1986). Thematically this chapter reviews father-son conflict when, with the imminent prospect of casting out and symbolically killing the father-king, that conflict had become implicitly cosmic. I repeat, therefore, the references to Winthrop D. Jordan, "Familial Politics: Thomas Paine and the Killing of the King," *Journal of American History* 60 (1973), 294–308, and Lynn Hunt, *Family Romance of the French Revolution* (Berkeley: Univ. of California Press, 1992).

PAGE NOTES

289   *This Paper. . . . may be also.*: June 3, 1774.

290   *if he was offended*: July 22, 1775.

290   **Old Stadler:** This music teacher worked a busy circuit in a wide area around Sabine Hall. He taught also at the house of Landon's nephew, Councilor Robert Carter of Nominy Hall. Fithian, the tutor there, thought him an old gentleman of great charm. See H. D. Farish, ed., *Journal and Letters of Philip Vickers Fithian, 1773–1774: A Plantation Tutor of the Old Dominion* (Charlottesville: UPVA, 1968), 189, 204.

291   *Proclamation. . . . his baseness*: Daybook, undated entries for 1774–1775; *And though*: ibid.

292   *How Lamentable*: ibid.

292   *Common Sense*: A pamphlet first published anonymously in Philadelphia in January of 1776. Its author, never known to Landon, was Thomas Paine (1737–1809), a recent immigration from England. Calling for immediate independence, it denounced as tyrannical the monarchical British constitution, under whose protection (with guarantees) the colonial rebels were still fighting to be reincorporated. During the spring of 1776, *Common Sense* acted as a catalyst to stiffen resolve in favor of revolution and republican government. It was many times reprinted, and also published as newspaper extracts in all major centers.

293   *And let me*: Feb. 15, 1776.

294   *But this Son*: Feb. 16, 1776; *If this is not*: Feb. 25, 1776.

295 *It is a melancholly thing. . . . old man's advice*: March 9, 1776.

296 *his friends. . . . a close confinement*: March 12, 1776.

297 *We owe. . . . doubtful at last*: March 12, 1776.

298 *I never saw*: March 16, 1776.

299 *It is to be*: March 28, 1776; *I went. . . . in 1763*: March 29, 1776.

299 **Elections**: The classic account is in Charles Sydnor, *American Revolutionaries in the Making: Political Practices in Washington's Virginia* (New York: Free Press, 1965).

300 **Shamefully turned out**: Francis Lightfoot Lee and RWC were defeated by gentlemen of no particular wealth or pedigree. The new representatives were Hudson Muse and Charles McCarty. Landon thought Muse *a worthless, though impudent, fellow*, and Mc-Carty, *a most silly though good natured fool*. He had long ago cold-shouldered *the famous Muse* because he believed he opened other persons' letters and made scandal about them (May 25, 1770). RWC had assisted in appointing both to the 1774 Richmond County Non-Importation Committee.

302 *It seems*: April 7, 1776; *One looks. . . . Suburbs of Hell*: April 8, 1776; *dread whether*: April 13, 1776.

303 *This is the language*: April 24, 1776; *going on*: April 25, 1776; *to please the Ladies*: May 10, 1774; *Certainly he*: April 25, 1776.

304 *This only shows*: May 1, 1776; *notorious Aims. . . . fools but madmen.*: May 2, 1776.

304 **G.R.**: Believed to be George Reynolds (d. 1781). He seems to have left no land to the wife and daughter who survived him (Robert K. Headley, Jr., *Wills of Richmond County, Virginia, 1699–1800* [Baltimore: Genealogical Publishing, 1983], 156).

305 *the peculiar genius. . . . God help us all*: May 18, 1776.

308 *even if Dunmore. . . . her success . . .*: May 29, 1776; *the rights of nature*: Feb. 23, 1777.

308 **The new order**: Jefferson at this moment was about to include a passionate denunciation of slavery in his draft Declaration of Independence (by way of denouncing the king for protecting slave-trading interests against Virginia's attempts to curb slave imports). Congress deleted that passage. See Garry Wills, *Inventing America: Jefferson's Declaration of Independence* (Garden City, N.Y.: Doubleday, 1978), 65–75.

309 *the first who opened*: July 14, 1776; *our battery's beginning*: July 13, 1776.

309 **Sigmund Freud**: a name that divides historians instantly into at least three camps. There are those who want to ban Freud's theory of psychology as a guide to interpreting the past; there are those who like it and want its paradigms applied extensively; and there are those who look pragmatically at what can be made of it in a particular context. I wish to be numbered in the third party. Like it or not, the name of Oedipus has come to be associated in our everyday understandings with a familiar kind of son-father antagonism. When I invoke Freud here, when I draw attention to Freud's own use of myth as embodied in literature, I once again affirm the importance for historians of attention to the mythic aspects of the struggles they recount.

309 **Patricide**: Freud took the name of Oedipus from the ancient Greek drama, the myth of the son who actually killed his father. The founder of psychoanalysis was in a sense driven back to the Greeks for this story, because literal patricide appears to have been suppressed, repressed, or forbidden in more modern European literature. Shakespeare told it repeatedly, but only in the transformed rendition (very relevant to Landon's post–Stamp Act rebellion anxieties) of casting down or killing the king. Yet, a twisted version of the primal story once existed in earlier British traditions: in the culmination of Malory's assemblage of Celtic legends, King Arthur had been killed by his son, Mordred. One literary historian, on whom I tried the hypothesis of the repressed patricide story, said: "Yes! And that's probably because everyone knew patricide to be more commonplace than they could bear to admit." He alluded to the countless times suspicion must have lurked that a son-and-heir had helped his father off in order to inherit sooner. The other side of the coin was the need for a son-and-heir to express ostentatious grief at the death of his father, lest he should be suspected by others (and himself?) of rejoicing at his coming into the succession. All this is properly to be designated as the nemesis of the old patrimonial patriarchy, and Landon's diary shows that he understood it well. Thanks to Harold Love for advice on this point.)

310 *Those who fancy entails. . . . arbitrary Principle.*: Daybook, undated entries for 1776.

310 **Law abolishing entails:** A sweeping measure that shows the radicalism of the American Revolution even in Virginia. By outlawing the fixing of a concentration of the property in one line only of a family, it had a determined equalizing effect—in the first instance within the family but ultimately in society. The importance of this measure has long been denied by historians committed to the view that the American Revolution was not so much a revolution as an independence struggle only. Recently in a very important article, Holly Brewer showed that these historians had misled themselves. The supposedly numerical demonstration of the unimportance of entail in Virginia daily life was based on invalid procedures. Brewer proved two main points: first, that a correct account showed that a high and steadily accumulating proportion of the valuable land in the colony was tied up in entails, and second, that the legislature enforced the practice strictly right up to the time of its sudden abolition. See Holly Brewer, "Entailing Aristocracy in Colonial Virginia: 'Ancient Feudal Restraints' and Revolutionary Reform," WMQ, 3d Ser. 54 (1997), 307–346. I have to make a retraction after this revelation. In *The Transformation of Virginia*, I declared that Jefferson's Statute for the Freedom of Religion, passed in 1786 after bitter contest, was the only important item in Jefferson's comprehensive revolutionary "Revisal of the Laws" to be adopted (Isaac, *Transformation of Virginia*, 273). I now know that the entail law, adopted at the outset, was very important. So, when Landon expostulated against Jefferson's new statute, he was indeed protesting the demolition of a vital protection of the continuing greatness of high families such as the Carters. For Jefferson's abolition of entail bill see Julian Boyd, ed., *The Papers of Jefferson* (Princeton: Princeton Univ. Press, 1950), 560–562.

311 LC to George Washington, Oct. 31, 1776, in Philander D. Chase, ed., *The Papers of George Washington, Revolutionary War Series*, 7 (Charlottesville: UPVA, 1997), 60–68, 64.

Chapter 13: Landon and Nassaw

I have not found a bibliography to guide me on this subject of the unequal two-sidedness of enslavement. I was, however, drawn into the study not just by the contemplation of the plight of Nassaw—though that certainly drove me—but also by engagement with large questions about the nature of history. How shall it get behind official versions to reach understandings of the terror by which power is ultimately enforced? Specifically, can such power be explicated by the methods of ethnographic history, which I and my colleagues of "The Melbourne Group" had developed? (Clifford Geertz assigned this label to the work of Inga Clendinnen, Greg Dening, and Rhys Isaac; see Clifford Geertz, "History and Anthropology," *New Literary History* 21 (1989–1990), 321–335.)

Questions about the method had been raised by Jean Christophe Agnew, "History and Anthropology: Scenes from a Marriage," *Yale Journal of Criticism: Interpretation in the Humanities* 3:2 (1993). My first version of Nassaw's story was my attempt to address deep issues about violence and power. I also wrote anoter essay in response, attaching my defense of the "ethnographic method" to a review of the demonstrable achievements of my colleagues Inga Clendinnen and Greg Dening. See Rhys Isaac, "On Explanation, Text and Terrifying Power in Ethnographic History," *Yale Journal of Criticism: Interpretation in the Humanities* 6:1 (1993), 217–236.

Bernard Bailyn, as so often, had led the way long before that. In 1974 he published a biography of Thomas Hutchinson, that same destroyed governor of Massachusetts whom Landon mocked as a fitting heraldic figure for George III's new coat of arms. History, Bailyn thought, might be truest in tragic rather than triumphal mode. Since then, contemplating the horrors of the slave trade, he has taken us to school with the great French historian and philosopher Pierre Nora. We must marry historical science and its objectifying "facts" to what Nora calls "memory," in which we acknowledge the unspeakable truths in the heritage of pain and suffering. It is in that grieving spirit that I believe the relationship of Nassaw and Landon Carter must be written into history. See Bernard Bailyn, "Considering the Slave Trade: History and Memory," WMQ, 3d. Ser. 58 (2001), 245–251.

PAGE NOTES

314 *His father's blasphemy*: We glimpse the ongoing intergenerational intimacies of plantation slavery. A father or a grandfather of the same name appears in the brief diary of Robert "King" Carter, Landon's father: "November 21, 1722 . . . Nassaw this Night told me he had Carted to the Landing 26 Load of wood."

314 **Corrie:** John Corrie (d. 1785) was a merchant at Hobb's Hole (Tappahannock), and a justice of the peace in Essex County (Greene, ed., *Diary*, 349). He, or rather his wife (née Rust), had a quarter in Richmond County, close to Sabine Hall. Landon had acquired part of the parcel of land, called Juggs, and had been at law with the Rust family about it, and he had plotted to acquire the whole parcel by a tough restricted-access policy (July 25, 1770). The field was still called Juggs in the twentieth century (personal communication from the late Mr. Robert Carter Wellford). Landon harbored the suspicion that this merchant, like all the rest, must be watched closely or he would cheat on quantities and prices.

315 *endeavours*: Sept. 11, 1775; *the best bleeder*: Feb. 26, 1774; *on every recovery*: July 14, 1777; *waked. . . . rational one.*: March 12, 1772; *I walkt about*: June 23, 1771.

315 **Meredith:** this child of Nassaw is only mentioned once in the surviving diary; but he is listed in LC 1779 Inventory.

316 *I believe*: Sept. 12, 1771; *strip*: March 31, 1770; *this whore's father*: Aug. 11, 1777.

316 **a man who came to Sabine Hall:** Described as *Jesse—John Carter's man*; he seems to be a white man in Landon's third son's employ.

317 *Though Nassaw . . .*: Sept. 23, 1773; see ch. 9; *giving a just account*: Oct. 31, 1770; *by drink*: April 2, 1772; *I have nobody. . . . sending for liquor.*: Sept. 23, 1773.

318 *I have threatened. . . . save his soul*: Sept. 23, 1773.

318 **Nassau:** The familiar spelling is used by the newspaper printer. It was the name of a province of the European Netherlands before it was applied to a Dutch Caribbean island. The same use of the correct spelling was made by Jack Greene in the published text of the diary. But "Nassaw" is the form used in manuscripts not only by Landon, but by his son and by the Richmond County inventory clerks.

319   *accused. . . . Narrow Passage*: Sept. 30, 1773; *Somebody must harbour him*: Oct. 1, 1773; *Talbot—Nassaw's son*: July 25, 1775.

320   *tied Neck & heels. . . . more soul Alive*: Sept. 11, 1775.

321   *so very drunk*: Sept. 28, 1775; *he will not eat. . . . capable servant*: Sept. 30, 1775; *cabbin door*: May 9, 1776; *for the last time*: April 4, 1777; *ordered to whip*: July 13, 1777; *drank up most*: Aug. 16, 1778.

322   *"Item . . ."*: Quotation from codicil to Landon's will, probated in Richmond County, February 1, 1779. Conveniently abstracted in Robert K. Headley, Jr., *Wills of Richmond County, Virginia, 1699–1800* (Baltimore: Genealogical Publishing, 1983), 152.

322   Quotation from RWC Diary, May 22, 1786.

322   These three Nassaws are listed among the slaves under 16 years of age; see RWC Taxable Property, 1783.

Chapter 14: Toward Death

For the politics of the continuing war, see John E. Selby, *The Revolution in Virginia, 1775–1783* (Charlottesville: UPVA, 1983).

PAGE NOTES

323   *sensibility*: Feb. 23, 1777; *a well behaved man*: Feb. 7, 1777; *Indeed I do think*: Feb. 9, 1777.

323   **Captain William Dennis**: The ship in which he was taken by the Baltimore privateer was one in which he had plied the Chesapeake trade on behalf of James Russell, a London merchant with whom Landon had some correspondence though he harbored deep suspicions concerning him (see March 24, 1770). It seems Landon and the ship's captain had never met before this, yet Landon had already written an extraordinary endorsement onto a letter by Dennis already noticed in chapter 9. Dennis had sent to his friend Giberne a copy of George III's November 30 speech; this Landon likened to a dead march played by a band of black musicians. Letters or a diary have not been found to give us Dennis's version of these visits to Sabine Hall.

324   *a Gentleman. . . . part with her son.*: Feb. 23, 1777; *Of course. . . . absolute or nothing*: Feb. 23, 1777.

325   *I heard Yesterday. . . . the temple of Hypocrisy*: Sept. 2, 1777.

325   *Albion*: A ship chartered by British persons and loyalists granted permission to leave Virginia. Her expected departure in early May was deferred with the permission of the Council of Virginia and then further delayed by order of the Royal Navy ships blockading the Chesapeake. It seems she finally left Norfolk on June 20, 1777, or soon after. (See *Virginia Gazette* [Dixon & Hunter], May 5, May 23, May 30, and June 20, 1777.)

325   **Captain Dennis' Villany**: No number of the *Virginia Gazette* survives with a report of this betrayal, whatever form it took.

326   *make such a request*: Feb. 3, 1777; *I every day see*: April 20, 1777; *astonished*: April 27, 1777.

327   *It came from clouds*: July 18, 1777; *July finished. . . . they are to be found.*: Aug. 1, 1778; *Grace and her*: Aug. 1, 1778.

328   *Is it not a Strange thing*: Aug. 2, 1778; *I don't know*: Sept. 2, 1778.

328   **Ben:** His record is short (especially when mentions of the other Ben from an outside quarter are separated). He appears first already as a horse rider, although then only a boy (Sept. 18, 1770). Three years later, when called from the stable yard to be a substitute waiter in the house he was deemed incompetent in that new role (Oct. 2, 1773). Now we find him a man with a wife on another gentleman's plantation. There were three Bens entered in LC 1779 Inventory and there were two (both over 16) in the RWC 1783 Taxable Property list.

328   **Captain Ball:** See Captain Williamson Ball, see ch. 3.

329   *I can give no:* Aug. 1, **1778**; *my Colic:* Aug. 3, 1778; *Nettle rash:* Aug. 7, 1778; *the faculty. . . . the body:* Aug. 28, 1778; *Freshwater:* Aug. 4, 1778; *Freshwater is again:* Aug. 5, 1778; *has given harbour. . . . bring them to me:* Aug. 8, 1778.

329   **Freshwater:** Tom Freshwater had been an overseer for Landon since 1770 at least—although at a down-river outlying quarter (May 29, 1770). He had been denounced and dismissed for sustaining an injury in a drunken Christmas escapade, but pleaded for by RWC (Jan. 8, 1772). Like so many in Landon's service, he was kept on to be constantly raged against. He came, as one might surmise, from a family of small property. He left no will in the Richmond County court records, though he may have been the Thomas who received land in 1754 from Thomas, his father, while brother George was cut off with a shilling (Robert K. Headley, Jr., *Wills of Richmond County, Virginia, 1699–1800* [Baltimore: Genealogical Publishing, 1983]). It was the custom under the old English Common Law for a parent who wished to exclude any of their offspring from a will to leave them a shilling. That way it was proved that they had not merely been omitted.

330   *would reserve. . . . set devils free:* Aug. 31, 1778; *I see it is vain:* Aug. 31, 1778; *This child chose:* Aug. 21, 1778; *I see:* Aug. 31, 1778; *A backwoods Visit. . . . only equally . . . :* Sept. 2, 1778.

330   **Quotation from family Bible, Sabine Hall.**

331   **Quotation from RWC Diary,** 1780. The cat's age was established by its having been given to the family when grandson George was a toddler. My guess is that it came from the Carter place at Corotoman, and Coorytang was an infant's attempt at this name.

Last Words

334   *spender spoon:* The *Oxford English Dictionary* is only indirectly of help. There is an obsolete noun "spender" for a steward who dispenses provisions. It is very likely that the utensil referred to came out of Landon's "Physick shop," where it would have been used in the dispensing of medicines.

About the Illustrations

Page iii. A reconstructed adaptation of the original design of the seal of Virginia. The Fifth Virginia Convention that drew up the first constitution of the new commonwealth in 1776 also ordained this seal. The die that was struck according to the original instructions has long since disappeared, and the surviving wax impressions of it affixed to documents are indistinct. The commonwealth reconstructed the image as seen here.

Page iv. Landon Carter portrait. Graham Hood, then director of the Colonial Williamsburg Foundation Department of Collections, made a careful study of the family portraits still hanging at Sabine Hall. In a letter of September 12, 1975, to Mr. and Mrs. Dabney Wellford he stated that, on several grounds, he attributed this portrait to the young John Hesselius (1728–1778). The dog makes no appearance in any diary—a canary that died in April 1758 is the only pet mentioned.

Page xvi. These surviving parts of the diary are reproduced from the Sabine Hall Papers (#1959), Special Collections, Alderman Library, University of Virginia.

Page 2. The lower Rappahannock River region. Taken from a map of Virginia prepared by Colonels Joshua Fry and Peter Jefferson, first published in 1754 by Thomas Jefferys of London. It was improved in a second edition published in 1755, which drew on further data collected by Fry, George Washington, and others.

Page 5. Sabine Hall. Although the flanking exensions are modern, there was in Landon's time a "communication building" extending to a kitchen on the east side.

Page 5. Reconstruction of the façade of Sabine Hall as it was when Landon built it. A Colonial Williamsburg Foundation architectural history team recently measured and minutely examined the remarkable and inventive workmanship in the construction of the building. (William Joseph Graham, Jr., prepared this drawing for the Colonial Williamsburg Foundation, which has kindly made it available for use in this book.)

Page 8. The York River at Yorktown. The Rappahannock River also would have had ships and boats plying to its port towns and plantation wharves.

Page 38. Carter lady's portrait. Graham Hood argues that this is a portrait of the first wife of Landon Carter, Elizabeth Wormeley, and that the painter was Charles Bridges. See Graham Hood, *Charles Bridges and William Dering: Two Virginia Painters, 1735–1750* (Charlottesville: University Press of Virginia, 1978).

Page 43. Pamela restored to her father. The English painter Joseph Highmore executed a series of paintings of scenes from Samuel Richardson's sensationally successful novel of 1743. These were then engraved so that hundreds of copies could be sold in England and the colonies. Since the novel was an international best seller, the captions to the plates were inscribed in French as well as English.

Page 56. Plate 1 of the collected plates for Diderot's *Encyclopédie*. Taken from *Recueil de planches sur les sciences . . . et les arts méchaniques*, Paris, 1762. The copperplate engraving was of immense importance in the visual education of western civilization. The emergent bourgeoisie had little access to the original paintings, but the prints went everywhere.

Page 81. A poultry-egg incubator with elaborate flues for the circulation of warm air. The book in which this appeared had matching plans for an "artificial mother"—a warmed space for the raising of the chicks (see Rhys Isaac, "Imagination and Material Culture").

Page 83. Drainage canals and tide gates: Landon Carter's diary makes recurrent reference to separate "drafts" that he did for his many construction projects that were part of his scientific improving of agriculture. These drawings executed on the pages of the 1750s notebook diary are the only ones to have survived. (From the Sabine Hall Papers [#1959], Special Collections, Alderman Library, University of Virginia.)

Page 95. A plate illustrating Book 12 of "Paradise Lost," in Landon Carter's own copy of volume III of *The Poetic Works of John Milton*, comp. Thomas Newton (London, 1761). (Sabine Hall Papers [#1959], Special Collections, Alderman Library, University of Virginia.)

Page 130. Speaker John Robinson in a mid-1750s portrait by John Wollaston, Jr. This long-serving Virginia politician was called a "very jewill of a man" at his death in 1766; but that was not Landon's sense of him as he dominated the proceedings of the House of Burgesses in 1752.

Page 138. Map from Le Page du Pratz, *Histoire de la Louisiane* (Paris, 1758). At the height of the war for North America, this French naturalist and geographer published an extensive account of the resources and the varieties of human and natural life in the vast territory then belonging to France. The map emphasizes the extent of this French possession.

Page 138. "Map of the British Colonies in North America . . . ," published by John Mitchell in London in February 1755, just as the war for North America was commencing. It revives old claims to all the lands from the Atlantic to the Pacifc Ocean.

Page 139. "Britain's right maintained" (London, 1755). This caricature was full of British professed contempt for French pretensions, including (on the right) the mocking "Ha Ha Ha" as the star of "Universal Monarchy" plummets into the sea.

Page 154. William Pitt, the Elder, in Roman garb. Charles Willson Peale, then an art student in London, was commissioned by gentlemen of Westmoreland County, Virginia, to make a portrait of one of the great patriots who had saved, they felt, both American and British liberty by seeing to the repeal of the Stamp Act. Peale sent back a canvas whose great size matched the stature of its subject. In 1768 he produced this smaller engraving in hopes of reaching a wider audience.

Page 162. Prime Minister Grenville hanging on the gallows. The notebook containing this captioned pen sketch has only lately come to the attention of scholars out of the papers surviving at Eyre Hall in Northampton County on Virginia's eastern shore. The contents are mostly the log of a 1765 journey to a mineral springs in what was then the far west of Virginia. The caricature deflects the charge of tyranny from the king to Grenville.

Page 166. Caricature of Grenville and Bute (London, February 1765). Hundreds of such satires lampooned this hated Scots adviser to George III. Bute is assumed to be in league with the exiled house of Stuart, then supported by France. Grenville is shown as part of this conspiracy. These supposed Jacobites dance on the tomb of the lately deceased uncle of the king, the Duke of Cumberland, who had ruthlessly suppressed the Scottish uprising in support of Bonnie Prince Charlie in 1745.

Page 170. Patrick Henry by Thomas Sully (1815). There are no depictions of Henry the man and orator that date from the time of his sudden rise. Here we see not the outrageous rebel of 1765 but the sublime patriot of American nationalist legend.

Page 177. Frontispiece to a *London Magazine* of 1768. A not-so-martial Britannia and a concerned-looking George III attend a female figure who is probably Liberty (though she has none of the insignia) as she grieves over the imperiled freedom of America and the sad state of Corsica, whose patriots had just been vanquished by the conquering French. The king can still be imagined as savior to these oppressed lands.

Page 180. Jean-Baptiste Greuze, "The Angry Wife" (French, c. 1786). This drawing resembles an engraving, and was evidently prepared for that purpose.

Page 193. Mrs. Fanny Berry. There were not many portraits of the ex-slaves interviewed in Virginia for the WPA project. This copy of a published photograph is one of the few to be found.

Page 216. "The Old Plantation" is the title that has been given to this well-known painting, believed to be made around 1800 in South Carolina. It shows a distinctive African American culture that was widespread in the American South. The figures and action seem to be taken seriously and not mocked in the racist manner that prevailed so long. The jars surely contain liquor; but that is matter of fact and is not stigmatized.

Page 260. "The Xmas Academics" is the title the artist gave this caricature, published in London in 1772. It is an almost affectionate treatment of the scandal generated by the taste for worldly pleasures of many clergymen. It is a match for Landon's stories of Parson Giberne, before the crisis of 1776 raised to frenzy the diarist's alarm at the trends of his times.

Page 275. Jean-Baptiste Greuze, "The Father's Curse, or the Ungrateful Son" (1777). This drawing (intended for engraving) captures dramatically the frenzied tone of Landon Carter's diary denunciation of his eldest son's ungrateful defiance.

Page 305. "La Destruction de la statue royale." This line engraving and etching was prepared by J. Cheveau, c. 1780, for the edification of a Continental European public stirred up by the war of the American Revolution. Soon the French would topple their own king's statues and behead Louis XVI.

Page 315. Plate xi of a collection of plates engraved for a manual of general knowledge. J. B. Basedow, *Elementarwerke für die Jugend und ihre Freunde* (Berlin, 1774).

Page 335. A hummingbird. This image comes from the rich series of engravings, colored by hand, that adorned the dedicated work on the plants and animals of southern North America and the British Caribbean published in Mark Catesby (1683–1749), *The Natural History of Carolina . . .* , (London: 1731–1743).

Acknowledgments

I have had crucial support during the long time of researching and writing this book from three academic homes that I still inhabit: The History Departments of LaTrobe University, Melbourne, Australia, and of the College of William & Mary, Williamsburg, Virgina; and the Department of Historical Research, The Colonial Williamsburg Foundation, and its associated John D. Rockefeller, Jr. Library, where Cathy Grosfils was especially helpful with the illustrations.

My work was greatly forwarded by research fellowships in: The Newberry Library, Chicago, where this work began; The Shelby Cullen Davis Center, Princeton University; The Woodrow Wilson International Center in the Smithsonian Institution; the Center for Historical Analysis, Rutgers University, New Brunswick, N.J.; the John Carter Brown Library at Brown University, Providence, R.I.; the Institute for the Humanities, University of Michigan at Ann Arbor; and the Center for Early Modern History, University of Minnesota, Minneapolis. I received special support also from the Australian Research Grants Council and the Harrison Chair Fund at the College of William & Mary.

Alton Becker, Megan Isaac, Kenneth Lockridge, and Carroll Smith-Rosenberg all read and commented most helpfully on the entire draft manuscript. Peter Ginna, the editor at O.U.P., together with his assistant, Furaha Norton, have been supportive critical readers and wonderfully creative proposers as we went from first complete draft to finished manuscript. I am immensely grateful to Joellyn Ausanka for her tireless efforts to produce this book magnificently. The following are just some of the other persons who have given me the vital assistance of critical readings of portions of this work and in the discussions ensuing: Roger D. Abrahams, Barbara and Cary Carson, John Cashmere, Inga Clendinnen, Greg Dening, John Gillis, Jack P. Greene, Norman Fiering, John Hust, Katie Holmes, Rowan Ireland, Gwynneth Hunter-Payne, Colleen Isaac, Lyned Isaac, Marilyn Lake, Philip Lisle, Donna Merwick, Lotte Mulligan, Angus McGillivery, Bernard Newsome, Lisa Norling, June Philipp, Judith Richards, Charles Rosenberg, Ron Schechter, Ron Southern, Alex Tyrell, Laurel Ulrich, Shane White, and Gordon Wood.

Index

Great Britain, 137, 153–54

Greek language, 90, 91

See also classical models

Greene, Jack P., 339, 341, 343 (n3), 344
(n11), 363, 364, 366 (nn129, 132),
368, 369 (n160), 373 (n177), 383
(n241), 384 (n244), 387 (n255), 389
(n277), 393 (n314)

Grenville, George, 162, 166, 398

hanged in effigy, 162, 163, 175

LC's opposition to, 176

North Briton seditious libel issue, 166

Pratt on, 178

Stamp Act, 162, 168, 369, 371 (n163)

subversion of, 155

Greuze, Jean-Baptiste, 275

Griffin, Major, 262, 389

Griffith, Lucille, 363, 365 (n124)

Griffith, Owen, xxiv, 219, 380–81

Griggs (overseer), 329–30

Guerrini, Anita, 360, 362 (n109)

Guthrie (tavern keeper), 11, 344 (n11)

Gwynn's Island, 2, 11, 308

Halifax, Lord, 165

Hall, Douglas, 354

Hamilton, Gilbert, 118–19

Harford, Henry, 244, 384 (n244)

Harris, John, 358 (n82)

Harry (Manuel's son), xxiv, 223

Harvey, William, 109–10, 361

Hawkesworth, J., 390 (n285)

Hayden, Brian, 380 (n219)

Headley, Robert K., Jr., 344 (n11), 347
(n27), 352 (n52), 353 (n54), 378
(n203), 384 (n246) 385 (n248), 391
(n304), 394 (n322), 395 (n329)

health

See also medical beliefs and practices

of family, 174, 270

of LC, 45, 143, 174, 224–25, 241, 273, 279,
290, 313–14, 327, 329, 381 (n224)

of Reuben Beale, 54

of slaves, 216–17

weather and, 77, 106

Heinemann, Ronald L., 375, 375 (n193)

Helen of Troy, 46

Hellier, Cathleene, 352 (n52)

Henry, Patrick, 170, 400

biographical sketch, 371 (n169)

defiance emphasized, 175

effect of, 172–74, 280

elections, 309

LC's rancor with, 288, 296

leadership of, 169–73, 174, 184

Herndon, G. Melvin, 356 (n66)

Herodotus, 85, 92, 93, 95, 99, 359 (nn85,
92, 93), 360 (n99)

Hertford, Henry. See Harford, Henry

Hickory Thicket Quarters, 6, 59

Hill, Aaron, 93, 95, 96, 97, 101, 351 (n44)

Hipkins, Samuel, 268, 390

Hippocrates, 106–7, 109

history, moral purpose of, xx, 334–35

History of Herodotus, 92, 93, 99, 359 (nn85,
92), 360 (nn 93, 99)

History of Scotland (Buchanan), 94–95

Hodges, Frances Beale Smith, 344 (n19),
349 (n37)

Hoffer, Peter Charles, 345–46 (n22)

Hoffman, Paul P., 340

Hoffman, Ronald, 340, 357 (n78)

Holton, Woody, 342

Home Quarter, 6, 59

Horace (poet), 58, 152, 355 (n58)

horses. See livestock

House of Burgesses

Boston Port Bill, 288–89

Committee of Propositions and Grievances, 128

Committee of the Whole, 130–33, 145,
149

defense funds, 144–46

elections, 174–75

House of Commons parallel, 125

LC's service in, xviii, **121–161**, 300

on pistole fee, 142

prayers for king's guidance, 259

reacting to Stamp Act, 169

role of, 127, 129–30

House of Commons (British), 125, 130–31